AN EIGHTEENTH–CENTURY JOURNAL

'NEWS FROM AMERICA' OR 'THE PATRIOTS IN THE DUMPS'
From 'The London Magazine', November 1776

AN

EIGHTEENTH-CENTURY JOURNAL

*Being a Record
of the Years
1774–1776*

Compiled by
JOHN HAMPDEN

LONDON
MACMILLAN & CO. LTD
1940

COPYRIGHT

PRINTED IN GREAT BRITAIN
BY R. & R. CLARK, LIMITED, EDINBURGH

FOR
DOREEN

CONTENTS

LIST OF ILLUSTRATIONS

List of Illustrations

INTRODUCTION

I. THE JOURNAL

THIS is such a Journal as might well have been kept in London during the years 1774, 1775 and 1776, a record day by day of the happenings, important or trivial, which were being most discussed in the Journalist's own circle, with an occasional anecdote that appealed to him and now and again a more personal note of a dinner party or a masquerade.

All the material [apart from a few editorial additions enclosed in square brackets] has been taken direct from contemporary sources, and much of it is contemporary in the strictest sense, coming from letters, newspaper reports, etc., which were written immediately after the events to which they refer. The remainder, though written later, is the work of writers who were adults in 1774 and in some cases eye-witnesses of the events or friends of the protagonists. No changes in the text have been made apart from the partial modernisation of spelling, capitals and punctuation, and omissions are indicated by dots . . . but some obvious misprints have been corrected without notice.

Except for a few letters taken from the Royal Archives at Windsor and the Archives of the Royal Society no manuscript material has been used, because the printed material alone is almost inexhaustible, even when the life of the provinces is excluded, as it has been here. It will be seen from the index of sources that only seventy-six works have been drawn upon, but several times this number have been examined in detail and many others have been skimmed, including for example nearly all the publications of the Historical Manuscripts Commission. The material collected in typescript amounted to three times that finally selected for inclusion. Two or three more journals covering the same years could be compiled without repetitions, and each of them would evoke protests, from any student of the period, at the inclusion of this item or the exclusion of that. Indeed the compiler's greatest difficulty has been that of choice, and since his choice had to be arbitrary he has been guided largely by the " news value " which events had at the time, as indicated by periodicals and private letters. To the modern historian of these momentous years the trial of the Duchess of Kingston may, quite rightly, be not worth even a footnote ; to many Londoners of 1776 it was a far more absorbing topic of conversation than what was happening obscurely along the distant coast of New England.

This volume is not, therefore, a work of scholarship in the sense of a new contribution to knowledge, nor is it a source-book which will serve for a systematic study of the period. It provides simply a picture of that period, as seen through contemporary eyes, which may be of interest to the general reader and of some value to the student.

The idea of the book first occurred to the compiler in 1924, when he was attempting an imaginative reconstruction of Lydia Languish's life in Bath ; he realised first that Lady Teazle's life in London would be even more interesting, and next that a much better Journalist than Lady Teazle could be postulated. The work had to be put aside more than once and was still further postponed by the popularity of Dr. G. B. Harrison's *Elizabethan Journals*, which followed a similar method. It has been changed a good deal in the course of compilation, but still shows signs of that interest in Sheridan, Goldsmith and Garrick which first attracted the compiler to the period. It is, however, a period which lends itself particularly well to this treatment, being so alive with multifarious interests and ideas, and so full of vivid contrasts ; and if the whole epoch of the War of American Independence can be covered in succeeding volumes the work should have a certain completeness.

The compiler's indebtedness to the many modern works which have dealt with this period is far too great to be acknowledged here in detail : they range from C. S. Terry's *John Christian Bach*, H. S. Altham's *History of Cricket*, Harvey Graham's *Surgeons All*, F. J. Weaver's *The Material of English History* and F. A. Mumby's *Publishing and Bookselling*, to the

Introduction

Times Handlist of Newspapers, the *Cambridge Modern History* and the *Oxford Companion to English Literature*. The compiler must, however, acknowledge his particular indebtedness to the work of Mrs. M. Dorothy George, G. Birkbeck Hill, Professor Allardyce Nicoll, Mr. W. Baring Pemberton, Mr. L. F. Powell, R. Crompton Rhodes, Sir Charles Grant Robertson, Miss D. M. Stuart, Mrs. Paget Toynbee, Mr. Brian Tunstall, Professor A. S. Turberville, and Mr. Carl van Doren.

His Majesty the King has graciously permitted the reproduction of letters from the George III Papers in the Archives of Windsor Castle. Grateful acknowledgments are due also to the Controller of His Majesty's Stationery Office for permission to use the extracts from Reports of the Historical Manuscripts Commission, and to the Editors (or their representatives) and the publishers for passages from the following books : *George III's Correspondence with Lord North*, edited by the Hon. Sir John Fortescue, Messrs. Macmillan & Co., Ltd. (for a letter of General Burgoyne's) ; *The Writings of Benjamin Franklin*, edited by A. H. Smyth, The Macmillan Company of New York : *The Private Letters of Edward Gibbon*, edited by R. E. Prothero, and *The Life and Letters of Lady Sarah Lennox*, both published by Mr. John Murray ; *The Early Diary of Fanny Burney*, edited by A. R. Ellis, Messrs. G. Bell & Sons, Ltd.; *The Letters of Horace Walpole*, edited by Mrs. Paget Toynbee, *Boswell's Life of Johnson*, edited by George Birkbeck Hill and revised by L. F. Powell, and *The Letters of David Hume*, edited by J. Y. T. Greig—all published by Oxford University Press ; *The Correspondence of General Thomas Gage*, edited by C. E. Carter, Yale University Press and Oxford University Press ; *The Journal of the Rev. John Wesley*, edited by F. W. Macdonald, Messrs. J. M. Dent & Sons, Ltd.; *The Cumberland Letters*, edited by Clementina Black, Messrs. Martin Secker & Warburg, Ltd.; and *George Selwyn, his Letters and his Life*, edited by E. S. Roscoe and Helen Clergue, Messrs. Ernest Benn, Ltd.

The compiler is deeply indebted also to the kindness of librarians of the Royal Library at Windsor, the British Museum, the Guildhall, the London Library, the Royal Society, the National Book Council and the British Drama League, and for invaluable help to Miss Barbara Lyall, Miss June Fletcher, his wife and his daughter.

Introduction

II. THE JOURNALIST

This Journal not only postulates a Journalist, it adumbrates him, as it proceeds, with growing distinctness. He cannot emerge from the shadows, to be given a local habitation and a name, but we become increasingly aware of his interests and limitations. He is evidently a man of means, of good standing and wide sympathies. We see him occasionally at St. James's, but more often at Carlisle House or Ranelagh, Covent Garden or Drury Lane, at Sir Joshua Reynolds' or at an informal gathering at Dr. Burney's, where he listens with joy to the Agujari or to a duet on the harpsichord and the " new-invented " pianoforte.

Much interested in contemporary literature, drama and music, an admirer of Goldsmith, Garrick, Gibbon, Gray and Mason, he has a prejudice against Dr. Johnson which we may ascribe to inadequate acquaintance or to an over-fastidious taste in small matters. He certainly shares Johnson's attachment to London, for he evidently does not leave it at all during these three years, even in the height of summer, and for him the provinces hardly seem to exist. He realises the need for reform in penal law, prisons and various social conditions ; he can sympathise with the chimney-sweeper's boy and the American negro slaves. He is hardly likely to have been a regular spectator of the executions at Tyburn which fascinated so many Londoners besides Selwyn, but he studies with quiet amusement the behaviour of the crowd when *The Crisis* is burned by the hangman. He seems free from those wild excesses in drinking and gambling which are so much the *ton*, and Wesley has left him equally untouched. In all things, indeed, he appears as spectator rather than participant, and especially in politics. His sympathies are obviously with the " Patriots." He detests Lord North's policy, and George III's dominance, but he realises that they have a majority in the country as well as in the House, and that the Opposition are too divided and ineffectual to avert the war between England and America which, even early in 1774, he regards as inevitable.

His view of these three crowded years is necessarily more limited in some ways than our own, but his record gives us a fresh glimpse of history which for us is made but for him was in the making.

J. H.

PROLOGUE

PROLOGUE

LONDON IN 1774

LONDON is a city and county of itself, in Middlesex ; the see of a Bishop, and the capital of Great Britain and of all the British Dominions. . . .

Within the city walls and its ancient bars and gates it takes in but a narrow compass : but, if in the general acceptation of London, we take in all that vast mass of buildings, reaching from Blackwall in the east to Tothill Fields in the west, from London Bridge or River south, to Islington north, and from Peterborough House on the Bank-side at Westminster to Cavendish Square and even to Marybone, and all the new buildings by and beyond Grosvenor and Hanover Squares to the Brentford Road one way, to the Acton Road another ; a prodigy all this, of such buildings as nothing in the world does or ever did surpass, except it was old Rome in Trajan's time. . . .

The figure of London . . . including the city of Westminster and borough of Southwark, is nearly oblong, being about five miles in length from west to east, if measured in a direct line from Hyde Park Corner to the end of Limehouse ; and upwards of six, if the streets be followed . . . London, including the buildings on both sides the water, is in some places three miles broad from south to north, as from St. George's in Southwark to Shoreditch in Middlesex ; or two miles, as from Peterborough House to Montague House in Great Russell Street ; and in some places not half a mile, as in Wapping, and less in Rotherhithe. Several villages, formerly standing at a great distance, are now joined to the streets by continued buildings ; and more are making haste to meet in like manner, as at Deptford, Islington, Mile End,

B

and Newington Butts in Surrey. But the act of Parliament obtained by the city of London in the session of 1760, for widening its passages, pulling down its crowded gates, and laying it more open in many places, will probably put a stop to the rapid progress of buildings in the extreme parts of the town ; since the city will be then as healthy to live in as any of the outskirts, and equally commodious ; and not be so liable to such dreadful conflagrations as have happened within these few years, from too much crowded buildings.

Besides, Westminster is in a fair way to join hands with Chelsea, as St. Giles's is with Marybone, and Great Russell Street by Montague House with Tottenham Court. The circuit of this large mass, as taken collectively, as consisting of the cities of London and Westminster, and by actual ad-measurement in straight lines, may on the Middlesex and Southwark sides amount to upwards of thirty-six miles, ex-clusive of Greenwich, Chelsea, Knightsbridge, and Kensington. . . . In the large circuit above mentioned . . . it may be reasonably concluded there are about 1,500,000 souls.

This city is under excellent regulations, particularly with regard to beggars, lights, pavements, etc. It is governed by a Lord Mayor, twenty-five Aldermen, two Sheriffs, the Recorder, and Common Council ; their jurisdiction being confined to the city and its liberties, as also to Southwark. They are conservators of the River Thames. . . . The government of the outparts is by Justices and the Sheriffs of London, who are likewise Sheriffs of Middlesex. . . . The streets are generally level, and the principal ones open, and extremely well-built ; the houses being generally of brick, and extending a considerable length. These are chiefly inhabited by trades-men, whose houses and shops make a much better appearance than commonly those do in any other city in Europe. Persons of rank commonly reside in large elegant squares, some few houses in which are of hewn-stone, or plaster in imitation of it ; and generally make a grand appearance. . . .

What adds most to the affluence and splendour of this great city, is its commodious port, though near forty miles from the main sea ; whither many thousand ships of burthen annually resort from all parts of the world : and those of

4

moderate bulk can come as far as London Bridge ; while large barges and west country boats can go through the bridge, and a great distance up the Thames, carrying goods of all kinds to and from the metropolis.

London is reckoned to have two-thirds of the whole trade in England. The strength of this city, having no sort of fortifications, unless we reckon the Tower of London as its citadel, consists in the number of its inhabitants, who are commonly computed to be one-seventh of all the people in England, and one-eighth of the whole in Great Britain. Here is one cathedral, two collegiate churches, three choirs of music, one hundred and forty-six parishes, seventy-four chapels for the established church, two churches at Deptford, twenty-eight foreign churches, besides Dissenters' meeting-houses of all persuasions, nearly equal to the number of established churches ; several Popish chapels, three Jewish synagogues, thirteen hospitals, besides a very large and magnificent one for all foundlings and exposed children, near Lamb's Conduit Fields, Red Lion Street ; three colleges, twenty-seven public prisons, eight public seminaries or free schools, one hundred and thirty-one charity schools in London and Westminster, and ten miles round ; fifteen markets for flesh, two for live cattle, two herb-markets, twenty-three other markets, fifteen inns of court or chancery for the study of the law, four fairs, twenty-seven squares, besides those within any single building, as the Temple, Somerset House, etc., three public bridges, including the very stately one at Westminster, and that built at Blackfriars ; a Town House or Guildhall, a Royal Exchange, a Custom-house, three artillery grounds, four pest-houses, two Bishop's palaces, namely, London and Ely ; and three Royal palaces, St. James's, Somerset, and, the most elegant of all, that part that remains unburnt of Whitehall.

The usual firing in this city, wood being scarce and dear, and that mostly used by the bakers, is pit-coal . . . whence the town appears always at a distance shrouded in smoke.

. . . In the streets ply daily about a thousand hackney coaches, besides a great number of sedan chairs. The penny-post, for carrying of letters, or small paper parcels within the bills of mortality, or ten miles round London every way, is a great conveniency.

Here is a Royal Society founded by King Charles II who hold their meetings under a president at their house in Crane Court, Fleet Street . . . and in 1751 a Society of Antiquaries obtained a charter. . . . The Bank of England began to be erected in 1732 . . . The Royal Exchange, in Cornhill, is generally allowed to be the finest structure of the kind in the world. . . . In the place where Stocks-market was held is the Mansion-house, for the Lord Mayor to reside in ; the first stone of which was laid in Oct. 1739 : it is a noble and magnificent structure, but too heavy, and too large for the use for which it was designed. . . . The General Post Office, in Lombard Street, is a large commodious place. — Bedlam, in Moorfields, is a spacious mad-house, and handsome building ; the two figures at the entrance, in allusion to the unhappy objects confined in this place, and done by Mr. Kyber, a German, and father of the late Colley Cibber, poet-laureate, are very well worth seeing. — St. Bride's, near Fleet-ditch, has an elegant steeple. St. Paul's Cathedral is allowed to be the finest Protestant church in the world.

We cannot dismiss this account without taking notice, that many of the nobility have houses superior to that of the King's favourite dwelling, the Queen's palace ; but St. James's is so disagreeable a habitation, that even some tradesmen would disdain to reside in it, unless it was on account of business.

A palace for our Kings ought certainly to be undertaken at the national expense, equal to the dignity of the greatest empire in the world. Both the honour and dignity of the nation require it ; for how disgraceful is it to see the Sovereign of Britain keeping his court in an old ruinous building, worse than the mansion of a Turkish bashaw. It is not enough to have only a palace. It would add a dignity to the state, and be an honour to the nation, to have, at the same time, proper edifices erected for the Secretaries of State, great officers, and even courts of justice. The Secretaries have their offices sometimes in houses hired by the week ; and our courts of justice are not much unlike hen-roosts in the corner of an old barn. It is enough to make us laugh when we hear the expense mentioned in a nation who, on the most trifling occasions, have squandered away millions in unnecessary expenses to little insignificant German Princes, merely to prevent their ragged soldiers from giving any disturbance to Hanover, when a few of our own regiments would have sent them into eternity.

SEVENTEEN SEVENTY FOUR

January 1774

Saturday, January 1st.

This day at noon, in the Council Chamber at St. James's, before their Majesties and the Royal Family, there was performed an Ode for the New Year, written by William Whitehead, Esq., Poet Laureate, and set to music by Dr. Boyce, Master of the King's Band of Musicians.

There was a very brilliant Court to pay the customary compliments; the Lord Chancellor, the Prime Minister [Lord North], Lords Gower, Bristol, Hertford, Talbot, Hinchinbrooke, and all the great officers attended, as did all the Foreign Ministers. Notwithstanding the fullness of the Drawing Room, however, nobody was presented but the Hon. Miss Phipps, only daughter to Lord Mulgrave. This young lady, though barely sixteen, is generally reckoned one of the most accomplished in the rising generation of the nobility. She was received with peculiar graciousness by their Majesties.

Wednesday, January 5th.

How prettily . . . do Premiers provide for their whole family! — Lord Guildford, the father of Lord North, is appointed Treasurer to the Queen, Lord Dartmouth, the brother-in-law of Lord North, one of the Principal Secretaries of State, Lady North, Ranger of Bushy Park, besides numberless cousin germans, etc. etc. of inferior note, which have been brought into office.

Thursday, January 6th.

Ever since the frost has set in, a number of women have all day infested the wide part of the Strand near Exeter 'change, collecting together a number of fellows to throw sticks at oranges, at a halfpenny a throw, to the general disturbance of the neighbourhood, and the utter disgrace of those magi-

strates and subordinate officers who are daily pestering the
public with acquainting them of the advantages they desire
of a well-regulated police.

Saturday, January 8th.

The inquest went out privately in Clare Market, in order
to examine the weights, etc. A person who sells butter, seeing
them coming, put a crown piece into a lump which she knew
to be short. A woman passing by, seeing her do it, bought it,
while the officers were round the stall, for nine-pence half-
penny per pound, and walked clear off with it.

Monday, January 10th.

At the Cockpit Royal, the south side of St. James's Park,
this day and all the week will be fought a main of cocks, between
the gentlemen of Essex and Northamptonshire, for five guineas
a battle and fifty the odd. To begin fighting each day at five.

Tuesday, January 11th.

To Carlisle House, which [Mr. John Christian] Bach has
taken for his concerts. The furniture, like Madame Cornelys,
is much on the decline, but it is in my opinion better for the
concert than Almack's.

Thursday, January 13th.

His Majesty, attended by his Grace the Duke of Ancaster
and the Earl of Pomfret, went in state to the House of Peers,
when the Commons being sent for and come, His Majesty
opened the sessions of Parliament with the following most
gracious speech from the throne :

My Lords and Gentlemen,

The unusual length of the last session of parliament made
me desirous of giving you as long a recess as the public service
would admit. I have, therefore, been glad to find myself
under no necessity of calling you from your respective counties
at an earlier season, and I doubt not but you are now met
together in the best disposition for applying yourselves to the
despatch of the public business.

You will, I am persuaded, agree with me in regretting that the peace, so long expected and so very desirable, is not yet effected between Russia and the Porte ; but it is with real satisfaction I can repeat, that other foreign powers continue still to have the same pacific dispositions with myself. I can have no other wish than to see the general tranquility restored : for the establishment and subsequent preservation of which no endeavours of mine, consistent with the honour of my crown and the interests of my people, shall ever be wanting.

In this state of foreign affairs, you will have full leisure to attend to the improvement of our internal and domestic situation. . . . Among the objects, which in this view will come under your consideration, none can better deserve your attention than the state of the gold coin . . . as well on account of its very high importance, as of the peculiar advantages which the present time affords for executing with success such measures as you may find it expedient to adopt with respect to this great national concern. . . .

Gentlemen of the House of Commons,
I have ordered the proper estimates for the current year to be laid before you ; and rely on your readiness to grant me such supplies as shall be found requisite in the present situation of affairs.

My Lords and Gentlemen,
The experience I have had of your past conduct leaves me no room to doubt, either of your zeal or prudence in your endeavours to promote the welfare of your country. You will not suffer any parts of the public service to escape your attention . . . and you can propose no measures that will serve either to secure or advance the happiness and prosperity of my people, in which you may not always depend on my most hearty concurrence.

Saturday, January 15th.
For sale by the candle at New Lloyd's Coffee House in Pope's Head Alley, Lombard Street. On Wednesday, the 19th January at twelve o'clock the good ship *Royal Charlotte,* a fast sailer, square stern, plantation built, burthen two hundred

and twenty tons, more or less, with exceeding good dimensions for the West India, Virginia, Carolina, or Baltic trade, and is well found, now lying off Wapping Old Stairs, John M'Kirdy, Commander. Inventories of William Tippell, Broker.

Monday, January 17th.

Lord Chatham is not to be in town this season. The Rockingham Party have lost all hopes. Temple himself has now despaired of being sent for. Burke thinks he belched his oratory for nothing. Clive reposes himself, like a seaman escaped from a storm, on a plank. Silence will prevail in St. Stephen's. Even Parliament Street will not have its pavement torn as usual with Jehu-like orators driving to the House. All is tranquillity and stillness. But this quiet serenity . . . may be the prelude to a storm.

Tuesday, January 18th.

This day being kept as the anniversary of Her Majesty's birthday, there was a very numerous and splendid appearance of the nobility, foreign ministers and other persons of distinction at court, to compliment their Majesties on the occasion.

We made our push through all the smug parsons in the outward room, got into the Drawing Room, were most graciously spoken to by His Majesty [and] got away with ease. . . . Benson Earle desired I would take him to the Ball, which I did. . . . The Duke of Devonshire and the Duchess of Grafton began ; they say there were seventy minuets. Never was anything so tiresome. Both their Majesties were at the Ball and stayed three country dances. We got away quite easily at half-past twelve, though the crowd was immense. The ladies' clothes were more elegant than fine ; chiefly plain silks, trimmed, some with sable, ermine, gauze and chenille. The gentlemen were very fine, particularly Mr. Hampden, Lord Egremont, and Mr. G. Hanger. . . .

Saturday, January 22nd.

The tea exported to America by the East India Company, in pursuance of an Act of Parliament passed last session, has already produced a ferment throughout that continent and is likely to be attended with more alarming consequences. . . .

On [December 14th] the body of the people of [Boston] and all the adjacent towns . . . assembled at the Old South Meeting House, to enquire the reason of the delay in sending the ship *Dartmouth*, with the East India tea, back to London . . . and appointed a committee of ten to see it performed . . . [but clearance for the ship was refused by the Governor]. . . . Behold what followed ! [On December 16th] a number of resolute men, dressed like Mohawks or Indians . . . in less than four hours emptied every chest of tea on board the three ships commanded by the Captains Hall, Bruce and Coffin . . . into the sea, without the least damage done to the ships or any other property. . . .

The patriotic inhabitants of Lexington . . . unanimously resolved against the use of bohea tea of all sorts, Dutch or English importation. . . . The following notice has been dispersed about [New York] : " Whereas our nation have lately been informed that the fetters which have been forged for us by Great Britain are hourly expected to arrive in a certain ship, belonging to or chartered by the East India Company, we do therefore declare that we are determined not to be enslaved by any power on earth. . . ." At a public meeting of the inhabitants [of Philadelphia] held at the State House on the 18th of October, the sense of the city was expressed in the resolves . . . " that the duty imposed by Parliament upon tea landed in America is a tax on the Americans, or levying contributions on them without their consent [and] . . . that it is the duty of every American to oppose this attempt. . . ."

Sunday, January 23rd.

[Lately published :]
Juliet Grenville, or the History of the Human Heart, by Mr. Brooke. [Author of *The Fool of Quality*] 12mo. 3 vols. 7s. 6d. sewed. Robinson.

A Letter from Mr. Peter Dollond to Nevil Maskelyne, F.R.S. and Astronomer Royal : describing some additions and alterations made to Hadley's Quadrant . . . in *Philosophical Transactions* [of the Royal Society], Vol. LXII, 4to. 14s. sewed. Davies.

Monday, January 24th.

Died, Saturday se'nnight, at Dartford, Mr. John Bell, master of the eleven cricketers there, the most noted cricketer in England.

Tuesday, January 25th.

Arrived safe in the river Thames, the ship *Polly*, Capt. Ayres, from Philadelphia, with 600 chests of tea, with which he was chartered by the East India Company for that port, but was not permitted to land the same.

Thursday, January 27th.

Letters from Boston complain much of the taste of their fish being altered : Four or five hundred chests of tea may have so contaminated the water in the harbour, that the fish may have contracted a disorder not unlike the nervous complaints of the human body. Should this misfortune extend itself as far as the banks of Newfoundland, our Spanish and Portugal fish trade may be much affected by it.

Friday, January 28th.

The tea thrown into the sea at Boston is valued at £18,000 at 1s. 6d. per pound. The whole sent to America is said to be about £300,000 worth, which is returning home, not being suffered to land.

The dispute with America is now become more serious than ever. It is reduced to the decisive question, whether the Right of Taxation be here or there ? There is no medium which can be adopted with honour or safety on either side. No problem of expediency can now be started, for the opposition in America is not to the sum levied, but to the right of levying it.

The Sheriffs of London and Middlesex sent an order to John Wilkes, Esq., to attend the House as Member for Middlesex, in consequence of the Speaker's letter, requiring the Sheriffs to give notice to all Members to attend.

THE ADELPHI FROM THE RIVER
From the print by Thomas Molton, 1796

Saturday, January 29th.

Our American affairs afford abundant matter of attention. Besides the resistance of the tea-duty, the Ministry appear desirous of taking up the affairs of Boston. The two Houses of Assembly petitioned the King, about six months since, for the removal of the Governor and the Lieutenant-governor, alleging their loss of public confidence and their incapacity to serve the King in general terms. The Petition was first laid aside, like the home remonstrances, but was on a sudden resumed and referred to the Privy Council ; who ordered the respective agents to attend with counsel, though not desired on the part of the province. . . . Thirty-five lords were assembled besides those in office. . . . Mr. Dunning asked, on the part of his clients, the reason of his being ordered to attend, and spoke shortly on the general object of the Petition, which meant no prosecution but to convey the sense of the people to the Throne. Mr. Wedderburn, under the pretext of reply, and the encouragement of the judges — the indecency of whose behaviour exceeded, as it is agreed on all hands, that of any committee of election — entered largely into the constitution and temper of the province and concluded by a most scurrilous invective against Dr. Franklin ; occasioned, as Dr. Franklin says, by some matter of private animosity ; as Mr. Wedderburn says, by his attachment to his deceased friend Mr. Whately, the publication of whose correspondence contributed to inflame the assembly to their late resolutions ; and others say, it is the opening of a new plan of American government. The resolution of Council is not yet public but is generally understood to be as much in favour of the Governor and as discouraging to the province, as words can make it. . . .

Various measures are talked of, for altering the constitution of the government of New England, and prosecuting individuals ; all tending to more or less enforcement. The opinion here is very general, that America will submit, that Government was taken by surprise when they repealed the Stamp Act, and that all may be recovered. . . .

Dr. Franklin is displaced from the office of Deputy Post-Master General for the Colonies, and the petition above-mentioned dismissed.

Sunday, January 30th.

I am now getting acquainted with authors, managers, etc. — good company to know but not to live with. [On Friday] I dined at the Br*ee*tish Coffee House with Garrick, Colman, Goldsmith, Macpherson, John Hume, etc. and yesterday went to Colman's *Man of Business*. We dined at the Shakespeare and went in a body to support it. . . . Though we got a verdict for our client his cause was but a bad one. It is a very confused miscellany of several plays and tales. . . .

[Some days ago] three macaroni bloods, on their ramble, called at the house of Miss Jones, the noted and celebrated courtesan. They were refused admittance, on which they broke the two parlour windows all to pieces and retreated in triumph.

Monday, January 31st.

King George . . . has ordered the pure, precise Dr. Dodd to be struck off the list of his chaplains, not for gallantry with a Magdalen, as you would expect, but for offering a thumping bribe to my Lord Chancellor [Apsley] for the fat living of St. George's, [Hanover Square]. It is droll that a young comely divine should have fallen into the sin, not of Mary the Penitent, nor of her host, Simon the Pharisee, but of Simon Magus, the founder of simony. Perhaps, as the Doctor married Lord Sandwich's mistress, he had had enough of *des filles repenties*.

FEBRUARY 1774

Tuesday, February 1st.

Lord Buckingham[shire] moved the House of Lords to address for copies of papers relative to the disturbances at Boston, on the teas. The Ministers pleaded that they had not yet obtained sufficient information, but would produce it as soon as they could. . . .

Yesterday a gentleman was robbed by a single highwayman near Hammersmith, of sixteen guineas, who refused his watch and returned him half a guinea to defray his expenses to town.

Friday, February 4th.

I had the pleasure to be at Carlisle House, and . . . the masquerade there was in every respect worthy of the noble subscribers. . . . Very early in the night most of the [people of fashion] unmasked ; several came with their masks off, and at supper they were generally so. . . . Most of the characters were better supported than usual. Bobadill, the hero of the play [*Every Man in his Humour*], was well-dressed but rather over-loud and over-active ; his voice surprised the gentlemen ; his sermon amazed the ladies ; and his arms and his jokes were terrible to all the little waiters. Two witches were properly equipped with scarfs, hoods and brooms. . . .

Several parties were engaged in different dances and other amusements, when a Dancing Bear arrived, his Keeper and Man, a lame Fiddler and another attendant who played excellently on the salt-box. . . . A witty Female Satire on her sex was much noticed ; her left side was dressed like a fine Lady, the other like a Beggar. . . . There were many rich and well-fancied dominoes : two Patagonians and two Otaheites. . . .

Between six and seven on Saturday morning the company were all gone.

Saturday, February 5th.

Yesterday came on to be heard before the House of Lords, by an appeal from the Court of Chancery, the long-contested cause between Donaldson and Becket, relative to literary property. The Attorney-General, who is counsel for the apellant, in a long and eloquent speech, declaimed against monopolies of that nature as repugnant to Law : after which the Lords adjourned the further hearing of this case till Monday next.

The House below the Bar was . . . exceedingly crowded. Mr. Edmund Burke, Dr. Goldsmith, David Garrick, Esq., and other literary characters, were among the hearers.

Sunday, February 6th.

I have made it my observation in this city, that in the course of one year some shops will alternately contain three different trades ; [Harlequin] scarce ever does more with the assistance of the very scene-shifters in one of Rich's best panto-mimes. I have known a shop open in a most glaring manner with trinkets and toys ; in three months again it has been changed into a linen-draper's, where every method of plaiting and folding handkerchiefs, placing black paper in the form of hearts under muslins, and other little drapery tricks to coax the girls to buy, have been practised without success. The draper courts and allures in vain, — he gives way to a Caledonian bookseller, who, with a load of Glasgow and Edinburgh pirated books gaudily gilt, promises to undersell all the trade ; and thus in succession does a house make its appearance in as motley a manner as [Harlequin's] coat. I suppose these sudden failures may arise from dissipation and extravagance. A young man becomes possessed of a small capital: he then resolves to enter into trade, to fall in love and marry as fast as possible. He gets a stock of goods upon nine months' credit, squanders away the cash as fast as it drops through the slit of the till, flies from pleasure to pleasure with his new wife, lives at all points, and burns his candles at both ends, and then his creditors for their credit given him take the residue of the goods unsold for the debt: they get ten shillings in the pound, and the young buck of a tradesman gets a child, which with a young wife without a shilling, he leaves to her parents to support, and he transmigrates to India or America. . . .

Monday, February 7th.

[The King has] seen Lieutenant-General Gage, who came to express his readiness, though so lately come from America, to return at a day's notice if the conduct of the Colonies should induce the directing coercive measures . . . He says they will be lions, whilst we are lambs, but if we take the resolute part they will undoubtedly prove very meek ; he thinks the four regiments intended to relieve as many regiments in America, if sent to Boston, are sufficient to prevent any disturbance. . . .

Tuesday, February 8th.

The Messrs. Adam being desirous of having their Lottery drawn in the most open and public manner, have made choice of a large room erected in 'Change Alley, on the spot where Jonathan's Coffee House formerly stood, being one of the most public places in the city of London, in the heart of business, and where the lottery wheels will be seen from the centre of the Royal Exchange. . . .

Thursday, February 10th.

In the House of Commons, Sir Edward Astley presented a bill to enable Thomas de Grey, Esq., to enclose several common lands and fields in the county of Norfolk. Mr. Sawbridge immediately presented a petition from William Tooke, Esq. praying that the bill to enable Mr. De Grey, etc. might not pass into an act. The petition was read, setting forth, that Mr. De Grey had not given proper notice to the inhabitants that occupied several of the lands he intended to enclose, and that the said enclosures would be highly prejudicial to the petitioner, and many others. The bill was, however, read a first time, and ordered to be read a second time on Tuesday se'ennight.

Friday, February 11th.

The hasty manner in which the enclosing bill was read [yesterday], produced a most virulent letter against the Speaker [Sir Fletcher Norton in today's] *Public Advertiser* [charging him with partiality]. . . .

The whole House seeming unanimous that the charge was groundless, Sir Fletcher arose, and said he was thoroughly satisfied that the House thought him innocent, and it was the height of his ambition to gain their esteem ; that, if he had their good word, he cared not what any faction said of him.

Mr. Herbert said, he thought it would be an impeachment of the understanding of that House to suffer such a libel to pass with impunity.

This produced a warm debate, and, in the conclusion, a motion was made, "That the letter in the *Public Advertiser* of this date, addressed to Sir Fletcher Norton, Knt., Speaker of this House, is a false, scandalous, and malicious libel, contrary to all law or justice, and in open violation of the privileges of this House." [This] was agreed to *nem. con.*

Mr. Herbert then moved, "That the printer of the *Public Advertiser* be ordered to attend this House on Monday next." And he was ordered accordingly.

Saturday, February 12th.

On Thursday last Mr. Matthews with a party of dragoons fell in with a gang of 80 smugglers within two miles of Maidstone, from whom he took a considerable quantity of tea and lace. Several of the men were wounded, and one of the horses threw his rider, and ran through Maidstone loaded with four bags of tea.

Sunday, February 13th.

Among other great works now introduced at Mr. Cox's Museum is an immense *barometer*, of so extraordinary a construction that by it the long-sought for and in all likelihood the only *perpetual motion* that ever will be discovered is obtained. The constant revolution of wheels moving in vertical, horizontal and other directions, is not only physically produced, but the indication of time from an union of the philosophic with the mechanic principles is effected. . . . [The clock] is kept constantly going by the rising and falling of the quicksilver in a most extraordinary barometer ; and there is no danger of its ever failing to go : for there is always such a quantity of moving power accumulated, as would keep the clock going for a year, even if the barometer should be taken quite away from it. . . .

Monday, February 14*th.*

The Printer of the *Public Advertiser* [Mr. Woodfall] attended the House of Commons today according to order ; when the *Public Advertiser* of Friday last being put into his hands, he was asked what reason he could urge in his vindication for having published the letter addressed to Sir Fletcher Norton, Knt., Speaker of the House of Commons.

The Printer made answer, that " Mr. Horne gave him that letter ; and that he published it in the hurry of business. He expressed his hopes that the House would make allowances for the great hurry the nature of his business subjected him to ; and what he had further to plead in his behalf was, that during a course of near twenty years he had never fallen under the displeasure of the House ; that he had attended according to their order ; and that in his unfortunate situation he must beg to throw himself on the mercy of the House."

On being asked Mr. Horne's Christian name, and where he lived, he said he believed his Christian name was John, and that the place of his residence was Brentford ; and being questioned of what profession Mr. Horne was, he answered, that he was deemed a clergyman.

The Printer was then ordered to withdraw from the bar, but not to go away.

The debate lasted till eight o'clock.

Upon a division, the numbers were as follow :

For Mr. Herbert's motion of " commitment to the custody of the Serjeant at Arms " .   .   152
For Mr. Fox's amendment of " committing to Newgate "   68

The printer was then taken into the custody of the Serjeant at Arms.

Mr. Horne was served with a notice to attend the House of Commons on the 16th, but he eluded it, by pretending that the notice must have been intended for some other John Horne, as there were many of that name in the city of London. However, he wrote to the clerk who signed the order, that, when he was properly summoned, he should think it his duty to attend.

Thursday, February 17th.

The Serjeant at Arms went to the house of Mr. Tooke, in Serjeant's inn, to take Mr. Horne into custody, who very readily accompanied him to the House ; and, when called to the bar, endeavoured to exculpate himself from holding the House in contempt. . . . He particularly wanted to know, whether what had been read to him was the charge or the evidence. The speaker said the charge. Mr. Horne then presumed the House meant that he should put in his plea ; and, after a short pause, he was answered in the affirmative. Then, he said, he should plead, as in other courts, NOT GUILTY. And there being no evidence against him but that of Mr. Woodfall, and Mr. Woodfall's evidence being judged incompetent, because in custody, Mr. Horne was discharged on paying his fees.

Saturday, February 19th.

Some gentlemen observing at the Smyrna Coffee House last week, what little prudence was made use of at the Worcester election, &c. a very popular member of Parliament present declared himself very pathetically, that corruption was become so universal, from the first Lord of the Realm down to the poorest member of a corporation, that we must in general expect that a candidate will bribe, and the voter be bribed ; and if there be yet any means of salvation left, it must be effected by men whose minds are enlarged and exalted, who will serve their country purely for the sake of preserving it, and not aggrandizing themselves. . . .

Wednesday, February 23rd.

[Yesterday was held] a very solemn trial in the House of

Lords upon literary property, which ended in the reversal of certainly a very extraordinary decree of Lord Mansfield's, who showed himself the merest Captain Bobadill that, I suppose, ever existed in real life. . . . Imagine the Bishop of Carlisle, an old metaphysical head of a college, reading a paper, not a speech, out of an old sermon book, with very bad sight, leaning on the table, Lord Mansfield sitting at it with eyes of fixed melancholy looking at him, knowing that the Bishop's eyes were the only eyes in the House who could not meet his ; the judges behind him full of rage at being drawn into so absurd an opinion and abandoned in it by their chief ; the bishops waking as . . . they do just before they vote and staring on finding something the matter ; while Lord Townshend was close to the bar getting Mr. Dunning to put up his glass to look at the head of criminal justice. He has not appeared since in the House of Lords, and all Westminster Hall behold his dejection without, I believe, one commiserating eye.

The question was put at half after five, when the decree was reversed, without costs ; so that the English booksellers have no other security in future for any literary purchase they may make, but the statute of the 8th of Queen Anne, which secures to the authors' assigns an exclusive property for fourteen years, to revert again to the author, and vest in him for fourteen years more.

Thursday, February 24th.

There is just published a very good dialogue between three persons of some note, namely, the partitioners of Poland. There is a great deal of wit and just satire in this piece ; but though the press can pass sentence I doubt it cannot see it executed. I do not know but part of it may be put in force. The rebellion in Russia still exists, which looks a little serious. How the Poles must pray that it may prosper ! The King of Prussia is so thorough-paced a villain that I should not be surprised if he had set it on foot. I am sure he will support it if he can see his interest in it. How happy would it be to have those three monsters punished by each other ! . . .

The famous Charles Fox was this morning turned out of

his place of Lord of the Treasury for great flippancies in the House towards Lord North. His parts will now have a full opportunity of showing whether they can balance his character, or whether patriotism can whitewash it.

The Queen was brought to bed this evening of another Prince.

Friday, February 25th.

The *Jupiter*, a large Guinea trader, belonging to [Liverpool], being at Old Olabar, on the coast of Africa, after taking on board 431 slaves, the crew mutinied, confined the officers, and put to sea, with an intent to sell the cargo at some of the Spanish settlements in the South Seas. But whilst they were considering how they should dispose of their commanders, a strong S.W. wind drove them within a small distance of the coast of Morocco, where they were taken by two pirate cruisers, and carried into Salee. The master and officers have been released, at the interposition of the French Consul, who kindly offered to pay their ransom ; but the rebellious crew, with the slaves, were immediately sold for the benefit of the captors.

Saturday, February 26th.

The Oratorio [*Omnipotence*] performed last night at the Haymarket having been declared a production of Handel *new* to the public, we expected, as no doubt the managers did, a very crowded house. We were however mistaken ; there was a very genteel company, but not a very numerous one.

The performance bore intrinsic marks of its inimitable author, and does honour to the memory of the composer of *Messiah*. The choruses are beyond expression great ; it is difficult to say whether the pleasure or astonishment of the audience exceeded. Their continued applause and encores prolonged the performance above half an hour after the usual time.

Monday, February 28th.

Mr. Woodfall was brought to the bar of the H. of C. and discharged, paying his fees. The Speaker, with great mildness, decency, and good temper, declaring that, as the matter

26

originated from an attack upon himself, he would not wish a thought should be entertained, that he held any malice either to him or Mr. Horne ; and that he had rather incur the displeasure of the House for being too lenient, than the resentment of the people for being too severe.

Mr. Alderman Harley presented a petition from the booksellers of London, etc. setting forth, that many of them would be ruined by the late decision in the House of Lords, unless some relief was given them.

Mr. Sawbridge seconded the motion, in which he said, that, by a decision in the year 1769, in favour of copyright, many of the booksellers had laid out their whole fortunes in that article, which right had now been taken from them by the determination of the Upper House ; and, if some redress was not given them, many families would be totally ruined.

It was referred to a committee.

MARCH 1774

Tuesday, March 1st.

The Court of Spain have been for some time past, and now are, very busy in their ports and dock-yards. The Court of Great Britain, 'tis said, desired to know their motive for what must be understood as warlike preparations : for answer they returned, they only followed the example of England in preventing their navy from going to decay, and that they did not mean to change their pacific intention.

Woodfall again petitioned the House to be discharged [and] was ordered to be discharged on paying his fees.

Wednesday, March 2nd.

[Extract of a letter from America to the Earl of Dartmouth:]

The report to be made upon the petition from the House of Representatives of the Massachusetts Bay against their governors will have so decisive an influence on the people of that province, that I feel myself compelled to address your Lordship on the subject.

A discovery is made, by letters under their own hands, that the Governor and the Lieutenant Governor had been secretly labouring to subvert the chartered rights of the colony, to subject the people to arbitrary government, and to subdue them by military force. It appeared, that to accomplish these ends they had painted the proceedings of the people in the most false and odious colours ; forging falsehoods where misrepresentation would not suffice.

All this was conducted under the cloak of secret and confidential correspondence, that the mischief might come upon them unforeseen, the causes unknown, and the authors undiscovered. The people were to be the victims of a secret information — they were to be condemned without being heard, and punished with the heaviest of all calamities, the loss of their rights and liberties, without being apprised of the accusation or a possibility of defence. . . .

It was natural that this discovery should exasperate the people to an extreme. . . . The ministry were sufficiently disposed to adopt every severity against them. Governor Bernard and the commissioners were sufficient to keep up their prejudices and passions. To poison the minds of those in opposition, and by that means deprive the people of every benefit, either from the efforts of that opposition or from a change of administration, was the diabolical plan of Mr. Hutchinson and Mr. Oliver. . . .

For some years past the people of America and those of Boston in particular have been abused, misrepresented, and oppressed beyond the example of the worst of times. They have seen for a series of years every representation against them received, every application for them rejected. . . .

The people of the Massachusetts Bay have asked humbly and waited patiently for justice against Mr. Hutchinson and Mr. Oliver. . . . I have not yet heard a denial or publication of the letters upon which their petition is founded ; but it is said that the letters cannot be admitted as evidence, unless the manner in which they were obtained be declared. This rule of evidence is of the first impression and as rational as it is new. . . . I have [not] heard it even insinuated by any reputable person that they were procured by any undue means. . . .

My Lord, the single question is, whether men who have rendered themselves universally obnoxious to the people shall be continued in authority over them ? To determine in the affirmative is to set the sentiments of the people at defiance. . . . An attempt to establish government in America by military force must be ultimately fatal to this country. It will commence in folly and injustice — it will end in distress and humiliation. RALEIGH.

Thursday, March 3rd.

Last week there were no less than four smuggling cutters riding at anchor near the Yorkshire coast, waiting a favourable opportunity to land their cargoes. The smuggling trade increases daily, and geneva is so plentiful in the North Riding of that County, that it may be bought at every day-labourer's house.

Friday, March 4th.

The House of Commons went into a Committee of Inquiry into abuses committed in gaols, by detaining persons for their fees, Sir Thomas Clavering, Chairman. Dr. Fothergill and Surgeon Potts were called in, and asked their opinions on the gaol-distemper ; they said, it proceeded from a number of persons being confined in a close place, and not kept clean ; that they recommended, as a preservative to the Courts of Judicature, for the prisoners to be well washed before they were brought into Court, and clean clothes provided for them to appear in ; that they would recommend the prisons to be often cleaned, scraped, white-washed, and painted, and gave it as their opinion that it was the clothes that carried the infection ; that the distemper was of a similar nature with the small-pox, no person could have it more than once ; and that hot and cold baths would be of great service in prisons.

Mr. Howard, Sheriff of Bedford, was called, and gave the House an account that he had seen thirty-eight out of forty-two gaols in the Lent circuit, besides others, as Bristol, Ely, Litchfield, etc. That those he had not seen, in a few days he should set out to visit. That he released a person out of Norwich city-gaol, who had been confined five weeks for the gaoler's fee of 13s. 4d. That at Launceston the keeper, deputy-keeper, and ten out of eleven prisoners lay ill of the gaol-distemper ; at Monmouth the keeper lay dangerously ill, and three of the prisoners were ill ; at Oxford eleven died last year of the small-pox. That as to fees, those in the Western counties were highest, as at Dorchester £1. 3s. 9d., Winchester £1. 7s. 4d., Salisbury £1. 6s. 4d., but in the county of York only 9s. That the gaols were generally close and confined, the felons wards nasty, dirty, confined and unhealthy ; that even York Castle, which, to a superficial observer, might be thought a very fine gaol, he thought quite otherwise : with regard to felons, their wards were dark, dirty, and small, no way proportioned to the number of unhappy persons confined there. Many others are the same, as Gloucester, Warwick, Hereford, Sussex, etc. The latter had not, for felons, or even for debtors, at their county gaol at Horsham, the least outlet ; but the poor unhappy creatures were ever confined within doors, without the least breath of fresh air.

He was asked his reasons for visiting the gaols, and answered, that he had seen and heard the distress of gaols, and had an earnest desire to relieve it in his own district, as well as others. He was then asked, if it was done at his own expense ; he answered, undoubtedly.

Saturday, March 5th.

It is now become quite fashionable for parties who partake in the regale of cake and caudle at the Queen's Palace, to adjourn to Mr. Cox's Museum at Spring Gardens, which, from its vicinity, allows them a happy opportunity of meeting with the politest company.

Sunday, March 6th.

[There died on Friday] at Sandwich, in Kent, William Boys, Esq., Lieutenant Governor of the Royal Hospital at Greenwich. When he was first mate of the *Luxemburgh*, a Jamaicaman, in her return to England, it was set on fire, by some accident, and the crew all perished, the above Capt. Boys and another Officer excepted, who escaped on the wreck. They lived many days in the most miserable manner, till the officer died, when Capt. Boys lived upon his dead corpse while it remained sweet, and then eat the flesh off his own shoulders, till they became quite bare ; and after living twenty-two days in this dreadful situation, he was happily relieved.

Monday, March 7th.

Lord North presented the following message from His Majesty :

" His Majesty, upon information of the unwarrantable practices which have been lately concerted and carried on in North America, and particularly of the violent and outrageous proceedings at the town and port of Boston, in the province of

31

Massachusetts Bay . . . hath thought fit to lay the whole matter before his two Houses of Parliament . . . that they will not only enable His Majesty effectually to take such measures as may be most likely to put an immediate stop to the present disorders, but will also take into their most serious consideration what further regulations and permanent provisions may be necessary to be established, for better securing the execution of the laws and the just dependence of the colonies upon the crown and parliament of Great Britain."

Lord North at the same time presented to the House the papers relative to the said outrageous proceedings. . . .

Mr. Rice, seconded by Lord Clare, moved an address of thanks. Rice said, the claims and pretensions of the Americans had gone beyond all example, and that the question now was whether the colonies were any longer to belong to Great Britain ; that the best blood of this country had been sacrificed in their defence, and yet that the expected advantages were not to be maintained without asserting our sovereignty. Lord Clare added, that if the measures to be proposed met with opposition, whatever should be the violences of North America, they must be submitted to. Dowdeswell, almost alone, objected to the conduct of the Administration, whose wise heads, he said, had brought to a crisis the trial for power between this country and America. . . . Wedderburn said . . . the question was now, whether America was to be ours or not. The declaratory clause . . . had passed almost without a dissenting voice. The right of taxation had been established ; but their joy on the repeal of the Stamp Act had been too riotous, too ostentatious their triumph. . . . The people would expect success from Administration when it had been trusted with full power so long. Colonel Barré said, if the Bostonians were so guilty as they had been represented, we ought to make war on them ; there could be no middle measures. A plan, it was said, was to be brought : let America appear at the bar with all her imperfections on her head, with all her sins, and all her merits and blessings to this country. If factious, still bone of our bone and flesh of our flesh. He was ready to follow any leader in that business that had determina-

32

tion nor meant to make a captious opposition ; our establish-
ments in that country were of too great consequence. Lord
North said the proper papers would be ready on the following
Friday ; on which the Attorney-General Thurlow said, so loud
as to be heard by Lord North, " I never heard anything so
impudent ; he has no plan yet ready." Lord George Germain
said he agreed there was no use in entering into the calamities
that had been brought on America, it had been owing to the
different conduct of different ministers (the consequence of
the King's changing them so often). The wisdom of Parliament was now requisite. It would not be right to let America
steal a constitution they had no right to. The mischiefs were
owing to the repeal of the Stamp Act and want of uniformity
in the proceedings of Parliament. Their laws must be revised,
their charters looked into. . . . General Conway said the
Parliament ought to assert its rights ; and he saw the necessity
of subordination ; our salvation depended on it. . . . One
word he would say for the Colonies, that short of taxation,
they were and would be loyal and dutiful subjects. The
Address was voted without a division.

Such an outset prognosticated ill for the Bostonians. . . .

Tuesday, March 8th.

Grenville's Election Bill was read for the last time in the
House of Lords. . . . The Bill was then passed — the best I
remember to have seen in my time, and a most unexpected
mound against corruption, though the more utility it shall
have, the more arts will be employed to undermine it.

Thursday, March 10th.

It is computed that near 300 people have flung themselves
into the different gaols of this metropolis, in hopes of being
discharged by an Act of Grace on the birth of Her Majesty's
tenth child.

We hear from Marblehead, that last Tuesday night the
inoculating Hospital for the small-pox, lately erected on Cat
Island, near that place, was entirely consumed by fire, together
with upwards of seventy beds, bedding, and all the other

furniture : it is supposed to have been purposely set on fire, owing to the dread of having that distemper spread among them.

Friday, March 11th.

The American correspondence, consisting of 109 letters, was read this day before the House of Commons.— By these letters it appears that the Bostonians were left entirely to themselves in the article of tea ; the governor and military were entirely passive, and suffered the inhabitants to take their own course.

Saturday, March 12th.

Lord Chatham is hourly expected in Town, not only to be present at the debates in a Great Assembly, but also (it is said) to endeavour to conciliate all differences between Great Britain and her colonies. . . .

We are assured, from tolerable good authority, that a treaty has been opened for some time between the Bedford, Rockingham, and Shelburne parties. If so, it will be impossible for the Minister to maintain his ground.

It is further asserted, that Lords Chatham and Temple mean to throw their whole weight to support the above triumvirate.

Sunday, March 13th.

[Yesterday] between the hours of two and three o'clock there was the highest tide at Westminster that has been known for forty years past ; it came in at the door of the wooden bridge in New Palace Yard, and reached within a half a yard of Hall Gate ; the Exchequer and Oliver's coffee-houses were filled with water. . . . In fact, the confusion was general from thence to Millbank, and all the lower part of Westminster. . . .

Monday, March 14th.

Lord North moved for leave to bring in a Bill for the immediate removal of the custom-house from Boston, and for discontinuing the landing or lading of goods, &c., at that port with an intended clause in the Bill to prevent restitution of the custom-house there till an adequate compensation should be made for the loss of the teas. The present disorders at Boston were one point, he said, to be attended to ; the second was to secure a proper dependence of the Colonies, a consideration for another day. Even this Bill was little resisted. . . . Dempster cavilled a little ; Sawbridge spoke out and said the Americans had been treated like slaves, their money was taken from them without their consent. . . . Lord John Cavendish doubted the efficacy of the measure : he and Dowdeswell had nothing better to propose, and did not deny the necessity of doing something. Colonel Barré, in a very different language from what he had been accustomed to use, declared the Americans ought to be punished for their ingratitude. He would co-operate with Lord North in this measure. . . .

The Bill was then read for the first time.

Tuesday, March 15*th.*

Before we proceed to any extremities with America we should recollect that the merchants of Great Britain have upwards of four millions of property there, which will be the first sacrifice ; that more than an hundred thousand of our manufacturers eat their daily bread from that trade which hostilities must destroy.

Thursday, March 17*th.*

Our coffee-house politicians are released from a world of anxiety, by the news of Lord Chatham's keeping winter quarter this warm campaign. Bets were calculating, whether he would join the English or the American forces. It was done at five to four, that he would once more " rejoice that America has resisted."

Sunday, March 20*th.*

A new species of entertainment . . . is now exhibiting at the Devil Tavern, by Dr. Kenrick, under the title of " The School of Shakespeare." This performance consists of a course of lectures upon the different productions of that immortal bard, in order to throw new lights upon them, and investigate the judgment of his different commentators. In an introductory address to the audience, he acknowledged the difficulty of throwing out any original elucidations upon an author who had already had so many commentators ; but as Theobald, Pope, Warburton, and even Johnson, had confined themselves merely to verbal criticism, he should examine Shakespeare as a poet and a moral philosopher. But though many of the observations were ingenious, I cannot think that he will be able to throw any new lights upon our great poet. He has laboured at two points . . . the first is that of Hamlet's madness being real, and not feigned ; the second, that Othello was not as represented, a black, but a tawny Moor. . . .

Wednesday, March 23rd.

[Extract of a letter from Benjamin Franklin to Thomas Cushing in America :]

I suppose we never had since we were a people so few friends in Britain. The violent destruction of the tea seems to have united all Parties here against our Province, so that the Bill now brought into Parliament for shutting up Boston as a port till satisfaction is made meets with no opposition. An alteration in our Charter relating to the choice of the Council is also talked of, but it is not certain that it will be proposed at present. I cannot but hope that the affair of the tea will have been considered in the Assembly before this time, and satisfaction proposed if not made ; for such a step will remove much of the prejudice now entertained against us and put us again on a fair footing in contending for our old privileges as occasion may require. . . .

Thursday, March 24th.

The House went into a Committee on [the Boston Port Bill yesterday], filled up the blanks, and reported it. It was immediately read again with slight opposition for about three hours, and with no division, all sides seeming to agree that the conduct of the Bostonians could not be defended. . . . Lord North said he was known to be no enemy to lenient measures ; but this was not the first offence of the Bostonians ; they had been guilty for three years past ; censure and warning had no effect. A measure of this sort alone could make them think this country in earnest. The general sense of the nation was with the House. He proposed to remove the port to Salem, seventeen miles from Boston. It would be in their power to shorten the operation of the Bill. The danger of fresh affronts was not to be risked. The inconvenience England would undergo must be borne. When the Stamp Act was repealed, the Americans did not pay their debts ; but if their debts were to be an argument against our taking any measures they were our masters. Four or five frigates would carry this measure into execution. He was free to confess that he would use even the military if necessary. The militia of Boston were no match for the force of this country. Lenient measures were at an end. Whether they were in rebellion or not he could not say ; nor was he answerable for the consequences. At least it would be clear to the world that the Bostonians brought on the rebellion themselves.

Friday, March 25th.

A petition was presented from the province of Massachusetts Bay in behalf of the said colony ; but that, and all intercession for their being heard in their own defence before they were condemned, was rejected, and the [Boston] Bill was read for the third time. Dowdeswell called it a Bill of pains and penalties ; Ellis said, that if England could not impose taxes, it could give no laws whatever to the Colonies. They had resisted the teas because interfering with smuggled teas. Edmund Burke made one of his painted orations, and said that, though he had not yet opposed the Bill, he would mark his heartfelt sorrow for it in that its last stage. The House had refused to hear the agents of the Colonies : the Ministers had had their songs of exultation, not even before victory but before battle. A combination of all the Colonies would ensue. . . . Sawbridge . . . told Lord North that he skulked behind the laws and came to Parliament, when he might have done the business himself by giving proper directions. This attack Lord North answered with much humour and wit, and ridiculed the complaint of a Minister being so arbitrary as to complain to Parliament rather than exert despotic power. Governor

Johnstone said he had warned the East India Company before they sent out their teas, and had foretold what had happened since. The Minister ought to have opened the whole of his plan ; it should have been known before this Bill was assented to. The sum of indemnification ought to have been specified, that the Bostonians might know when they have expiated their crime. The House was sowing seeds of rebellion in that country. . . . The Bill, however, passed without one division on it.

Saturday, March 26th.

[Lord Chatham has written to Lord Shelburne :]

I am extremely anxious about the measures now depending with regard to America, and I consider the fate of Old England as being at stake, not less than that of the New. The violence committed upon the tea-cargo is certainly criminal ; nor would it be real kindness to the Americans to adopt their passions and wild pretensions, where they manifestly violate the most indispensable ties of civil society. Boston, therefore, appears to me to owe reparation for such a destruction of the property of the East India Company. This is, to my mind, clear and evident ; but I confess, it is equally clear to me, that in pursuing this just object, government may become unjust ; if they attempt to blend the enforcement of general declared rights of the British Parliament (which I must for ever treat as rights in theory only) with a due satisfaction for a tumultuous act of a very criminal nature. The methods, too, proposed by way of coercion, appear to me too severe, as well as highly exceptionable in order of time : for reparation ought first to be demanded in a solemn manner, and refused by the town and magistracy of Boston, before such a bill of pains and penalties can be called just.

The whole of this unhappy business is beset with dangers of the most complicated and lasting nature ; and the point of true wisdom for the mother-country seems to be in such nice and exact limits, (accurately distinguished and embraced with a large and generous moderation of spirit,) as narrow, short-sighted councils of state are not likely to hit. Perhaps a fatal desire to take advantage of this guilty tumult of the

Bostonians, in order to crush the spirit of liberty among the Americans in general, has taken possession of the Government. If that mad and cruel measure should be pushed, one need not be a prophet to say, England has seen her best days. Boston, I hope and believe, would make reparation for a heinous wrong in the tea-cargo ; but to consent quietly to have no right over their own purse, I conceive the people of America will never be brought to do. Laws of navigation and trade, for regulation not for revenue, I should hope and believe America, once at ease about internal taxation, would also acquiesce under, and friendly intercourse be again opened ; without which, we, not they, shall be undone. . . .

Sunday, March 27th.

[Lately published :]

The Works of Benjamin Hoadly, D.D. late Lord Bishop of Winchester. Collected and published by his son John Hoadly, LL.D., Chancellor of the Diocese of Winchester. 3 vols. folio.

While truth, virtue and religion are esteemed and revered among us, and while the rights of princes and of subjects are understood and preserved in this free and protestant country, all future ages will look up [to this author] with gratitude, as the great defender and assertor of all that is truly valuable to them, as men, Christians, and Britons ; or, in his son's words, " as a public benefactor to his King and country." . . .

An enquiry into the moving powers employed in the circulation of the blood ; in a lecture delivered at Newcastle the 28th of December, 1773, to a large company of the gentlemen of the faculty and others. By Andrew Wilson, M.D. 8vo. 1s. 6d. Dilly.

The Inflexible Captive : a tragedy. By Miss Hannah More. 8vo. 1s. 6d. Cadell.

The History of English Poetry, from the close of the eleventh century. To which are prefixed, two dissertations, 1. On the origin of romantic fiction in Europe, 2. On the introduction of learning into England. By Thomas Warton, B.D. Fellow of Trinity College, Oxford, and of the Society of Antiquaries. Vol. 1. 4to. £1, 1s. boards. Dodsley.

Letters written by the late Rt. Hon. Philip Dormer Stanhope, Earl of Chesterfield, to his son Philip Stanhope, Esq ; late Envoy Extra-ordinary at the Court of Dresden. Published by Mrs. Eugenia Stanhope. 2 vols. 8vo.

The reader is informed, in an advertisement prefixed to these letters, that the late Earl of Chesterfield had a natural son, whom he loved with the most unbounding affection, and whose education was for many years the chief engagement of his life. After furnishing him with the most valuable treasures of ancient and modern learning, to those acquisitions he was desirous of adding that knowledge of men and things which he himself had acquired by long and great experience. With this view these Letters were written. The editor is Mr. Stanhope's widow. . . .

Plays and Poems by William Whitehead, Esq. 2 vols. 8vo. Price 8s. sewed. Dodsley.

A correct edition of this gentleman's works, which prove with how just a title he claims the seat of Poet Laureate.

Monday, March 28th.

Lord North moved for leave to bring in a Bill for regulating the government of Massachusetts Bay. . . . His Lordship said there must be something radically wrong in the constitution of the Massachusetts Bay, when the civil magistrates could not act on any occasion. He wished to take away the executive from the democratic part, and lodge it in officers appointed by the Crown, and to have justices of the peace *ex officio*. He would have the Governor name the Judges, &c., belonging to the courts of justice, and all to be removeable, except the Chief Justice and Judges of superior Courts, and then not without a sign manual ; and no town meetings to be held without leave of the Governor. Charter rights would be sufficiently entered into in the course of the Bill. George Byng disapproved of the motion as heaping provocation on provocation. Sir Fletcher Norton, the Speaker (for the House was in Committee), desired to know whether it was the intention to leave the province with a Council and Assembly or not ? Lord North replied, he meant nothing that would affect the Assembly or election of the Council. Stephen Fox approved vigorous measures, but said

the disorders had arisen neither from the Stamp Act nor its
repeal ; but that all colonies, as they acquire strength, look
with a jealous eye on the mother-country.

Lord George Sackville Germain made a much admired
speech in favour of the motion — and of himself.   It was
impossible, he said, to understand the purport of the Bill at
the first opening.   He would ask if this was all that was to be
done this session ?   As far as it went, he had no objection.   The
present Council in the Massachusetts was a council of control,
not of advice.   He would put that council on the same foot as
in other royal governments abroad.   It was absurd to let the
people choose the Council.   The intended Bill ought to prevent
their having a power of calling their town meetings which
were now only political.   Lord North had expressed doubts
as to the alteration of juries ; perhaps the House did not know
that their grand juries were appointed with a salary and
chosen annually : the petty juries were elected by the different
townships.   The sheriff's was also a lucrative office.   What a
situation were the army and navy in, triable by such a jury !
God forbid those juries should be trusted, when Scotch juries
were not suffered to try the rebels, nor Sussex juries the
smugglers !   But it would be said, will you bring them hither
to be tried ?   Perhaps not, but he would not have them tried
on the spot.   He would bring the constitution of that country
as near to our own as he could.   It was perpetually asked in
the House, would you infringe their Charters ?   He would
answer, he would not only assert the power of this country in
words, whilst they were counteracting us with deeds. . . .
Governor Pownall owned the mob governed in the Massachusetts, but that they were sober, religious, and fond of
government.   The Bill was ordered in without a division.
However, nothing farther was done then, except ordering a
Committee to inquire into the proceedings of the Colony. . . .

Tuesday, March 29th.

We are in profound tranquillity. . . . Even America gives
us no pain, at least it makes little sensation, for the Opposition
have not taken up the cause ; in the first place because the
Opposition is very feeble ; and secondly, because it has a great

mind to be less ; that is, they are, many of the few, endeavouring to wriggle into court by different doors. The general tone against the Bostonians is threats. It remains to see whether America will be as pliant as we say they must be. . . . But we could even afford to lose America. Every day gives us more East Indies. Advice has just come that we have taken Tanjore, and a General Smith has got £150,000 for his own share. Spaniards are forced to dig in mines before they are the better for the gold of Potosi ; we have nothing to do but to break a truce and plunder a city, and we find the pretty metal ready coined and brilliants ready cut and mounted. . . . Depredation is authorised by Act of Parliament, at least by the vote of the House of Commons that acquitted and applauded Lord Clive. . . .

The Duke of Devonshire marries Lady Georgiana Spencer ; she is a lovely girl, natural and full of grace ; he the first match in England. . . . Lord Pelham is made Justice in Eyre.

Sir John Moore, Bart., is appointed a Cornet in the first or Royal regiment of Dragoons, commanded by the Earl of Pembroke.

Wednesday, March 30th.

The Boston Port Bill . . . underwent a fuller, and by all accounts a fairer discussion [yesterday] in the House of Lords than it did in the House of Commons. . . . The remarkable features of the day were the notorious division among the Ministry, which was very near avowed, some calling what passed in Boston commotion, others open rebellion, a more than disregard to Lord Dartmouth, and somewhat of the same sort towards Lord North. Lord Mansfield took upon himself a considerable lead ; alleged that it was the last over-act of high treason, proceeding from over lenity and want of foresight ; that it was, however, the luckiest event that could befall this country, for that all might be recovered, for compensation to the India Company he regarded as no object of the Bill ; that if this Act passed, we should be passed the Rubicon ; that the Americans would then know that we should temporise no longer ; and if it passed with tolerable unanimity, Boston would submit and all would pass *sine caede*.

Thursday, March 31st.

His Majesty went in state to the House of Peers, and gave the royal assent to . . . the bill for removing the officers of customs from Boston in Massachusetts Bay ; for continuing several free ports in Jamaica ; . . . for allowing further time for enrolment of deeds and wills made by papists ; for dissolving the marriage of Richard Heatley ; for making perpetual the acts for regulating the trials of controverted elections ; for the pay and clothing of the militia ; for relieving prisoners acquitted of felonies, but retained for fees ; . . . for the preservation of turnpike-roads ; for improving lands in the Isle of Ely ; for lighting, paving, and watching the parish of St. James, Clerkenwell ; and to several private bills. The House adjourned to the 12th of April ; and the House of Lords to the 14th.

Being Maundy Thursday, his Majesty's alms were distributed to thirty-five poor men and women, three ells of holland, a piece of woollen cloth, a pair of shoes and stockings, 20 shillings in a purse, 35 silver pence, a loaf of bread, and a platter of fish to each.

[Tomorrow will be] published *The Poems of Ossian,* translated by James Macpherson, Esq., printed for W. Strahan and T. Becket, the corner of the Adelphi, in the Strand,—a new edition, corrected . . . in two volumes octavo, price 12s. bound.

April 1774

Good Friday, April 1st.

Information having been given to Sir John Fielding, that a company of coiners made a business of coining halfpence in a house on Fish-street-hill, that magistrate applied [yesterday] to the Lord Mayor for his warrant to apprehend them, which he obtained and sent five of his people, well-armed, to take them by surprize. There were no less than eight of them at work, who, when they found themselves discovered, endeavoured to make resistance, and one of them received a ball in his head before he surrendered. The night before they had sent a child for some beer, with new halfpence to pay for it; and the landlord observing to the child that they were warm, she innocently replied that her daddy had just made them. A cart-load of implements were found in the house, and carried to Bow-street.

Saturday, April 2nd.

Thomas Hutchinson, Esq., Governor of the province of Massachusetts Bay, in North America, having humbly requested his Majesty's leave to come to England, the King has been graciously pleased to comply therewith, and to appoint Thomas Gage, Esq., Lieutenant-General of his Majesty's forces, to be Captain-General and Governor in Chief of the said province, and Vice-Admiral of the same during his Majesty's pleasure.

Tuesday, April 5th.

Yesterday morning died, much and deservedly regretted, at his chambers in Brick Court in the Temple, Dr. Oliver Goldsmith, author of the poems of the *Traveller* and *Deserted Village* and many ingenious works in prose. He was seized

44

on Friday se'nnight with a nervous fever in his brain which occasioned his death.

Thursday, April 7th.

At a coachmaker's on the Surrey side of Blackfriars Bridge, a new invented carriage is making, to contain twelve people, and is to go without horses. A man is to sit on the box, and turn an iron bar, which communicates to some springs which set it in motion.

Sunday, April 10th.

I have read Mr. Warton's [*History of English Poetry*, Volume the First]. I never saw so many entertaining particulars crowded together with so little entertainment and vivacity. The facts are overwhelmed by one another, as Johnson's sense is by words ; they are all equally strong. Mr. Warton has amassed all the parts and learning of four centuries and all the impression that remains is that those four ages had no parts or learning at all. There is not a gleam of poetry in their compositions between the Scalds and Chaucer : nay, I question whether they took their metres for anything more than rules for writing prose. In short, it may be the genealogy of versification with all its intermarriages and anecdotes of the family. . . . I am sorry Mr. Warton has contracted such an affection for his materials that he seems almost to think that not only Pope but Dryden himself have added few beauties to Chaucer. . . .

Wednesday, April 13th.

Sir Joshua [Reynolds] was much affected by the death of Goldsmith, to whom he had been a very sincere friend. He did not touch the pencil for that day, a circumstance most extraordinary for him, who passed no day without a line. He acted as executor and managed in the best manner the confused state of the Doctor's affairs. At first he intended to have made a grand funeral for him, assisted by several subscriptions to that intent, and to have buried him in the Abbey ; his pall-bearers to have been Lord Shelburne, Lord Louth, Sir Joshua himself, Burke, Garrick, etc. ; but on second thoughts, he resolved to have him buried in the plainest and most private manner possible, observing that the most pompous funerals are soon past and forgotten ; and that it would be much more prudent to apply what money could be procured to the purpose of a more substantial and more lasting memorial of his departed friend, by a monument ; and he was accordingly privately interred in the Temple burying-ground. . . .

A lady, who was a great friend of Dr. Goldsmith, earnestly desired to have a lock of his hair to keep as a memorial of him ; and his coffin was opened again, after it had been closed up, to procure this lock of hair from his head. . . .

Soon after Goldsmith's death, certain persons dining with Sir Joshua were commenting rather freely on some part of his works, which, in their opinion, neither discovered talent nor originality. To this Dr. Johnson listened in his usual growling manner for some time ; when at length, his patience being exhausted, he rose with great dignity, looked them full in the face and exclaimed, " If nobody was suffered to abuse poor Goldy, but those who could write as well, he would have few censors."

A monument will be erected to perpetuate the memory of Dr. Goldsmith. Sir Joshua Reynolds will draw the design ; Mr. Wilton has offered to be the statuary ; and Dr. Johnson is to write the epitaph. The monument is intended to be placed in the Poets' Corner in Westminster Abbey, and the expense proposed to be defrayed by a public subscription.

Friday, April 15*th*.

Sir Charles Whitworth presented the Bill for the better regulating the Government of . . . Massachusetts Bay . . . and after a short debate, the Bill was read a first time, and ordered to be read a second time next Friday. Lord North then presented to the House several more papers relative to the present state of some of His Majesty's Colonies in North America, which was read by the Clerks of the House, and took up near an hour reading. . . .

General Conway was the only man who spoke out on these Bills, which he did with firmness, though without bitterness.

He said the Administration had boasted of sending a sword in one hand and the olive in the other : he saw the sword but could not discover the olive-branch.   They were going to take away juries from Boston, though Colonel Preston, in the midst of a town exasperated at the deaths of eleven persons, had had a fair trial and had been acquitted.   There was one peaceable measure sure of success, and that was not tried, repealing the Tea Bill : he would second Mr. Rose Fuller in moving for such repeal.

Sunday, April 17th.

[I have] got Lord Chesterfield's Letters, which without being well entertained, I sat up reading last night till between one and two and devoured above 140.   To my great surprise they seem really written from the heart, not for the honour of his head, and in truth they do no great honour to the last, nor show much feeling in the first, except in wishing for his son's fine gentlemanhood. . . . The repetitions are endless and tiresome. . . . The more curious part of all is that one perceives by what infinite assiduity and attention his Lordship's own great character was raised and supported, and yet in all that great character what was there worth remembering but his *bons mots*? . . . From politics he rather escaped well, than succeeded by them.   In short the diamond owed more to being brillianted and polished and well set than to any intrinsic worth or solidity. . . .

He seems to have been determined to indemnify himself for the falsehood and constraint of his whole life by owning what an impostor he had been.   The work is a most proper book of laws for the generation in which it is published, and has reduced the folly and worthlessness of the age to a regular system, in which nothing but the outside of the body and the superficies of the mind are considered.   If a semblance of morality is recommended, it is to be painted and curled and Hippolytus himself may keep a w——, provided she is married and a woman of quality.   In short, if the idea were not an old one, I would write on the back of this code, *The whole duty of man, adapted to the meanest capacities.*

Monday, April 18*th.*

A Hackney coachman driving furiously down Holborn, and turning short into Hatton Garden, overset an apothecary's man with a basket of medicines hanging over his arm, and broke the phials all to pieces, and nobody was so kind as to take the man's number, by which means he escaped paying for his carelessness. These fellows should always be punished severely; for where they do mischief once by accident, they do it twice on purpose, and then call out with "Kicksey, who's afraid?"

Tuesday, April 19*th.*

A motion was made by Mr. Fuller in the House of Commons that on Tuesday next the House would resolve itself into a Committee to take into consideration the 3d. per pound weight duty laid upon teas in all his Majesty's dominions in N. America, with the appropriation of said duty, which upon a division was rejected 182 to 49. On this occasion Mr. E. Burke distinguished himself in a masterly manner.

[In Danzig] the Prussians now carry everything with a very high hand, and seem resolved to convince the inhabitants of this city, that if they do not submit in quietness, force will be used. . . .

Wednesday, April 20*th.*

This day the sessions ended at the Old Bailey. At this sessions 16 prisoners were capitally convicted ; 42 sentenced to be transported for seven years : one for 14 years : 18 to be branded : 15 to be whipped : and 40 were discharged by proclamation.

Thursday, April 21*st.*

Hawke, the highwayman, who broke gaol in August last, being put to the Bar [yesterday at Bow Street], a variety of facts, committed since his being at large, were sworn to. It appeared that Mr. Smith, Keeper of Tothill-fields Bridewell, having received some information concerning the prisoner, went to Uxbridge, where he learnt the name and place of abode of a man in whose coach Mr. Hawke had been a few days before conveyed to that town. Mr. Smith then returned, and, in company with Mr. Bond, went to a coach-yard near Hatton Garden ; and having previously been informed that Hawke's lodging was in that neighbourhood, very properly enticed [the coach-yard keeper] into a house in Hockley in the Hole, to prevent the possibility of any communication between him and the prisoner. Here the business was opened ; and after much difficulty, the man (who was not present yesterday) was prevailed upon to confess that Hawke's horse stood in his stables, and to give a direction to his habitation. They then procured further assistance, and proceeded to a house in a court in Shoe-Lane : Mr. Smith searched the first floor, while Mr. Bond went to a room above, where seeing Hawke in bed, he immediately leaped upon him, and gave an alarm, upon which Mr. Smith came in just time enough to prevent the prisoner catching up a loaded pistol. After he was secured, he said they might congratulate themselves upon having acted with great caution and intrepidity, which had prevented them being blown to atoms. Five loaded pistols and a great number of watches were found in his apartment. Mr. Hart deposed, that on Monday the 29th of March, as he and Captain Cunningham of the 20th Regiment of Guards, were going in a hackney coach towards Fulham, they were stopped by the prisoner a little on the other side of Knightsbridge, who thrusted a pistol against Mr. Hart's breast and demanded his money, upon which he delivered one shilling and sixpence and some halfpence ; that Captain Cunningham having the value of £500 about him, was endeavouring to secure his pocket-book, which being observed by the highwayman, he threatened to fire unless it was immediately delivered ; the Captain refused to give up his property, and bid him " fire away," upon which he instantly discharged a pistol, but happily without effect. After this they got out of the carriage, and endeavoured to annoy the villain with their sticks, and by throwing stones ; but were not able to prevent his escape. Mr. Boyde, Mr. Lemotte, Mr. Ladbroke, Mr. Ward, Mr. Walter, Mr. Spence, Mr. Barnsley, Mr. Mackie, &c., &c. exhibited separate charges of highway robbery against the prisoner, and were accordingly bound over to prosecute.

Friday, April 22nd.

The Committee sat on the second reading of the Bill for regulating the Civil Jurisdiction in America. . . . Sir George Savile said he had trembled at every step that had been taken on the affair of Boston : he had argued ill from the time the House had refused to hear Mr. Bolland, agent for that Colony, and till now had withdrawn himself from that whole business. Ellis affirmed that the King, Lords, and Commons have a right to alter charters given by the Crown. General Conway said, that though it had been alleged that the Americans had no right to be heard at the bar of the House, yet it had been the universal practice, on alteration of charters, to hear the party, and in matters of right it could not be refused. . . .

Lord North replied, that it was fit in courts of law to hear the parties ; but charters were the regulations of the Crown and under the control of Government. Was it the idea that we should send over to summon them to attend their rights, which did not exist, whilst they go on plundering your merchantmen, and tarring and feathering your subjects ? Were we, in that state, to take no steps to restore government ? He was persuaded they would send word they would not appear at the bar. . . .

Sir George Yonge and Governor Johnstone blamed the injustice of Administration. The latter complained that the new Bill would make the Governor of Massachusetts absolute, and the Americans become the slaves of Ministers. The latter had better speak out and say at once that they meant to establish despotism all over the Empire. . . . Governor Pownall . . . said there was an end of opinions, it would come to action with the Americans. They would immediately hold a Congress of the different provinces ; they would unite, and consider how they should proceed most to their advantage. . . .

The Bill was then read a second time without a division and ordered to be committed. . . .

The booksellers' bill for the security of literary property was read the first time, and ordered to be read again on Wednesday the 4th of May, when counsel is to be heard on both sides.

Saturday, April 23rd.

A few nights ago at the Club at Almack's, the conversation happening to turn on the ensuing general election, several eminent artists and men of letters were talked of as candidates for a seat in Parliament ; and amongst others it was mentioned that Sir Joshua Reynolds had canvassed the Borough of Plympton. Most of the young Macaronies seemed to think that he had not the slightest chance ; upon which George Selwyn said, " If Sir Joshua was to try, he certainly must carry it against any man in England, for surely there was nobody equal to him on a canvas."

[Yesterday] the five malefactors under sentence of death in Newgate were executed at Tyburn. Of these Thomas Ives, for high treason in coining and counterfeiting the current silver coin, was drawn on a sledge, and after hanging some time his body was opened and his bowels and heart taken out and burnt.

Monday, April 25th.

Vienna, March 31*st.*—All the accounts from the Ottoman empire mention the vast preparations making by the Turks to continue the war against Russia with vigour. The grand Vizier's army is preparing to approach the Danube. . . .

Tuesday, April 26th.

[Lately published :]
Sketches of the History of Man. 2 vols. 4to. £1, 16s. Cadell.

This work [by Lord Kames] . . . considers the progress of men as individuals, with respect to language, food, property, commerce, the arts and population . . . the progress of men in society . . . [and] the progress of sciences, including the principles and progress of reason, of morality and of theology. . . .

The author hath displayed great reading and abilities. His style is very correct and perspicacious, a few Scotticisms excepted. . . .

51   E

Wednesday, April 27th.

PROCEEDINGS AGAINST

EDINBURGH	BOSTON
Began the 10th of February, 1737, and ended the 21st of June, having continued near four months.	Began the 14th, and ended the 31st of March, 1774, being in all seventeen days.
The Provost and magistrates of Edinburgh, the judges of Scotland and many other witnesses at the bar.	Witnesses examined at the Privy Council, and their evidence suppressed.
Council and evidences for the magistrates and city fully heard at the bar.	The agent refused a hearing at the bar.
Two members for Edinburgh, forty-five for Scotland in the Lower House and sixteen in the Upper House.	Not one member for Boston in either House, nor for all or any part of America, nor even a voice in electing one.
Charge — an overt act of rebellion and an atrocious murder — proved on a full hearing, and by competent evidence.	Charge — a riot and trespass — no evidence and no hearing.
Frequent conferences held between the two Houses to compare the evidence, etc.	Not one conference.
Punishment — A fine of £2,000.	Punishment — The loss of their port, to the injury of the town, at the lowest and the most favourable estimate, of £500,000. The restoration of their port, and the use of their property, left at the King's mercy, after they shall have paid for rotten tea the full price of that which is found, and all damages to the amount, we may presume, of £30,000.
For proof, see the Journals of the Lords and Commons in 1737, and the Bill against Edinburgh.	Journals of the Lords and Commons 1774, and the Boston Port Bill.

AN ABLE DOCTOR

Thursday, April 28th.

At [Shrewsbury] Assizes bills of indictment were preferred
by Capt. Chilcot, late of the *Charming Jenny*, against three
opulent inhabitants of the isle of Anglesea (one of whom is
said to be possessed of a considerable estate, and to have
offered £5,000 bail) in order to their being tried at the next
assizes on a charge of piracy, when the bills were found. It
appeared in the course of the depositions, that on the 11th of
September last, in very bad weather, in consequence of false
lights being discovered, the captain bore for shore, when his
vessel, whose cargo was valued at £19,000, went to pieces
and all the crew, except the captain and his wife, perished,
whom the waves had brought on shore upon part of the wreck.
Nearly exhausted they lay for some time, till the savages of the
adjacent places rushed down upon the devoted victims. The
lady was just able to lift a handkerchief up to her head, when
her husband was torn from her side. They cut his buckles
from his shoes, and deprived him of every covering. Happy
to escape with life, he hasted to the beach in search of his wife,
when, horrible to tell ! her half-naked and plundered corpse
presented itself to his view. What to do, Captain Chilcot was
at a loss. Providence, however, conducted him to the roof of a
venerable pair, who bestowed upon him every assistance that
his hard case required, who, in a short space, had been reduced
from affluence to a most deplorable state. The captain's wife,
it seems, at the time the ship went to pieces, had two bank bills
of a considerable value, and 70 guineas in her pocket. There
were five others concerned.

Friday, April 29th.

The report is revived, that Parliament will be dissolved
this summer ; but many people believe it to be only a report.
The matter which gives it countenance is the Civil List being
five quarters in arrear. The odious step of paying this debt is
reserved to be the first work of a new parliament ; it is too
obnoxious to be the last of an old one. Considering the immense
revenue of the King, it staggers every dispassionate man how
this happens. None can account for it. The official ministers

are kept as totally in the dark concerning the King's expenses, as they are concerning all important public measures ; which they know nothing of until the scheme is produced to them, when they are not at liberty to make any alteration, nor dare they deviate, in an iota, from their instructions.   The tenure by which they hold their offices is to receive entirely, and to obey implicitly.   Their slavish submission to hourly insults of this kind gives them a sort of claim to ask for places, as they fall, for their poor relations.

Saturday, April 30th.

A gentleman just arrived from Plymouth informs [me] that whilst he was there, a small vessel was purchased, in order to be sunk under water four or five fathom deep, in which a man has undertaken to live thirty hours ; great wagers are depending upon this undertaking.   However, if we can believe Derham, in his *Treatise on Experimental Philosophy*, we may suppose the experiment very practicable.   He says, that a boat was so contrived as to be rowed under water, in the reign of King James the First, for many hours, by six men, whilst one man was in the steerage, who (as the air became condensed, and unfit for respiration) let a certain chemical fluid out of a cask, which so rarified the air, that the crew breathed as well as if they had been on land.

MAY 1774

Sunday, May 1st.

Next to gaming, which subsides a little from want of materials, the predominant folly is pictures. . . . Sir George Colbroke, a citizen and martyr to what is called *speculation*, had his pictures sold by auction last week. A view of Nimeguen, by Cuyp, not large and which he had bought very dearly for seventy guineas sold for two hundred and ninety ! . . . One Guido for two thousand pounds to Mr. Duncombe. The 'Doctors' at Houghton, the first picture in England and equal to any in Italy but Raphael's, cost but a little above six hundred pounds. . . .

Miss Davis, the *Inglesina*, is more admired than anything I remember of late years in Operas ; but though music is so much in fashion, that some of our fine gentlemen learn to sing, it holds no proportion with hazard and Newmarket. The Cuzzoni and Faustina would not be paid higher than a race-horse.

Monday, May 2nd.

Some gentlemen of the Society of Antiquaries, being desirous to see how far the actual state of Edward I's body answered to the methods taken to preserve it, by writs issued from time to time, in the reigns of Edward III and Henry IV to the treasury, to renew the wax about it, several of which are printed in Rymer's *Foedera*, obtained leave to open the large stone sarcophagus, in which it was deposited, on the north side of Edward the Confessor's chapel. This was accordingly done this morning, when, in a coffin of yellow stone, they found the royal body, in perfect preservation, wrapt in two wrappers, one of them of gold tissue, strongly waxed, and fresh ; the outermost more decayed. The corpse was habited in a rich mantle of purple, paned with white, and adorned with orna-

55

ments of gilt metal, studded with red and blue stones and pearls. Two similar ornaments lay on his hands. The mantle was fastened on the right shoulder by a magnificent fibula of the same metal, with the same stones and pearls. His face had over it a silken covering, so fine, and so closely fitted to it, as to preserve the features entire. Round his temples was a gilt coronet of *fleurs de lys*. In his hands, which were also entire, were two sceptres of gilt metal ; that in the right surmounted by a cross *fleuri*, that in the left by three clusters of oak leaves, and a dove on a globe ; this sceptre was about five feet long. The feet were enveloped in the mantle and other coverings, but sound, and the toes distinct. The whole length of the corpse was six feet two inches. As it does not appear that any of the above-mentioned writs were issued since the reign of Henry IV the body must have been preserved above three centuries and an half, in the state in which was now found, by virtue of the embalment originally bestowed on it ; and, as every thing was restored with the strictest care, and the tomb secured beyond a possibility of ever being opened again, it may continue, at least, as many centuries longer.— Edward I died at Burgh upon Sands, in Cumberland, on his way to Scotland, July 7, 1307, in the 68th year of his age.

Tuesday, May 3rd.

Sir George Savile [yesterday] presented a petition from several inhabitants of North America . . . resident in London, praying to be heard against sending troops against them, and against the proceedings then carrying on in Parliament. All the favour shown to that petition was to suffer it to lie on the table. . . .

The Bill for regulating the Massachusetts [was read] the third time and a very long debate, though not a very new or lively one, ensued, which lasted till past two in the morning, when the Bill was carried by 239 to 64. . . .

Among the great collection of pictures sold by Mr. Christie, in Pall Mall, on Saturday last, were a few by the most distinguished artists. The feast of Bacchus and Ariadne, by Molinari, was knocked down at 90 guineas ; David, with a head of Goliath, by Preti Genoese, commonly called Capucino, went for 120 guineas, and a fine piece of the Lord's Supper, by Titian, for 130 guineas.

Wednesday, May 4th.

Last night was the triumph of Boodle's. [The] Masquerade [at the Pantheon] cost two thousand guineas : a sum that might have fertilised a province . . . vanished in a few hours, but not without leaving behind it the fame of the most splendid and elegant fête that was perhaps ever given in a seat of the arts and opulence. It would be as difficult to describe the magnificence of the scene as it would be easy to record the humour of the night. The one was above, the other below all relation. I left the Pantheon about five this morning. . . .

Thursday, May 5th.

The Duchess of Gloucester received masks, but with tickets only, which gave a dullness to the scene peculiar to regularity ; and if one dullness surpasses another, royal dullness takes the lead of even city dullness.

Friday, May 6th.

Whilst the men upon the *ton* take every possible means to appear effeminate, the women . . . assume the most masculine air in their power. The fashion of riding in the forenoon in Hyde Park will convince any bystander of this observation : the Macaronies in their riding-dresses seem but half-whelped . . . whilst the truly female Amazonians appear like heroes and . . . wear the breeches literally as well as metaphorically. This indeed is a fine time for the women . . . but I would have the men . . . prove themselves at least noun substantives in public as well as in private. A *thing* with a large nosegay, a laced tucker and a perfumed toupée is of the doubtful gender and might, at least, be shown as a hermaphrodite at Bartholomew Fair. . . .

Saturday, May 7th.

Yesterday printed proposals were delivered at the door of the House of Commons, " for putting the open vaults and churchyards, in and about this metropolis, under proper regulations " ; the writer supposes that the great increase of putrid fevers is owing to this great nuisance. The greatest evil is what he calls the parish or poors' graves ; these pits, as he justly observes, are kept open till they are full, and the stench is such, that the minister is often obliged to stand at a considerable distance when he reads the burial service over these poor creatures.

Sunday, May 8th.

Mr. Hawes attended the late Dr. Goldsmith as an apothecary during his late illness, of the circumstances of which he has lately published a fair, candid and accurate account. . . . He has been treated in an injurious manner in the newspapers. The cause of this is sufficiently apparent. Mr. Hawes was thoroughly convinced that Dr. James's Powder [which Dr. Goldsmith insisted upon taking against all advice] had been highly injurious in Dr. Goldsmith's case and he very frankly published that opinion . . . but at the same time he candidly acknowledged that this Medicine, in many cases of fevers was highly beneficial and . . . he has treated Dr. James himself with great decency and politeness. . . .

The part which Mr. Hawes has taken is perfectly consistent with the general humanity of his character, and which has led him with Dr. Cogan to be so assiduous in establishing in this kingdom an institution for the recovery of persons apparently dead by drowning. . . .

" It was supposed [says Mr. Hawes] that my publication might be prejudicial to the sale of this famous medicine. . . . I was indeed somewhat prepared for the scurrility which has been thrown out against me by a very expressive declaration which Mr. Francis Newbery, jun., made to me . . . that ' say what I would, the fever-powder was his property and he would defend it.' "

Monday, May 9th.

A whimsical thing happened on Friday in St. James's Park ; a domestic of the French Ambassador was running in a great hurry down the Birdcage Walk. " Why in that haste ?

What is the matter ? " cried a drill sergeant, stopping him.
" Sad news ! we are all ruined ! " cries the Frenchman, " the
King of France is dead ! " " You lie, you traitor," returns
the drill sergeant, and knocks him down, " the King of France
is alive and merry, God be thanked, at the end of the Mall."

Wednesday, May 11th.

I paid my half-crown and walked into Ranelagh. . . . The
people of the true *ton*, who visit this dove court of delight, come
in about eleven, stare about them for half an hour, laugh at
the other fools who are drenching and scalding themselves
with coffee and tea, abuse everybody, despise all they have
seen and then they trail home again to sup.   The citizens, on
the other hand, who are the apes of the nobleman's fashions
without either the grace or the vivacity of the animal, run like
children after the sound of a puppet-show drum, at the name
of the Duke of Gloucester, or Lady Almeria Carpenter, or any
other woman of quality that is either celebrated for wit or
beauty, or any other nobleman, though he be as dull as the
rest of the ―― family.   The sight of great folks is what they
come to see, and how they are dressed, and how they walk,
and how they talk ! . . .

Thursday, May 12th.

Monday upwards of two hundred pounds worth of smuggled
tea were seized in the cellar of a house in Petticoat Lane, White-
chapel, and carried to the custom house.   At the same place
were found two barrels of new counterfeit half-pence.

The iron rails in St. James's Park, in the room of the brick
wall, has such a delightful effect from the street that application will be made to His Majesty that the Green Park wall,
Piccadilly, may be taken down and iron rails upon a stone
basis erected in its stead.   This mean brick wall, excluding the
beauty of the Parks, has been long lamented as an inelegant
nuisance.

Saturday, May 14th.

I shall here insert a table by which the comparative merit
of the British singing birds may be examined, the idea of which

I have borrowed from Mons. de Piles, in his *Cours de Peinture par Principes*. I shall not be surprised however, if, as he suggests, many may disagree with me about particular birds, as he supposes they will do with him, concerning the merits of painters.

As I have five columns, instead of the four which M. de Piles uses, I make 20 the point of absolute perfection, instead of 16, which is his standard.

	Mellowness of tone	Sprightly notes	Plaintive notes	Compass	Execution
Nightingale . .	19	14	19	19	19
Skylark . .	4	19	4	18	18
Woodlark . .	18	4	17	12	8
Titlark . .	12	12	12	12	12
Linnet . . .	12	16	12	16	18
Goldfinch . .	4	19	4	12	12
Chaffinch . .	4	12	4	8	8
Greenfinch . .	4	4	4	4	6
Hedge-sparrow .	6	0	6	4	4
Aberdavine (or Siskin) . .	2	4	0	4	4
Redpoll . .	0	4	0	4	4
Thrush . .	4	4	4	4	4
Blackbird . .	4	4	0	2	2
Robin . . .	6	16	12	12	12
Wren . . .	0	12	0	4	4
Reed-sparrow .	0	4	0	2	2
Black-cap, or the Norfolk mock-nightingale .	14	12	12	14	14

I have made no mention of the bullfinch in this table, which is commonly considered as a singing bird ; because its wild note, without instruction, is a most jarring and disagreeable noise.

I have likewise omitted the redstart (which is called by the French *le Rossignol de Muraille*), as I am not sufficiently acquainted with its song, though it is admired by many ; I should rather conceive, however, with Zinanni, that there is no very extraordinary merit in the notes.

The London bird-catchers also sell sometimes the yellow hammer, twite, and brambling as singing birds ; but none of these will come within my definition of what may be deemed so.

Most people, who have not attended to the notes of birds, suppose that those of every species sing exactly the same notes and passages, which is by no means true, though it is admitted that there is a general resemblance.

Thus the London bird-catchers prefer the song of the Kentish goldfinches, but Essex chaffinches ; and when they sell the bird to those who can thus distinguish, inform the buyer that it hath such a note, which is very well understood between them.

These are the names which they give to some of the nightingale's notes : Sweet, Sweet jug, Jug sweet, Water bubble, Pipe rattle, Bell pipe, Scroty, Skeg, skeg, skeg, Swat swat swaty, whitlow whitlow whitlow, from some distant affinity to such words.

Some of the nightingale fanciers also prefer a Surrey bird to those of Middlesex.

These differences in the song of birds of the same species cannot, perhaps, be compared to anything more apposite than the varieties of the provincial dialects.

Sunday, May 15th.

We [do not] know actually yet that Louis Quinze is dead, but we conclude so. Lord Stormont's courier arrived on Wednesday and had left Paris on Sunday night at eleven, when the hiccup was begun. He said he might not be able to write again soon, as all horses would be stopped. Some pretend to say the King died on Tuesday, others conclude he is recovered, but horses would not be stopped on that account, — on the contrary. Many foretell war, not on knowledge. The Dauphin is little known.

The Duke and Duchess of Cumberland have been landed this week. . . . The honeymoon was waned to less than half a moon before he left England. . . .

Lord Ilchester has had a stroke of palsy and it is not the first. How thick calamities fall on that family ! Lord Holland drags on a wretched life and Lady Holland is dying of a cancer. Their youngest and only good son is just gone with his regiment to America. . . .

Monday, May 16th.

The purser of the *Duke of Kingston*, Indiaman, arrived at the India-house, with an account of the arrival of that ship at Falmouth, from Canton, in China. She sailed from the Downs, Jan. 4. 1773, having been little more than 16 months absent.

Tuesday, May 17th.

Sunday not less than two thousand people assembled in and about the church and churchyard of St. Olave's, Tooly Street, in order to see the wife of Mr. J—— B——, a carman (who had a share in the last £20,000 [lottery] prize), perform penance, for calling the woman a whore with whom her husband lives and cohabits. The reason of Mrs. B——'s calling her so being well known to the populace, they seemed determined, if the woman who was called whore had made her appearance, to have stripped her, and given her a severe ducking in the Thames, but happily for her, she thought it most advisable to keep out of the way. After the ceremony was performed, Mrs. B—— was accompanied to a friend's house, with no less a number than above mentioned.

Wednesday, May 18th.

Yesterday's Gazette confirms the death of the French King [Louis XV] who expired, at three o'clock in the afternoon of the 10th instant, of the small-pox, at his palace of Versailles, in the 64th year of his age, and the 59th of his reign.

The dauphin of France, who succeeds to the crown, is grandson to the late King, is named Louis Augustus, was born August 23, 1754, and married Maria Antonietta, of Austria, on May 16, 1770.

Thursday, May 19th.

The intentions of administration with regard to America, are now apparent. The bill they have brought in, called the Quebec Bill, is to enlarge that province so as to take in half America, to establish in it the Roman Catholic religion, the French law, and to make the King with the Governor and Council the Legislature of the Province. Thus, at one stroke, they meditate the subversion of the Church, the Law, and the

Constitution of England. The King of England is to be put in the place of the King of France, and have a taste of what is deemed so delicious, arbitrary power. Lord Mansfield will have at length the pleasure of triumphing over what he so much hates, the Trial by Jury. The first west wind may blow this arbitrary system over to this country, when once it is established in that. Yet we are so absurd as to countenance the scheme, and aid in digging the pit for America into which we ourselves must fall.

Saturday, May 21st.

On Monday last Resolutions were moved in the Committee of Ways and Means, for increasing the licences of hawkers and pedlars, from £4, 4s. (a rate already too high) to £5, 5s. if they walked afoot, and still higher if they used a horse or cart. It seemed intended to have passed those Resolutions unobserved, by their being moved early, and neither introduced with speech nor notice. They were accidentally overheard by Mr. William Burke, and Mr. Dempster, who called the House to attend, when they were taken up by those gentlemen, Mr. Edmund Burke, Mr. Pulteney, Lord Frederick Campbell, Mr. Thomas Townshend, and Mr. Cavendish, with much spirit. They were shown to be uncommercial, crude, and surreptitious ; and at length, after a feeble defence from the Treasury Bench, they were negatived without a division. Much is this nation indebted to gentlemen who watch ministerial jobs at all times, particularly on the eve of a General Election. None of his Majesty's subjects have a better claim to the protection of Parliament than hawkers and pedlars. They increase the consumption of our manufactures, by supplying the lower classes of the community with them at a cheap rate. To their utility we may presume they owe their preservation, for they have long been the objects of the jealousy and the dislike of all shopkeepers ; and they are rarely either freeholders in counties or electors in any of our towns.

Sunday, May 22nd.

The danger of catching the smallpox the common way is so very great, that no fewer than one in six surely die thereof, and the hazard from inoculation is so very small, that not one in a thousand are lost thereby. . . .

The earlier in life the better, (and of the measles likewise) as they would wish well to their immediate issue, and their succeeding posterity also : by this means, in time, they might extirpate both entirely out of the land. O what would former ages have given for so fortunate a discovery !

Monday, May 23rd.

Captain Elphiston arrived in town express from Sir Peter Denis, Commander-in-chief of the King's ships in the Mediterranean, with an account that the Dey of Algiers had behaved with the utmost insolence and contempt to our Flag, and peremptorily refused to receive Mr. Fraser as Consul from hence, nor would he suffer him to remain in the city. He concluded by ordering the English men of war to leave the Bay directly, which the Admiral complied with. . . . Poor Old England, how art thou fallen since the glorious days of George the Second ! . . .

Economy is now so much the cry at St. James's, that there is very little doubt but the honour of the Nation will be sacrificed to it, and that the Minister will advise the king to submit to the insult . . . and appease his wrath by presents ! So Christian-like and forgiving are we become.

Thursday, May 26th.

The present Queen of France is a great enemy to paint, and is determined to discountenance the use of it as much as possible. She never was known to have the least touch of it on her face, nor would she allow any of her ladies, attendants, to paint. We may therefore expect to see the natural complexion of the French ladies in a short time, which, perhaps will be an inducement for those of England to abuse Dame Nature less, by using less rouge.

Mr. Colman took his leave of the performers of Covent Garden Theatre, having given up the management, sold his share in the patent, and retired to a private station.

Friday, May 27th.

Yesterday came on according to order in the Upper
Assembly the third reading of the Bill for providing quarters
for the officers and troops in North America.   The bill was
accordingly read a third time by the clerk, and upon the question being put, whether the bill should pass, Lord Chatham
got up and spoke for upwards of an hour in a very nervous and
sensible manner.   During the course of his speech his Lordship
highly condemned the refractory behaviour of the Americans,
but at the same time disapproved of the measures taken by
administration, looking upon them as harsh, oppressive and
tyrannical.

Lord Chatham was so infirm, that he was obliged to support
himself with a crutch. . . .

Saturday, May 28th.

A chimney-sweeper's boy was sent up a stove in White-
chapel which was on fire, in order to extinguish it, but when
he had got half-way up he stuck and was suffocated before
they could get him out.

Sunday, May 29th.

[Lately published:]
The Search after Happiness.   A Pastoral Drama.   By Miss
Hannah More, of Bristol.   Cadell.

This pleasing, instructive little poem has already passed
into a third edition.   " It was composed . . . several years
ago, (the author's age eighteen) and recited at that time and
since by a party of young ladies, for which purpose it was
originally written."   Four young ladies, who are in search of
happiness, are introduced by Florella, a young shepherdess, to
Urania, a matron, by whom she has been protected and
educated.   This old shepherdess, who with her two daughters,
Sylvia and Eliza, are all the characters of the pastoral, upon
hearing that they were in search of happiness, and enquiring
where they sought it, after being told by Euphelia, that she
had sought it in courts, balls, and drawing-rooms ; by Cleona,
that fame, literary fame was her object, poetry and philosophy
her study and pursuit ; by Pastorella, that novels and romances

65

were her taste, a victim to fancy and imagination ; and by Laurinda, that all her misfortunes were owing to a vacancy of thought, to folly and ignorance ; proceeds to correct their errors, and to convince them that the chief happiness and misery of mortals are owing to a good or bad education, and that wisdom, virtue and religion, are the unerring paths of pleasantness and peace. The important truths are conveyed in most elegant numbers.

America vindicated from the high charge of ingratitude and rebellion : with a plan of legislation proposed to the consideration of both Houses. 8vo. 1s. Ridley.

The Report of the Lords Committees appointed by the House of Lords to enquire into the several proceedings in the Colony of Massachusett's Bay, in opposition to the sovereignty of His Majesty in his Parliament of Great Britain over that Province ; and also what has passed in that House relative thereto, from the first day of January, 1774. 2s. 6d. Bingley.

Experiments and Observations on different kinds of Air. By Joseph Priestley, LL.D. 5s. 8vo. Johnson.

Retaliation ; a poem by Dr. Goldsmith ; including epitaphs on the distinguished wits of the metropolis. 4to. 1s. 6d. Kearsley. [From which I take this extract:]

Here lies David Garrick, describe me who can,
An abridgement of all that was pleasant in man :
As an actor, confess'd without rival to shine ;
As a wit, if not first, in the very first line.
Yet, with talents like these, and an excellent heart,
The man had his failings, a dupe to his art :
Like an ill-judging beauty, his colours he spread,
And be-plaster'd with rouge his own natural red.
On the stage he was natural, simple, affecting,
'Twas only that when he was off he was acting.
With no reason on earth to go out of his way,
He turned and he varied full ten times a day :
Tho' secure of our hearts, yet confoundedly sick
If they were not his own by finessing and trick.
He cast off his friends, as a huntsman his pack,
For he knew, when he pleased, he could whistle them back :

Of praise a mere glutton, he swallow'd what came,
And the puff of a dunce he mistook it for fame ;
'Till his relish grown callous, almost to disease,
Who pepper'd the highest was surest to please.
But let us be candid, and speak out our mind,
If dunces applauded, he paid them in kind.
Ye Kenricks, ye Kellys, and Woodfalls, so grave,
What a commerce was yours, while you got and you gave ?
How did Grub-street re-echo the shouts that you raised,
While he was be-Rosciused, and you were be-praised ?
But peace to his spirit, wherever it flies,
To act as an angel, and mix with the skies :
Those poets who owe their best fame to his skill,
Shall still be his flatterers, go where he will ;
Old Shakespeare receive him with praise and with love,
And Beaumonts and Bens be his Kellys above.

Monday, May 30th.

This day the Society of Arts voted a gold medal to Mr.
Pinchbeck of Cockspur-street, for his invention of a plough
for mending the roads ; and a silver medal to Mr. Phillips of
Tottenham-Court-Road, for a new invention for raising water
to the tops of houses.

JUNE 1774

Wednesday, June 1st.

Monday evening, about seven o'clock, one of the most daring riots happened in the town of Greenwich that perhaps ever was committed in a civilised country. . . . The *Cumberland* Man of War, lately launched at Portsmouth, a number of sailors from the guard-ships lying at Portsmouth and Chatham, were sent to navigate her round ; but the winds having been contrary for some time, and these people being under no kind of discipline, have committed great ravages in the gardens in and about Deptford and Greenwich ; insomuch, that they have gone into the Gardens in the evenings by fifty in a gang, and filled each man his sack with cabbages, or whatever else they thought proper ; and into the farmers' yards, and took whatever they liked, such as pigs, ducks or fowls, and carried them on board in triumph ; and complaint having been made to the Justices at Greenwich, Justice Russel directed the constables of the neighbouring villages to be very vigilant in assisting to bring these lawless plunderers to justice. Accordingly on Monday morning five out of a great many were secured, and put into the watch-houses in Deptford and Greenwich ; and as there was a Review that morning on Blackheath by his Majesty, their comrades on board did not think it prudent to stir out of the ship till all the guards were gone, and the roads clear ; when about 300 sailors came on shore out of the *Cumberland*, armed with crows, handspikes, hatchets, iron bolts, staves and cutlasses, and immediately broke down the watch-house at Deptford, and released their comrades. Then they made enquiry where the Justice and Constables lived that dared to imprison one of their body ; and being informed at Greenwich, where two of their mess-mates were also confined, they immediately left Deptford, and set off for that place, swearing most bitter oaths they would hang in the market place at Greenwich every magistrate and constable they could find. Accordingly this lawless gang, attended with a great mob, entered the town about seven o'clock, when the number amounted to about 2,000. . . . They directly attacked the watch-house, which being very strong, took them some time to demolish ; but after robbing a butcher's shop in Church Street of the cleavers, and a blacksmith's of hammers, they soon broke it down. During this time the inhabitants shut their shops, and barricaded their houses, expecting they would search every house for the magistrates and constables, to put their infernal intentions against them in execution, as they brought halters with them ; but about ten o'clock a report being spread by an arch boy, an apprentice to a druggist, that Justice Russel, at the head of a company of the Guards from the Tower, was upon the road coming to secure them, they directly fled, threatening to return again and set the town on fire. All the inhabitants kept watch all night, and many of the ladies of the town were terribly frightened, and in fits. . . .

Thursday, June 2nd.

A Bill which had passed the Commons, to relieve book-sellers who had bought property in copies, was thrown out by the Lords by 21 to 11.

The Parliament of Ireland was prorogued till the 26th of July next. . . .

Friday, June 3rd.

The City of London presented a strong petition against the Quebec Bill, but it was only ordered to lie on the table. The Opposition, however, prevailed to have witnesses examined, which the Lords had not done ; but though great evidence appeared of the bad consequences the Bill would have, the tight majority overruled all conviction. . . .

Saturday, June 4th.

A gentleman asking Dr. Johnson the other day what he thought of Lord Chesterfield's letters to his son, " Why, Sir (says he) they are written in the true style and spirit of the age, for they inculcate the morals of a w——e, and the manners of a dancing master."

Sunday, June 5th.

Observed by Mr. Pennant, in his late *Tour in Scotland and Voyage to the Hebrides*, at Crasthwaite Church in the vale of Keswick, Cumberland . . . which hath five chapels belonging to it, the minister's stipend was five pounds per annum, a *goose-grass*, or the right of commoning his goose ; a *whittle gait*, or the valuable privilege of using his knife for a week at a time at any table in the parish ; and lastly, a *hardened sark*, or a shirt of coarse linen : whereas the rectory of Winwick, a small village in Lancashire, is the richest living in England. The rector is Lord of the Manor, and has a glebe of £1,300 annual rent ; the whole living is worth £2,300 per annum.

Tuesday, June 7th.

Lord North persisting at past eleven at night to go on with the [Quebec] Bill, Burke made an angry speech and complaint of the heat and fatigue, and left the House, followed by others of the Opposition. This alarmed Lord North and he suffered the House to break up. It was time to grow alarmed, for accounts had been just received that New York had taken almost as warm a part as Boston, and had seized and sent away a cargo of tea. The example of so great and potent a province was likely to have great influence on the other Colonies. At the same time came advice that at Philadelphia they had burnt the effigies of Alexander Wedderburn, Solicitor-General, for his aspersing Dr. Franklin ; and of Governor Hutchinson for his evil intentions.

Wednesday, June 8th.

The celebrated Dr. Samuel Johnson is about making the tour of France and Italy, in the suite of his friends Dr. Thrale and lady. They are to be accompanied by Signor Barretti (author of *Travels through Italy*, &c.) who is to be what is generally called Bear Leader upon this occasion.

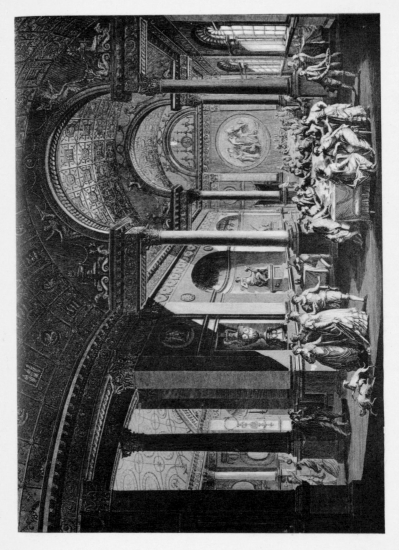

THE SUPPER ROOM AND PART OF THE BALLROOM AT THE
FÊTE CHAMPÊTRE, JUNE 9TH, 1774

Friday, June 10th.

The Fête Champêtre [held yesterday] at the Oaks, in Surrey [is said to be] the first of the kind given in England. . . .

The company began to make their appearance about half past six o'clock, and continued pouring in till past nine. As soon as any carriage had let down a party, and they had got within the gate which led upon the lawn, they were saluted by French-horns placed in a retreat so obscure as not to be observed by the company. The front lawn soon became crowded with fancy dresses ; and the ladies, by their pastoral appearance and simplicity, made beauty appear with additional charms, and by their elegant fancy-habits meant certainly to outvie each other in taste and magnificence.

About eight o'clock a signal was given for the company to attend the *Masque* on the back lawn ; accordingly, General Burgoyne, who was the principal manager and conductor, and for whose skill and abilities on the occasion the greatest compliments are due, came forward, and conducted the nobility and others, the visitors, through the house to the voluptuous scene on the back lawn. No sooner did the rural picture present itself, but amazement seized the whole company ; the first thing that caught their attention was the concourse of people on each side the road, and the branches of trees bending with the weight of heads that appeared as thick as codlings on a tree in a plentiful season. At the upper end of the back lawn was a most superb and beautiful *orangerie*, or plantation of orange-trees, inter-mixed with a great variety of greenhouse plants ; behind the *orangerie* lay concealed a capital band of music, under the sole direction of Mr. Barthélemon, the composer of the masque. On the right from the company, swains appeared in fancy-dresses, amusing themselves at the game of nine-pins, whilst shepherdesses, neatly attired, were at the swing. On the left side were other swains with their bows and arrows, shooting at a bird which had perched itself upon a maypole ; whilst others were shewing their agility by dancing and kicking at a *tambour de basque*, which hung decorated with ribbands, from a bough of a tree.— In short, every rural pastime was exhibited.

In the centre of the *orangerie* sat Mrs. Barthélemon and Mr. Vernon, making wreaths of flowers, and continued in that employment till after the company had taken their seats upon the benches, placed in a circular form on the green. As soon as the ladies and gentlemen were thus arranged, two Cupids went round with a basket of the most rich flowers, and presented each lady with an elegant *bouquet* ; the gentlemen had likewise a similar present. When the Cupids had distributed the flowers, nimble shepherdesses supplied their baskets with fresh assortments. Thus, whilst the attention of the company was taken up with admiring the agility and pretty manner of these little attendants accommodating the nobility and others with their nosegays, they were on a sudden surprised with a harmonious sound from the instrumental band, which being conveyed to the company through the orange plantation and shrubbery, created a most happy and pleasing effect, and which was still the more heightened by the company not being able to distinguish from what quarter it came.

This symphony, whose sweetness of sound had given every face a smile of approbation, being ended, Mr. Vernon got up, and with a light and rustic air called the nymphs and swains to celebrate the festivity of the day, informing them, that Stanley, as Lord of the Oaks, had given the invitation, and on that account he commanded their appearance to join the festive song and dance. After this air followed a grand chorus, which was composed in so remarkable a style, and carried with it so much jollity, that the company could scarce be prevailed upon to keep their seats. Next followed a dance by Sylvans ; then a song by Mrs. Barthélemon ; afterwards, a different dance by the whole assembly of *figurantes* was executed in a masterly style, and was succeeded by a most elegant and pleasing duet by Mrs. Barthélemon and Mr. Vernon, which concluded with a dance. The next air consisted of four verses, sung by Mr. Vernon ; at the end of each line was a chorus. The dance of the Sylvans continued during the whole time of the chorus, and had an excellent effect. . . .

The first *Masque* being over, the company amused themselves with walking about till the temporary room was illuminated, and upon a signal given another procession was made. Lord Stanley, supported by Lady Betty Hamilton, the Queen of the Oaks, and Miss Stanley led the way, the rest of the company following two by two. The noble visitors were first conducted through a beautiful and magnificent octagon hall, with transparent windows, painted suitable to the occasion : at the end of the great room hung six superb curtains, supposed to cover the same number of large windows ; they were of crimson colour, richly ornamented with deep gold fringe. Colonnades appeared on each side of the room, with wreaths of flowers running up the columns ; and the whole building was lined chair-back high with white Persian and gold fringe ; the seats around were covered with deep crimson. The company amused themselves with dancing minuets and cotillons, till half-past eleven, when an explosion, similar to the going off of a large quantity of rockets, put the whole lively group into a consternation. This was occasioned by a signal given for the curtains, which we have before described, to fly up and exhibit to the company a large supper-room, with tables spread with the most costly dainties, all hot and tempting.

The company took their seats in an instant, without the least interruption, and partook of the entertainment. They no sooner appeared satisfied than the whole was removed instantaneously, and a handsome dessert spread on the table, without their being able to account for the sudden change. When the ladies seemed tired with this second piece of luxury, the band were heard tuning their instruments in the octagon hall. This was another signal for the company to leave the supper-room and adjourn to the ball-room. No sooner was the above chamber cleared, when again, to the astonishment of all present, down flew the large curtains, and made the ball-room appear in its first state of elegance.

The ceremony of arranging the company next took place, and was executed by the General, who having placed Lady Betty Hamilton in the centre, formed the rest of the company into a circular group. This done, a Druid of the Oaks, represented by Captain Pigott, came forward from the octagon hall, with a few complimentary lines, suitable to the occasion, summoning the fauns and wood-nymphs to attend the ceremony within. A grand chorus was then sung by the nymphs, fauns and sylvans, led on by Cupids. After this chorus, another speech by the Druid. Mrs. Barthélemon, in the character of a wood-nymph, sang a pleasing air, the words in praise of conjugal felicity. This produced, at the conclusion, a *chaconne*, which was executed by eight principal dancers with great ease and agility. The Druid made another speech, and having finished, Mr. Vernon sung an air in praise of the oak. Next was an allemande, by sixteen principal dancers, and afterwards a speech relative to the Oaks, by the Druid. Mrs. Barthélemon and Mr. Vernon then sung a duet, which was likewise in praise of the oak, its prosperity and advantage, finished with a few complimentary lines to Lady Betty by the Druid and a grand chorus of vocal and instrumental music : during which a device in transparency was introduced, with two Hymeneal torches lighted on the top and a shield representing the Hamilton crest (an oak with a saw through it, and a ducal coronet). After a chorus, the Druid, fauns, and wood-nymphs went to the altar ; and two Cupids, the Cupid of Love, and the Hymenean Cupid, ascending the steps, crowned the shield with the wreath of Love and Hymen. . . .

The third part was opened by minuets composed on the occasion by the Earl of Kelly. Lord Stanley and Lady Betty Hamilton opened the second ball, and the rest of the nobility danced in their turns ; when the minuets were ended, country dances struck up, and continued till past three o'clock. The company were highly entertained by the illuminations in the gardens, which had a fine effect from the front wing of the house. Facing the temporary room was erected a large Ionic portico, supported by four large transparent columns of a bright pink colour. On a scroll on the pediment were the following words, " Sacred to propitious Venus." In the centre of the pediment was a shield, with the Hamilton and Stanley arms quartered, the whole supported by a band of Cupids, who appeared to great advantage by the assistance of four pyramids of lights. Several pyramids of lights were likewise erected in different parts of the garden.

The whole of this festival was conducted by General Burgoyne.

It is said that [it] . . . will cost Lord Stanley twelve thousand pounds. A very magnificent amphitheatre was built by Messrs. Adam. . . .

Monday, June 13th.

Mr. John Malcomb, an officer of the customs at Boston, who was tarred and feathered and led to the gallows with a rope about his neck, and threatened to be hanged and whose house and furniture were destroyed, is arrived in town. He came on board the *Active*, man-of-war. After he got on board, it is said, he was offered £300 sterling by the people of Boston, in satisfaction of his damages.

Wednesday, June 15th.

By the new building Act it is enacted that every parish within the cities of London and Westminster, and the liberties thereof, and the other parishes, precincts and places within the bills of mortality, the parishes of St. Marylebone, Paddington, St. Pancras and St. Luke at Chelsea, in Middlesex, shall at all times, after the 24th of June instant, have and keep in some known and public place within each parish three or more proper ladders, of one, two and three stories high, for assisting persons in houses on fire to escape therefrom. . . .

Thursday, June 16th.

The late risings among the German sugar-bakers were owing to some discontents they had conceived against their masters, a few of whom had not improbably been guilty of oppressions towards them ; but as all meetings in large bodies of journeymen, and other workmen, for the raising of wages, &c. are in the eye of the Law riotous combinations, and therefore illegal, instead of obtaining a redress of injuries, these poor ill-advised fellows have only incurred the punishment inflicted on such associations.

Friday, June 17th.

The Lord Mayor received a counterfeit letter as from the Admiralty, informing his Lordship, that there was a pressing necessity for manning a large fleet, and desiring his opinion officially on the speediest method of raising men to man it. This letter had a temporary effect upon the stocks, for which purpose it was calculated. They fell considerably.

Monday, June 20th.

On Friday Lord Chatham attended the House of Peers, when the amendments in the Bill for the government of Quebec were taken into consideration. His Lordship stated, with great force, many objections to the clause giving to the French Canadians so advantageous a part of the fisheries of cod on the Labrador Coast, to the great prejudice of the English Fishermen on the Banks of Newfoundland, considering the said fisheries of Labrador as a nursery of French Canadian seamen, to man, in case of a French War, any squadrons of France in those seas. . . . He further maintained, unanswered, that the dangerous innovations of this Bill were at variance with all the safe-guards and barriers against the return of Popery and Popish influence, so wisely provided by all the oaths of Offices of Trust, from the Constable up to the members of both Houses, even to the sovereign in his Coronation Oath. . . .

It is curious enough to hear an abandoned Administration pleading for the full enjoyment of the Roman Catholic religion in Canada, while they do not even tolerate the Protestant religion there. If they were rational and liberal in divine opinions, they ought to tolerate the Catholics here when they establish their tenets abroad. But to persecute Catholics here, and to persecute Protestants in another part of the Empire, is consistent with the rest of their politics.

Wednesday, June 22nd.

The Lord Mayor, the Aldermen Crosby, Lewis Plomer, and Sawbridge, the Recorder, city officers, and upwards of 150 of the common council, in coaches, went in procession from Guildhall to St. James's, in order to present their address and petition against signing the bill for the better government of Quebec. . . . Lord Hertford delivered to the Lord Mayor the following paper :

" As your petition relates to a bill agreed on by the two Houses of Parliament, of which His Majesty cannot take public notice until it is presented to him for His Royal assent in Parliament, I am commanded by the King to inform you, that you are not to expect an answer."

The Lord Mayor, immediately on reading it, sent the remembrancer to present his duty to the King, and to inform His Majesty, that he waited officially to present to His Majesty an address from the City of London, agreeable to His Majesty's appointment signified to the sheriffs ; on which after some little hesitation, they were admitted, and the same was read by the Recorder.

The King went immediately to the House of Lords, as it was the last day of the session, passed the Bill, and prorogued the Parliament, but only to the 4th of August, to be ready against bad news from America. Those that were actually received were not entirely satisfactory : though General Gage had been quietly received at Boston, the inhabitants had assembled in council and voted to invite the other colonies to unite with them in stopping all trade with England. . . .

His Majesty was much insulted in his way to the House of Peers. The cry of " No Popery " was re-echoed from every quarter, and the noisy expressions of displeasure were greater than His Majesty ever yet heard.

Friday, June 24th.

The Parliament should regulate the height of houses in narrow streets, by providing that where the street is not of more than such width no house shall be carried more than so many feet high. At the end of Chancery Lane, towards Fleet Street, a grocer has lately erected a tall house, which is a public nuisance. The street there was too narrow, dark and confined before ; and this is one of the greatest thoroughfares from Holborn, and sluices down such a multitude of carriages of all sorts that it greatly contributes to the frequent stoppages at Temple Bar. . . . In truth, Chancery Lane wants widening throughout, from Holborn to Fleet Street, but particularly near Temple Bar, where it is now dangerous passing for foot people by the crowd of carriages, the frequent stops, and the smallness of space. The grocers' carts add to the distress, for they very commonly prevent any passing at the foot of this lane for twenty minutes together, and lives are daily in danger. Where St. Martin's Lane empties itself into the Strand, another very great pass, it is often with no little peril that foot-passengers can get along. Such thoroughfares as St. Martin's and Chancery Lanes, when they discharge into another frequented passage, like the Strand and Fleet Street, should have their corners rounded off in the manner of the North East End of St. Paul's Churchyard upon the turning into Cheapside. Security and conveniency plead for this, as it would prevent the accidents which now happen at sharp turnings or the corners of crowded passages, by surprise and persons not being able to see two yards before them.

The Bars at Saville Row, Hanover Square, Southampton Street in the Strand, and other places, should be taken away ; for the public convenience ought to overbear private ease.

Some new streets should be made for communication in different parts of the town. At the end of Saville Row there should be a carriage-way to St. George's, which might easily be effected by removing a cane shop and an auction room. There should be a street leading from St. Clement's or Arundel Street along Lincoln's Inn fields through the turnstile into Holborn. So likewise from the Mansion House to Moorfields . . . a wider gate and carriage-way into the Temple, by taking in part of the Mitre Tavern, Brick and Fountain Courts, raising the bottom part of Temple Lane, and enlarging the gate-way and passage from thence to the King's Bench Walks, and carrying a street from the back gate of the Temple through Whitefriars to Blackfriars Bridge.

Saturday, June 25th.

Yesterday the report was made to His Majesty of the prisoners under sentence of death in Newgate, when William Hawke, William Jones, and John Charles, were ordered for execution on Friday next.

Sunday, June 26th.

[Lately published :]
The advantages of an alliance with the Great Mogul : in which

are principally considered three points of the highest importance to the British nation, &c. By John Morrison Esq., Ambassador Extraordinary and Plenipotentiary to His Majesty George III, King of Great Britain &c. 8vo. 2s. Cadell.

Macbeth. A tragedy. By William Shakespeare. Collated with the old and modern editions. 8vo. 3s. sewed. Owen.

Medical Memoirs of the General Dispensary in London for the years 1773 and 1774. By John Coakley Lettsom, M.D., F.R. & A.S.S. 8vo. 4s. Dilly.

The General Dispensary was established in the year 1770, the design of which is to administer advice and medicines to the poor, both at the Dispensary and at their own habitations. These Memoirs contain the most remarkable cases that fell under the author's observation during the above period, with a variety of reflections upon them. . . .

The Ides of June. A Poem. To the Fair Sex. 6d. Wilkie.

Good sentiments and tolerable poetry. The author thinks June to be a month of great temptation and therefore endeavours to guard the fair sex against it. . . .

The Grecian History from the earliest State to the Death of Alexander the Great. By Dr. Goldsmith. 2 vols. 8vo. 10s. Rivington.

Wednesday, June 29th.

Governor Hutchinson of Massachusetts Bay, before he dissolved the General Assembly, refused his consent to the grants which passed the House, for the payment of the salaries due to the agents of the province at the court of Great Britain, one of whom Benjamin Franklin, Esq, was expressly recognised in that character by His Majesty's Secretary for American Affairs. . . .

General Gage, on his arrival at Boston, on the 13th of May, was received as Governor and Commander in Chief with all possible honours and respect. He was complimented on his arrival by His Majesty's Council, by the gentlemen in the commission of the peace, by the episcopal and dissenting clergy, by the military officers and town magistrates, and afterwards sumptuously entertained at the Town Hall.

Next day, there was a numerous meeting of the inhabitants legally assembled at Feneuil Hall, to consider an Act of the

British Parliament for shutting up their port, when they came to the following resolutions :

" That it is the opinion of this town, that if the other colonies come into a joint resolution, to stop all importations from and exportations to Great Britain and every part of the West Indies, till the Act for blocking up this harbour be repealed, the same will prove the salvation of North America and her liberties. . . ."

JULY 1774

Friday, July 1st.

[Yesterday] the wife of Hawke the highwayman presented a petition into Lord Rochford's own hands, at his office at Whitehall, praying for a reprieve for her husband, but his Lordship, after perusing it, told her with great tenderness, that he was sorry the unfortunate man's crimes were of such a nature that His Majesty's clemency could not be hoped for.

Saturday, July 2nd.

Early in the morning [yesterday] the prisoners [who were to be executed] employed themselves in singing psalms and other acts of devotion. Exactly at seven o'clock they were brought from the cells into the Press-yard, in order to the taking off their irons.— Jones trembled as if his frame was dissolving, while Hawke appeared, if not with unconcern, with a fortitude very unusual. While the irons were taking off, an acquaintance of Hawke accosted him with a " How d'ye, Billy ? " — which the other replied to with cheerfulness, and enquired after an old acquaintance whom he had heard was indisposed. From Newgate to the place of execution Hawke behaved with much calm resignation, while Jones prayed and wept incessantly. When they came within 200 yards of Oxford Street Turnpike, Hawke looked round him, as if he rather wished than feared the journey at an end. When they arrived at the place of execution about 20 minutes were spent in devotion, and then they were tied up. A number of pigeons were now thrown into the air, as were others at stated periods during the melancholy ceremony. About a minute before they were turned off Hawke kicked off his shoes with great violence, and at the instant the cart moved he drew up his knees to his breast, so as to fall with a violent jerk, which almost instantly deprived him of life. There was a hearse in waiting, with a handsome black coffin with yellow nails, on which was the following inscription :

MR. WILLIAM HAWKE,
Died July 1st,
1774
Aged 24

Hawke has desired that a tombstone may be erected to his memory, with an epitaph from a stone in Stepney Churchyard, beginning thus :

" Adieu, vain world ! I've had enough of thee ! "

Just as the unhappy men were turned off, a young fellow, a shoe-maker by trade, was detected picking a gentleman's pocket of a gold watch, and consigned to the care of the constables, who carried him before a magistrate.

Much has been said with great humanity and truth on the dreadful frequency of executions at Tyburn, and nothing is more evident than that they have very little effect in restraining men from committing depredations on the public. A reformation in our criminal laws has been long and loudly called for : In the opinion of the celebrated H. Fielding Esq, the lives of those executed are thrown away. It is not so much the severity as the certainty of punishment which deters men of bad morals. He who is about to commit a robbery estimates the numbers whom the jury will not convict from a proper reluctance to hang men for a petty act of pilfering, those who escape, because no evidence but the most certain will convict for a capital offence, with the numbers who are pardoned at the report, where it is become a kind of maxim to hang none but those who have been guilty of repeated offences, and laughs at the danger when there are so many chances of escaping. The beneficial effects of the severities of Pope Sextus the Fifth must convince every man that legal severity is real mercy. Our Laws should be carefully reviewed and the number of capital offences greatly lessened ; but when that is done, the sentence of the law should be the voice of fate.

Sunday, July 3rd.

The new act for the regulation of madhouses declares that if, after the 20th of November, 1774, any person shall conceal or confine more than one lunatic without having a licence, such person shall forfeit £500. The Royal College of Physicians are to elect yearly, on the last day of September, five of their own body as commissioners for granting licences to the keepers of madhouses. . . . The commissioners, or any three of them, are required, once at least in every year, to visit and inspect such houses as they have licensed and to examine the lunatics, and make minutes of the state of such houses. . . .

Monday, July 4th.

[Extract of a letter from Plymouth, June 28, Ten o'clock at night :]

I have waited till the last moment before the post sets off, to give you an account of an affair, perhaps as remarkable as the whole history of gaming can produce, viz. the sinking of a vessel in 17 fathom water, by a man within it, without any assistance but such as himself alone could furnish. The wager was, that he was also to remain twelve hours beneath at that depth, then to raise the vessel to the surface again, and himself to be produced alive. . . . The people . . . say her going down was very swift, and that, in about five minutes after, or less, the water seemed to rise and be much agitated.

The affair soon got wind ; numbers flocked to the Hoe and the Point at the Long Rooms, expecting his raising of the vessel ; however, night came without any appearance of her ; several indeed, whose curiosity was very predominant, stayed all night ; others went home, it having been suggested he would stay to the end of the time fixed for the wager, i.e. twelve hours ; however, the time arrived, two o'clock this morning, and no signs of the vessel — to this present time. Several of the launches from the Dockyard have been down sweeping for her, and thought they had got a cable under her, and hove thereon, but it broke. They are gone back to the yard for fresh ones and more assistance, and in this state the affair now stands.

'Tis almost impossible to describe to you the consternation Plymouth is in, among all ranks of people, on account of the fate of this unhappy man, though the folly of him is so evidently glaring. . . . Mr. [Blake] is said to feel, and very strongly, on his being the cause thereof, in promoting the wager.

Mr. [Blake] says, he has air (I suppose in casks) on board sufficient for three days. People still out on the Hoe.

Tuesday, July 5th.

The fate of the vessel that was sunk for experiment, is at last determined,— irrecoverably lost. (Plymouth, July 1st.) It is still believed that the project is feasible, and would have succeeded, but on account of the badness of the bottom, there being rocks upwards of sixty feet high near the spot where the vessel was sunk.

Thursday, July 7th.

I could not help smiling on a procession of watermen the other day, who were walking to the sound of music, with that true kind of John Bull-face, which seemed to be ashamed of that which gave it pleasure. The sight of these buttock-of-beef visages threw me into deep thought about the characters of the present race of Englishmen ; and, after revolving over and over again their various merits and faults, I summed up the business with a perfect conviction that Watermen, Carmen, Porters, Chairmen, and Hackney-coachmen, were the only classes that had retained their ancient manners and characters unseduced, unrefined and unmelted, down to this present period of dissipation, hurry and mutation. These boisterous and unceremonious sons of bluntness and integrity retain their original vulgarity, uncontaminated of its primitive pollution.

Friday, July 8th.

A dreadful affray began [on Sunday] and continued all Monday and Tuesday between the English and Irish haymakers employed in the neighbourhood of Hyde, Mill Hill, Hendon, and other places adjacent to the Edgware Road.

Several on both sides have been dangerously wounded ; and a man, woman, and child, are said to have lost their lives in the confusion.

And on Wednesday, eleven of the rioters, who had beat and wounded, in a very desperate manner, many of the poor Irish haymakers, were apprehended by the spirit and union of the farmers in that neighbourhood, and were brought to Bow Street, Covent Garden ; where, after a long examination by Sir John Fielding, Knt., Sampson Wright, and William Addington, Esqrs. they were all committed to Newgate, being separately charged with different offences. The poor Irish haymakers have been treated with great cruelty. It seems this quarrel began from a resolution on the side of the English labourers, to prevent those poor industrious Irishmen from working at haymaking, as has long been the custom, and without whose assistance the hay round London could not be got in in time.

Saturday, July 9th.

The great use of an opposition in Parliament was never more clearly demonstrated than in the progress of the [Quebec] Bill. Tho' on every division the Minister had a majority of two to one, yet the opponents of the bill by the force of their arguments, and the persevering spirit of their resistance, have so far prevailed as to introduce several material clauses, by which it is rendered much less hostile to the liberties of mankind than in its original form. It was observed in the beginning of the debates, that as the noble Lord seemed so much in earnest, it was evident that the bill must pass ; yet it was still the duty of those who disapproved the whole principle to endeavour to render it as little obnoxious as possible. On settling the limits of Canada, the opposition prevailed. . . .

Sunday, July 10th.

Lord Holland is at last dead, and Lady Holland is at the point of death. . . .

Christina, Duchess of Kingston, is arrived, in a great fright, I believe, for the Duke's nephews are going to prove her first marriage, and hope to set the will aside. It is a pity her friendship with the Pope had not begun earlier; he might have given her a dispensation. . . .

There is just returned a Mr. Bruce, who has lived three years in the court of Abyssinia, and breakfasted every morning with the Maids of Honour on live oxen. . . .

Monday, July 11*th.*

Friday the Duke of Northumberland sent, as a present to the British Museum, a curious Roman altar-piece (which had been found on the estate in Northumberland) for the inspection of the curious.

Thursday, July 14*th.*

Captain Furneaux, of his Majesty's sloop the *Adventure*, who sailed from Plymouth the 31st of July, 1772, in company with Capt. Cook, of his Majesty's sloop the *Resolution*, upon a voyage to make discoveries in the southern hemisphere, arrived at Spithead, having penetrated as far towards the south pole as the latitude of 67 deg. 10 min. and circumnavigated the globe chiefly between the latitudes of 55 and 60, in which tract he met with much ice, but no land. The *Adventure* parted company with the *Resolution* on the 29th November last, off the coast of New Zealand, and Capt. Furneaux does not expect the latter will return to England this year. Capt. Furneaux brought with him a native of Otaheite [Omiah], who was desirous of seeing the great King. When they arrived at Charlotte Bay, in New Zealand, they found a note in a bottle informing them that the *Resolution* had been there : their boat went on shore for vegetables, when a mate (Mr. Rowe), a midshipman, and six seamen were cut off by the savages, and afterwards roasted and devoured ; their bones were only left.

According to an estimate lately laid before both Houses of Parliament, the manufactures exported from Great Britain in the year 1773, to different parts, amounted to thirteen millions, two hundred twenty-six thousand, seven hundred and forty pounds sterling ; and the value of those imported from foreign countries during the same year, amounted to the sum of £11,832,469, so that there was a balance in our favour of £1,394,271.

The commodities exported from Great Britain to America, on an average of three years, have amounted to £3,370,900. The commodities imported into Great Britain from the colonies, for the same period of time, have amounted to £3,924,606, 13s. 4d.

Friday, July 15th.

Mr. Foote hath again spurred his Pegasus and produced a new comedy of three acts, called *The Cozeners*, which was performed for the first time [this night] at the Haymarket.

It is founded on two recent events that have made much noise in the polite world. The first was the artifice of a female adventurer, who, under pretence of procuring places and employments from the government, obtained considerable sums of money from the credulous and unwary. . . . The other occurrence, was the application made by the wife of a certain celebrated preacher, to a nobleman in considerable power, for a living of great value in his gift ; the sale of which being refused, the doctor got into disgrace at court and became the subject of public ridicule. These two circumstances are very ingeniously blended together, and afford our author great scope for his comic abilities. . . .

A very humorous and entertaining representation, abounding with incidents drawn from real life, and finely touched by a master pencil. It may be justly called a general caricature of the times and a fine satire upon the credulity, absurdity and turpitude of the present era.

Wednesday, July 20th.

A letter from Boston says, that the gentlemen of New York have contracted with the manufacturers of that and Connecticut Government for 50,000 yards of woollen cloth, being determined never to wear those British manufactures any more which may be had in America.

Thursday, July 21st.

Yesterday a fellow was detected picking the pocket of a gentleman on Tower Hill, who was standing by a mountebank's stage ; he was carried to Tower-ditch, where he underwent so severe a ducking and whipping, that his recovery is doubtful.

Monday, July 25th.

[Lately published :]

A Letter to the Right Hon. Frederic Lord North, first Lord of the Treasury. 1s. Bell.

A fulsome panegyric of his lordship, composed of trifles and bad grammar. The production of a young place-hunter.

Le Taureau Blanc : or The White Bull. From the French. Translated from the Syriac by M. de Voltaire. 1s. 6d. Murray.

One more proof of the old man's constancy in infidelity. A weak though impious attack on revelation, particularly levelled at the Old Testament history and some of the prophets.

The Life of Dr. Oliver Goldsmith, written from personal Knowledge, authentic Papers and other indubitable Authorities. To which are added copious extracts from such Parts of the Doctor's Works as tend to amuse the Imagination, enlarge the Ideas and amend the Heart. 1s. 6d. Swan.

A Philosophical Essay on Space. In which are exploded those commonly received, though contradictory, Notions that Space is Nothing or that it is the Sensorium of the Deity. In a Letter to a Friend. By Richard Yate, Gentleman. 1s. Snagg.

Tuesday, July 26th.

Yesterday morning early a duel was fought in a field near Pancras by two Hibernian hairdressers ; their seconds were two journeymen tailors, who charged their pistols, unknown to them, with potatoes half boiled.

Wednesday, July 27th.

By advices just received from the theatre of war between the Russians and the Turks, we are told that the latter are very unsuccessful and that the Russian arms bear down everything before them.

The refusal of the Danzigers to submit to the Prussian eagle has greatly irritated that prince ; and it is probable that as soon as he shall have gained by private treaty the promise of the Germanic electors not to meddle in that affair, that those unhappy citizens will feel the weight of his avenging hand. The King of England, as one of the electors, is said to have promised not to interfere.

Friday, July 29th.

There never was so much company at the election at Eton, since the reign of the celebrated Dr. Barnard, as there was last Monday : the upper school could scarcely contain them. Lords North, Suffolk, Granby, Scarborough, Boston, Spencer, Hamilton, the Bishop of Bath and Wells, and several other persons of distinction were present ; gentlemen out of number, and more than a hundred ladies. The speeches began at 12 o'clock. The young orators performed to admiration in general,— but Master Blount, in Satan's address to the sun, in Milton, was inimitable : So striking and proper was his manner, so pleasing his tones, so expressive his eye and features of all the passions, so various and graceful his action, that, joined to an elegance of person, won the hearts of his auditors, and of the finer part of it more especially. In short, such a combination of excellencies can scarcely be imagined ; but owing to the excessive heat and the greatness of his exertion, it was with difficulty he could pronounce the last line of the speech, had barely strength to reach one of the desks, and there fainted away.

Saturday, July 30th.

Very intelligent people affirm, that the Premier's augury of a " Ten Years' Peace " will prove a false one, and still more intelligent people assert, that he himself is now fully sensible of it.

Sunday, July 31st.

On the first day of June, the port of Boston was blocked up in the terms of the Act of Parliament ; and to mark the general sympathy on that event, the same day was observed throughout the British colonies as a day of general prayer, fasting and humiliation. On the 14th, a Solemn League and Covenant was entered into by the Americans to take place on the 31st of August. . . .

August 1774

Thursday, August 4th.

Her Grace of Kingston [has] . . . gone again, with much precipitation, and with none of the pomp of her usual progresses. In short, she had missed her lawyer's letters, which warned her against returning. A prosecution for bigamy was ready to meet her. She decamped in the middle of the night ; and six hours after the officers of justice were at her door to seize her. This is but an unheroic catastrophe of her romance ; and though she is as thorough a comedian as Sixtus Quintus, it would be a little awkward to take possession of his villa, after being burnt in the hand. What will be the issue of the suit and lawsuit I cannot tell. As so vast an estate is the prize, the lawyers will probably protract it beyond this century. . . .

In France they are persuaded the old Parliament will be restored. . . . However, the old spirit remains at least in one quarter, and they continue butchering the poor Corsicans. Is it true that the King of Sardinia is to have that island ? How unfortunate it is that little countries should retain a spirit of independence, which they have not strength to preserve ; and that great nations, who might throw it off, court the yoke ! . . .

The King of Prussia has been amazingly gracious to General Conway, and ordered him to attend him to all his reviews. This is most astonishing favour to an Englishman. . . .

Wednesday, August 10th.

Fresh accounts of the unsettled state of affairs in Sicily and on the Continent. At Palermo the people still continue very riotous ; and in some parts of Poland the election of deputies at the Dietines has been so very tumultuous, that the opposite parties fired on each other. The pretended rupture, however, between Prussia and Malta, is now said to be without foundation, and that the preparations making at the latter are only by way of precaution, to prevent the like disturbances as have lately happened in Sicily, the Island of Malta labouring at present under a scarcity of corn.

The King of Prussia lays claim to the city of Danzig without the least shadow of right. It is said that he intends to purchase the pretended claim upon the city of Hamburgh of Count Schomberg ; and it is certain he has claimed a debt, amounting to an immense sum, of the States of Holland, which debt their High Mightinesses assert was discharged above seventy years ago.

The new subjects which the King of Prussia has acquired in Polish Prussia, are reduced to the same condition with the rest of his people ; all the males are born military slaves, they are obliged to wear an uniform, and to learn the military exercises ; nay, it is said, that every male child, when born, receives a military collar and ten dollars, by which he is ever after considered as a soldier in the King's service, and liable to all the rigour of arbitrary laws. Blessed effects of arbitrary power !

Thursday, August 11*th.*

Tuesday a great cricket match was played on Seven Oaks Vine, for one thousand guineas, between the Duke of Dorset and ten men on the side of Kent, and —— Ridge, Esq., and ten men on the side of Hampshire, which was won with great ease by the former.

Saturday, August 13*th.*

The children at the Foundling Hospital had but very few lessons in music before it was found to be expressly against Act of Parliament, and a stop put to its intended progress by order of the Governors at the last general meeting, for whom the musicians ought ever to pray.

Sunday, August 14*th.*

A numerous meeting of the inhabitants [of New York, on June 13th] resolved that the statute commonly called the Boston Port Act is oppressive to the inhabitants of that town, unconstitutional in its principles and dangerous to the liberties of

America ; and that a joint resolution to stop all importation from and exportation to Great Britain, till that Act shall be repealed, will prove the salvation of North America and her liberties : for this purpose it is farther resolved that deputies be sent to meet deputies from other colonies, to agree about the means to be used for carrying this measure into execution. . . .

Monday, August 15*th.*

Letters from Boston bring accounts that all hopes of accommodation with the Mother Country are over. If any hopes had remained, General Gage would only have prorogued, and not dissolved, the General Assembly. The consequences are evident ; their non-importation scheme will likely become general all over America ; so that blocking up the port of Boston, instead of being a punishment on the Americans, will, in fact, annihilate our export trade to America, and fall heavy on our British merchants and manufacturers.

Tuesday, August 16*th.*

On Tuesday last a teacher at an eminent boarding school on the Chelsea Road having occasion to correct one of the young ladies (her scholar) and having accordingly turned her over her knee in a convenient attitude to receive the chastisement of the birch rod, being of some age and high spirit, grew obstropulous ; and after receiving a few strokes, being impatient to endure any longer the smart, in struggling kicked the teacher with her heel so violently on one eye, that she has ever since been confined to her bed, and is judged by the faculty in no small danger of losing the use of it.

Thursday, August 18*th.*

Since the prospect of Dr. Falck's being able to raise the vessel lately lost off Plymouth, wagers to a considerable amount were laid at two coffee-houses in Pall-Mall, this week, about what position the unfortunate man who perished in her will be found in.

Friday, August 19*th.*

Mr. Garrick gave a splendid entertainment or *Fête Cham-*

pêtre, at his gardens at Hampton. Signor Torre conducted a most brilliant fire-work ; and an elegant concert of music was performed. The Temple of Shakespeare, and gardens, were illuminated with 6,000 lamps, and the Forge of Vulcan made a splendid appearance.

Saturday, August 20th.

Sir Robert Barker, late Commander in Chief of the Company's forces in the East Indies, who is every day expected home, has been near eighteen years in the service in Asia, and is asserted to be the richest Englishman, except Lord Clive, that ever returned from that part of the world.

Sunday, August 21st.

The Turks and Russians after having sacrificed near 60,000 of their subjects in each campaign, have at last signed a peace without any very material advantage to the victorious party. . . .

The Prussian eagle has long cast a jealous eye on the power of the Russians, the recent smart of whose rod he has not yet forgotten. He has for some time past beheld with secret pleasure that empire exhausting its military strength in a contest in which he artfully evaded engaging as a party. He seems to have considered it as much more to his advantage to make himself master of the most fruitful parts of Poland, than to engage in an uncertain war from which no profits could be reaped. It is probable that the Russian empress began at last to see into the views of that enterprising monarch, and was therefore desirous of concluding a treaty as soon as possible with the Turks. . . .

Monday, August 22nd.

Vice-Admiral Graves arrived at Boston on the 30th of June, in His Majesty's ship *Preston*, and assumed the command of the squadron ; which, exclusive of the flag-ship, consisted of seventeen ships and vessels, of which eight only were at Boston, the rest being dispersed from the Gulf of St. Lawrence to Georgia. . . . The *Preston* and all the other ships on this station [are] manned only according to the lowest peace establishment. . . .

When Admiral Graves was under a necessity of recalling some of his cruisers, the better to block up the port of Boston, in terms of the Act of Parliament, the Americans availed themselves of the weakness of the squadron and procured supplies to an astonishing degree ; so that it required more ships than the Admiral could spare to carry the Boston Port Act into proper execution. To render this Act of as little effect as possible, most of the provinces to the southward of Boston [have] contributed to the relief of that town and appointed committees for transmitting their donations of rice and other provisions to its inhabitants.

Tuesday, August 23rd.

It is a general observation in the country . . . that candidates never, at any former election, showed half so much anxiety for a seat as they do at present ; there are few electors but receive a dish of fish, &c. every now and then, and hares and partridges are expected to be very plentiful at the tables of freemen the ensuing winter, so that it is now a common saying, " We shall have our bellies full of venison, fish and game every seven years."

Wednesday, August 24th.

The [Quebec] Bill has nothing terrible in it but in imagination. Some few thousands of the King's Subjects desired leave to continue Catholics, and the favour is granted, which is only permitting, with a good grace, what could not have been avoided ; for nothing could have robbed them of their private religious sentiments.

The whole business of America at present appears to consist in associating, resolving, signing solemn covenants, and writing circular letters ; in short, anything but carrying on that trade by which Great Britain and her Colonies hope to be mutually benefitted.

Thursday, August 25th.

The experiments making at Landguard fort, under the direction of General Williamson, &c. we hear are likely to be of great utility and saving to government, by making shot

weighing 42 lb. (in the shape of a pear) do as much execution,
fired out of an eighteen pounder, with a third of the quantity
of powder, as can be effected by round balls of the same weight
that are fired from a forty-two pounder, the piece of ordnance
hitherto used for that purpose.

Friday, August 26th.

If London Bridge should fall the first hard frost, which is
expected by all the engineers, 'tis imagined the New River
Company will give the proprietors of the London Bridge shares
an indemnity, and no wheels to be established upon the reconstruction of that bridge.

Monday, August 29th.

At his seat at Johnson Hall, in the province of New York,
in America, [died on July 11th] the very brave and worthy
Sir William Johnson, Bart. not more celebrated for his conduct
in the last war, than remarkable for the ascendancy he had
gained over the Indian nations. He has left a large sum of
money to be employed in presents to the Indians of the Mohawk
castles, through whose faithful and invariable attachment the
worthy Baronet was enabled to conduct the business of his
department with admirable ability, justice and humanity. All
the inhabitants, men, women, and children, of those castles,
had mourning presented to them on the much lamented death
of their beloved patron.

Tuesday, August 30th.

There has not been so universal a dullness in town as there
now is, since the eve of the last election. The streets are almost
without passengers. The quality have left St. James's for the
sake of visiting their seats and their boroughs ; and the tradesmen seem in general to have deserted their shop-boards and
counters for Margate and Brighthelmstone. At the west end
of the town an old house-keeper mumbles out an answer to
enquiries ; and in the city, beardless apprentices are posted as
sentinels, to tell customers their masters are out of Town.
This want of bustle is but as a calm before a storm. The
parliamentary session will not be a long one ; America and

the Continent must however of necessity afford some subjects which will demand immediate and serious consideration. No sooner will the Minister have patched up the political sores of the day, than he will have his hands full in providing such an aimable senate as will content themselves without probing these sores to see if they are properly cured.

Wednesday, August 31st.

A war is talked of abroad, in which Great Britain, Russia, and Prussia, are to act against France, Spain, Austria, and Sardinia . . . Circumstances seem to give credit to the reports. Sardinia has entered into an alliance, offensive and defensive, with France, and Corsica is to be delivered up before Christmas. The Prince of Piedmont is to marry the Princess Adelaide of France ; preparations are already making for the marriage. The Chevalier Charles Edward Stuart (vulgarly called the Pretender) and his consort were lately received in the Grand Duchy of Tuscany, in the greatest pomp and magnificence. The Empress Queen has made several complaints against the House of Hanover, at an assembly of the Plenipotentiaries at Regensburgh, and sent letters to her ambassadors at the different Courts of Europe to notify the same, to which complaints an answer is daily expected. The King of Prussia has ordered a powerful army to enter Poland, and is set out for Silesia himself, attended by the Crown Prince, the Prince of Brunswick, and General Lentulus, which appears very suspicious. The King of Sweden, who is known to be in the interest of France, is uncommonly active in augmenting his army, to be a check upon Russia in the North ; the warlike Choiseul is at the head of the French ministry, and the immense treasures of Spain are laid open to him ; from all which it is predicted that a war will soon break out in Europe.

SEPTEMBER 1774

Friday, September 2nd.

A set of young Bloods have for some time past paraded the streets in this metropolis in the evening, and for want of better diversion have amused themselves with throwing spirits of vitriol over the clothes of people, in particular the fair sex, by which several rich silk gowns have been utterly spoilt.

Tuesday, September 6th.

A person having invented a liquid as a preventative of bad effects ensuing from libidinous gratifications, and having solicited a patent for the sole vending the same ; when it came to the Great Seal the Lord Chancellor would not suffer it to proceed any further, such an invention, instead of being useful, in his opinion, tending to the encouragement of vice, and therefore should not have his sanction.

Wednesday, September 7th.

Complaint was lately made to the Deputy Ranger of St. James's Park, by several of the nobility whose houses look out on Constitution Hill, complaining of the great obstruction they met with by the number of horses, cows, &c. now in the said Park, since which palisades have been erected from the Queen's Library to the upper part of Constitution Hill, by which the nuisance complained of has been removed.

Friday, September 9th.

The Town has been so dull and barren of subjects these three months, that the papers have been filled with advices from Spain which never were received, and letters from Boston written by persons who never were in America. A few days will furnish something real to talk about. The alterations in the theatrical companies will be shortly newspaper topics, to them will succeed the city election, after that the meeting of Parliament, and after a short but busy sessions the General Election.

Saturday, September 10th.

Mr. Maskelyne, Astronomer Royal, and Mr. Reuben Burrow are now in Scotland making observations to determine the attraction of mountains, at the request of the Royal Society.

Wednesday, September 14th.

[The King has written to Lord North,] The die is now cast, the Colonies must either submit or triumph ; I do not wish to come to severer measures but we must not retreat ; by coolness and an unremitted pursuit of the measures that have been adopted I trust they will come to submit ; I have no objection afterwards to their seeing that there is no inclination for the present to lay fresh taxes on them, but I am clear there must always be one tax to keep up the right and as such I approve of the Tea Duty.

Friday, September 16th.

They write from Gosport that on the 30th of January 1774, his Majesty's store-ship, the *Endeavour*, Lieut. James Gordon commander, sailed from the Downs, as was supposed, for Boston in America ; but arriving off the Lizard, the orders were opened, and the commander found he was to proceed, without delay or loss of time, for Falkland's Islands, though they had but four months' provision on board. . . . On the 22nd of April she arrived at Port Egmont on Falkland's Islands . . . and large sheets of lead were fixed up with this inscription engraved : " Be it known to all nations, that Falkland Islands, with this fort, the storehouses, wharfs, harbours, bays and creeks thereunto belonging, are the sole right and property of his most sacred Majesty George the Third, of Great Britain, France, and Ireland, Defender of the Faith, &c. in witness whereof this plate is set up, and his Britannic Majesty's colours left flying, as a mark of possession, by Samuel William Clayton, commanding officer at Falkland Islands, May 22, Anno Domini 1774. . . ."

The *Endeavour*, in her return home, met with very severe weather, in which the master (Mr. Allen) and two men were washed overboard. They saw no land from the 23rd of May till the 29th of August, when at six o'clock they saw Fyall, one of the Azores, which they steered for, being very short of water, and reduced to an allowance of one quart per man per day for some time. The next day they got into Fyall Road, where they procured water, and some fresh provisions, and the next day sailed for England, being obliged to cut her cable. . . . She had a good passage from Fyall to Spithead, where she arrived on Friday last.

Sunday, September 18th.

[Lately published :]

Plays written by Thomas Southerne, Esq ; now first collected. With an account of the life and writings of the author. 3 vols. 9s. Evans.

The Ambulator, or the Stranger's Companion in a Tour round London ; within the circuit of twenty-five miles ; describing whatever is remarkable, either for grandeur, use or curiosity ; and comprehending catalogues of the pictures by eminent artists. To which is prefixed, a concise description of London, Southwark, and Westminster. 12mo. 2s. 6d. Bew.

Edward. A Novel. 2 vols. 5s. Davies.

Chaste, sensible and entertaining. The fair sex will meet with many good lessons of instruction in this novel. . . .

An Abridgment of the History of England, from the Invasion of Julius Caesar to the Death of George the Second. By Dr. Goldsmith. 3s. 6d. Kearsley.

Sunday, September 25th.

Both theatres are now opened for the winter season, and great expectations are entertained that the town will be agreeably amused, as a strong exertion is expected on both sides. Mr. Garrick, with his extensive judgment in scenic lore, will, doubtless, be induced to display his emulation against so formidable a company as the opposite managers have prepared against him. Mr. Garrick opened his theatre on Saturday, September 17, with the comedy of *The Drummer, or The Haunted*

House, and a new prelude, entitled, *The Meeting of the Company, or Bayes's Art of Acting.* . . .

Covent Garden Theatre opened the succeeding Monday, when Mr. Woodward spoke an occasional prologue that met with great applause. The house is new painted and decorated, in a simple, but pleasing style ; the front boxes are much enlarged, and upon the whole the theatre is greatly improved. We have much reason to expect a great share of entertainment, from this sample given of the desire the managers have of gratifying the wishes of the town, and believe that their expectations will be crowned with success.

Mr. Foote, as usual, concluded his season the 15th September ; and Aristophanes is now upon a tour to Paris, from whence he will probably import some new characters for the amusement of the public next year.

Tuesday, September 27th.

[Extract of a letter of Mr. Edmund Burke's to the Marquis of Rockingham :]

I agree with your Lordship entirely, the American and foreign affairs will not come to any crisis, sufficient to rouse the public from its present stupefaction, during the course of the next session. I have my doubts whether those at least of America, will do it for some years to come. I don't know whether the London papers have taken in the Pennsylvania instructions to their representatives. Lest they should not, I send your Lordship the Philadelphia paper which contains them. It is evident from the spirit of these instructions, as well as by the measure of a Congress and consequent embassy, that the affair will draw out into great length. If it does, I look upon it as next to impossible, that the present temper and unanimity of America can be kept up, popular remedies must be quick and sharp, or they are very ineffectual. The people there can only work on Ministry through the people here, and the people here will be little affected by the sight of half-a-dozen gentlemen from America, dangling at the levées of Lord Dartmouth and Lord North or negotiating with Mr. Pownall. If they had chosen the non-importation measure as the leading card, they would have put themselves on a par with us, and we should be in as much haste to negotiate ourselves out of our commercial, as they out of their constitutional difficulties. But in the present temper of the nation, and with the character of the present administration, the disorder and discontent of all America and the more remote future mischiefs which may arise from those causes, operate as little as the division of Poland. The insensibility of the merchants of London is of a degree and kind scarcely to be conceived. Even those who are most likely to be overwhelmed by any real American confusion are amongst the most supine. The character of the Ministry either produces or perfectly coincides with, the disposition of the public. . . .

Thursday, September 29th.

By authentic letters received by the *Scarborough* man-of-war, in twenty-four days, from Boston, it appears that the Massachusetts province was in a very disordered and tumultuous state, more so than has ever yet been known. . . .

What most irritated the people, next to seizing their arms and ammunition, was the apprehending six gentlemen, Select Men of the town of Salem, who had assembled in a town meeting, according to the old custom, though contrary to the new acts of Parliament, to choose some public officers ; upon which General Gage sent for and cautioned them, threatening them that he would enforce the acts if they persisted to carry matters to the last extremity. He was answered, that they should be governed by the laws of the province, and accordingly went on with the business of the meeting : meantime a company of soldiers were ordered into the town, who came prepared as for an engagement, but before their arrival the meeting had got through with their business and were broke up. The Select Men, however, were apprehended and three of them admitted to bail, to stand trial at the next court, and three were sent to gaol, who, on their arrival, were by the keeper refused admittance and remained under arrest when the *Scarborough* sailed. . . .

Friday, September 30th.

The parliament of Great Britain was dissolved by royal

proclamation, being the only parliament that has received its dissolution before the expiration of the term of seven years since his present Majesty's accession to the throne [in 1760]. There was but one such dissolution during the long reign of George II, viz. in 1746.

OCTOBER 1774

Thursday, October 6th.

The chief motive [of the dissolution of Parliament] is supposed to be the ugly state of North America, and the effects that a cross winter might have on the next elections. . . . Such a ferment in London as is seldom seen at this dead season of the year! Couriers, dispatches, post-chaises, post-horses, hurrying every way! Sixty messengers passed through one single turnpike on Friday. The whole island is by this time in equal agitation ; but less wine and money will be shed than have been at any such period for these fifty years. . . .

The first symptoms are not favourable to the court ; the great towns are casting off submission, and declaring for popular members. London, Westminster, Middlesex seem to have no monarch but Wilkes, who is at the same time pushing for the mayoralty of London, with hitherto a majority on the poll. It is strange how this man, like a phoenix, always revives from his embers! America, I doubt, is still more unpromising. There are whispers of their having assembled an armed force, and of earnest supplications arrived for succours of men and ships. . . . Our Parliaments are subjected to America and India, and must be influenced by their politics ; yet I do not believe our senators are more universal than formerly. . . .

Our roads are so infested by highwaymen, that it is dangerous stirring out almost by day. Lady Hertford was attacked on Hounslow Heath at three in the afternoon. Dr. Eliot was shot at three days ago, without having resisted ; and the day before yesterday we were near losing our Prime Minister, Lord North ; the robbers shot at the postillion, and wounded the latter. In short, all the freebooters, that are not in India, have taken to the highway. The Ladies of the Bedchamber dare not go to the Queen at Kew in an evening. . . .

Friday, October 7th.

John Wilkes, Esq., was declared duly elected [Lord Mayor of London]. . . . The joy of the populace was so great that they took the horses from the coach, and in the struggle for the honour of drawing it to the mansion-house one man lost his life and another was much hurt.

At a numerous meeting of the inhabitants of Westminster [on Tuesday] the Lords Mountmorres and Mahon were put in nomination . . . to represent that city in Parliament, and at the same time Humphrey Cotes offered his services. They have since been opposed by Lord Percy and Lord Thomas Pelham Clinton.

Saturday, October 8th.

The Coroner's inquest sat on the body of the man who was trampled to death in attempting to assist in drawing the Lord Mayor's coach, as already mentioned, and brought in their verdict Accidental Death. The law, nevertheless, exacts the forfeiture of the moving body towards the death of a subject ; in consequence of which the jury adjudged the near fore-wheel of the Lord Mayor's coach the moving body, and valued the same at 40s.

Sunday, October 9th.

[Extract of a letter from Dr. Benjamin Franklin to Thomas Cushing in America :]

As yet it does not appear that there is any intention of changing measures : but all intelligent men are of opinion, that if the American Congress should resolve on the non-consumption of the manufactures of Great Britain this Ministry must go out, and their late measures be all reversed. As such a resolution, firmly adhered to, would in a peaceable and justifiable way do everything for us that we can wish, I am grieved to hear of mobs and violence, and the pulling down the houses, which our friends cannot justify, and which give great advantage against us to our enemies. . . .

Wednesday, October 12th.

Many think the new Parliament will be for reversing the

late proceedings ; but that depends on the Court, on which every Parliament seems to be dependent ; so much so, that I begin to think a Parliament . . . of little use to the people : for since a Parliament is always to do as a ministry would have it, why should we not be governed by the ministry in the first instance ? They could afford to govern us cheaper, the Parliament being a very expensive machine that requires a vast deal of oiling and greasing at the people's charge ; for they finally pay all the enormous salaries of places, the pensions, and the bribes, now by custom become necessary to induce the members to vote according to their consciences. . . .

Thursday, October 13th.

Orders have been issued to the Officers of the three regiments of Foot Guards, the Horse Guards, and Horse Grenadiers, to poll for those ministerial candidates, the absent Lord Percy and Lord Tommy Clinton ; and commands are laid upon everybody under the influence of Administration. . . .

The new senate . . . will be a curious assemblage of patricians and plebeians and knights — of the post. An old-clothes man, who, George Selwyn says, certainly stood for Monmouth, was a candidate, but unsuccessful. Bob [Macreth], formerly a waiter at White's, was set up by [Lord Orford] for two boroughs, and actually is returned for Castle Rising with Mr. Wedderburn. . . . For my part, waiter for waiter, I see little difference ; they are all equally ready to cry, " Coming, coming, Sir."

Friday, October 14th.

Mr. Garrick appeared last night for the first time this season in Lusignan, in the *Tragedy of Zara* ; and though he has but just recovered from a severe fit of the gout, it was remarked he never acted the part better, or more affected the audience.

Tuesday, October 18th.

The College of Physicians held their grand anniversary feast, at their hall in Warwick-lane, when the Harveian oration was delivered by Dr. James.

Friday, October 21st.

Orders are given, we hear, for several recruiting parties to be sent into different parts of the country, to get hands with all expedition. This does not look as if we are at peace.

Saturday, October 22nd.

Yesterday morning many of the Brentford electors were brought to town in coaches and four ; they made a droll appearance as they passed through the city, some asleep, some discharging out of the coach-door what they, like brutes, had gorged themselves with at Brentford. Some were singing and hallooing out " Wilkes, Glynn, and Liberty ! " and their coachmen so drunk, that they could with difficulty keep upon their boxes. . . .

Elections are almost over. Wilkes has taken possession of Middlesex without an enemy appearing against him ; and, being as puissant a monarch as Henry the Eighth, and as little scrupulous, should, like him, date his acts *From our Palace of Bridewell, in the tenth year of our reign.* He has, however, met with a heroine to stem the tide of his conquests ; who, though not of Arc, nor a pucelle, is a true Joan in spirit, style, and manners. This is her Grace of Northumberland, who has carried the mob of Westminster from him, sitting daily in the midst of Covent Garden, and will elect her son and Lord Thomas Clinton, against Wilkes's two candidates, Lord Mahon and Lord Mountmorres. She puts me in mind of what Charles the Second said of a foolish preacher, who was very popular in his parish : " I suppose his nonsense suits their nonsense."

Sunday, October 23rd.

[Lately published :]
A Voyage towards the North Pole undertaken by his Majesty's Command, 1773. By Constantine John Phipps. 4to. Price 12s. 6d. boards. Nourse.

The honourable author was appointed to make this voyage by the lords of the Admiralty, in consequence of an application from the Royal Society, in order to ascertain how far a navigation could be extended towards the North Pole ; and we find Captain Phipps could not advance within seven degrees of it, notwithstanding the season of the year was the most favourable for this voyage. He, nevertheless, conducted the undertaking with skill and resolution, and has in this performance approved himself a very accurate journalist.

Thursday, October 27th.

At the final close of the poll yesterday at Covent Garden, for representatives in Parliament for Westminster, the numbers were, for Earl Percy, 4,994 ; Lord Pelham Clinton, 4,744 ; Lord Mountmorres, 2,531 ; Lord Mahon, 2,342 ; Humphrey Cotes, Esq., 130 : whereupon the two former were declared duly elected.

Friday, October 28th.

This day the following advices were received from Boston, dated Sept. 24.

Four 24 pounders, and eight 9 pounders, have been transported from Castle-William by order of General Gage, and placed against the fortifications of this town. The 59th regiment is arrived from Salem, and stationed on Boston Neck. The Select Men of Boston have waited on General Gage, desiring to know what he means by placing cannon at the avenues of the town and digging trenches round the town ; to which he returned for answer, that he had no hostile intention, and only meant to have them in readiness in case of an attack from the Provincials.— Other letters add, that the troops are marching from all quarters towards Boston, and that General Gage's intention seems to be, when his army is strong enough, to rob the people of their lives and liberties.

The Deputies assembled in Congress approve the conduct of their brethren at Boston, and trust, that the effect of the united endeavours of North America will carry such conviction to the British nation of the unwise, unjust, and ruinous policy of the present Administration, as quickly to introduce better men, and wiser measures.

Sunday, October 30th.

[Lately published :]
The Minstrel ; or the Progress of Genius. A Poem. Book II.
By James Beattie, LL.D. 4to. Dilly.

> What cannot Art and Industry perform,
> When Science plans the progress of their toil !
> They smile at penury, disease, and storm ;
> And oceans from their mighty mounds recoil.
> When tyrants scourge, or demagogues embroil
> A land, or when the rabble's headlong rage
> Order transforms to anarchy and spoil,
> Deep vers'd in man, the philosophic sage
> Prepares with lenient hand their frenzy to assuage.
>
> 'Tis he alone, whose comprehensive mind,
> From situation, temper, soil and clime
> Explored, a nation's various powers can bind,
> And various orders, in one form sublime
> Of polity, that, 'midst the wrecks of time,
> Secure shall lift its head on high, nor fear
> Th' assault of foreign or domestic crime,
> While public faith, and public love sincere,
> And industry and law maintain their sway severe.

A Letter to Dr. William Hunter, Physician Extraordinary to the Queen, Professor of Anatomy in the Royal Academy, and Fellow of the Royal and Antiquarian Societies, on the dangerous tendency of medical vanity ; occasioned by the death of Lady Hollan. By Wm. Rowley, M.D. and man-midwife. 8vo. 1s.

Thoughts upon Slavery. By John Wesley, M.A. 1s. Hawes.

A Proposal for the Establishment of public Examinations in the University of Cambridge, with occasional remarks. By the Rev. John Jebb. 6d. Wilkie.

The Patriot. Addressed to the Electors of Great Britain. 6d. Cadell.

Our author's style is agreeable, and many of his sentiments just, particularly this : " Too many neither suspect, nor fear, nor care for the public, but hope to force their way to riches by virulence and invective and are vehement and clamorous, only that they may be *sooner hired to be silent.*" There are other sentiments, however, which are false and pernicious, and may be confuted by a schoolboy. " As we have always protected the Americans, we may therefore subject them to government." But by what means, and to what kind of government ? Again, " The less is included in the greater ; that power which can take away life may *seize upon property*," though it be to make *American purses* pay the pensions of *Jacobite doctors*. Pity, that great abilities should be prostituted, and classical merit so debased for *a pension*.

Monday, October 31st.

Mr. Groome, of the Red Lion, in Drury-lane, being on a visit on board a ship in the river, had the misfortune to fall overboard, and, before the body could be recovered, he was supposed to be quite dead ; but one of the medical assistants to the newly established society for the recovery of persons supposed to be drowned, being sent for, he was, after two hours labour, brought to life.— This is the tenth person so restored by means of the bounty allowed by this humane society.

NOVEMBER 1774

Wednesday, November 2nd.

Tomorrow evening will be debated at the Crown Tavern, Bow Lane, the following questions :—

1. Do the Scriptures countenance a free or a despotic government ?
2. Whether living characters are proper subjects for the satire of the stage.

Thursday, November 3rd.

Should a civil war (says an evening paper) be kindled in America (as there are too many grounds for apprehending, from the accounts received from thence, and also from the Royal Proclamation for prohibiting arms and ammunition from being sent abroad) it will not only be very fatal to the trade and commerce of this kingdom, but must probably involve it in a new war with France and Spain. How could this nation support at once a war with those powers, and its own colonies ? The proclamation against sending guns and gunpowder out of this kingdom will be of very little use or effect, because the Americans will certainly procure whatever quantity of them they want from France or Spain ; and if orders were given to stop and seize such ships as were laden with those commodities by those nations, it would bring on an immediate war with them. Nay, indeed, our good friends the Dutch will be ready enough to supply them with such things, or any sort of warlike stores they may have occasion for. The Ministry, by their arbitrary and unconstitutional proceedings, have brought this kingdom into a dreadful and most dangerous condition. Burdened already with heavy and innumerable taxes, and deprived of all trade and commerce, how is it possible for the people of England to support a double war, a war against the House of Bourbon and a war against their fellow

subjects in America ? It is absolutely impossible for the people
to raise money sufficient for such purposes ; they have it not
to give ; and surely our Egyptian task-masters will not compel
us to make brick without straw. Perhaps the creditors of
the public may have occasion to tremble at this unhappy
crisis. Those who have not regarded and spared the Charters
of the East India Company, or the Charters of the City of
London, or the Charters of our American colonies, may not
regard the faith of parliament and spare the creditors of the
public. . . .

Saturday, November 5th.

When it was under consideration in the Cabinet, whether
John Wilkes, Esq. should be approved of as Lord Mayor by
the Chancellor, a Member observed, " It was much better to
permit him to be Lord Mayor for one year, than King of the
City for life."

Monday, November 7th.

Died suddenly, Thomas Bradshaw, that low but useful tool
of Administration. His vanity had carried him to great
excesses of profusion, and, being overwhelmed with debts, he
shot himself.

Tuesday, November 8th.

[Mr. Edmund Burke has been elected member for Bristol]
by a majority of 251, after one of the longest and warmest
contests that has been remembered. . . . The election has
lasted a month. . . . This is the second city in the Kingdom,
and to be invited and chosen for it . . . at no expense to
[himself] but with much charge and trouble to every public-
spirited gentleman is an honour. . . .

[Dr. Johnson has] had always a very great personal regard
and particular affection for Mr. Edmund Burke . . . and
when the general election . . . broke up the delightful society
. . . at Beaconsfield Dr. Johnson shook the hospitable master
of the house [Mr. Burke] kindly by the hand and said, " Farewell, my dear Sir, and remember that I wish you all the

success which ought to be wished you, which can possibly be wished you indeed — *by an honest man."*

Wednesday, November 9th.

Being Lord Mayor's Day, about twelve o'clock, the new Lord Mayor, the old Lord Mayor, several of the aldermen, city officers, etc., preceded by the Joiners and Salters Companies, went in procession from Guildhall to the Three Cranes stairs, where they took water and proceeded to Westminster. After paying their respects to the different courts who were then sitting, the Lord Mayor was sworn into his office by the barons of the Exchequer. After which they again took water, and about half after three landed at Blackfriars, from whence they proceeded through the city to Guildhall ; but it was five before the procession could reach Guildhall on account of the crowd of people, who, by their continual loud acclamations, frightened the horses in the state coach, so that it was with difficulty they could be made to move on. . . .

Thursday, November 10th.

On Wednesday night, at Guildhall, the ball was opened by Lord Mahon and Miss Wilkes ; the dancing continued until one o'clock, soon after which the greatest part of the company departed, much pleased with the elegance of the entertainment. Some young gentlemen, who stayed after the rest of the company, got upon the hustings, and being heated with liquor, quarrelled, and threw bottles at each other, upon which the officers prevailed upon them to quit the hall about three o'clock.

Wednesday morning their Royal Highnesses The Dukes of Gloucester and Cumberland, the Lord Chancellor, Chief Justices of the King's Bench and Common Pleas, Secretaries of State, and most of the nobility were suddenly *taken ill,* which prevented them accepting the Lord Mayor's invitation to dine at Guildhall.

Friday, November 11th.

As Lord Berkeley was passing over Hounslow-Heath, in the dusk of the evening, in his post-chaise, the driver was called

AN EXECUTION AT TYBURN

to stop by a young fellow genteelly dressed and mounted ; but the driver not readily obeying the summons, the fellow discharged his pistol at the chaise, which Lord Berkeley returned; and in the instant, a servant came up, and shot the fellow dead. By means of the horse, which he had that morning hired, he was traced, and his lodgings in Mercer-street, Long-Acre, discovered ; where Sir John Fielding's men were scarce entered, when a youth, booted and spurred, came to enquire for the deceased by the name of Evan Jones. This youth, upon examination, proved to be an accomplice, and impeached two other young men belonging to the same gang, one of whom was clerk to a lace-man in Bury-street, St. James's, after whom an immediate search being made, he was traced along the road to Portsmouth, and, at three in the morning, was surprized in bed at Farnham, and brought back to London, by Mr. Bond and other assistants. The other accomplice was also apprehended, and all three were carried before Sir John Fielding, when it appeared that these youths, all of good families, had lately committed a number of robberies in the neighbourhood of London ; that their names were Peter Houltum, John Richard Sauer and William Sampson ; that Sampson, in particular, had 50 guineas due to him for wages when he was apprehended, and that he had frequently been entrusted with effects to the amount of £10,000. An evening paper says that there are no less than *seven* of these youths in custody, from 18 to 20 years of age ; some of whose parents are in easy, some affluent circumstances, all of them overwhelmed with sorrow by the vices of their unhappy sons.

Sunday, November 13th.

There has been a foolish riot at Winchester, and forty of the middle class of commoners have set off . . . Dr. Warton locked up. . . . It all arose from some boy dressing up like the housekeeper, who has a humpback, and she desired the assistant, Huntingford, to order them all to bed before their usual time. That they would not comply with. Then Dr. Warton came into the hall ; the boys hissed him and said either Huntingford or they must quit the house. . . .

Monday, November 14th.

[Today the State] Lottery began drawing at Guildhall.

Tuesday, November 15th.

Application having been made by General Gage to the workmen in Boston and New York to assist in completing the fortifications on Boston Neck, by means of which the soldiery would become sole masters of the passages into the town, the same had been unanimously rejected, and not a man was to be found base enough to assist in an erection which would probably be improved to spill the blood of their fellow-subjects. An application of the like kind was made to the merchants of Philadelphia to supply the troops with necessary provisions and clothing and met with the same repulse. . . .

At New York a party has been formed in opposition to the country party, which has occasioned great confusion, and is supported by the merchants and traders chiefly against the gentlemen and freeholders. This division is fomented by the friends of government as the most likely means of ruining the common cause, and defeating the struggle for American liberty. . . .

Monday, November 21st.

[The King has written to Lord North,] I am not sorry that the line of conduct seems now chalked out. . . . The New England Governments are in a state of rebellion ; blows must decide whether they are to be subject to this country or independent. . . .

Tuesday, November 22nd.

The influence of the Crown in Parliament, by means of its Minister, is, rightly considered, but a grateful exchange of compliment ; for, as by the Act of Settlement the Kings of England are Parliamentary Kings, so, as one good turn deserves another, our Parliaments are become Royal Parliaments.

Wednesday, November 23rd.

[Lately published :]

An Examination of Dr. Reid's Enquiry into the human Mind on the Principles of common Sense, Dr. Beattie's Essay on the Nature and Immutability of Truth, and Dr. Oswald's Appeal to common Sense in Behalf of Religion. By Joseph Priestley, LL.D. F.R.S. 5s. Johnson.

A New Essay on the constitutional Power of Great Britain over the Colonies in America. By the Pennsylvania Farmer.

The Works of George Lillo ; Author of the Tragedy of George Barnwell. 6s. Davies.

The Maid of the Oaks ; a pastoral entertainment, in five acts, [*by Major-General John Burgoyne*], *as it is performed at the Theatre-Royal, in Drury Lane.* 1s. 6d. Becket.

Thursday, November 24th.

A great event happened two days ago — a political and moral event, the sudden death of that second Kouli Khan, Lord Clive. There was certainly illness in the case : the world thinks more than illness. His constitution was exceedingly broken and disordered, and grown subject to violent pains and convulsions. He came unexpectedly to town last Monday, and they say, ill. On Tuesday his physician gave him a dose of laudanum, which had not the desired effect. On the rest there are two stories ; one that the physician repeated the dose ; the other, that he doubled it himself, contrary to advice. In short he has terminated at fifty a life of so much glory, reproach, art, wealth and ostentation ! He had just named ten members for the new Parliament.

Friday, November 25th.

Next Tuesday Parliament is to meet — and a deep game it has to play ! few Parliaments a greater. The world is in amaze that no account is arrived from America of the result of their General Congress — if any is come it is very secret ; and *that* has no favourable aspect. The combination and spirit there seem to be universal, and is very alarming. . . .

The next Augustan age will dawn on the other side of the

Atlantic. There will, perhaps, be a Thucydides at Boston, a Xenophon at New York, and, in time, a Virgil at Mexico, and a Newton at Peru. At last, some curious traveller from Lima will visit England and give a description of the ruins of St. Paul's, like the editions of Balbec and Palmyra. . . .

Saturday, November 26th.

Our unnatural warfare with the Americans is good for nothing but to create famine, ruin our manufactures, cripple our commerce, facilitate the designs of our natural enemies, by weakening our mutual strength, promote emigration, and in a word, render us the scorn and derision of not only all Europe, but all the world, for our invincible ignorance and impolitic folly.

Though it is whispered in many places that the Pretender, in the character of a private gentleman, is very busy in America, in spurring the rebellious people to revenge themselves, and is daily supplying them with materials for that purpose ; yet we cannot think these whispers founded on truth. . . .

Sunday, November 27th.

A memorial from the British Court has been circulated throughout the ports of France, in order to discountenance every species of illicit commerce between the subjects of His Most Christian Majesty, and those of the King of Great Britain in America. By this memorial, owners of ships, or merchandize, who engage in this contraband trade, are given to understand that their ships will be strictly searched, and that offenders will be rigorously punished for their breach of treaties, without involving the two nations in the contest, or disturbing in the least the public tranquillity. A like memorial has been communicated to the Dutch traders.

Monday, November 28th.

The ecclesiastical Court are come to a resolution that the Duchess of Kingston is Mrs. Hervey ; and the sentence will be public in a fortnight. It is not so certain that she will lose the estate. . . .

Lord Clive certainly cut the jugular vein with a pen knife.— It is called a fever frenzy. . . .

Tuesday, November 29th.

The writs for calling a new parliament being returnable this day, His Majesty came to the House of Peers, and being in his royal robes seated on the throne, commanded the attendance of the House of Commons in the House of Peers ; who being come, His Majesty by his Chancellor signified his pleasure that they should return and choose a Speaker, to be presented next day for His Majesty's approbation. They returned accordingly and unanimously chose Sir Fletcher Norton.

Wednesday, November 30th.

This day His Majesty came again in state to the House of Peers and having approved of the Commons' choice, opened the session with the following speech :

My Lords and Gentlemen,

It gives me much concern that I am obliged, at the opening of this Parliament, to inform you that a most daring spirit of resistance and disobedience to the law still unhappily prevails in the province of the Massachusetts Bay, and has, in divers parts of it, broke forth in fresh violences of a very criminal nature. These proceedings have been countenanced and encouraged in other of my colonies and unwarrantable attempts have been made to obstruct the commerce of this Kingdom by unlawful combinations. I have taken such measures and given such orders as I judged most proper and effectual for carrying into execution the laws which were passed in the last session of the late Parliament, for the protection and security of the commerce of my subjects, and for the restoring and preserving peace, order, and good government in the province of the Massachusetts Bay ; and you may depend upon my firm and steadfast resolution to withstand every attempt to weaken or impair the supreme authority of this legislature over all the dominions of my Crown ; the maintenance of which I consider as essential to the dignity, the safety and the welfare of the British Empire ; assuring myself that while I act upon these principles, I shall never fail to receive your assistance and support.

I have the greatest satisfaction in being able to inform you that a treaty of peace is concluded between Russia and the Porte. By this happy event, the troubles which have so long prevailed in one part of Europe are composed and the general tranquillity rendered complete. . . .

As soon as [His Majesty had retired and] the House was cleared of the Ladies, and several Lords had taken the oaths, the above speech was read by the Chancellor, as Speaker of the House of Peers; and then Lord Hillsborough, after a long speech, chiefly respecting the refractory conduct of the American colonies, moved for an address of thanks to His Majesty for his most gracious speech from the throne, and was seconded by Lord Buckinghamshire, who likewise expatiated on the daring spirit of resistance that prevailed throughout the colonies, more particularly in the province of Massachusetts Bay. . . . The Duke of Richmond got up and after censuring the severe and precipitate Acts of the last parliament, moved for an amendment in the address, which occasioned a long and warm debate, but on the question being put the amendment was rejected by 63 to 13, and the address as at first proposed, passed by a majority of 46 against 9. . . .

December 1774

Thursday, December 1st.

The present *Lion* of the times . . . is [Omiah] the native of Otaheite ; and next to him . . . Mr. Bruce, a gentleman who has been abroad twelve years and spent four of them in Abyssinia and other places in Africa, where no Englishman before has gained admission. His adventures are very marvellous. He is expected to publish them. . . . His figure is almost gigantic . . . and exceedingly well made. . . . He seems rather arrogant and to have so large a share of good opinion of himself as to have nothing left for the rest of the world but contempt. . . .

[Tonight at Dr. Burney's] I found Omiah seated on the great chair . . . and [James Burney] next to him, and talking Otaheite as fast as possible. . . . As [Omiah] had been at Court he was very fine. He had on a suit of Manchester velvet, lined with white satin, a *bag*, lace ruffles, and a very handsome sword which the King had given to him. He is tall and very well made, much darker than I expected to see him, but has a pleasing countenance. . . . Indeed he seems to shame education, for his manners are so extremely graceful, and he is so polite, attentive and easy, that you would have thought he came from some foreign court. . . . He committed not the slightest blunder at table. . . . [He speaks a good many words of English.] I only wish I could have spoke his language. Lord Sandwich has actually studied it so as to make himself understood in it. His hands are very much tattooed, but his face is not at all. . . .

Friday, December 2nd.

The Lord Mayor of London [Mr. Wilkes] was sworn into parliament, as member for Middlesex, and delivered in his qualification upon oath accordingly.

Saturday, December 3rd.

As soon as the news was received of the Bishop of Worcester's death, Lord North went immediately to the King, to ask the vacant Bishopric for his brother the Bishop of Lichfield and Coventry, and there is no doubt of his succeeding to the vacant See.

It is expected that a strict and severe enquiry will immediately be made into the means by which gentlemen returning from India have acquired such monstrous and overgrown fortunes. . . . It must end in bringing the plunderers of the East to that condign punishment which, to the disgrace of the national character, has so long been withheld from them through the influence of a noble Lord deceased, and the parliamentary abilities of the celebrated Caledonian Orator, who will no longer feel himself interested in the preservation of Nabobs, now that his noble friend is no more.

Sunday, December 4th.

An estimate of the number of souls in the following provinces, made in Congress, Sept. 1774.

In Massachusetts, 400,000. New Hampshire, 150,000. Rhode Island, 59,678. Connecticut, 192,000. New York, 250,000. New Jersey, 130,000. Pennsylvania, including the lower counties, 350,000. Maryland, 320,000. Virginia, 650,000. North Carolina, 300,000. South Carolina, 225,000. Total 3,026,678.

Monday, December 5th.

Being the day appointed to take His Majesty's speech into consideration, the gallery doors were kept shut, contrary to the usual custom, till after three o'clock ; and when opened, near 200 crowded in ; but were no sooner seated than a member rose and insisted that all strangers should withdraw, which was opposed by Mr. Burke and others ; but at length the House was ordered to be cleared and the Speaker called for the key. The House being now called to order, Lord Beauchamp moved for an address of thanks for His Majesty's most gracious speech from the throne. Besides the usual form

of addressing his Lordship introduced several pertinent
observations on the present spirit of the colonists, their resolves,
meetings, and in particular, their intended non-importation
agreement. His speech was much approved. His Lordship
was seconded by Mr. De Grey, jun. Lord John Cavendish
then rose, and, after condemning the conduct of administration,
and the turbulent spirit of the colonies, moved an amendment,
in calling for such papers relative to America as had been
received since the last sessions, without which, his Lordship
said, it would be impossible for the House to determine with
propriety or certainty, whether it might or might not be
necessary to adopt such measures. Lord North answered
Lord Cavendish in a short speech, and [many other members
also spoke]. . . .

The question being put at about half after ten, the House
divided — for the amendment 73, against it 264 ; and the
question for the address being then put, it passed, of course, in
the affirmative.

Tuesday, December 6th.

At a general court of proprietors of East India stock held
on Thursday . . . a letter was read from Warren Hastings,
Esq., Governor of Bengal, in which he gave a very satisfactory
account of the progress he had made in forming a new code
of laws, for the better administration of justice in the Company's
territorial acquisitions. . . .

Wednesday, December 7th.

There are twenty-one men of war and frigates now building
at the different dock-yards of this kingdom. At Deptford,
three 70 gun ships, and two frigates ; at Woolwich, two of 60,
and one of 54 ; at Sheerness, two frigates ; at Chatham, five
men of war, and frigates ; at Portsmouth, six ditto, besides two
beginning at Plymouth.

Friday, December 9th.

Yesterday morning a bill of indictment was presented to
the Grand Jury for the county of Middlesex, at Hick's-Hall,
against the Duchess of Kingston for felony, in marrying the late

Duke of Kingston, at the time she was actually the wife of the Hon. Augustus Hervey. . . . She must appear to take her trial at the Old Bailey as a felon, or an outlawry will issue against her.

Sunday, December 11th.

It is a very great insult to respectable citizens and gentlemen of moderate fortunes, who from principles of economy choose to sit in the first gallery [of our theatres], that they admit too men in liveries. The prices of admittance have been raised within these thirty years, and every art practised for the interest of the managers ; and in these times, when every necessary and convenience of life is considerably enhanced, it is a matter of prudence in persons of the middle rank of life to prefer the gallery to the pit. But this is no reason why livery servants should be allowed to place themselves by the wives and daughters of private gentlemen and reputable tradesmen, to whom they often behave with great insolence and indecency. [It is desirable] to know why a constable does not make his appearance in the back row of the first, as well as the second, gallery, being frequently as much wanted in the one as the other. A drunken man and a livery servant were both very troublesome in the first gallery at Covent-Garden Theatre on Saturday night.

Monday, December 12th.

Last Saturday being the anniversary of the institution of the Royal Academy, a general assembly of the Academicians was held at Somerset-House. . . . [Gold medals were given] to Mr James Jefferys for the best picture in oil colours, the subject Seleucus and Stratonice . . . to Mr Charles Banks, for the best medal of a bas-relief, the story Pygmalion . . . [and] to Mr Thomas Whetten, for the best design in architecture. . . .

After the medals were given, the President, as usual, read to the Students a discourse, the subject of which was imitation, and the advantage to be drawn from studying the works of other masters. After the President had finished his discourse, the assembly proceeded to elect the officers for the year ensuing, when Sir Joshua Reynolds was re-elected President.

Council	Visitors
Edward Burch,	Francisco Bartolozzi,
G. M. Mozer,	James Barry,
Joseph Nollekens,	Nathaniel Hone,
Thomas Sandby,	Joseph Nollekens,
James Barry,	Peter Toms,
Richard Cosway,	Edward Burch,
Tho. Gainsborough,	Charles Catton,
Jer. Meyers, Esqrs.	Nathaniel Dance,
	Benj. West, Esqrs.

Tuesday, December 13*th.*

[On] Sunday two funeral sermons were preached at Cripplegate Church, by the Rev. Messrs. Goldwyer and Parry, in commemoration of that truly pious and able divine the late Rev. Dr. Nicolls. The dead march in *Saul* was played by an excellent band of music from the Theatre Royal in Drury-Lane, conducted by Mr. Smart, and the organ by the ingenious Mr. Battishell. Some select anthems and choruses from Mr. Handel's *Messiah,* viz. " I know that my Redeemer liveth," " For as in Adam all die," " The Trumpet shall sound," " O Death where is thy sting," " But thanks to God," " Worthy is the Lamb," &c. were sung by Messrs. Hudson, Dyne, J. Burton, and a number of the best chorus singers. To do justice to the performers, the whole was admirably performed, and conducted with the greatest solemnity, to the entire satisfaction of upwards of ten thousand people, assembled on that occasion ; and . . . no material accident happened.

Wednesday, December 14*th.*

A gentleman, who is a member of a certain assembly, asked the Lord Mayor, a few days ago, how he liked the King's speech. " What speech ? " answers the Lord Mayor. " Why that printed speech in your hand," replied the member. " You mistake," cries my Lord, " it is the American Death Warrant." " You are merry," cries the member. " Yes," returns the Lord Mayor, " I thank God it is not my death warrant." " But, to be serious," says the member, " don't

you think that the speech is a good one ? " " Yes," returns
the Lord Mayor, " it is a *bloody* good one."

Thursday, December 15*th.*

The long-expected sloop is arrived at last, and is, indeed, a
man of war ! The General Congress have voted a non-importation, a non-exportation, a non-consumption ; that, in case of
hostilities committed by the troops at Boston, the several
provinces will march to the assistance of their countrymen ;
that the cargoes of ships now at sea shall be sold on their
arrival, and the money arising thence given to the poor at
Boston ; that a letter, in the nature of a petition of rights,
shall be sent to the King ; another to the House of Commons ;
a third to the people of England ; a demand of the repeal of
all the Acts of Parliament affecting North America passed
during this reign, as also of the Quebec Bill : and these resolutions not to be altered till such repeal is obtained. . . .

We are at our wit's end — which was no great journey. . . .
Lord Chatham's crutch [may] be supposed a wand, and be
sent for . . . [but] the stile is a little too high to help them
over. His Lordship is a little fitter for raising a storm than
laying one, and of late seems to have lost both virtues. The
Americans at least have acted like men, gone to the bottom at
once, and set the whole upon the whole. Our conduct has
been that of pert children : we have thrown a pebble at a
mastiff, and are surprised it was not frightened. Now we
must be worried by it, or must kill the guardian of the house,
which will be plundered the moment little master has nothing
but the old nurse to defend it.

Monday, December 19*th.*

A new comedy called *The Choleric Man*, written by Mr.
Cumberland, was performed for the first time at Drury Lane
Theatre. The characters are Mr. Nightshade, *Mr. King* : Mr.
Manlove, his brother, *Mr. Aickin* : Young Manlove, *Mr.
Reddish* : Young Nightshade, *Mr. Weston* : Stapleton, *Mr.
Packer* : Dibble, *Mr. Baddeley* : Gregory, *Mr. Moody* : Laetitia
Fairfax, *Mrs. Abington* : Mrs. Stapleton, *Mrs. Hopkins* : Lucy,
Miss Pope. . . .

Thursday, December 22nd.

Mr. Edmund Burke's celebrated speech, April 19, 1774 . . . has been for some months ready for the press ; but the friends of administration having been used to attribute a great deal of their opposition to their measures in America to the writings published in England, the publication has been delayed till the measures of Government have had their full operation. . . .

Christmas Day, Sunday.

There was a numerous and splendid appearance at court to compliment their Majesties, when the Knights-Companions of the several orders appeared in their several collars. At noon their Majesties went to the Chapel-Royal and heard a sermon from the Rev. Dr. Kaye, Sub-almoner : after which their Majesties received the sacrament from the hands of the Lord Bishop of London, Dean of the Chapel, assisted by the Lord Bishop of Winchester, Clerk of the Closet to the King. The sword of state was carried to and from chapel by Lord Cathcart.

Monday, December 26th.

Josiah Wedgwood, Potter to her Majesty, [has] been obliged to remove his warehouse from Newport Street to Greek Street, Soho, for the sake of more room and better accommodation. . . .

Wednesday, December 28th.

THE LONDON GENERAL BILL OF CHRISTENINGS AND BURIALS
FROM DECEMBER 14, 1773, TO DECEMBER 13, 1774

Christened	Males . 8,711	Buried	Males . 10,366	Decreased in the Burials this year . 772
	Females 8,287		Females 10,518	

Died under 2 Years	. 7,742	Between 20 and 30 .	. 1,578
Between 2 and 5 .	. 2,119	,, 30 ,, 40 .	. 1,721
,, 5 ,, 10 .	. 826	,, 40 ,, 50 .	. 1,838
,, 10 ,, 20 .	. 712	,, 50 ,, 60 .	. 1,630

Between 60 and 70	. 1,256	101	1
,, 70 ,, 80	. 974	102	6
,, 80 ,, 90	. 422	103	3
,, 90 ,, 100	. 53	104	1
100	. 1	106	1

Diseases

Abortive & stillborn	. 581	shoehead & water in	
Aged . . .	. 1,294	the head . . .	15
Ague	9	Jaundice . . .	114
Apoplexy & sudden	. 209	Imposthume . .	8
Asthma & tissick .	. 311	Inflammation . .	96
Bedridden . .	7	Itch	0
Bleeding . .	9	Leprosy . . .	0
Bloody flux . .	4	Lethargy . . .	1
Bursten & rupture	9	Livergrown . . .	1
Cancer . . .	49	Lunatic . . .	59
Canker . . .	3	Measles . . .	121
Chicken pox . .	8	Miscarriage . . .	4
Cholic, gripes, twist of		Mortification . .	193
the guts . . .	63	Palsy	73
Cold	2	Pleurisy . . .	20
Consumption .	. 4,242	Quinsy . . .	4
Cough & whooping		Rash	0
cough . . .	554	Rheumatism . .	5
Convulsions . .	. 5,457	Rickets . . .	3
Diabetes . . .	1	Rising of the lights .	1
Dropsy . . .	743	Scald-head . . .	4
Evil	17	Scurvy . . .	6
Fever, malignant fever,		Small pox . . .	2,479
scarlet fever, spotted		Sores & ulcers . .	12
fever, & purples	. 2,607	Sore throat . . .	4
Fistula . . .	4	St Anthony's fire . .	2
Flux	13	Stoppage in the stomach	16
French pox . . .	57	Surfeit . . .	3
Gout	54	Swelling . . .	7
Gravel, stranguary &		Teeth	780
stone . . .	27	Thrush . . .	88
Grief	1	Tympany . . .	0
Headache . . .	1	Vomitting and looseness	5
Headmouldshot, horse-		Worms . . .	1

Casualties

Bit by mad dog . .	0	Killed themselves . .	22
Broken limbs . .	0	Murdered . . .	7
Bruised . . .	2	Overlaid . . .	4
Burnt	8	Poisoned . . .	1
Choked . . .	0	Scalded . . .	0
Drowned . . .	82	Smothered . . .	0
Excessive drinking .	3	Stabbed . . .	1
Executed . . .	13	Starved . . .	4
Fractured . . .	0	Suffocated . . .	5
Found dead . . .	3		
Killed by falls & several		Total . .	220
other accidents . .	65		

Friday, December 30th.

During the course of the month past application has been
made to the Court of Session in Scotland, on the part of Mr.
Dodsley, bookseller in London, against certain booksellers and
printers in Edinburgh, who had printed an edition of Lord
Chesterfield's Letters. Mr. Dodsley announced that he had
paid £1,500, for the copyright of that book, and that this
edition was printed contrary to the statute of Q. Anne, and
therefore prayed that the sale might be stopt for ten days, till
Mr. Dodsley had time to produce his title. It was answered
that the statute of Queen Anne only gives a right to authors
and their assigns, and that this copyright had never been
assigned to Mr. Dodsley by Lord Chesterfield. The court was
pleased to grant a sist to stop the sale for ten days, upon Mr.
Dodsley's finding caution for £500, to pay for damages that
might be sustained by the sale of the book being stopped.

Saturday, December 31st.

On Saturday last the Lord Mayor issued warrants for
apprehending all rogues, vagabonds, and disorderly women,
in consequence of which a great number of vagrants, &c. have
been committed to the different jails.

" If the worthy chief magistrate goes on at this rate, in a
very short time he will not have a single friend left at large."

SEVENTEEN SEVENTY FIVE

January 1775

Sunday, January 1st.

Being New Year's Day, the Rev. Dr. Kaye preached before their Majesties at the Chapel Royal. The sword of state was carried to and from Chapel by Lord Willoughby de Brooke. There was a numerous court to compliment their Majesties, which did not break up till five o'clock. At the same time, according to annual custom, the forty boys educated in navigation, mathematics, &c. in Christ's Hospital were presented to His Majesty by their president.

Wednesday, January 4th.

His Majesties' servants and tradespeople are five quarters in arrears tomorrow ; the want of which is most severely known to many who have large families to maintain, with small salaries, so long due before paid.

Saturday, January 7th.

[From] Charlestown, Nov. 6. A few days ago arrived the *Britannia*, Capt. Ball, from London. Notice having been received, that he had six chests of tea on board, near a thousand people were assembled on the wharf. They had prepared a scaffold two feet high to run on wheels ; had placed the Pope, Lord N——, and the Pretender, in order to burn the tea ; but as soon as the tea was brought upon deck, the owners were ready with hatchets, and chopped the chests to pieces, and threw the tea overboard. The people then drew the scaffold about the town ; and when it became dark there was computed to be 2500 men with each a candle in his hand, who retired to the out parts of the town, where they set fire to the scaffold ; in the meantime some of them took the Pope's cap and went round to the ladies in the town, who emptied the tea out of their canisters into the cap ; they then burnt Lord

N——, the Pope, and Pretender, with the cap full of tea, all together.

Monday, January 9th.

The last Non-importation agreement of the Americans did not last entire three months. The Americans themselves agreed to admit many articles, which, from their nature, it would have been folly to except against, particularly books, which the Quakers at Philadelphia very early admitted to be imported, from an honest man in their Assembly remarking, that not importing of books was like excluding knowledge and learning from the Continent. There were several other articles very early admitted.

Tuesday, January 10th.

[Today] was published Mr. Burke's famous speech on the proposed repeal of the Tea Duty, in the last Parliament. . . . With the quickest conception and amazing facility of elocution, with great strength of argumentation, and with all the powers of imagination and memory, the speech has . . . great defects. The redundancy of images, the pursuit of wit, even to puerility, the want of judgment and sobriety, and the still greater want of art to touch the passions, rank this great composition (which was the greater, as it was spoken unpremeditated) but with the species of imperfect eloquence. . . .

Wednesday, January 11th.

A correspondent says, a few days since he heard with horror the moving solicitation of a chimney-sweeper's boy to a neighbour of his, begging for God's sake he might be permitted to sweep the chimneys for the soot ; that if he did not carry home a bushel he should be half murdered. He says he enquired, and found the boy's report in general too true, in respect to the unreasonable and inhuman severity used by some master chimney-sweepers on these their unfortunate vassals. . . . It is a great reflexion on many of our parochial officers in this metropolis, that they bind out the children of the poor to any, even the most wretched employments, without bestowing the least care and concern for what becomes of them, or how they are used.

Thursday, January 12th.

Much hath been said of late concerning the treatment which those unfortunate beings, the negro slaves, meet with at the hands of their masters in the British Colonies. It seems, indeed, wondrous strange, that those very people who so loudly complain of infringements of their liberties, and so speciously declaim about the natural rights of mankind, should themselves have so little consideration for the sufferings of [those] of their fellow creatures who have the misfortune to fall into their power. The Rev. Mr. Wesley, in a letter to the monthly reviewers, has given two remarkable instances of this notable inconsistency in the Colonists, exemplified in copies of two advertisements, published in the newspapers of Virginia and North Carolina. They are as under — " Ran away on the 10th inst. a lusty negro, named Bob. The said fellow is outlawed, and I will give ten pounds for his head, severed from his body ; and forty shillings if brought alive." The second advertisement breathes the same diabolical spirit of revenge. " Ran away from the subscriber, a negro fellow named Zeb. aged 36. As he is outlawed, I will pay twenty pounds currency to any person who shall produce his head severed from his body ; and five pounds if brought home alive. John Mosely."

However cheap these advertising tyrants may hold the liberties of others, and even the lives of those who happen to wear a complexion darker than their own, surely the souls of their poor slaves can never be half so black as those of their inhuman task-masters ; whose cruelties can only be equalled by the unfeeling barbarity of drovers and carmen, the very scum and outcasts of a civilised nation !

Monday, January 16th.

[On Wednesday last] the keeper of an alehouse in Bishopsgate ward was complained of . . . for harbouring the watchmen of that ward during their hours of duty ; and being convicted . . . for suffering tippling in his house paid the penalty of ten shillings, besides being disabled from keeping an alehouse for the space of three years.

The *Paris Gazette* hath an article, dated from Civita Vecchia, which announces the safe arrival of the Duchess of Kingston, and declares it to be her intention to reside for several years at Rome.

Tuesday, January 17th.

[This] night was performed, for the first time, at Covent Garden Theatre, a comedy called *The Rivals*. . . .

[It] requires much castigation, and the pruning hand of judgment, before it ever can pass on the town as even a tolerable piece. In language it is defective to an extreme, in plot outré, and one of the characters is an absolute exotic in the wilds of nature. . . . If *The Rivals* rests its claim to public favour solely on the basis of merit, the hisses of the auditors . . . give reason to suspect a most fatal disappointment. . . .

Some of that stage-art, much of which Cibber derived from his connection with the theatre, would have taught our juvenile poet to give more effect to the part of Jack Absolute which is, in some sort, a second Atall in *The Double Gallant*. . . . The characters of Faulkland and Julia are beyond the pitch of sentimental comedy, and may not improperly be styled metaphysical. What evil spirit could influence the writer and the managers to assign the part of Sir Lucius O'Trigger to Mr. Lee, or Mr. Lee himself to receive it ? . . .

I think I never saw a performance more disgraceful to a Theatre-Royal. . . . None of the performers seemed to be tolerably perfect except Mrs. Bulkley and Miss Barsanti ; Shuter did not know any two lines together, and when ever he was out he tried to fill the interval with oaths and buffoonery ; in all his scenes with Woodward he put him out ; and for the Irishman, of all disgusting attempts that ever was damned in a strolling company, nothing ever came up to this. . . .

This comedy is said to be written by Mr. Sheridan, jun. . . .

[I] observed that instead of the social question . . . after a new piece of, " Well, sir, how have you been entertained ? " it was " Well, sir, have not you been vastly fatigued tonight ? " This question bodes no good to the young author.

Wednesday, January 18th.

The Court at St. James's [for] Her Majesty's birthday was very numerous and splendid. His Majesty sat to receive the compliments of the nobility and gentry in a suit of light blue velvet and silver, with spangles ; and the Queen was dressed in an elegant brocaded full suit of clothes, and a new elegant diamond stomacher, with necklace and earrings. The Ball began soon after nine o'clock ; the Queen's brother danced the first minuet with the Duchess of Grafton, and the second with the Duchess of Devonshire. Minuets continued till eleven, and only two country dances were called for ; and while the last was dancing, their Majesties retired, and the Ball ended at half-past eleven. The jewels worn by the ladies were of immense value ; those of the Duchess of Devonshire alone were estimated at seventy thousand pounds ; her dress was a blossom-coloured full suit of clothes, with silver spangles and white ermine. . . . The dresses of the gentlemen were extremely rich. . . .

The crowd . . . squeezed and shoved and pressed upon the Queen in the most hoyden manner. As she went out of the Drawing-room somebody said in flattery, " The crowd was very great." — " Yes," said the Queen, " and wherever one went, the Queen was in everybody's way."

Amongst the various luminary exhibitions . . . there was one in Long Acre that set all others at a contemptible distance ; it represented her M——y's profile, with a fiery nose a foot long, and a hare-lip of the same splendid irradiation, " grinning horribly a ghastly smile ! " — Above were a variety of the cherubimical order, playing round the royal head, and ever and anon dropping a libation of boiling oil into her princely mouth. — The whole cut a capital figure, and was much admired by the *cognoscenti* in the art of illuminations : the credit of the piece is given to the ingenious dapper Doctor of Marybone ; but we will not answer for the authenticity of the report.

Thursday, January 19th.

The House of Commons met pursuant to their adjournment,

when Lord North presented to the House several bundles of American papers. . . .

Friday, January 20th.

[In the] House of Lords the Earl of Dartmouth, Secretary of State for America, produced the official American papers.

The Earl of Chatham, after strongly inveighing against the dilatoriness of administration, &c. proceeded as follows :

But as I have not the honour of access to his Majesty, I will endeavour to transmit to him, through the constitutional channel of this House, my ideas of America, to rescue him from the misadvice of his present ministers. I congratulate your Lordships that the business is *at last* entered upon, by the noble Lord's laying the papers before you. As I suppose your Lordships too well apprised of their contents, I hope I am not premature, in submitting to you my present motion :

" That an humble address be presented to his Majesty, humbly to desire and beseech his Majesty, that in order to open the way towards a happy settlement of the dangerous troubles in America, by beginning to allay ferments and soften animosities there ; and above all, for preventing in the meantime any sudden and fatal catastrophe at Boston, now suffering under the daily irritation of an army before their eyes, posted in their town ; it may graciously please his Majesty that immediate orders may be dispatched to General Gage, for removing his Majesty's forces from the town of Boston as soon as the rigour of the season, and other circumstances indispensable to the safety and the accommodation of the said troops, may render the same practicable."

I wish, my Lords, not to lose a day in this urgent and pressing crisis ; an hour now lost in allaying the ferment in America, may produce years of calamity ; for my own part, I will not desert for a moment the conduct of this mighty business, from the first to the last ; unless nailed to my bed by the extremity of sickness, I will give it unremitted attention ; I will knock at the door of this sleeping and confounded Ministry, and will rouse them to a sense of their important danger.

When I state the importance of the Colonies to this country, and the magnitude of danger hanging over this country, from the present plan of misadministration practised against them, I desire not to be understood to argue a reciprocity of indulgence between England and America. I contend not for indulgence, but justice to America : and I shall ever contend that the Americans justly owe obedience to us in a limited degree :— they owe obedience to our ordinances of trade and navigation ; but let the line be skilfully drawn between the objects of those ordinances, and their private internal property ; let the sacredness of their property remain inviolate ; let it be taxable only by their own consent, given in their provincial assemblies ; else, *it will cease to be property.* . . .

Resistance to your acts was necessary as it was just ; and your vain declarations of the omnipotence of parliament, and your imperious doctrines of the necessity of submission will be found equally impotent to convince or enslave your fellow subjects in America, who feel that tyranny, whether *ambitioned* by an individual part of the legislature or the bodies who compose it, is equally intolerable to British subjects.

The means of enforcing this thraldom are found to be as ridiculous and weak in practice, as they are unjust in principle. Indeed I cannot but feel the most anxious sensibility for the situation of General Gage and the troops under his command ; thinking him, as I do, a man of humanity and understanding ; and entertaining, as I ever will, the highest respect, the warmest love, for the British troops. Their situation is truly unworthy, penned up — pining in inglorious inactivity : — They are an army of impotence, you may call them an army of safety and of guard, but they are in truth an army of impotence and contempt ; and to make the folly equal to the disgrace, they are an army of irritation and vexation. . . .

But his Majesty is advised that the union in America cannot last. Ministers have more eyes than I, and should have more ears ; but from all the information I have been able to procure, I can pronounce it, an union, solid, permanent and effectual. . . .

I remember some years ago when the Stamp Act was in agitation, conversing in a friendly confidence with a person of undoubted respect and authenticity, on that subject, and he assured me, with a certainty which his judgment and opportunities gave him, that these were the prevalent and steady principles of America : — That you might destroy their towns and cut them off from the superfluities, perhaps the conveniencies of life ; but that they were prepared to despise your power, and would not lament their loss, whilst they have — what, my Lords ? Their *woods* and their *liberty*. The name of my authority, if I am called upon, will authenticate the opinion irrefragably.

If illegal violences have been, as it is said, committed in America, prepare the way, open the door of possibility for acknowledgment and satisfaction ; but proceed not to such coercion, such proscription ; cease your indiscriminate inflictions ; amerce not thirty thousand — oppress not three millions for the fault of forty or fifty. Such severity of injustice must for ever render incurable the wounds you have already given your Colonies ; you irritate them to unappeasable rancour. What though you march from town to town, and from province to province ; though you should be able to enforce a temporary and local submission — which I only suppose, not admit — how shall you be able to secure the obedience of the country you leave behind you in your progress ? — to grasp the dominion of eighteen hundred miles of continent, populous in valour, liberty and resistance ! . . .

The spirit which now resists your taxation in America, is the same which formerly opposed loans, benevolences, and ship-money in England : — the same spirit which called all England *on its legs*, and by the Bill of Rights vindicated the English constitution : — the same principle which established the great, fundamental, essential maxim of our liberties, *that no subject of England shall be taxed but by his own consent*. . . .

When your Lordships look at the papers transmitted us from America, when you consider their decency, firmness and wisdom, you cannot but respect their cause and wish to make it your own. For myself, I must declare and avow, that in all my reading and observation — and it has been my favourite study ; I have read Thucydides, and have studied and admired the master-states of the world — that for solidity of reasoning,

force of sagacity and wisdom of conclusion in such a complication of difficult circumstances, no nation or body of men can
stand in preference to the general Congress at Philadelphia. I
trust it is obvious to your Lordships, that all attempts to impose
servitude upon such men, to establish despotism over such a
mighty continental *nation*, must be vain, must be fatal. We
shall be *forced ultimately to retract* ; let us retract while we can,
not when we must. I say we must necessarily undo these
violent oppressive acts : *they must be repealed, — you will repeal
them ; I pledge myself for it, that you will in the end repeal them ; I
stake my reputation on it : — I will consent to be taken for an idiot, if
they are not finally repealed.* Avoid then this humiliating, disgraceful necessity. With a dignity becoming your exalted
situation, make the first advances to concord, to peace and to
happiness. . . .

Every motive therefore of justice and of policy, of dignity
and of prudence, urges you to allay the ferment in America,
by a removal of your troops from Boston, by a repeal of your
acts of parliament, and by demonstration of amicable dispositions towards your Colonies. On the other hand, every
danger and every hazard impend, to deter you from perseverance in your present ruinous measures : — Foreign war
hanging over your heads by a slight and brittle thread : —
France and Spain watching your conduct, and waiting for the
maturity of your errors, with a vigilant eye to America, and the
temper of your Colonies, more than to their own concerns, be
they what they may.

To conclude, my Lords : if the Ministers thus persevere in
misadvising and misleading the King, I will not say they *can*
alienate the affections of his subjects from his crown ; but I
will affirm *that they will make the crown not worth his wearing.* I
will not say that the King is betrayed ; but I will pronounce,
that the kingdom is undone. . . .

[The division was, against the question, 68 ; for it, 18.]

Saturday, January 21*st.*

A few days ago died, at Birmingham, Mr. John Baskerville, very eminent as a Printer, for the beauty of his types
and ink.

Sunday, January 22nd.

[Copy of a letter from Dr. Samuel Johnson to Mr. James Macpherson, the translator of Ossian and Homer, who has threatened Johnson with violence for denying the authenticity of the Ossian poems :]

I received your foolish and impudent note. Whatever insult is offered me I will do my best to repel, and what I cannot do for myself the law will do for me. I will not desist from detecting what I think a cheat from any fear of the menaces of a Ruffian.

You want me to retract. What shall I retract ? I thought your book an imposture from the beginning. I think it upon yet surer reasons an imposture still. For this opinion I give the public my reasons which I here dare you to refute. But however I may despise you, I reverence truth and if you can prove the genuineness of the work I will confess it. Your rage I defy, your abilities since your Homer are not so formidable, and what I have heard of your morals disposes me to pay regard not to what you shall say, but to what you can prove.

You may print this if you will. SAM: JOHNSON.

Monday, January 23rd.

Lord Chatham is as warm as ever in the cause of America, and he intends to be early in the House of Lords upon their meeting. He has had the delegates from America with him, and all the papers laid before him ; which have made him more strenuous than ever in a determined resolution to procure the repeal of these unnatural Acts passed against the Americans.

Tuesday, January 24th.

The literary dispute between Dr. J[ohnson] and Mr. M[acpherson] it is apprehended will end rather tragical than otherwise ; the rigid philosophy of the former has so far forsaken him upon this occasion, that he has actually challenged his Scotch disputant to meet him on a particular mountain in one of the Western Islands, there to decide by pistol shot this momentous affair.

The Doctor is in regular training and fires already without

blinking : Mr. M. has accepted the Doctor's challenge and given Becket orders to make up half a dozen cartridges with the sacred manuscript of his beloved Ossian, as the certain means of carrying conviction to the heart of the philosophical infidel.

Wednesday, January 25th.

[On the 18th] Turnbull and Latimer's instrument for taking the distance of the moon from the sun was tried and proved upon Gateshead Fell, near Newcastle, by Mr. William Hope, an experienced mariner, who declared that by means of that instrument at sea the longitude might be determined with the greatest exactness.

This day is published in seven volumes, 8vo, price two guineas, bound in calf and lettered, the *Complete Works* of the Rev. George Whitefield, A.M., late of Pembroke College, Oxford, and Chaplain to the Rt. Hon. the Countess of Huntingdon, containing all his sermons and tracts which have been already published, with a select collection of letters . . . from the year 1734 to 1770, including the whole period of his ministry. . . . Edward and Charles Dilly.

Thursday, January 26th.

It is high time the Parliament should take cognisance of the numerous buildings daily increasing round the suburbs of the city. Politicians of all nations have ever agreed in opinion that an overgrown metropolis was one of the melancholy proofs of a sinking nation ; the great scarcity of labourers that has been experienced at our late harvests may be properly imputed to this cause. . . .

Friday, January 27th.

The publication of a speech said to be Lord Chatham's, having offended his Lordship, the sale of it is stopped. The publisher received it of a very respectable member of the House of Commons, and had not, in printing it, the least idea of incurring his Lordship's displeasure.

Saturday, January 28th.

Mr. Sheridan's comedy of *The Rivals* was performed for the second time with additions and alterations at the Theatre-Royal, Covent Garden. Its present state is widely different from that . . . on the first night's representation. Sir Lucius O'Trigger being retouched has now the appearance of a character ; and his assigning Beverley's reflection on his country as the grounds for his desire to quarrel with him is a reasonable pretence, and wipes off the former stigma undeservedly thrown on the sister kingdom. . . . Mr. Clinch did the strictest justice to the part. . . .

An alteration of a principal incident gave a very favourable turn to the fable and the whole piece, viz. that where young Acres now delivers his challenge to his friend Absolute, begging him to carry it to his rival Beverley, not knowing the two characters composed but one man ; its being at first given to Sir Lucius, the person who indited it, was highly inconsistent. The cuttings have been everywhere judicious. . . .

The performers were very attentive to the discharge of their duty . . . Shuter has now wiped off the odium. . . .

It was received with the warmest bursts of approbation by a crowded and apparently impartial audience. . . .

Sunday, January 29th.

Dr. Johnson's *Tour to the Western Isles.* What a heap of words to express very little ! and though it is the least cumbrous of any style he ever used, how far from easy and natural ! He hopes nobody but is glad that a boatful of sacrilege, a diverting sin ! was shipwrecked. He believes in second sight, and laughs at poor Pennant for credulity ! The King sent for the book in MS., and then wondering, said, " I protest, Johnson seems to be a Papist and a Jacobite ! " — so he did not know why he had been made to give him a pension ! . . .

Monday, January 30th.

Advices received from America, by a ship from New York, bring a confirmation of the unanimous concurrence of all the colonies in the measures recommended by the General Congress.

The town of Birmingham has petitioned the Parliament to enforce the American Acts, that is, make war, for they have a manufacture of swords and muskets. I believe the Dutch will petition too, for much such a reason !

Tuesday, January 31st.

THEATRICAL ENTERTAINMENTS
Drury Lane

Dec. 30. Choleric Man [Richard Cumberland] — Deserter [Charles Dibdin]

Jan. 4. Distressed Mother [Ambrose Philips] — Harlequin's Jacket

    5. Maid of the Oaks [Gen. John Burgoyne]

    6. Provoked Wife [Sir John Vanbrugh] — Deserter

    7. Distressed Mother — Harlequin's Jacket

    9. Ditto — Ditto

  10. Much Ado about Nothing [Shakespeare]

  11. Twelfth Night [Shakespeare] — Harlequin's Jacket

  12. Choleric Man

  13. Maid of the Oaks — Guardian [David Garrick]

  14. Choleric Man — Harlequin's Jacket

  16. Distressed Mother — Ditto

  17. Choleric Man

  18. Wonder [Susannah Centlivre] — Cobbler [Charles Dibdin]

  23. Matilda [Thomas Francklin] — Male Coquet [David Garrick]

  24. Wonder — Deuce is in him [George Colman the elder]

  27. Choleric Man — Harlequin's Jacket

Covent Garden

Dec. 30. Loves makes a Man [Colley Cibber] — Druids

  31. Richard III [Shakespeare]

Jan. 4. Grecian Daughter [Arthur Murphy] — Druids
     5. She Would and She Would not [Colley Cibber]
     6. Maid of the Mill [Isaac Bickerstaffe] — Druids
     7. Distressed Mother
     9. Ditto — Druids
   10. Busy Body [Susannah Centlivre]
   11. Distressed Mother — Druids
   12. Artaxerxes [Thomas Arne]
   13. She Stoops to Conquer [Goldsmith] — Druids
   14. Distressed Mother
   16. Ditto — Druids
   17. The Rivals [Sheridan]
   18. Ditto — Druids
   23. Alexander — Two Misers [Kane O'Hara]
   25. Love in a Village [Isaac Bickerstaffe] — Druids
   27. Elfrida [William Mason, altered by George Colman] — Druids

FEBRUARY 1775

Wednesday, February 1st.

[Yesterday to] Bach's Concert. It was the opening of his new room, which . . . is by much the most elegant room in town ; it is larger than that at Almack's. The statue of Apollo is placed just behind the orchestra, but it is thought too large and clumsy. There are ten other figures or pictures bigger than life. They are painted by some of our most eminent artists ; such as West, Gainsborough, Cipriani, &c. These pictures are all transparent and are lighted behind ; and that light is sufficient to illuminate the room without lustres or any candles appearing. The ceiling is domed, and beautifully painted with alto-relievos in all the piers. The pictures are chiefly fanciful ; a Comic Muse painted by Gainsborough is most highly spoken of. 'Tis a great stroke of Bach's to entertain the town so very elegantly. Nevertheless Lord Hillsborough, Sir James Porter, and some others, have entered into a subscription to prosecute Bach for a nuisance and I was told the jury had found a Bill against him. One would scarce imagine his house could molest either of these men, for Bach's is at the corner of Hanover Street. . . .

Thursday, February 2nd.

Yesterday . . . Lord Chatham offered a bill for pacifying America by abrogating the Declaratory Law and the late Acts ; and, they say, recalled the memory of his ancient lustre. . . . Lord Shelburne was violent, and Lord Mansfield so violently frightened, that he was not there ; on which I hear King George joked before all his servants, when he was told it after the play. The newspapers . . . now are very accurate in recounting debates. . . . When the last Prime Minister designs to open his plan I do not know ; the present produces his today. There is a great deal of bravery and a great deal of terror stirring ; and the address of today, I am told, has a layer of each. . . .

Friday, February 3rd.

[Yesterday] Lord North . . . produced part of his plan for carrying on the war. The most memorable topics of his speech, which was larded with violence and moderation, as his own humour or the plan that had been given him took their turn, were these : that jurisdiction must be kept up with legislation ; that it was essential *at present* not to repeal the Acts of the last session as it was necessary to maintain authority, which was well worth all the exertion of every force in this country. The non-importation and non-exportation agreement, he maintained, was not likely to be observed. That the nation must contribute to relieve the distresses of its traders, should there be any. . . . He would move an Address to the King to take all proper means of reducing America, but would acquaint the House that he had other measures to propose on a future day. It was determined to reinforce General Gage ; four regiments were to go, and his army to be increased to 10,000 men. There would also be regulations with regard to their trade. If they would not trade with us, it was just they should not trade with others. The object was great, the attempt honest ; no better means had been proposed. He meant to prevent the refractory Colonies from fishing in our seas. . . . The Address . . . was carried, and it was a *vote for a civil war*, by 304 to 105. . . .

Saturday, February 4th.

A most immense crowd [at the opera]. In the last dance . . . there were a hundred [gentlemen] on the stage ; two hundred people were sent away. All this crowd is for the Sestina, who is by far the best comic actress and singer we ever had. . . .

Three Major-generals are ordered to go to America in March — Howe, Burgoyne, and Clinton ; they had their orders Friday night last. I am very sorry for Mrs. Howe, who I believe would most willingly have gone with her husband had it been possible.

Sunday, February 5th.

At present the ministers are encouraged to proceed by the
assurances they receive from America that the people are not
unanimous ; that a very great part of them disapprove the
proceedings of the Congress, and would break through them if
there was in the country an army sufficient to support these
friends, as they are called, of Government. They rely, too,
on being able to divide [the Americans] still farther by various
means ; for they seem to have no conception that such a thing
as public spirit or public virtue anywhere exists. I trust they
will find themselves totally mistaken. The Congress is in high
esteem here among all the friends of liberty, and their papers
much admired ; perhaps nothing of the kind has been more
thoroughly published or more universally read. . . .

Monday, February 6th.

[Extract of a letter of General Charles Lee's from America
to Edmund Burke, Esq. :]

I have now run through almost the whole Colonies from
the north to the south. I have conversed with every order of
men, from the first estated gentleman to the poorest planters,
and cannot express my astonishment at the unanimous, ardent
spirit reigning through the whole. They are determined to
sacrifice everything, their property, their wives, children, and
blood, rather than cede a tittle of what they conceive to be
their rights. The tyranny exercised over Boston, indeed, seems
to be resented by the other Colonies in a greater degree than
by the Bostonians themselves. . . .

As to their capacity for war, the want of attention to certain
circumstances has led the regular officers who served in America
into a very great mistake on this head. . . . They shut their
eyes to all the evidences of the reverse ; to their promptness
to action, their superiority in marching, and address in the
use of all military instruments ; but above all, their ardour
and zeal for the service. . . . Formerly they had a slouching,
slovenly air. Now every peasant has his hair smartly dressed, is
erect and soldier-like in his air and gait. This change struck me
very much in passing through the provinces of Massachusetts

and Connecticut. It must be attributed to the military spirit which they breathe, and their companies of cadets formed in all the towns of any considerable size. . . . I shall say nothing of the formidable numbers of light infantry (undoubtedly the best in the world) which their back provinces can produce. In short, sir, it is my persuasion, that should the people of England be infatuated enough to suffer their misrulers to proceed in their measures, this country may scorch her fingers, but they themselves will perish in the flames. . . .

Tuesday, February 7th.

I believe Mr. Hawkins Brown will lose his election. He is to pay £1,200 towards the expenses if he loses it ; should he gain the cause, he is to add a thousand more. Giving £2,200 for a seat in Parliament, is as the times go, very well, but to pay £1,200 for nothing but trying Mr. Walter's right seems to me not a little hard.

Thursday, February 9th.

[Now published :]
Experiments and Observations on Electricity, made at Philadelphia in America, by Benjamin Franklin, LL.D and F.R.S. . . . Illustrated with copper plates. The fifth edition. . . . Newbery, at the Corner of St. Paul's Churchyard. . . . 10s. 6d.

Friday, February 10th.

Lord North moved for leave to bring in a Bill for putting the trade of America with England and Ireland and the West Indies under temporary restrictions, and for restraining the refractory provinces from fishing on the banks of Newfoundland. As this Bill was founded on the supposed rebellion of the Massachusetts, the evidence of such rebellion was much contested by Dunning, Burke, Glynn, T. Townshend, Lord J. Cavendish, and Sir George Savile, and maintained by the Attorney and Solicitor General and Sir Fletcher Norton, the Speaker. . . . Leave was granted to bring in the Bill at twelve at night by 261 against 85. . . .

Saturday, February 11th.

Mr. Howard has lately inspected the several gaols and bridewells in the north of England ; from thence went into Scotland and crossed to Ireland, where he attentively visited several of their county gaols, as well as every prison in Edinburgh and Dublin, and having collected the several statutes relative thereto, is on his return to England.

Tuesday, February 14th.

[The King finds] that the preparations the three Major Generals must inevitably make for their expedition to N. America cannot cost them less than £500 each ; they have behaved so very properly and are so poor, that [the King wishes] Lord Barrington to allow them that sum. . . .

This day is published, price one shilling and sixpence, *The Rivals*, a comedy, as it is now performing with universal applause at the Theatre-Royal, Covent Garden, printed for J. Wilkie, No. 71 St. Paul's Churchyard, and J. Walter, Charing Cross.

Wednesday, February 15th.

The war with our colonies, which is now declared, is a proof how much influence jargon has on human actions. A war on our own trade is *popular* ! Both Houses are as eager for it as they were for conquering the Indies — which acquits them a little of rapine, when they are as glad of what will impoverish them as of what they fancied was to enrich them — so like are the great vulgar and the small. . . . We are raising soldiers and seamen — so are the Americans, and, unluckily, can find a troop as easily as we a trooper. But we are above descending to calculation : one would think the whole legislature were of the club at Almack's, and imagined, like Charles Fox, that our fame was to rise in proportion to our losses. . . . In the meantime bad news pours in from America. . . .

Thursday, February 16th.

[Yesterday] four convicts were executed at Tyburn . . . one for robbing a farmer's boy of sixpence.

Friday, February 17th.

Lord Carysfort has purchased the celebrated picture representing " The Triumph of David," by Nicholas Poussin,
esteemed one of the most capital pieces in Europe of that much
admired master.

A new thing last night at Bach's room, in Hanover Square,
called the Festino ; 'tis under the direction of Gallini, and is
to be weekly like Almack's. . . . As I understand, the plan
is a dinner for gentlemen. At eight or nine the ladies are to
come, then catches and glees till supper, and after supper they
dance. . . .

Saturday, February 18th.

Braganza [by Robert Jephson] was acted last night [at
Drury Lane] with prodigious success. The audience, the most
impartial I ever saw, sat mute for two acts, and seemed determined to judge for themselves and not be the dupes of the
encomiums that had been so lavishly trumpeted. At the third
act, they grew pleased, and interested : at the fourth they were
cooled and deadened by two unnecessary scenes, but at the
catastrophe in the fifth, they were transported. They clapped,
shouted, huzzaed, cried bravo, and thundered out applause
both at the end, and when given out again ; yet the action
was not worthy of the poet. Mrs. Yates shone in the dignified
scenes, but had not variety enough ; Smith, recalling Garrick
in *Richard III*, played the Viceroy with great spirit ; but
Reddish was pitiful and whining in the Duke ; Aickin ridiculous
in the first old conspirator, and the Friar totally insignificant,
though engaged in the principal scene in the play, where indeed
he has too little to say. The charming beauties of the poetry
were not yet discovered, and the faults in the conduct may be
easily mended. . . . I trust, if this tragedy does not inspire
better writers, that it will at least preserve the town from hearing with patience the stuff we have had for these fifty years.
There was an excellent prologue written by Murphy well
delivered by Mrs. Yates . . . [and an epilogue by Horace
Walpole Esq.].

Monday, February 20th.

An Account of the Receipts of " Matilda "
[by Dr. T. Francklin, acted at Drury Lane Theatre]

	£	s.	d.		£	s.	d.
				Author's Nights			
Jan. 21st 1st Night .	220	7	6	Jan. 24th 3rd Night	196	9	0
„ 23rd 2nd do. .	153	13	0	Feb. 3rd 8th do.	170	8	0
„ 26th 4th do. .	174	9	6	„ 7th 9th do.	190	0	0
„ 28th 5th do. .	205	14	0				
„ 31st 6th do. .	165	1	0		556	17	0
Feb. 2nd 7th do. .	221	4	0				
				Three nights charged			
Manager's Six Nights	1,140	9	0	at £73 : 10 : 0 per			
Ditto charges at £100				night . . .	220	10	0
per night . .	600	0	0				
	540	9	0	Author's Balance . £336	7	0	
Loss by Author's three							
nights under-							
charged . .	79	10	0				
Manager's Balance . £460	19	0					

Tuesday, February 21st.

The operas are much in fashion, both for serious and comic. . . . Such crowds every night that you must go by six or have no place in the pit ; you cannot even get your coach to the door.

Friday, February 24th.

A petition was presented to the House of Commons from the Corporation of London against the Bill to restrain the trade and commerce of [the American colonies] . . . on the ground of its being an unjust, cruel, partial and oppressive Bill, injurious to the trade of Great Britain and tending to increase the wealth and strength of her rivals and enemies.

Saturday, February 25th.

[Lately published :]
Miscellanies in Prose and Verse. By Mrs. Chapone. Small 8vo. Pp. 178. Dilly.

Thoughts upon the present contest between Administration and the British colonies in America. Addressed to the merchants of the city of London, and all the sea ports, trading and manufacturing towns in Great Britain and Ireland. 1s. J. Browne.

Monday, February 27th.

To Sir Joshua Reynolds' to see his pictures. Here we were very much delighted. The ease and elegance of this painter . . . seem unrivalled among English artists. Among other portraits we saw Signor Sacchini, which is taken for the Duke of Dorset. It is finely done and makes a most charming picture. Sir Joshua himself . . . said that Sacchini was the highest type of manly beauty. But what most delighted me was the beautiful Mrs. Sheridan, who is taken seated at a harp, a whole figure in character of Saint Cecilia ; a denomination she greatly merits. . . .

Tuesday, February 28th.

High Phaetons are now creeping into fashion among the Young Bloods of the whip ; one of a most extraordinary nature, with a coachman no less extraordinary, was seen yesterday on the Turnham Green Road ; men, women and children stood in groups gaping at this most absurd and ridiculous vehicle. The charioteer on his return stopped at Turnham Green, drew up to the door, and with the greatest ease stepped into the balcony, drank a gill of wine ; then, with a becoming carelessness, walked in again and drove to town.

On Thursday night an engine belonging to one of the offices attempted to go through St. James's park in order to get at the fire in Petty France, Westminster, but was stopped by the sentry at the Horse Guards, who refused to let it pass ; on which a fireman knocked him down with his axe and drove through, and the engine going over him, bruised him in so shocking a manner that his life is despaired of.

MARCH 1775

Sunday, March 5th.

A large party [at Mr. Burney's house in St. Martin's Street, Leicester Square]. . . . Mr. Bruce, who is very fond of music, had appointed . . . to hear Mr. Burney play upon [the] Merlin harpsichord. . . . We had music for above two hours. Mr. Burney played delightfully ; and [his daughter] Hetty accompanied him in a very fine duet for the harpsichord and piano forte. . . .

Mr. Bruce . . . has favoured him with two delightful original drawings, done by himself, of instruments which he found at the Egyptian Thebes . . . and also with a long letter concerning them, which is to be printed in the History.

Wednesday, March 8th.

The burning of [*The Crisis* papers] at the Royal Exchange yesterday [by order of the House of Commons] was abundantly more diverting than the [burning] at Westminster on Monday. Soon after twelve o'clock more than a thousand people were assembled. The constables formed their ring at half-past twelve, and the city Marshal made his appearance before one, sustaining with great intrepidity the insults of the mob. At a quarter past one the sheriffs arrived — and the Hangman produced his links and faggots, and the opprobrious papers were committed to the flames. The top of the Royal Exchange was crowded, and the windows of that and all the neighbouring buildings filled with people. Two dead cats were thrown from the tops of houses, which were immediately circulated among the mob. This was but a prelude — waistcoats, hats, wigs, dishclouts and cats, alternately flew through the air, while Mr. Oates paraded round the fire fearless of consequences. The flames now subsiding, the half-burnt faggots were thrown from one end of the Royal Exchange to the other. The whole was a comedy of diverting incidents, filled with the essential requisites of time, place and character.

Sunday, March 12th.

A NEW OFFICE OF INITIATION FOR ALL YOUTHS
OF THE SUPERIOR CLASS

Lord Chesterfield's Creed

I believe that this world is the object of my hopes and morals and that the little prettinesses of life will answer all the ends of human existence. I believe that we are to succeed in all things by the graces of civility and attention ; that there is no sin but against good manners, and that all religion and virtue consist in outward appearance. I believe that all women are children, and all men fools, except a few cunning people who see through the rest and make their use of them. I believe that hypocrisy, fornication, and adultery are within the lines of morality ; that a woman may be honourable when she has lost her honour, and virtuous when she has lost her virtue.

This and whatever else is necessary to obtain my own ends and bring me into repute, I resolve to follow ; and to avoid all moral offences, such as scratching my head before company, spitting upon the floor, and omitting to pick up a lady's fan ; and in this persuasion I will persevere without any regard to the resurrection of the body or the life everlasting. Amen.

Q. Wilt thou be initiated into these principles ?

A. That is my inclination.

Q. Wilt thou keep up to the rules of the Chesterfield morality ?

A. I will, Lord Chesterfield being my admonisher.

Then the Officiator shall say,

Name this child.

A. *A Fine Gentleman.*

Then he shall say,

I introduce thee to the world, the flesh and the devil, that thou mayest triumph over all awkwardness and grow up in all politeness ; that thou mayest be acceptable to the ladies, celebrated for fine breeding, able to speak French and read Italian, invested with some public supernumerary character in a foreign court, get into Parliament, perhaps into the privy council ; and that, when thou art dead, the letters written to thy bastards may be published in five editions for the instruction of all sober families.

Ye are to take care that this child when he is of a proper age be sent to Genevato be confirmed.

Monday, March 13th.

Mr. Sheridan's comedy of *The Rivals* was performed for the first time at [Bath on March 8th]. . . . It was received with every mark of approbation and applause from a numerous and polite audience.

Tuesday, March 14th.

This day I called at Mr. Thrale's, where I was received with all respect by Mr. and Mrs. Thrale. She is a very learned lady and joins to the charms of her own sex, the manly understanding of ours. The immensity of the brewery astonished me. One large house contains . . . four store vessels, each of which contains fifteen hundred barrels, and in one of which one hundred persons have dined with ease. There are beside, in other houses, thirty-six of the same construction, but of one half the contents. . . .

Wednesday, March 15th.

[Yesterday] afternoon, Robert Rous, one of the turnkeys of the New Gaol, Southwark, seeing a prisoner, who was committed there for different highway robberies had tied rags round his fetters, ordered him to take them off, which he refused ; Rous immediately cut them off and found both his irons sawed through ; upon which he secured him, and then sent up Charles Davis and Symonds to overlook a great number of prisoners who were in the strong room, when the rioters immediately secured the former in the room and all fell on him with their irons, which they had knocked off. Rous hearing of it went up with a horse pistol, and extricated his fellow turnkey from their fury and then locked the door : all the turnkeys as well as constables surrounded the door and the yard, and the prisoners fired several pistols loaded with powder and ball at two of the constables ; the balls went through their hats. After which a sergeants' guard was sent for from the Tower. In the interim, the outrages continuing, one of the constables who had a blunderbuss loaded with shot, fired through the iron grates at the window, which dangerously wounded one fellow committed for a burglary in the Mint. When the soldiers arrived and their muskets were loaded, the room was opened and the prisoners were all secured, 21 of whom are chained down to the floor in the condemned room, and all yoked. Some of the people belonging to the prison were wounded.

Thursday, March 16th.

The people called Quakers presented a petition to His Majesty in favour of the Americans, since which some of that persuasion have been in conference with Lord Dartmouth.

Friday, March 17th.

A very fine new cantata, composed by Rauzzini, was performed last night for his benefit, to a house not half full ; all the consolation the good-humoured man had was that he had the very best company in town. The Duchess of Devonshire had two plumes sixteen inches long besides three small ones ; this has so far outdone all other plumes, that Mrs. Damer, Lady Harriet Stanhope, &c., looked nothing.

Sunday, March 19th.

Stepped into St. Martin's in the Strand, which I saw lighted up, but I could get no further than the door ; such a crowd I never saw under one roof. . . . There was one Harrison (as I learned) in the pulpit. . . . No bombast-player in *Tom Thumb* or *Chrononhoton*, etc., ever so roared and so bellowed as he did, and his matter was as lifeless as his manner was hyper-tragic. A man at the door, from whom I learned his name, told me he was a very good liver and a fine preacher, if he had not those ways with him, yet here the poor fellow was deceived, for it was those ways (as he called it) which made him pass for a fine preacher. . . .

Monday, March 20th.

There have been many long days in Parliament . . . but long days make small sensation, when the majorities are very great, and always on the same side. The Houses go on fulminating against America ; we shall see whether their edicts are regarded, or rather their troops and generals. The province of New York seems to be better disposed than the other colonies ; but we must wait for the re-echo of our new Acts, and for the Congress in May. In three months we shall hear whether it will be war or peace. The nation will stare a little if it is the former. It is little expected, and less thought of. We are given up to profusion, extravagance, and pleasure : heroism is not at all in fashion. Cincinnatus will be found at the hazard-table, and Camillus at a ball. The vivacity of the young Queen of France has reached hither. Our young ladies are covered with more plumes than any nation that has no other covering. The first people of fashion are going to act plays, in which comedians, singers, dancers, figurantes, might all walk at a coronation. The summer is to open with a masquerade on the Thames. I am glad the American enthusiasts are so far off ; I don't think we should be a match for them. We want more Indies ; we cannot afford to lose any. . . .

Lord Bristol is dead at the Bath. He was born to the gout from his mother's family, but starved himself to keep it off. This brought on paralytic strokes, which have dispatched him. Will her Grace of Kingston now pass eldest, and condescend to be, as she really is, Countess of Bristol ? or will she come over and take her trial for the becoming dignity of the exhibition in Westminster Hall ? How it would sound, " Elizabeth, Countess of Bristol, *alias* Duchess of Kingston, come into court ! " . . . It shows genius to strike out anything so new as her achievements. . . .

Tuesday, March 21st.

Strolled into the Chapter Coffee House, Ave Mary Lane . . . remarkable for a large collection of books and a reading society. I subscribed a shilling for the right of a year's reading, and found all the new publications I sought. . . .

Here I saw a specimen of English freedom, viz. a whitesmith in his apron, and some of his saws under his arm, came in and sat down and called for his glass of punch and the paper, both which he used with as much ease as a lord. Such a man in . . . almost any other country would not have shown himself with his hat on, nor anyway unless sent for by some gentleman. . . .

In the evening . . . to the Pantheon. . . . Nothing worth going there for but the Agujari. She is a most surprising singer, and in my opinion a pleasing one ; she goes two notes higher in her voice than the notes of the harpsichord. The *ton* is to say " she is more surprising than pleasing," but I do not subscribe to that, for she has a very good method. They have a story . . . that when she was three years old she fell asleep on a dunghill, and that a pig came and ate all the flesh from her hips to her neck : that she screamed so violently from the pain she suffered, that it is imagined she broke something in her throat, which has caused her voice to be so very high and clear ; they farther add that she was so eaten by the pig that she moves entirely by the help of silver springs, which are fixed under her stays. This woman always fills the Pantheon with a great mixture of company. The best company goes off soon after the concert is over. . . . Then it is beyond all things deplorable. . . .

Wednesday, March 22nd.

Mr. Edmund Burke, in a speech that lasted three hours, opened to the House of Commons a plan he had drawn for pacifying America. . . . The plan was rejected at half an hour after eleven at night by 270 to 78.

[Extract of Mr. Burke's Speech :]
First, Sir, permit me to observe, that the use of force alone is but *temporary*. It may subdue for a moment ; but it does not remove the necessity of subduing again : and a nation is not governed, which is perpetually to be conquered.

My next objection is *uncertainty*. Terror is not always the effect of force ; and an armament is not a victory. If you do not succeed, you are without resource ; for, conciliation failing, force remains ; but, force failing, no further hope of reconciliation is left.   Power and authority are sometimes bought by kindness ; but they can never be begged as alms, by an impoverished and defeated violence.

A further objection to force is, that you *impair the object* by your very endeavours to preserve it.   The thing you fought for is not the thing which you recover ; but depreciated, sunk, wasted, and consumed in the contest.   Nothing less will content me, than *whole America*.   I do not choose to consume its strength along with our own ; because in all parts it is the British strength that I consume.   I do not choose to be caught by a foreign enemy at the end of this exhausting conflict, and still less in the midst of it.   I may escape ; but I can make no insurance against such an event.   Let me add, that I do not choose wholly to break the American spirit, because it is the spirit that has made the country.

Lastly, we have no sort of *experience* in favour of force as an instrument in the rule of our colonies.   Their growth and their utility has been owing to methods altogether different. Our ancient indulgence has been said to be pursued to a fault. It may be so.   But we know, if feeling is evidence, that our fault was more tolerable than our attempt to mend it ; and our sin far more salutary than our penitence.   These, Sir, are my reasons for not entertaining that high opinion of untried force, by which many gentlemen, for whose sentiments in other particulars I have great respect, seem to be so greatly captivated.   But there is still behind a third consideration concerning this object, which serves to determine my opinion on the sort of policy which ought to be pursued in the management of America, even more than its population and its commerce,— I mean its *temper and character*.

In this character of the Americans, a love of freedom is the predominating feature which marks and distinguishes the whole ; and as an ardent is always a jealous affection, your colonies become suspicious, restive, and untractable, whenever they see the least attempt to wrest from them by force, or shuffle from them by chicane, what they think the only advantage worth living for.   This fierce spirit of liberty is stronger in the English colonies probably than in any other people of the earth. . . .

Thursday, March 23rd.

The London, Bristol, and Bath machines, will begin flying in one day on Sunday, April 2nd, and continue every Sunday, Tuesday, and Thursday nights, from the Saracen's Head Inn, Friday Street and Bell Savage Inn, Ludgate Hill ; and every Monday Wednesday and Friday nights from the Gerrard's Hall Inn, Basing Lane, Three Cups Inn, Bread Street, and Swan Inn, Holborn Bridge, London, precisely at half after nine o'clock for Bath and Bristol : and every night (Saturday excepted) from the White Lion Inn, Broad Street, and every Sunday, Tuesday and Thursday nights, from the White Hart Inn in Broad Street, and every Monday, Wednesday and Friday nights, from the Rummer Tavern, Bristol, precisely at nine o'clock, for London : and every night (Saturday excepted) from the White Lion and Greyhound Inns, in the Market Place, and every Sunday, Tuesday and Thursday nights, from the White Hart Inn, Stall Street, Bath, precisely at eleven o'clock, for London.

Two days' machine as usual, from the Christopher Inn, Bath, and The One Bell, in the Strand, London.

The Post chaises as usual, from the White Hart and White Lion, Bath, at eight o'clock : and from the Rose Inn, Holborn Bridge, and Golden Cross, Charing Cross, London, at eight o'clock.

Prices in the above machines, etc. as follows : Inside to and from Bristol in one day, £1, 10s. Children in lap and outside ditto, 15/-. Inside to and from Bath ditto, £1, 8s. Children in lap and outside ditto, 14/-. Inside to and from Bath in two days, £1, 5s. Children in lap and outside ditto, 12/6. Inside by post-coach £1, 8s. Children in lap and outside ditto, 14/-. Half the money to be paid on taking the places, the other half on entering the machines or post-coaches. Each inside passenger to be allowed 14 lb. ; children in lap and outside passengers 7 lb. of luggage ; all above to pay in the one day machines and post-coaches three halfpence, and in the two day machines a penny per lb.

They all call at the Old and New White Horse Cellars, the Black and White Bear Inns, in Piccadilly, London, both going out and coming in of town.

The proprietors will not be accountable for any jewels, plate, money, writings, etc. (if lost), unless entered and paid for as such.

Performed by John Glazier, Richard Maltby, Bath ; Thomas Lawrence, Devizes ; James White, Thomas Hancock, Marlborough ; Mess. Halliwell's, Joseph Cookman, William Summersby, William Clark, John Edgley, Speenhamland ; Ann Bannister, Reading ; John March, Maidenhead ; William Day, Hounslow.

Friday, March 24th.

[Lately published :]

Travels through the Middle Settlements in North America, in the Years 1759 and 1760. With Observations upon the State of the Colonies. By Andrew Burnaby, M.A., Vicar of Greenwich. 4to. Pp. 106. Payne.

Taxation no Tyranny : an Answer to the Resolutions and Address of the American Congress. 8vo. 1s. 6d. Cadell.

Common fame attributes the merit of this performance to the celebrated Dr. Johnson, and every page of it confirms the truth of the report. That gentleman has been charged, in his former political productions, with writing by compulsion ; in this it is plain he has written from the heart. The fundamental principle he endeavours to establish is, " that the supreme power of every community has the right of requiring from all its subjects such contributions as are necessary to the public safety, or public prosperity " ; a position, he says, considered by all mankind, as comprising the primary and essential condition of all political society, till it became disputed by those zealots of anarchy, who have denied to the parliament of · Britain the right of taxing the American colonies. . . .

Saturday, March 25th.

Saturday last, no less than seven public places of entertainment were open at one time : the Italian Opera-house, Drury Lane, Covent Garden, and Foote's theatres. Bach and Abel's concert, Almack's Assembly, and Ranelagh House.

Sunday, March 26th.

The public was near being entertained with a singular duel between Doctors Johnson and Franklin, on account of the former insinuating in plain terms in *Taxation no Tyranny*, that the latter was an electrical master of mischief. We suppose Dr. Johnson's weapon would be a folio dictionary of political language and Dr. Franklin's an electrical apparatus. The first is experienced in knocking down booksellers and the latter would oppose him with fire from heaven.

Monday, March 27th.

Sir Joshua Reynolds, at Mrs. Abington's request, had promised to bring a body of wits to her benefit ; and having secured forty places in the front boxes, had done me the honour to put me in the group. Johnson sat on the seat directly behind me ; and as he could neither see nor hear at such a distance from the stage, he was wrapped up in grave abstraction and seemed quite a cloud, amidst all the sunshine of glitter and gaiety. I wondered at his patience in sitting out a play of five acts, and a farce of two. He said very little ; but after the prologue to *Bon Ton* had been spoken, which he could hear pretty well from the more slow and distinct utterance, he talked of prologue-writing, and observed, " Dryden has written prologues superior to any that David Garrick has written ; but David Garrick has written more good prologues than Dryden has done. It is wonderful that he has been able to write such a variety of them."

Tuesday, March 28th.

On Sunday se'nnight, Dr. Benjamin Franklin, Agent for Philadelphia, set out from his house in Craven Street, in order to embark for North America. Two days before he had received the melancholy account of the death of his wife, which is supposed to have hastened his departure. Other advices say, that the Ministry had at last applied to him, soliciting his good offices at the ensuing Congress, in order to heal the present unhappy divisions and bring about a recon-

ciliation between the Colonies and the Mother country.
Certainly no man living is more able to effect this than the
great American philosopher, who has been unjustly persecuted
by some persons in power and deprived of his office merely
because he was an American, and because he openly and
uniformly asserted the rights and liberties of America.

Thursday, March 30th.

On Tuesday [February 14th] Cardinal Braschi was unanimously elected Pope. . . . He has now assumed the name
of Pius VI. Everybody is surprised at the sudden election. . . .
The conclave has, however, lasted four months. The election
was brought about by the Zealots, who found means to unite
a majority of suffrages. . . .

Friday, March 31st.

The facts in the case of the Shaftesbury election are more
curious, if possible, and the corruption more indecent than in
the notorious case of Hindon. Four thousand new guineas are
brought in triumph into the town, with shouts of joy, " the
election money is come," the bells are set a-ringing ; a little
after Punch arrives, and public notice is given that he will
dance at such a time and his goldfinches will fly ; the voters
attend in shoals for three successive nights ; they go up into
a room, contiguous to Punch's, two by two ; they sign a note
of hand for twenty guineas, payable to Punch, under the name
of Glen Bucket, and then, through a hole in the partition,
receive out of the adjoining room, from an invisible Punch,
twenty guineas per man in exchange for the note. Declarations
repeatedly made by the agents that all this money had been
distributed. The Petitioner declares that he should tender the
bribery oath to the voters ; they are alarmed and some
actually receive another twenty guineas, upon condition of
Punch's delivering up the note ; the agents then tell them they
can swear safely, however some are conscientious and refuse.
In the hall at the poll when the bribery oath is again mentioned,
the Mayor and forty constables rise up and almost kill the man
who proposes it. . . .

APRIL 1775

Saturday, April 1st.

[Samuel Johnson] this morning received his Diploma as Doctor of Laws from the University of Oxford. . . .

Sunday, April 2nd.

JOHNSON : "Fleet Street has a very animated appearance ; but I think the full tide of human existence is at Charing Cross."

Monday, April 3rd.

Van Burtchell, a tooth-drawer, has had his wife embalmed by the famous Hunter. [He keeps her in a glass case in his drawing-room] and though she has been dead three months she looks as well as when alive. . . .

Tuesday, April 4th.

This evening, (for the benefit of Mr. Lee) *She Stoops to Conquer ; or, The Mistakes of a Night* [was performed at Covent Garden] : Hardcastle, Mr. Shuter ; Miss Hardcastle, Mrs. Bulkeley ; with the *Stratford Jubilee.*

Wednesday, April 5th.

At a church near Piccadilly . . . a lady of a military officer, and the wife of a brandy merchant in that neighbourhood, sit in a pew adjoining to each other ; the latter, it seems, has lately worn a bunch of feathers in her hair of such an amazing height, as well as breadth, as to obscure the other's sight of the parson, as they generally unluckily sat parallel to each other : the captain's lady in vain remonstrated ; till last Sunday, after sermon, they coming to high words, the former, who is a little spirited woman, got upon a hassock, and in pulling the other's finery off, brought down her hair and a large quantity of wool, and other combustibles. The congregation not being half out, it occasioned a loud laugh, and the poor female, stripped of her borrowed plumes, was obliged to wait in the sexton's room till after dark, before she could go home ; and she has been the ridicule of the neighbourhood ever since. The military lady plumes herself on being protected by a bit of red cloth, while the other lady and her spouse threaten a prosecution in the most vehement terms.

Thursday, April 6th.

A fine young lion was landed at the Tower, as a present to His Majesty, from Senegal. He was taken in the woods out of a snare by a private soldier, who being set upon by two savages that had laid the snare, he killed them both and brought away his game. His Majesty, for his bravery, has ordered his discharge and a pension for life of £50 a year.

Monday, April 10th.

[The] Oxford Machine, every day to and from London, licensed by the Rev. the Vice-Chancellor, to carry six passengers at 10s. each, sets out from the " Star Inn," in the Corn-market, Oxford, at eight in the morning, to the " New Inn," in the Old Bailey, London ; leaves the " New Inn " at half-past seven, and Jenkin's " Green Man and Still " at eight, will not stop on the road to breakfast ; each inside passenger allowed 20 lbs. luggage, and all above to pay 1d per pound ; Outside Passengers half price. Performed by Richard Whiten.

The PATENT ALARM, for instantly stopping sedans, chariots, coaches and post-chaises, and causing the attendants to assemble in cases of danger or necessity, may be seen at Mr. Pinchbeck's, in Cockspur Street ; Mr. O'Keeffe's, Coachmaker, in Long-Acre ; and at Mr. Jacob's, Coachmaker, in St. Mary-Axe, who vend them for the Patentee.

Tuesday, April 11th.

At two o'clock [yesterday] the Lord Mayor, accompanied by the Sheriffs, and Aldermen Bull, Sawbridge, Hayley, Lewes, and Newenham, went up to St. James's, with the Address,

Remonstrance and Petition of the Lord Mayor, Aldermen and Livery in Common-Hall assembled, " praying for the removal of his present Ministers for their iniquitous measures respecting our fellow subjects in America."

The King's Answer [was] delivered to the Lord Mayor by the Earl of Hertford, Lord Chamberlain : " It is with the utmost astonishment that I find any of my subjects capable of encouraging the rebellious disposition which unhappily exists in some of my Colonies in North America.

" Having entire confidence in the wisdom of my Parliament, the Great Council of the Nation, I will steadily pursue those measures which they have recommended for the support of the Constitutional Rights of Great Britain, and the protection of the commercial interests of my kingdoms."

I never saw so shabby an appearance as they made, for except the Lord Mayor's coach and Mr. Sawbridge's chariot, no equipage had even the show of belonging to a gentleman. They dispersed handbills, Sunday, to assemble a mob ; and some blackguard fellows got together, but they would not cheer, though the Lord Mayor's servants called to them so to do. The Duke of Queensberry had his pocket picked, in the Drawing-room, of a gold snuff-box. . . .

Thursday, April 13th.

His Majesty went to the House of Peers, and gave the royal assent to the Bill for restraining the trade of New Jersey, Pennyslvania, &c. ; to the Bill for punishing mutiny and desertion in America ; the Bill for appointing commissioners of land tax ; for indemnifying persons who have omitted to qualify for offices ; the Bill for preventing frauds in the manufacture of hats, &c. ; and to several private Bills.

The House of Commons agreed to the report of their committee of supply,

That it is the opinion of this committee, that a sum not exceeding £262,537, 7s. 10d. be granted to His Majesty for extraordinary expenses of the army, for the service of the year 1774, and not provided for by Parliament.

That £3,000 be granted to the trustees of the British

Museum. That £5,000 be granted to the Turkey Company.
That £4,346, 10s. 5d. be granted to the civil establishment of
Nova Scotia.   £3,086 for the civil establishment of Georgia.
£4,590 for the civil establishment of East Florida.   £5,450 for
the civil establishment of West Florida.

That £6,336 be granted for the civil establishment of
Senegambia.

That £1,886 be granted for the expenses attending general
surveys in North America, for the service of the year 1775.

And £1,250,000 for paying off Exchequer bills made out
pursuant to an Act of the last session.

Resolved, that it appears to this committee, that the sum of
£895,686, 13s. 10¼d., remaining in the Exchequer on the 5th
of April, 1775, for the disposition of Parliament, of the produce
of the overplus moneys arising out of the fund, commonly
called the sinking fund, be granted to make good the supply
granted to His Majesty.

[The Houses adjourned for Easter.]

Easter Sunday, April 16th.

[Lately published :]
The Poems of Mr. [Thomas] Gray. To which are prefixed
memoirs of his life and writings, by William Mason, M.A.
4to.   15s.   Dodsley. . . .

The style is excellent, simple, unaffected : the method
admirable, artful, and judicious. He has *framed* the fragments
(as a person said) so well, that they are fine drawings, if not
finished pictures. . . . I shall certainly read it over and over.
I do not find that is likely to be the case with many *yet*. Never
was a book, which people pretended to expect so much with
impatience, less devoured — at least in London, where quartos
are not of quick digestion.

The Canterbury Tales of Chaucer. To which are added an
essay upon his language and versification, an introduction discourse and notes [by Thomas Tyrwhitt]. 4 vols. 8vo.   13s. in
boards. Payne.

I have waded through Mr. Tyrwhitt's most tedious notes to
the *Canterbury Tales*, for a true antiquary can still be zealous

to settle the genuine shape of a lump of mineral from which Dryden extracted all the gold and converted into beautiful medals. . . .

Monday, April 17th.

Lord North has it in contemplation to dissolve the South Sea Company, and to throw their savings, amounting to near a million of money, into the sinking fund, and apply it to the service of the current year. The above savings, having arisen entirely from the exorbitant charge of £500 for each million of the funds managed by the South Sea Company, may very honourably be applied to the public use.

Lady Gertrude Hotham (Lord Chesterfield's sister) . . . is dead ; she set her ruffle, and thence the rest of her dress, on fire, and died of it in ten days. She had wit like all her brothers, but for many years had been a Methodist. About two years ago, as the Earl was ill, she went with her Primate, Lady Huntingdon, to try to tempt him to one of their seminaries in Wales, hoping to get at his soul by a cranny in his health. They extolled the prospects, and then there were such charming mountains ! " Hold, ladies," said he ; " I don't love mountains, — when your Ladyships' faith has removed the mountains, I will go thither with all my heart ! " . . .

Tuesday, April 18th.

Dr. Johnson, his fellow-traveller through the Scotch Western Isles, Mr. Boswell, and Sir Joshua Reynolds dined here. . . . [Dr. Johnson's] conversation is the same as his writing, but a dreadful voice and manner. He is certainly amusing as a novelty but seems not possessed of any benevolence, is beyond all description awkward, and more beastly in his dress and person than anything I ever beheld. He feeds nastily and ferociously and eats quantities most unthankfully. As to Boswell, he appears a low-bred kind of being.

Wednesday, April 19th.

[On] Monday afternoon a very severe battle was fought in the field behind Montague House, between an Irishman and a

THE BALL AT THE MANSION HOUSE
APRIL XVII. MDCCLXXV
BLE
THE RIGHT HON. IOHN WILKES, LORD MAYOR

G.B. Cipriani inv. et del.   F. Bartolozzi sculp. 1775.

Welshman, both hairdressers, for eight guineas, which lasted about an hour, when victory declared in favour of the former.

Immediately after, on the same spot, another was fought between a carpenter and one well known by the name of Harry, the Fighting Coachman, for two guineas, which after a smart contest, was won by the former.

Saturday, April 22nd.

I dined today at the Exhibition of Pictures, with the Royal Academicians. We do not beat Titian or Guido yet. Zoffany has sent over a wretched Holy Family. . . . He is the Hogarth of Dutch painting, but, no more than Hogarth, can shine out of his own way. He might have drawn the Holy Family well if he had seen them *in statu quo.* Sir Joshua Reynolds is a great painter, but, unfortunately, his colours seldom stand longer than crayons. . . . Loutherbourg . . . would paint landscape and cattle excellently if he did not in every picture indulge some one colour inordinately. . . . The prices of all are outrageous, and the numbers of professors still greater. An American, West, deals in high history, and is vastly admired, but he is heavier than Guercino, and has still less grace, and is very inferior. . . .

Sunday, April 23rd.

Lord North [has transmitted] to His Majesty Sergeant Kempe's report upon the petition of Martha Latimer who was condemned at the last Kingston Assizes to be burnt for coining. Lord North . . . has had a pretty general application in her favour from his neighbours at Kingston ; he understands that the woman was only a servant to Harris the principal criminal, who is likewise condemned and whose death will answer the purpose of example. Lord North, therefore, submits to His Majesty whether he may not safely extend his Royal mercy to Martha Latimer, and respite her from the horrid punishment of burning. . . . If, as she was certainly guilty of the fact laid to her charge, she should not be thought an object of pardon, she may be afterwards transported. . . .

[The King to Lord North :] " As you seem to interest yourself in favour of Martha Latimer ; I authorize you to direct Mr. Eden to have her respited and the punishment transmuted to transportation. . . ."

Tuesday, April 25th.

Last Monday se'nnight was brought into the port of Newcastle, by Capt. Ford, of the *Hazard* sloop of war, a smuggling shallop, called the *Friend's Delight*, Thomas Johnson, master, with 218 half ankers of geneva, six ankers of brandy, 1160 lb. of tea, a quantity of light gold, and some silver, the whole cargo amounting together to £1,000.

The above vessel is the noted Irish smuggler, burthen seventy tons, commanded by the Old Smoker, that has for a long time openly carried on a great trade along this coast. She was well armed, mounting four carriage guns and ten swivels, and so remarkable a sailor as to defy all attempts to take her. She was last October chased for several hours by the *Hazard*, and had not now been taken but by stratagem ; and it is even thought, that if all her hands had been on board, she would have again escaped.

Wednesday, April 26th.

Yesterday the House of Commons having met pursuant to their last adjournment . . . Mr. Watt's Steam Engine Bill was reported and . . . ordered to be engrossed.

Thursday, April 27th.

Lord North made the following motions in a committee of the whole House appointed to consider what encouragement ought to be given to the fisheries of Great Britain and Ireland — " That a bounty of £40 be given to the first 100 ships that arrive with a cargo of 10,000 cod-fish caught on the banks of Newfoundland ; £20 for the next 100 ships ; and £10 for the next 100 ships.— That a bounty of £500 be given to the ship that arrives with the greatest quantity of whale-oil ; £400 for the next greatest quantity ; £300 for the next ; £200 for the next ; and £100 for the next.— That Ireland have liberty to import blubber and whale-fins, the same as England.— That the duty on seal-skins imported into Ireland do cease, and be no longer paid.— That Ireland have leave to export clothing to America, for so much of the army as they supply and pay for.— That a bounty of 5s. per ton be given to all flax-seed imported into Ireland."— The encouragement to be given to the linen manufactory of that kingdom was postponed.

Friday, April 28th.

Captain Shads, of the *Cerberus,* who [sailed for Boston on the 20th instant and] carried out the three Generals, Burgoyne, Clinton and Howe, was the very person who landed the brave General Wolfe at Quebec, and afterwards brought him off dead in his boat.

Saturday, April 29th.

Letters from Bohemia speak of a dangerous revolt among the peasants of that Kingdom, who being incensed against the oppressions of the nobility, have risen and commit most terrible ravages. To redress their grievances, it is said, the Emperor has interposed, and it is thought, will secure to them their privileges.

By authority of Parliament, Cox's Museum Lottery, to begin drawing May 1st, 1775. Tickets with or without admission, are now selling as cheap as at any office in London, by Hornsby and Pearce, at their offices, No. 19, corner of Pope's Head Alley, Cornhill. . . . The two capital prizes of £5,000 each will be paid at the bank in money if desired. . . .

Sunday, April 30th.

[Lately published :]
An Answer to a Pamphlet, entitled " Taxation no Tyranny." Addressed to the Author and to Persons in Power. Almon.
Tyranny unmasked ; an answer to a late pamphlet entitled, " Taxation no Tyranny." 2s. 6d. Flexney.
" Taxation no Tyranny " candidly considered and its arguments and pernicious doctrines exposed and refuted. 2s. W. Davies.

MAY 1775

Monday, May 1st.

[Being May Day] the girls were seen tripping across the fields with their companions by four o'clock in the morning; the blind fiddlers attended, according to annual custom, at the different places leading to Kentish Town, Mary-le-bone and Lisson Green. The tea-drinking houses and gardens were open by five o'clock, as were also the public houses within five miles round the metropolis : a greater havoc among the hot rolls and buns has not been known for many years past. At eight o'clock the company were seen coming in pairs to town, some rather enlivened by the refreshing glasses that went round as soon as the tea-equipages were removed.

Tuesday, May 2nd.

The new farce called *St. Patrick's Day or The Scheming Lieutenant* [was] performed . . . at Covent Garden Theatre. . . . This piece was professedly presented as a farce and . . . declared in the Prologue to be a hasty production, designed merely to assist a performer at his benefit. . . .

It afforded as much laugh as any theatrical exhibition at which we have for some time been present. . . . Rosy and Credulous are very laughable examples of the extravagant in dramatic portrait painting. . . . The language in general shows the author a man of humour and observation . . . [but] his jests are occasionally too low and vulgar and his scene too extravagantly absurd. . . . *St. Patrick's Day* was better acted than benefit novelties usually are.

Wednesday, May 3rd.

Lord North opened the budget, and stated in a very masterly manner the minutiae of the public accounts, debtor and creditor. The supplies, he said, would amount to

£5,562,000, the ways and means would amount to upwards of £6,500,000, consequently there would be a surplus of £1,000,000. His Lordship proposed to pay off £1,000,000 of 3 per cents. at 88 per cent. and to have a lottery of 60,000 tickets, the same as last year, to be subscribed for by such persons as held stock prior to the 24th April, 1775. . . .

Thursday, May 4th.

At the Mansion-house dinner on Easter Monday, Mr. Boswell, who had taken care to secure good room at the table, seeing Mr. Colman in want of a place, called to him, and gave him one beside himself, saying " You see what it is to have a Scotsman for your friend at Mr. Wilkes's tables." A little time after there came a foreign waiter, with something : Mr. Boswell talked to him in German ; upon which Mr. Colman observed, " I have certainly mistaken the place today ; I thought I was at the Mansion-House ; but I must surely be at St. James's ; for here are none but Germans and Scots."

Monday, May 8th.

It was generally observed that his Majesty never looked better than he did on Friday last, at Drury-Lane theatre. He is not near so corpulent as he was, and looks much more healthy ; this is attributed to his abstemious method of living ; having eaten very little flesh meat for some months.

Tuesday, May 9th.

[Mr. James Watt writes :] I have at last got an Act of Parliament vesting the property of my new fire-engines in me and my assigns throughout Great Britain and the Plantations for twenty-five years to come. . . . This affair has been attended with great expense and anxiety and without many friends of great interest I should never have been able to carry it through, as many of the most powerful people in the House of Commons opposed it. It has been in Parliament ever since the 22nd of February. . . .

Wednesday, May 10th.

By a letter from Florence . . . the situation of the Pretender is truly deplorable. His finances are limited almost to poverty, and the Cardinal York squanders his ecclesiastical revenues upon the church without administering much to the wants of his brother. Thus circumstanced, the Pretender is little more than able to keep a carriage, and on this carriage, he is not allowed any ensign armorial. He is exceedingly corpulent owing to a total disuse of exercise, and his face is remarkably carbuncled, from an excessive indulgence of the bottle, to which he constantly flies as a refuge from reflection.

Friday, May 12th.

House of Commons. Thursday. The common business of the day being over, the Bill for extending the patent of the Bristol china came up. Sir William Bagot desired leave to bring up a petition from Mr. Wedgwood, the Staffordshire potter, against the Bill ; which being granted, it was read and set forth that the patent granted by the Crown to Mr. Cookworthy was illegal and void . . . that this Bill would be granting a monopoly of a raw material in Cornwall against all the potters of the Kingdom. . . .

Saturday, May 13th.

On Monday evening, at the Robin Hood, the adjourned question of the existence of ghosts came on, and was decided almost *nem. con.* against such existence. . . . The chairman attempted to read Mr. Wesley's testimony of ghosts, appearing to and conversing with some of his disciples (in his *Journal* lately published) ; but as this was only second-hand evidence . . . the testimony was not read.

Sunday, May 14th.

A meeting, something of Arcadian-like institution, is held weekly at the seat of a Mr. Miller, at Bath Easton, near Bath, where the beaux and belles esprits carry their several *bouts rimez*, etc., and secretly deposit them in an urn placed in the gardens for their reception. At an appointed hour the vase gives up its literary treasures, which are all publicly read before a committee appointed to decide on their different merits and adjudge the various prizes of bouquets, etc., to those, who, stepping forward, acknowledge the signatures of the successful pieces.

Monday, May 15th.

Mr. Burke presented to the Hon. House of Commons a representation and remonstrance from the General Assembly of New York, which, after a warm debate in which Mr. Cruger, Member for Bristol, distinguished himself, was rejected.

Wednesday, May 17th.

To Beauclerk's villa. . . . It is delightful, just at Highgate. He has one of the most numerous and splendid private libraries that I ever saw, greenhouses, hothouses, observatory, laboratory for chemical experiments, in short everything princely.

Thursday, May 18th.

Five of the pirates who were concerned in the murder of the captain, mate and carpenter of the Guineaman called the *Little Will*, of Liverpool, were examined at Doctors Commons, by the judge of the High Court of Admiralty, for the above murders, and also for running away with the ship and cargo on the coast of Guinea ; when they were all five, by the evidences of several other of the sailors who were on board the said ship, and who would not assist in the said murders and robbery, clearly proved to be guilty and immediately committed to the Marshalsea prison in the Borough, in order to their being tried at the Admiralty sessions at the Old Bailey. They were headed, when taken at sea, by the boatswain, who fought in a very desperate manner after the back part of his head was taken off, and was also wounded in several places in his body and even in that condition tumbled one of his adversaries overboard, by which he was drowned, and was at length cut to pieces and died on the deck.

Friday, May 19th.

Lord Camden moved for a repeal of the Quebec Bill and made a great figure, as Lord Mansfield, who defended it, made an artful one, pleading that it was better to have that Bill than no constitution at all there. . . . The chief part of the debate turned, however, on the great military preparations and fleets assembling in Spain, which Lord Lyttelton called on the Ministers to declare the intent of, as did the Duke of Richmond. . . . Lord Rochford said, no Lord had a right to call on him, yet declared the Court of Spain had given assurances of having no hostile designs against us ; but Lord Sandwich succeeded worse, for it came out that we had but 17 ships at home, and they wanted 4,000 men.

The Quebec Bill was upheld by 88 to 28. . . .

Mr. Burke printed his speech and plan for the pacification of America. It was much more sober, judicious, and chaste from flights than the former.

Saturday, May 20th.

On Saturday last died near Margate, Mr. Beale, one of the people called Quakers. He was the first person who erected a bathing machine at Margate.

Monday, May 22nd.

Yesterday the great cricket match between Kent and All England was begun to be played in the Artillery Ground. The Duke of Dorset, Lord Cholmondeley, and about twelve more noblemen and gentlemen met about half after eleven o'clock, when the wickets were pitched, and at twelve the Kent people went in, who got thirty-seven notches. At three o'clock the opposite party went in, and Small, the first man on that side, got what is almost incredible, seventy-five notches, and was at last bowled out just before eight o'clock.

[In the] afternoon many persons got on the wall of Bunhill-fields Burying Ground to see the cricket match . . . and pelting the crowd with brick-bats, etc., a battle royal ensued in which several persons were terribly wounded.

Tuesday, May 23rd.

The following bills received the royal assent, viz. The bill to enable the different Universities in Great Britain and the colleges of Eton, Westminster, and Winchester, to hold in perpetuity their copyright in books given or bequeathed to them for the advancement of learning. . . . The bill for completing and maintaining the pier of Megavissey in Cornwall. . . . The bill to enable His Majesty to license a play-house in Manchester. . . . The bill to dissolve the marriage of Robert Green, Esq. with his now wife. And also to several road, enclosure and private bills.

Wednesday, May 24th.

The Duchess of Kingston, who has returned from Italy to answer the charge of bigamy, appeared unexpectedly in the King's Bench, and surrendered herself. Lord Mansfield treated her with great respect. She gave bond in £5,000 for her appearance to her trial, and was bailed in £1,000 each by the Duke of Newcastle, whom she had got named in the Duke of Kingston's will, Lord Mountstewart, son of Lady Bute, first cousin of that Duke, Sir Thomas Clarges, and M. la Roche. The charge was then read, which she heard with amazing intrepidity of countenance, and then was dismissed on her bail.

Capt. O'Kelly lately sold one of his Eclipse colts for 1,000 guineas down, and 500 more if he wins the first time he starts.

Friday, May 26th.

Both Houses of Parliament were prorogued by the Lord Chancellor to Thursday, the 27th day of July next.

Tuesday, May 30th.

[Last night] it was divulged by a London *Evening Post* extraordinary, that a ship on its way to Lisbon happened to call *at* England, and left some very wonderful accounts, nay, and affidavits, saying, to wit, that General Gage had sent nine hundred men to nail up the cannon and seize a magazine at Concord ; of which the accidental captain owns, two cannon were spiked or damaged. An hundred and fifty Americans, who swear they were fired on first, disliked the proceeding, returned blows, and drove back the party. . . . The captain was sent for to be examined, but refused. He says Gage sent away a sloop four days before he sailed, which sloop, I suppose, is gone to Lisbon, for in eight days no news of it. The public were desired by authority to suspend their belief ; but their patience is out, and they persist in believing the first account, which seems the rather probable, in that another account is come of the mob having risen at New York, between anger and triumph, and have seized, unloaded, and destroyed the cargoes of two ships that were going with supplies to Gage ; and, by all accounts, that whole continent is in a flame.

So here is this fatal war commenced !

Wednesday, May 31st.

In the workhouse at Camberwell in Surrey [there is] a woman named Jones, aged 125 years, who remembers her being at service when King Charles the Second was crowned in 1660, and at this time enjoys her perfect senses ; and, what is full as observable, the nurse who attends her is aged 101. . . .

Died lately at Sheltington near Tamworth in Warwickshire, aged fifty-seven, Mr. Spooner, farmer, of that place. He was thought to be the fattest man in England, weighing, four or five weeks before his death, forty stone and nine pounds. He had not been able to walk for several years, but had a little cart and able horse to draw him abroad for air. He measured, after his death, four feet three inches across the shoulders. . . . His fatness some years ago saved his life ; for, being at Atherstone market, and some difference arising between him and a Jew, the Jew stabbed him in the body with a pen-knife ; but the blade, being short, did not pierce his bowels or even pass through the fat which defended them.

JUNE 1775

Thursday, June 1st.

The trials of the two Perreaus . . . for forgery came on at
the Old Bailey.

A discovery was made [three months since] of a very uncommon kind of forgery, carried on for some time past, by
[this] Robert and Daniel Perreau, twins, the former an apothecary in high practice in Golden Square ; the other living in
genteel life in Pall Mall. These two in confederacy with a
Mrs. Rudd, who co-habited with Daniel and generally passed
for his wife, have from time to time raised considerable sums
by means of bonds forged in the name of the well-known agent,
William Adair, Esq. ; which they have imposed upon several
gentlemen of character and fortune, as collateral securities
with their own notes for the payment of the said sums. The
occasion that led to the discovery was as follows : Robert
Perreau, the apothecary, who bore an irreproachable character,
applied to Mr. Drummond, the banker, for the loan of £5,000
and offered a bond, which he said Mr. Adair had given to his
brother for £7,500 as a pledge for the payment. It should,
however, be remarked that to give colour to these bonds it
had been artfully given out, that Mrs. Rudd, the pretended
wife of Daniel, was nearly connected with Mr. Adair, and
even insinuated that she was his natural daughter ; but Mr.
Drummond who was well acquainted with the handwriting
of Mr. Adair, on examining the signature, doubted the authenticity of it, and with the utmost delicacy asked Mr. Perreau if
he had seen Mr. Adair sign it, who frankly answered that he
had not, but added that he could not entertain the least doubt,
considering the connection, but that it was authentic. Mr.
Drummond [having] more narrowly examined the bond, told
Mr. Perreau frankly, that he believed he had been imposed

upon ; but added that to remove all doubt, if he would go with him to Mr. Adair and procure from that gentleman an acknowledgment of its validity, he would then immediately advance the money : to this Mr. Perreau readily consented. They went, found Mr. Adair at home, asked the question and were answered in the negative ; on which Mr. Perreau put on an affected smile, and told him he jested. But Mr. Adair accosting him with a very different air, told him it was no jesting matter, and that it behoved him to clear it up. Mr. Perreau then said, if that was the fact he had been sent upon a fine errand indeed ! Desired to have the bond and added that he should make the proper enquiries. This request, how-ever, was refused ; and it was thought advisable not to lose sight of Robert, till he had produced Daniel and his pretended wife.

On his return home, it is probable that he had acquainted the parties with what had happened and that in their first agitation, it had been consulted either to make their escape or in case that should be found impracticable, that Mrs. Rudd should acknowledge the signature, as most likely to escape punishment and to procure for the two brothers their liberty. Be that as it may, they all three took coach together ; and it should seem by the evidence of Mrs. Rudd that she had taken with her what money and other movables she could con-veniently carry. . . . Instead, however, of escaping, an in-formation was laid against them ; and they were obliged to appear before Sir John Fielding, by whom they were com-mitted to different prisons for further examination. In the meantime, their story had taken air, and as they were all three well known, the concourse of people was so great on the day appointed for hearing them, that the justices were obliged to adjourn from Bow Street to Guild Hall, Westminster ; where the facts already related were attested by Mr. Adair, Mr. Drummond and others, with several additional charges, par-ticularly by Admiral Sir Thomas Frankland, from whom they had obtained £4,000 on the first application, which they honestly repaid before the money became due ; afterwards £5,000 and lastly £4,000 upon similar bonds, all signed with the name of Mr. Adair ; of which bonds a Mr. Watson, money-scrivener, said he had drawn to the number of eight, all of them by order of one or other of the brothers, but which, he could not, he said be certain, they were both so much alike. Being pressed to make a positive declaration, he at last fixed upon Daniel.

Dr. Brooke likewise charged them with obtaining from him 15 Bank of Ayr bonds, each of the value of a hundred pounds, upon the security of a similar bond with the rest for £3,100.

The facts being made appear, the brothers were remanded to prison, and the parties bound to prosecute. But Mrs. Rudd, being advised by her counsel to become King's evidence, was afterwards admitted to bail. On her future examination, she declared that she was the daughter of a nobleman in Scotland ; that she married when young a Mr. Rudd, an officer in the army, against her friends' consent ; that she had a very considerable fortune ; and that upon some disagreement, when her husband and she determined to part, she made a reserve of money, jewels, and effects to the amount of £1,300, all of which she gave to Daniel Perreau, whom she loved she said with the tenderness of a wife ; that she had had three children by him ; that he had returned her kindness in every respect till lately. When having been unfortunate in gaming in the Alley, he had become uneasy, peevish and much altered towards her ; that he cruelly constrained her to sign the bond now in question, by holding a knife to her throat, and swearing he would murder her if she did not comply, that being struck with remorse, she had acquainted Mr. Adair with what she had done, and that she was now willing to declare every transaction with which she was acquainted, whenever she should be called upon by law so to do.

Friday, June 2nd.

Insurrections have been general in France, on account of the dearness of corn ; many of the ringleaders have been seized and executed without trial, but the cry for bread is yet unredressed.

Monday, June 5th.

Government keep the disagreeable news they have received

from America so close that nothing of consequence has yet transpired, though there seems no reason to doubt the authenticity of what has already appeared in the public prints.

King Louis is gone to be crowned. He was besieged for three days in Versailles by twenty thousand men, and in danger of Lord Peterborough's *sacre*, who, when he was shown the *Sainte Ampoule* at Rheims, and the monk asked him, " *Monsieur, est-ce que vous sacrez vos Rois?* " replied, " *Non, Monsieur, nous les massacrons.*" Insurrections in France ! insurrections in Bohemia ! insurrections in America !

Wednesday, June 7th.

The sessions ended at the Old Bailey, when fifteen convicts received sentence of death, [among them] Robert and Daniel Perreau.

Friday, June 9th.

At length — we have heard Agujari ! . . . I could compare her to nothing I ever heard. . . . Such a powerful voice ! so astonishing a compass, reaching from C. in the middle of the harpsichord to two notes above the harpsichord ! Every tone so clear, so full, so charming ! Then her *shake* — so *plump* — so true, so open ! It is as strong and distinct as Mr. Burney's upon the harpsichord. Besides its great power, her voice is all sweetness, and when she pleases, all softness and delicacy. She sings in the highest style of taste, and with an expression so pathetic, that it is impossible to hear it unmoved. . . . She sung in twenty different styles. The greatest was *son regina* and *son amante*, from Didone. Good God ! what a song and how sung ! Then she gave us two or three *Cantabiles*, sung divinely, then she chanted some church music, in a style so nobly simple and unadorned, that it stole into one's very soul ! Then she gave us a *bravura*, with difficulties which seemed only possible for an instrument in the hands of a great master ; then she spoke some recitative, so nobly ! In short, whether she most astonished, or most delighted us, I cannot say, but she is really a sublime singer ! . . .

Saturday, June 10th.

Lieutenant Nunn, of the navy, arrived this morning at Lord Dartmouth's office, and has brought letters from General Gage, Lord Percy, and Lieutenant-Colonel Smith containing the following particulars of what passed on the 19th of April last between a detachment of the King's troops in the province of Massachusetts Bay, and several parties of rebel Provincials.

General Gage having received intelligence of a large quantity of military stores being collected at Concord for the avowed purpose of supplying a body of troops to act in opposition to His Majesty's government detached on the 18th of April at night, the Grenadiers of his army and the light infantry, under the command of Lieutenant-colonel Smith, of the 10th regiment, and Major Pitcairne of the Marines, with orders to destroy the said stores ; and the next morning eight companies of the 4th, the same number of the 23rd, and 49th, and some marines, marched under the command of Lord Percy to support the other detachment.

Lieutenant-colonel Smith finding, after he had advanced some miles on his march, the country had been alarmed by the firing of guns and ringing of bells, dispatched six companies of light infantry in order to secure two bridges on different roads beyond Concord, who, upon their arrival at Lexington found a body of the country people drawn up under arms on a green close to the road ; and upon the King's troops marching up to them, in order to enquire the reason of their being so assembled, they went off in great confusion and several guns were fired upon the King's troops from behind a stone wall, and also from the meeting house and other houses by which one man was wounded, and Major Pitcairne's horse shot in two places. In consequence of this attack by the rebels, the troops returned the fire and killed several of them ; after which the detachment marched on to Concord, without anything further happening, where they effected the purpose for which they were sent ; having knocked off the trunions of three pieces of iron ordnance, burnt some new gun-carriages, and a great number of carriage wheels and thrown into the river a considerable quantity of flour, gunpowder, musketballs and other articles. Whilst this service was performing, great numbers of the rebels assembled in many parts and a considerable body of them attacked the light infantry posted at one of the bridges, on which an action ensued and some few were killed and wounded.

On the return of the troops from Concord, they were very much annoyed and had several men killed and wounded by the rebels firing from behind walls, ditches, trees, and other ambushes ; but the brigade under the command of Lord Percy having joined them at Lexington, with two pieces of cannon, the rebels were for a while dispersed : but, as soon as the troops resumed their march, they began again to fire upon them from behind stone walls and houses, and kept up in that manner a scattering fire during the whole of their march of fifteen miles, by which means several were killed and wounded ; and such was the cruelty and barbarity of the rebels that they scalped and cut off the ears of some of the wounded men, who fell into their hands.

It is not known what number of the rebels were killed and wounded ; but, it is supposed that their loss was very considerable.

General Gage says that too much praise cannot be given to Lord Percy, for his remarkable activity during the whole day ; and that Lieut.-Col. Smith and Major Pitcairne did everything that men could do, as did all the officers in general; and that the men behaved with their usual intrepidity.

Sunday, June 11*th.*

From the day on which the skirmish at Lexington happened all intercourse between the country and the garrison of Boston was cut off, and the town was completely blocked up on the land side. General Putnam was ordered to assume the command of such of the rebels' troops as had assembled at Roxbury and its environs, to the amount of fifteen thousand men : all supplies of provision or fuel were strictly prohibited from being carried into Boston, and every step was taken to distress the King's troops as much as possible. . . .

Exaggerated accounts of the action near Lexington flew with the greatest rapidity to every province in North America ;

and together with the comments which accompanied them, did infinite mischief to his Majesty's authority in that country. The people prepared for resistance, instantly flew to arms and in every province where the spirit of disaffection prevailed, it was resolved not to supply the King's ships or troops with provisions, stores, or even with fuel. Some of the most violent proceeded so far, as to declare offenders against these resolutions to be enemies of their country, and others threatened such with the punishment of death.

Thursday, June 15th.

Yesterday at the public office in Bow-street, before Sir John Fielding and the rest of the Justices, Henry M'Allester and Archibald Girdwood were put to the bar, when Mr. John Christian Bach deposed, that on the 7th instant about ten o'clock at night he was robbed near Hammersmith by two men of a guinea, a gold watch, chain and seals. A constable produced a chain and seals found upon Girdwood ; and Mr. Bond produced a gold watch found in M'Allester's lodgings ; all which Mr. Bach swore were his property, taken from him at the above time. Mr. Thomas Gainsborough swore, that about the same time and near the same place, he was robbed of a metal watch (which he borrowed that morning from his nephew) and some money. Dinmore, a constable, produced a watch that he found in Girdwood's possession, which Mr. Gainsborough's nephew proved to be the one he lent his uncle. . . . The ostler of the Star in Blackman-street proved that the prisoners often had horses from their inn, particularly on the 7th of June . . . on which they were remanded and the several parties bound to prosecute.

Monday, June 19th.

[The Rev. John Wesley has written to Lord Dartmouth :]

All my prejudices are against the Americans, for I am an High Churchman, the son of an High Churchman, bred up from my childhood in the highest notions of passive obedience and non-resistance ; and yet in spite of all my rooted prejudice, I cannot avoid thinking (if I think at all) that an oppressed people asked for nothing more than their legal rights and that in the most modest and inoffensive manner which the nature of the thing would allow.

But waiving this, waiving all considerations of right and wrong, I ask, is it common sense to use force towards the Americans ? . . . They are divided among themselves ? So you are informed by various letters and memorials. . . . No, my Lord, they are terribly united : not in the Province of New England only, but down as low as the Jerseys and Pennsylvania the bulk of the people are so united that to speak a word in favour of the present English measures would almost endanger a man's life. . . .

Tuesday, June 20th.

[There has] appeared in the public papers the copy of a proclamation issued by General Gage at Boston on the 12th of last month, offering His Majesty's pardon to all persons who should immediately lay down their arms, except Samuel Adams and John Hancock ; declaring all those rebels who should not comply with these terms ; and all persons to be traitors who should aid and assist, or hold any correspondence with the rebels ; and moreover, ordering martial law to be in force within the province of Massachusetts Bay so long as the present unhappy occasion shall require it.

Wednesday, June 21st.

Advice was this day received that the Pennsylvania packet from London was safe arrived at Philadelphia, with Dr. Franklin on board. The General Assembly of Philadelphia was sitting when his arrival was made known ; and his consent being first asked, he was chosen one of their delegates to the Continental Congress and took his seat accordingly.

Thursday, June 22nd.

Being the day appointed for keeping the anniversary of His Majesty's birthday, who entered into the thirty-eighth year of his age on the 4th instant, it was celebrated with the usual joy and splendour. Lord Stormont's St. Andrew's cross, set round with diamonds, and appended to his riband of the Order of the Thistle, was cut from it at Court by some sharpers who made off with it undiscovered.   It was worth several hundred pounds.

Mr. Garrick, Mr. Colman, Mr. Foote, Mr. Harris, and other gentlemen, who either have or now do preside over the entertainments of the public, were at Court. . . . Mr. Garrick and Mr. Colman (the modern Beaumont and Fletcher) went in the same carriage, which was a very elegant one and belonged to Mr. Garrick, whose servants appeared in new liveries. . . .

Friday, June 23rd.

The Lord Mayor laid before the Court of Common Council a letter addressed to the Lord Mayor, Aldermen and Common Council of the city of London from the committee of New York, in which they say, " The minions of power here may now inform administration, if they can ever speak the language of truth, that this city is as one man in the cause of liberty. Assure yourselves," say they, " that we speak the real sentiments of the confederated colonies on the continent, when we declare, that all the horrors of a civil war will never compel America to submit to taxation by the authority of parliament.   But should His Majesty be graciously pleased, upon suitable emergencies, to make requisitions in ancient form, the colonies have expressed their willingness to contribute to the support of the empire, but to contribute of their voluntary gift as Englishmen ; and when our unexampled grievances are redressed, our Prince will find his American subjects testifying on all proper occasions by as ample aids as their circumstances will permit, the most unshaken fidelity to their sovereign and inviolable attachment to the welfare of his realm."

Saturday, June 24th.

By the ship *Watt* just arrived from Virginia, in 32 days, there is advice that Lord Dunmore had suppressed an insurrection at Williamsburgh that was of a dangerous tendency, 150 men from the back-settlements having attempted with Mr. Patrick Henry, one of the delegates, at their head, to oblige the Governor to bring on shore a quantity of gunpowder belonging to the King, which he, for security, had put on board one of the men of war. . . .

Sunday, June 25th.

The Clubs at the Savoir Vivre, Almack's, White's and Guthrie's, [yesterday] gave a new diversion invented by Lord Lyttelton or rather borrowed from the Venetians, a race of boats called a Regatta. Lord Lyttelton and Temple Luttrell, one of the Duchess of Cumberland's brothers, were the chief managers. . . .

Notwithstanding the unfavourable aspect of the morning, the managers hoisted the St. George's standard upon the centre arch of Westminster Bridge, about one o'clock, as a signal to the public that the Regatta would be celebrated that evening. . . . The Thames, by six o'clock, was overspread with vessels and boats ornamented with divers colours. . . . At half past seven, the several candidates for the Regatta honours started at Westminster Bridge ; twelve boats, two men in each, in three divisions, habited in white, red, and blue, rowed down to Waterman's Hall, and went round a vessel placed there for the purpose, and then made up again for the goal, which was gained by one of the red squadrons. . . .

As soon as the winners were declared, and their prizes awarded, the whole procession began to move from Westminster Bridge for Ranelagh : the director's barge at the head of the whole squadron, with grand bands of music playing in each. Unfortunately . . . before the divisions could arrive at Ranelagh, it was nearly dark, and to aggravate the misfortune the wind got up and it began to rain.

The company landed at the stairs about nine o'clock, when they joined the assembly which came by land in the Temple of Neptune, a temporary octagon kind of building erected about twenty yards below the Rotunda, lined with striped linen of the different coloured flags of the navy, with light pillars near the centre, ornamented with streamers of the same kind loosely flowing, and lustres hanging between each. . . .

At half after ten the Rotunda was opened for supper, which discovered three circular tables, of different elevations, elegantly set out, though not profusely covered : the Rotunda was finely illuminated with parti-coloured lamps, and those displayed with great taste and delicacy ; the centre was solely appropriated for one of the fullest and finest bands of music, vocal and instrumental, ever collected in these kingdoms ; the number being 240, in which were included the first masters led by Giardini, and the whole directed by Mr. Simpson. . . . It was opened with a grand new piece composed for the occasion, after which various catches and glees were admirably sung by Messrs. Vernon, Reinhold, &c. &c. But the illumination of the orchestra had been unfortunately overlooked, which gave that part of the design a gloomy appearance.

Supper being over, a part of the company retired to the Temple, where they danced minuets, cotillions, &c. without any regard to precedence ; while others entertained themselves in the great room. . . . The company consisted of about 2,000 among which were . . . their Royal Highnesses the Dukes of Gloucester and Cumberland, Duke of Northumberland, Lords North, Harrington, Stanley, Tyrconnel, Lincoln, their respective ladies . . . the French, Spanish, Prussian, Russian, and Neapolitan Ambassadors, etc., etc.

Wednesday, June 28th.

The Sheriffs Plomer and Hart waited on His Majesty at St. James's, in consequence of the King's appointment last Saturday at Kew. Mr. Sheriff Plomer addressed His Majesty in the following words : " May it please your Majesty, we are ordered by the Lord Mayor, Aldermen and Livery of the city of London, in Common Hall assembled, to wait upon your Majesty, humbly to know your Majesty's royal will and pleasure, when your Majesty will be pleased to receive upon the throne their humble address, remonstrance and petition." His Majesty replied, " You will be pleased to take notice that I will receive their address, remonstrance and petition, on Friday next at the levée." Mr. Sheriff Plomer then said, " Your Majesty will permit us to inform you that the Livery in Common Hall assembled have resolved not to present their address, remonstrance and petition, unless your Majesty shall be pleased to receive it sitting on the throne." The King answered, " I am ever ready to receive addresses and petitions, but I am the judge where." . . .

July 1775

Monday, July 3rd.

The gentlemen who went last from England [to India] seem to be in the right with respect to the Rohilla war in which transaction Mr. Hastings's conduct is not quite free from suspicion, but he appears in other matters to have been a very able and useful servant to the Company, and in particular to have put their finances in Bengal into a much better situation than they were before his time. The worst part of the business is that the two parties in the council appear too much irritated against one another to act together with any cordiality for the future. . . .

Tuesday, July 4th.

Mrs. Rudd came in custody of the Keeper of Newgate before the Court of King's Bench, in order to be bailed, on the ground of having been admitted a King's evidence in the case of the two Perreaus, and thereby entitled to the protection of the law. But it appearing that she did not come under the definition of an accomplice legally entitled to pardon, and that, moreover, she was not detained in custody for any crime that she had confessed herself a party in committing, but for crimes she had concealed, the Court ordered her to be remanded to prison.

Wednesday, July 5th.

The Sheriffs waited on His Majesty at St. James's, when Mr. Sheriff Plomer addressed the King in the following words : " May it please your Majesty, we are ordered by the Mayor, Aldermen, and Livery of the city of London, in Common Hall assembled, to wait upon your Majesty, humbly to deliver into your Majesty's hands, in their name, their resolutions agreed to in Common Hall on the 24th of June last and of the 4th

MRS. RUDD, DRAWN FROM THE LIFE

From 'The Town and Country Magazine', September 1775

instant." Mr. Sheriff Plomer then delivered a copy of the resolutions only, but not the address, petition and remonstrance, into the King's hands which he received without saying a word.

The resolutions of the 4th were as follows :

July 4. " Resolved, That the King is bound to hear the petitions of his people, it being the undoubted right of the subject to be heard and not a matter of grace and favour.

" Resolved, That His Majesty's answer is a direct denial of the right of this court to have their petitions heard.

" Resolved, That such denial renders the right of petitioning the Throne, recognised and established by the Revolution, of no effect.

" Resolved, That whoever advised His Majesty, directly or indirectly, to refuse hearing the humble address, remonstrance and petition of this court, on the throne, is equally an enemy to the happiness and security of the King, and to the peace and liberties of the people.

" Ordered, That the address, remonstrance and petition, which His Majesty refused to hear on the throne, be printed in the public papers and signed by the town-clerk.

" Resolved, That the following instruction be given to our representatives in parliament :

" *Gentlemen*, you are instructed by the Livery in Common Hall assembled, to move immediately on the next meeting of parliament, for an humble address from the House of Commons to His Majesty, requesting to know who were the advisers of those fatal measures, which have planted popery and arbitrary power in America, and have plunged us into a most unnatural civil war, to the subversion of the fundamental principles of English liberty, and the ruin of our most valuable commerce, and the destruction of His Majesty's subjects : to know who were the advisers of a measure so dangerous to His Majesty's happiness, and the rights of his people, as refusing to hear the petitions and complaints of his subjects. You are further instructed, gentlemen, to move for an impeachment of the authors and advisers of those measures that, by bringing them to public justice, evil counsellors may be removed from before the King, his throne may be established, the rights of the people vindicated, and the whole empire restored to the enjoyment of peace, liberty and safety."

Saturday, July 8th.

[The King to Lord North :]

I have no doubt but the nation at large sees the conduct of America in its true light and I am certain any other conduct but compelling obedience would be ruinous and culpable, therefore no consideration could bring me to swerve from the present path, which I think myself in duty bound to follow.

Monday, July 10th.

A very eminent physician who attended a publican that died in Fleet-market on Thursday, said that he had visited 160 publicans, who had died within a year, all of fevers, which he attributed to their drinking out of glasses or pots after persons who had lately been discharged from prisons ; and he advised the washing of pots or glasses before they are used.

Tuesday, July 11th.

Accounts from New York, dated June the 7th . . . mention that the Congress have determined to raise troops and raise money, &c., and also to make one more effort for conciliation by an application *to the King* and *people of England.* The account I saw was so worded, and I think they are emphatical words. I think *Parliament* is purposely omitted.

I am told this morning that an account came last night, that the Congress' mode of application is by a *Petition*, as they call it, *of Right.* That they insist upon its being agreed to, and with a threat, that otherwise they shall immediately publish a manifesto to all Europe and declare themselves independent.

Saturday, July 15th.

Yesterday the Lord Mayor, attended by the two Sheriffs, and the following Aldermen : viz. Frederick Bull, Esq., Samuel Lee, Esq., and Sir Watkin Lewis ; the City Remembrancer, (the Recorder not being there) the Town Clerk, and about sixty Livery, waited on his Majesty at St. James's, with their humble petition and address. They arrived there about two

o'clock. As soon as his Majesty came, the Town Clerk read
the petition, which his Majesty received very graciously, but
gave for answer, that he could not comply with their request.
The Lord Chancellor, Lord Talbot, and several other Lords
were present. No throne was erected.

Tuesday, July 25th.

This morning arrived Captain Chadds, of His Majesty's
ship *Cerberus*, with the following letter, from the Honourable
Lieutenant-General Gage, to the Earl of Dartmouth, one of
His Majesty's principal Secretaries of State. . . . Dated Boston,
June 25, 1775.

My Lord,

I am to acquaint your lordship of an action that happened
on the 17th instant between His Majesty's troops and a large
body of the rebel forces.

An alarm was given at break of day, on the 17th instant,
by a firing from the *Lively* ship of war ; and advice was soon
after received that the rebels had broke ground, and were
raising a battery on the heights of the peninsula of Charlestown, against the town of Boston. They were plainly seen at
work, and in a few hours, a battery of six guns played upon
their works. Preparations were instantly made for landing a
body of men to drive them off, and ten companies of the
grenadiers, ten of light infantry, with the 5th, 38th, 43rd and
52nd battalions, with a proportion of field artillery, under the
command of Major-General Howe and Brigadier-General
Pigot, were embarked with great expedition and landed on the
peninsula without opposition, under the protection of some
ships of war, armed vessels and boats, by whose fire the rebels
were kept within their works.

The troops formed as soon as landed ; the light infantry
posted on the right, and the grenadiers upon their left. The
5th and 38th battalions drew up on the rear of those corps,
and the 43rd and 52nd battalions made a third line. The rebels
upon the heights were perceived to be in great force and strongly
posted. A redoubt, thrown up on the 16th at night, and other
works full of men, defended with cannon, and a large body
posted in the houses in Charlestown, covered their right flank ;

and their centre and left were covered by a breast-work, part of it cannon proof, which reached from the left of the redoubt to the Mystic or Medford river.

This appearance of the rebels' strength, and the large columns seen pouring in to their assistance, occasioned an application for the troops to be reinforced with some companies of light infantry and grenadiers, the 47th battalion and the 1st battalion of marines ; the whole, when in conjunction, making a body of something above 2,000 men. These troops advanced, formed in two lines, and the attack began by a sharp cannonade from our field pieces and howitzers, the lines advancing slowly, and frequently halting to give time for the artillery to fire.

The light infantry was directed to force the left point of the breast-work, to take the rebel line in flank, and the grenadiers to attack in front supported by the 5th and 52nd battalions. These orders were executed with perseverance, under a heavy fire from the vast number of the rebels ; and notwithstanding various impediments before the troops could reach the works, and though the left under Brigadier-General Pigot was engaged also with the rebels, at Charlestown, which at a critical moment was set on fire, the Brigadier pursued his point, and carried the redoubt.

The rebels were then forced from their strongholds and pursued till they were drove clear off the peninsula, leaving five pieces of cannon behind them.

The loss the rebels sustained must have been considerable from the great numbers they carried off during the time of action, and buried in holes, since discovered, exclusive of what they suffered by the shipping and boats ; near one hundred were buried the day after, and thirty found wounded in the field, three of which are since dead.

I enclose, your lordship, a return of the killed and wounded of His Majesty's troops.

This action has shown the superiority of the King's troops, who, under every disadvantage, attacked and defeated above three times their own number, strongly posted and covered by breast-works.

The conduct of Major-General Howe was conspicuous on

this occasion and his example spirited the troops in which Major-General Clinton assisted, who followed the reinforcement. And in justice to Brigadier-General Pigot, I am to add, that the success of the day must in a great measure be attributed to his firmness and gallantry.

Lieutenant-Colonels Nesbit, Abercrombie and Clarke ; Majors Butler, Williams, Bruce, Spendlove, Smelt, Mitchel, Pitcairne and Short exerted themselves remarkably ; and the valour of the British officers and soldiers in general was at no time more conspicuous than in this action.

I have the honour to be, etc.

Tho. Gage

Total killed and wounded.

1 Lieutenant-colonel, 2 majors, 7 captains, 9 lieutenants, 5 sergeants, 1 drummer, 91 rank and file killed. 3 Majors, 27 captains, 32 lieutenants, 8 ensigns, 40 sergeants, 12 drummers, 706 rank and file, wounded. . . .

Wednesday, July 26th.

Dick Goodenough . . . has written a kind of parody of Puffy Pensioner's *Taxation no Tyranny* under the noble title of *Resistance no Rebellion* which, I hear, is well received. He has bound them together and sent them to me by the coach. I wonder they did not quarrel in the boot and tear the binding to pieces. . . . I am sorry, like Sir Roger de Coverley's head upon the sign-post, that so much may be said *on both sides.* . . .

Thursday, July 27th.

A private letter from Philadelphia . . . dated June 5th, mentions, " That the Congress had concluded upon never submitting to the late Acts and had resolved upon repelling force by force, and [on May 15th] had appointed Colonel George Washington General and Commander-in-Chief of all the forces in America ; and that he had set out to join the Provincial troops before Boston."

Both Houses of Parliament met pursuant to their last prorogation, and were further prorogued to Thursday, the 14th of September.

Saturday, July 29th.

The Treasurer of his Majesty's Chamber, yesterday, had money from the Treasury to pay the King's Household a quarter's allowance, due the fifth of July, 1774 : and his Majesty in consideration of their being so much in arrears has . . . given positive orders that the hundred thousand pounds given him by Parliament for Somerset and Buckingham houses, last sessions, shall be paid to his servants for wages and allowances due, in consequence of which another quarter's payment is expected to take place in August next.

Monday, July 31st.

This morning an express arrived at the Admiralty office, with an account of the [*Resolution*], Capt. Cook, being safe arrived off Portsmouth, from the South Seas, after a fine short passage from St. Helena.

All private letters that come with the Government's dispatches from America are opened before delivered.

[General Gage has written to Lord Dartmouth :] The trials we have had show that the rebels are not the despicable rabble too many have supposed them to be, and I find it owing to a military spirit encouraged amongst them for a few years past, joined with an uncommon degree of zeal and enthusiasm. . . . In all their wars against the French they never showed so much conduct, attention and perseverance as they do now.

August 1775

Tuesday, August 1st.

The Coat and Badge given by the will of Doggett the player was rowed for by six watermen, from the Old Swan at London Bridge to the Swan at Chelsea. At twelve o'clock a number of cutters and other boats with flags, streamers, and awnings, &c. had assembled on the river, in many of which were drums, fifes and other music, which had a very agreeable effect. A flag was hoisted on the steeple of St. John's, Southwark. The candidates for the prize assembled at twelve and at five minutes before one started on a signal given by the firing of a pistol. A general shout now cheered the contending parties, who rowed against wind and tide. . . . There were not above 200 boats attending, but it was a cheerful sight to behold them all in motion. . . . Some of the rowers were without shirts, and they all struggled hard for the prize. . . . Doggett and Alleyn, two players, have immortalized their names, the first by an annual rowing match, the latter by founding a college.

Thursday, August 3rd.

Lord Grosvenor offered Count O'Kelly 11,000 guineas for his celebrated stallion Eclipse the last July meeting at Newmarket.

The heroine Kingston is almost forgotten. Foote had a mind to have revived her story on the stage ; but Lord Hertford would not license his piece. It is still thought she will be tried and convicted, but her Countess-hood will save her Duchess-hood from being burnt in its hand.

Friday, August 4th.

Four companies of the Royal regiment of Artillery embarked at Woolwich . . . for America.

Sunday, August 6th.

[On Thursday] an extraordinary match at cricket was played at Moulsey Hurst between six unmarried against the same number of married women ; and was won by the former, though one of the latter ran seventeen notches. There were great bets depending.

Monday, August 7th.

It is still confidently asserted by some who pretend to be in the secret, that Boston is reduced to ashes, and that General Gage is on his return to England.

Wednesday, August 9th.

What a figure do two great empires make at this moment ! Spain, mistress of Peru and Mexico, amazes Europe with an invincible armada ; at last it sails to Algiers, and disbarks its whole contents, even to the provisions of the fleet. It is beaten shamefully, loses all its stores, and has scarce bread left to last till it gets back into its own ports !

Mrs. Britannia orders her senate to proclaim America a continent of cowards, and vote it should be starved unless it will drink tea with her. She sends her only army to be besieged in one of their towns, and half her fleet to besiege the terra firma ; but orders her army to do nothing, in hopes that the American senate at Philadelphia will be so frightened at the British army being besieged in Boston, that it will sue for peace. At last she gives her army leave to sally out, but being twice defeated, she determines to carry on the war so vigorously till she has not a man left, that all England will be satisfied with the total loss of America ; and if everybody is satisfied, who can be blamed ?

Friday, August 11th.

The Journals of Captain Cook, on his third time of circumnavigating the globe, together with the charts, drawings, and observations which he has made in his passage, were on Wednesday presented to his Majesty by the Earl of Sandwich.

Saturday, August 12th.

On Tuesday the Water Bailiff, with assistants, seized two unlawful nets near Strand on the Green but the fishermen rose in a body and took the nets by force from them, whereupon the Water Bailiff applied to the Lord Mayor who granted a warrant against several of them, made it special to Mr. Gates and had it backed by Sir John Fielding. On Thursday Mr. Gates, with assistants, went and took the principal person, but he was soon rescued, ran into the Thames and swam till he was taken into a boat and by that means escaped. Mr. Gates and his people waited all night, but were not able to take any of the men. They however re-took one of the nets, after a severe battle, in which some of Mr. Gates's men were terribly beaten. Strict search is making after the fishermen.

Monday, August 14th.

On Wednesday evening the Rev. Mr. John Wesley preached to a very crowded auditory at West Street Chapel, from Jeremiah XI. ver. 6 and 7. . . . In his discourse he displayed the national sins of England to be swearing, luxury, and murmuring against their rulers, for which the judgments of God hung over this land ; he farther observed, " Except in some large towns, he had never, in the course of his life, seen such general want and penury as appeared among the lower order of people, which, added to the present disturbances in America, was truly alarming, and concluded with exhorting everyone in particular to break off their sins by repentance, that so it might, as in the case of Nineveh, please the Lord to return the sword into its scabbard."

Tuesday, August 15th.

About the middle of [last] month, Col. Guy Johnson, His Majesty's Superintendent of Indian affairs, arrived at Montreal accompanied by a considerable number of chiefs and warriors of the six nations : after which he held a general congress with the chiefs and warriors of the Canada confederacy, to the amount of 1700, who, in presence of his Excellency General Carleton, unanimously resolved to support their engagements with His Majesty, and remove all intruders on the several communications.

Wednesday, August 16th.

The birthday of the Bishop of Osnaburg, [their Majesties' second son], who then entered into the 13th year of his age. Their Majesties received the usual compliments on that occasion.

Thursday, August 17th.

Extract of a letter from Hanover, August 8.

" The Regency of this Electorate have received orders for the regiments of Prince Ernest of Mecklenburgh-Strelitz, Goldacker, Hardenberg, Rhoden and De la Mothe, to march immediately to Stade, in order to embark there on the first day of September, and sail with the first fair wind, to replace the English regiments at Gibraltar and Port Mahon. . . .

Friday, August 18th.

A very elaborate dissertation has lately been presented to Lord North, upon the political propriety of establishing colonies in the new discoveries in the south seas ; the author founds his arguments upon the probability of our losing those we possess in North America ; if not at present, certainly in a future period not very distant, and he shows the necessity of providing new markets for the manufactures of Britain, when the old ones decline.

The institution of a new order of knighthood, to be called the Order of Merit, which was so much talked of about three years ago, is again on the carpet ; the ribbond is to be a straw-coloured one. Such an institution would render a monarch, desirous of encouraging merit, more popular than perhaps any measure that could be devised.

Saturday, August 19th.

ADVERTISEMENT [in the *Public Advertiser*]

Bugs destroyed by ANDREW COOKE, at the King's Arms, Holborn Hill, opposite the Dog's Head in the Pottage Pot ;

Cooke being universally known amongst the first rank in the City and suburbs of London, after twenty years' practice, and having cured sixteen thousand beds with great applause, the Bugs not returning for a number of years, being the oldest Bug-destroyer in England ; if any complaints should happen, he visits again gratis ; my abilities in my profession may be known by enquiring at the Asylum, Westminster Bridge, the Swan with Two Necks, in Lad Lane, the Rev. Mr. French's, at Bow, and sundry others, not room to mention here. And whereas a set of people style themselves Bug-destroyer to his Majesty, which serves for no other purpose than to draw in the unwary ; please to refer to the Court-Calendar for twenty years back. You'll find that no person was ever appointed to that office ; if any has a right, it is myself, having worked at sundry apartments in the King's Palace.

I remain, with due respect, the Public's most humble servant at command,

ANDREW COOKE

KING'S ARMS, HOLBORN HILL, the Old Three Fishes over the door.

Sunday, August 20th.

[Lately published :]
Sterne's Letters to his Friends on various Occasions. To which is added, his History of a Watch-Coat, with explanatory Notes. Kearsley. 12mo. Pp. 176. 2s.
Speech of Edmund Burke, Esq. ; on moving his Resolutions for Conciliation with the Colonies, March 22, 1775. Dodsley.
The History of Great Britain. By James Macpherson. 2 vols. 4to. £2, 2s. Strahan.

Monday, August 21st.

Mrs. Howe is vastly better since the General was made Commander-in-Chief, for he is at least safe for a time, and safe from bush-fighting, which seemed the most to be dreaded as being more frequent than a regular action ; besides she flatters herself his advice will be a little attended to, and she knows he wishes to have a peace that is creditable to both. I don't know if their avoiding him is true enough, but it's very moving if it is. . . .

Tuesday, August 22nd.

[Mr. Edmund Burke has] been chosen Agent by the General Assembly of New York. . . .

The transactions of the American Congress, though conducted with the greatest secrecy, begin to be disclosed. We now discover that the seizing of Ticonderoga and Crown Point, which was given out as the rash attempt of a few private desperadoes, was a preconcerted measure ; that a friendly address to the Canadians preceded the execution, and that, by securing those passes, the intent was to prevent the Indians from falling suddenly upon the back-settlements, and to check General Carleton in his progress should he attempt an irruption on that side. . . .

The Congress have once more petitioned the Throne . . . [and] sent [an] address to their fellow subjects in Britain, in which the title is no less remarkable than the matter :

The Twelve United Colonies, by their Delegates in Congress, to the Inhabitants of Great Britain. . . .

Wednesday, August 23rd.

The King issued a Proclamation declaring the Americans rebels, and forbidding to assist them. The Opposition made no noise on this stretch of power.

Thursday, August 24th.

We are at length actually involved in war. . . . If any indication is to be taken from external appearances the King is entirely satisfied with the present state of his Government. His spirits at his levées, at the play, everywhere, seem to be remarkably good. His Ministers, too, are perfectly at their ease. Most of them are amusing themselves in the country, while England is disfurnished of its forces in the face of armed Europe, and Gibraltar and Minorca are delivered over to the custody of foreigners. . . .

As to the good people of England, they seem to partake every day more and more of the character of that administration which they have been induced to tolerate. . . . We look to the merchants in vain, they are gone from us, and from themselves. They consider America as lost and they look to administration for an indemnity. Hopes are accordingly held out to them that some equivalent for their debts will be provided. In the meantime, the leading men among them are kept full fed with contracts and remittances and jobs of all descriptions ; and they are indefatigable in their endeavours to keep the others quiet, with the prospect of their share in those emoluments, of which they see their advisers already so amply in possession. They all, or the greatest number of them, begin to snuff the cadaverous *haut goût* of lucrative war. War, indeed, is become a sort of substitute for commerce. The freighting business never was so lively, on account of the prodigious taking up for transport service. Great orders for provisions and stores of all kinds, new clothing for the troops, and the intended six thousand Canadians, puts life into the woollen manufacture ; and a number of men-of-war, ordered to be equipped, has given a pretence for such a quantity of nails and other iron work, as to keep the midland parts tolerably quiet. All this, with the incredible increase of the northern market since the peace between Russia and the Porte, keeps up the spirits of the mercantile world, and induces them to consider the American war, not so much their calamity as their resource in an inevitable distress. This is the state of *most*, not of *all* the merchants. . . .

Friday, August 25th.

Wednesday a small ship, from Bristol to America, was stopped in the Bristol Channel, on an information given that she was carrying out some warlike ammunition to the Provincials, and on searching her, there were found thirty thousand muskets.

Saturday, August 26th.

[Extract of a letter from Dr. Benjamin Franklin to Joseph Priestley, dated Philadelphia, July 7th :]

The Congress met at a time when all minds were so exasperated by the perfidy of General Gage, and his attack on the country people, that propositions of attempting an accommodation were not much relished ; and it has been with difficulty that we have carried another humble petition to the Crown to give Britain one more chance, one opportunity more, of recovering the friendship of the colonies ; which, however, I think she has not sense enough to embrace, and so I conclude she has lost them for ever.

She has begun to burn our seaport towns ; secure, I suppose, that we shall never be able to return the outrage in kind. She may doubtless destroy them all ; but if she wishes to recover our commerce are these the probable means ? . . .

You will have heard, before this reaches you, of the treacherous conduct [of General Gage] to the remaining people in Boston, in detaining their *goods*, after stipulating to let them go out with their *effects*, on pretence that merchants' goods were not effects ; the defeat of a great body of his troops by the country people at Lexington ; some other small advantages gained in skirmishes with their troops ; and the action at Bunker's Hill, in which they were twice repulsed and the third time gained a dear victory. Enough has happened, one would think, to convince your ministers that the Americans will fight, and that it is a harder nut to crack than they imagined.

We have not yet applied to any foreign power for assistance, nor offered our commerce for their friendship. Perhaps we never may ; yet it is natural to think of it if we are pressed. . . .

Sunday, August 27th.

[Sheridan's play, *The Rivals*,] has been acted at Southampton. Above a hundred people were turned away the first night. They say there was never anything so universally liked. They have very good success at Bristol, and have played *The Rivals* several times ; — Miss Barsanti, Lydia, and Mrs. Canning, Julia.

Monday, August 28th.

Saturday night between the hours of eleven and twelve o'clock as Dr. A —— was returning home peaceably to his lodgings, he was accosted by one of those wandering females, who ply at every corner of this city after dusk. As the Doctor passed the evening with a jovial catch party, he was rather mellow, therefore began to joke with his new acquaintance, till he came to the corner of St. Martin's Lane. Finding now he had no mind to treat her, she seized him by the collar, bellowing out, " Watch, watch ! A rape, a rape ! Help ! or this villain will ruin me ! " Five or six watchmen in an instant came to her assistance, and among the rest an ill-looking fellow, who said he was her husband. The first thing he seized was the trembling composer's nose, which unfortunately is none of the shortest, holding it in contact with his chin for above ten minutes, and swore horribly he'd instantly do himself justice for the injury intended his bed. In vain did the poor Doctor expostulate, until at length one of the watchmen whispered the Doctor and told him he knew the husband was altogether as avaricious as jealous and therefore advised him to tempt him with a little money ; the affrighted Doctor took the hint, clapped five guineas into his hand and was instantly released for his bounty.

Tuesday, August 29th.

[Today the King's Proclamation declaring the Americans rebels] was read in Palace Yard, Westminster, and at Temple Bar by the heralds, etc., as also at the Royal Exchange by one of the Lord Mayor's officers, accompanied only by the Common Crier. The Lord Mayor would not permit the officers to have horses, or the mace to be carried, as is usual on such occasions.

September 1775

Saturday, September 2nd.

A Proclamation was [yesterday] issued for proroguing the Parliament to Thursday the 26th day of October, then to sit for the dispatch of business.

Monday, September 4th.

The slave trade having been greatly affected by the late Order of Council for prohibiting the exportation of gunpowder, etc. the sailors of Liverpool, who are unemployed on that account, assembled in a body [last week] and threatened destruction to the whole town. They had got several pieces of cannon which they fired, but a party of light horse being sent for from Manchester, they were soon dispersed and about 40 of them lodged in gaol.

Wednesday, September 13th.

[The King to Lord North :]

If the Opposition is powerful next session it will much surprise me, for I am fighting the battle of the legislature, therefore have a right to expect an almost unanimous support ; if there should arise difficulties they will not dismay me for I know the uprightness of my intentions and therefore am ready to stand every attack of ever so dangerous a kind with the firmness that honesty and attachment to the constitution will support. . . .

Friday, September 15th.

The Prussians now [stop] all vessels destined for Danzig, whether coming in or going out, and [insist] on their unloading before they enter the Fahr-Wasser, and paying the custom-house duties, piece by piece, of their cargoes ; but none of the burghers of that unhappy place, nor any foreign masters, [have] as yet consented to this ; choosing rather to go back with their lading than submit to such an exaction. In consequence of this and other grievances the city of Danzig [is] now going to ruin apace. . . .

Saturday, September 16th.

This morning came on at the Sessions House in the Old Bailey, the trial of Mrs. Rudd for forgery ; when after some debates by the counsel on both sides, which lasted two hours . . . a special verdict was given, and the matter will be determined by the twelve Judges ; she was remanded to Newgate.

Sunday, September 17th.

[Last Sunday] a woman-preacher, who accompanied Mr. John Wesley to Plymouth, held forth upon the Parade and brought together the greatest concourse of people that had ever been seen there ; the novelty of a woman Methodist-preacher having drawn half Plymouth to hear her.

Tuesday, September 19th.

The influence Mrs. Rudd gains over her acquaintance is by no means owing to her beauty, of which she has a very small portion. She is of the middling size, and was always exceedingly thin, with rather a sallow complexion, a dark piercing eye and fine teeth. Her dress and tone of voice are very distinguishing and captivating, and such as would make her an object of attention in the politest circle : to these she adds an uncommon degree of understanding and presence of mind, which never forsake her on any exigency. There is no doubt but what she must stand trial ; for out of the twelve judges six have already given their opinion against her ; the four Judges of the King's Bench, and Barons Burland and Hotham ; their opinions cannot be taken till November, so that she must remain in Newgate till December.

Wednesday, September 20th.

Covent Garden Theatre opened [tonight] for the first time this season, with a new Prelude, *The Suspicious Husband*, and *The Padlock*. In the Prelude, the curtain rising, discovered the different performers of the theatre, comparing notes together on their various successes, cast of parts, droll accidents, etc. etc. which they experienced during their different summer excursions : — Mattocks gives an account of the sailors levelling their great guns at the Liverpool theatre ; when Dunstall humorously replies, " they would point them much truer at a Frenchman or Spaniard." — Lee Lewes diverts them with the manner of their performing *Hamlet* in a company that he belonged to, when the hero who was to play the principal character had absconded with an innkeeper's daughter ; and that when he came forward to give out the play, he added, " the part of Hamlet to be left out, for that night."

Thursday, September 21st.

The weather proving unfavourable on Tuesday last the managers of [Marybone] Gardens have indulged the waiters with another night, which will be this present evening . . . when there will be a variety of entertainments [and] a very capital firework under the direction of Signor Caillot . . . the whole to conclude with a representation of the Forge of Vulcan under Mount Aetna, the Cavern of the Cyclops and Flowing of the Lava, after which will be a large Air Balloon, illuminated with blazing stars.

Friday, September 22nd.

[Lately published :]

The Defects of Police the Cause of Immorality, and the continual Robberies committed, particularly in and about the Metropolis : with various proposals for preventing Hanging and Transportation : likewise for the Establishment of several Plans of Police on a permanent Basis with respect to common Beggars ; the regulation of Paupers ; the peaceful Security of Subjects ; and the moral and political Conduct of the People ; Observations on the Rev. Mr. Hetherington's Charity ; and the most probable Means of relieving the Blind. By Jonas Hanway, Esq. 4to. 6s. Dodsley.

Number 1, — to be continued in 24 weekly numbers, price 6d. each, — [of] the *Works of Alexander Pope, Esq.*, with his last corrections, additions and improvements . . . printed ver-

THE NEW FRONT OF DRURY LANE THEATRE

Architects: R. and J. Adam, 1775

batim from the octavo edition of William Warburton, now Lord Bishop of Gloucester. . . . Each number . . . adorned with an elegant engraving. . . .

Saturday, September 23rd.

On opening the theatre in Drury Lane this evening, for the first time this season, it appeared more like a new than an old theatre in consequence of the great alterations made in it during the last summer. The new front is simple and elegant and considerably improved by the addition of eight grand lamps. The most useful alterations within doors consist in the heightening of the ceiling twelve feet ; the removal of all the old side boxes, top and bottom, and substituting others on a larger scale, supported by light elegant pillars ; the addition of different passages to the upper and lower boxes, and spacious entrances from Bridges Street to every part of the house ; with directions, in large letters, to each. The chief ornamental improvements within doors consist of numberless decorations which cannot fail to strike the beholder. The roof is covered with a circular painting, finely executed, and remarkable for its well-studied simplicity. The light airy pillars that support the upper boxes, galleries, etc., are inlaid with plate-glass on green and crimson ground, which being finely contrasted afford a happy and elegant effect. Around each of these are some pretty fancied open paintings, with various borders, which, together with the crimson spotted lining of the boxes, and the light festoon curtain painted underneath the whole, relieve them finely. The stage doors, for united elegance and delicacy, are superior to anything of the kind we have seen or heard of in this country. The old chandeliers are taken down ; those on the sides are replaced by neat gilt branches on the pillars, holding two candles each ; in the front are four new chandeliers, of a more light and fashionable construction ; and there is no slit to be in the new curtain. — The alterations, as well within as without, are such, in short, as do great honour to the taste of Mr. Adam, the artist who designed them, and the spirit of the managers who have now converted an old barn into the most splendid and complete theatre in Europe.

Sunday, September 24th.

The violent measures towards America are fairly adopted and countenanced by a majority of individuals of all ranks, professions or occupations in this country. . . . The generality of the nation are aiding and assisting in their own destruction ; and I conceive that nothing but a degree of experience of the evils can bring about a right judgment in the public at large. . . .

Monday, September 25th.

[Yesterday] Mr. Viney, Master of the Wheel Manufactory on the Surrey side of Blackfriars Bridge, went as far up as Putney and back again in a machine with a pair of small wheels, made to go without rowing. It carries one person, who works it with his feet with springs.

Wednesday, September 27th.

[Extract of a letter from General Burgoyne, from Boston, August 10th and 18th, 1775 :]

Our station here is exceedingly disagreeable, without an army fit to undertake any business of consequence against the rebels opposed to us. They are strongly entrenched and very numerous in every part in which they are assailable, and we could not muster above 3,600 men for an attack on their army, after leaving a proper number for the defence of Boston and these lines at the head of this camp. . . .

Fresh provision for the army without which we shall probably lose a great many men in the winter — our sickness increasing daily in fluxes — the wounded recover slowly and many of them dying — now belonging to this camp there are 900 sick and wounded, rank and file — and about 1,900 fit for duty, exclusive of artillery, and about 100 recruits who do not carry arms — change of air and fresh provisions would probably save a great many men. But should it be thought to carry on the war without a *very large* addition to this army they need not flatter themselves with any expectation of its being terminated soon in our favour — and were I to advise those in that way of thinking, it should be to withdraw the army entirely from the rebellious Colonies and send such part of it as is not wanted in Europe to Canada, Halifax, and E. Florida, leaving these Colonies to quarrel and fight among themselves, what I think would be the immediate case, in consequence of that measure, and from those places you could give assistance to such as you thought proper.

But should the coercive plan be adopted, there should not be less than 5,000 men (rank and file I always mean when I talk of numbers) for the preservation of this place with a fleet commanded by a Commodore or Rear-Admiral — the Admiral being at New York, where there should be 15,000 with an additional battalion of artillery, now much wanted — about 500 at Halifax — and 2,000 or more for Canada to be added to as many Canadians and Indians as could be had from thence.

A Viceroy with full powers.

There is no possibility of carrying on a war so complicated as this will be, at the distance we are from the fountain head, without these full powers being at hand. . . .

Thursday, September 28th.

They write from Hamburg that it is no longer to be doubted that a considerable body of Russian troops have received orders to go to Danzig in order to protect that city from the attempts of the King of Prussia. The public is impatient to know how his Prussian majesty will relish this proceeding.

Friday, September 29th.

At Guildhall [Alderman Sawbridge was duly elected as Lord Mayor, and afterwards] laid before the Court the following letter from the Congress at Philadelphia :

MY LORD,

Permit the Delegates of the people of twelve ancient colonies, to pay your Lordship and the very respectable body of which you are the head, the just tribute of gratitude and thanks for the virtuous and unsolicited resentment you have shown to the violated rights of a free people. The city of London, my lord, having in all ages approved itself the patron of liberty, and the support of just government, against lawless tyranny and oppression, cannot fail to make us deeply sensible of the powerful aid our cause must receive from such advocates. A cause, my lord, worthy the support of the first city in the world, as it involves the fate of a great continent and threatens to shake the foundations of a flourishing, and, until lately, a happy empire.

North America, my lord, wishes most ardently for a lasting connection with Great Britain, on terms of just and equal liberty ; less than which generous minds will not offer, nor brave and free ones be willing to receive.

A cruel war has at length been opened against us, and whilst we prepare to defend ourselves like the descendants of Britons, we still hope that the mediation of wise and good citizens will at length prevail and restore harmony and peace, on permanent principles, to an oppressed and divided empire.

We have the honour to be, my lord, with great esteem, your lordship's faithful friends and fellow-subjects.

By order of the Congress,

JOHN HANCOCK, President

PHILADELPHIA, July 8, 1775.

Mr. Stavely moved that the above letter should be entered on the records of the city, and printed in the papers. [This was carried.]

October 1775

Monday, October 2nd.

Mr. Wilkes, if he has derived no real, has at least some personal consequence from serving the office of Lord Mayor ; for before his Mayoralty he was as thin as a shotten herring, but now he sports a belly truly aldermanic.

Friday, October 6th.

The Gentlemen who are members of the society called " The London Association," met on Wednesday at the Globe Tavern, Fleet Street, when they came to several resolutions for rescuing the press from the shackles of ministerial slavery, and for affording protection to those Printers who may otherwise suffer in the cause of Liberty.

The report of a skirmish between the Provincials and Regulars gains ground every hour. Ministry are in possession of the particulars, 'tis said some days, which we think is an infallible sign that it has been decided against the King's troops, otherwise they would be the first to announce it. . . .

Saturday, October 7th.

A very succinct and impartial account has been dispatched to government of the number of Americans now absolutely in arms in the different provinces, which makes them to be 53,000, officers included.

Monday, October 9th.

Sentimental Comedy has so vitiated the taste of the town, that it ceases to be a matter of surprise why Congreve's pieces are not more frequently laid before the public. . . . *The Way of the World*, though confessedly replete with wit and character, is not the most entertaining play in representation. It is so full of plot and intrigue, that it demands an unusual degree of attention in the performers and audience to excite admiration ;

on Saturday they both seemed averse to assist the author. Mr. King in Witwou'd was as entertaining and full of spirits as usual. Mr. Jefferson, in the gay admired Mirabel, (independent of the antique mode of his wig, and formal cut of his clothes, which surely were both uncharacteristic,) seemed, in attempting to be quite natural, to keep the entire plot of the play in his own bosom, looked more like the father than the Mirabel of Congreve. Mr. Reddish was a contrast to his friend Mirabel ; he seemed attentive, nervous, and played the latter part of his character well ; and had he but a little more the ease of comedy in the former part, and the address of a gentleman through the whole, he would have appeared to considerable advantage. . . . Mrs. Abington's person, manner, and dress were fashionable and elegant ; but though the character was certainly a fine one, there was a want of that spirit best calculated to call her powers into action : her delivery was tediously formal ; and had the audience been deprived of their sight, they would conclude that Capt. Bobadill had got into petticoats. Her dress was no more decent than Madam Hidon's was on her first appearance last year ; stays so low cut before puts modesty to the blush ; and will not be countenanced by an English audience, though made after the French fashion. . . . Mrs. Greville, to convince the town that she could keep a secret, whispered it only to a few friends in the pit. This lady behaves as if she were a princess in disguise, that had been ousted of her dominions, and took up with her present profession until she was restored : her indifference is intolerable, and should be noticed by her employer.

Friday, October 13*th.*

A detail of the forces to be employed in America for the year 1776.

British {	1 Regiment of light cavalry . . .	250
	30 Regiment of inf. at 12 comp. each .	22,300
	Artillery	800
	Marines	2,200
	To be raised by General Carleton . . .	15,000
	Germans now raising	4,000
	Total . .	44,550

To add to this those raising in Ireland, and a large fleet of ships well manned, complete and fit for service.

Monday, October 16th.

Lord Mansfield's House at Caen Wood and Mr. Garrick's at Hampton, are beautifully new fronted with the terras invented by the Messrs. Adams ; and it is imagined, from its durability, that most new houses will be finished with it.

Saturday, October 21st.

A new grand ballet called *The Savage Hunters* was produced last night at Drury Lane Theatre, in which Signora Paccini made her first appearance as principal woman dancer, and met with universal applause. She is rather of the under size, but is so graceful, and active, that she charmed all the cognoscenti :— Mr. Slingsby was very capital : Grimaldi, was very great in the satyr :—The different movements of the music, which were composed for the occasion, are very pleasing.—In a word, the whole dance is characteristic, and had a fine effect.

Monday, October 23rd.

On the 5th and 6th of this month the five battalions of the Hanoverian troops, destined for Gibraltar and Port Mahon embarked at Ritzebuttel, but the contrary wind has prevented their sailing yet.

Wednesday, October 25th.

Some letters from Malta mention that two frigates of that Order which served in the Spanish fleet against Algiers, in returning from Alicante to Malta met off Bona in Africa, with two Turkish caravelles and one chebeck laden with ammunition for the use of the Algerines. As soon as these vessels came within reach a most furious combat ensued, during which the chebeck sailed off but the two caravelles, after fighting for three days, were obliged to surrender and were brought into Malta. This action cost the Maltese 300 men killed and wounded and the Turks lost 700.

Thursday, October 26th.

The King opened the session with a very extraordinary speech. . . . The most striking part was the King's notification of a design of sending Commissaries to treat with any provinces that should wish to return to their duty. . . .

In the Commons Lord John Cavendish and Sir James Lowther moved to correct the Address and were briskly seconded. . . . Charles Fox said . . . " not Lord Chatham, not the Duke of Marlborough, no, not Alexander nor Caesar, had ever conquered so much territory as Lord North had lost in one campaign." . . .

The House sat till past four in the morning, when the Address was carried by 278 to 108.

We hear that some of the ministers have proposed in Council that both fleet and army be withdrawn from America, and these colonists be left entirely to themselves. . . . I should have said that this measure only anticipates the necessary course of events a few years ; that a forced and every day more precarious monopoly of about £6 or £700,000 a year of manufactures was not worth contending for ; that we should preserve the greater part of this trade even if the ports of America were open to all nations ; that it was very likely, in our method of proceeding, that we should be disappointed in our scheme of conquering the Colonies ; and that we ought to think beforehand how we were to govern them after they were conquered. Arbitrary power can extend its oppressive arm to the Antipodes ; but a limited government can never long be upheld at a distance, even where no disgusts have intervened : much less where such violent animosities have taken place. We must, therefore, annul all the Charters ; abolish every democratical power in every colony ; repeal the Habeas Corpus Act with regard to them ; invest every Governor with full discretionary or arbitrary powers ; confiscate the estates of all the chief planters ; and hang three fourths of their clergy. To execute such acts of destructive violence twenty thousand men will not be sufficient ; nor thirty thousand to maintain them, in so wide and disjointed a territory. And who are to pay so great an army ? The colonists cannot at any time, much less after reducing them to such a state of desolation : we ought not, and indeed cannot, in the over-loaded or rather overwhelmed and totally ruined state of our finances. Let us, therefore, lay aside all anger ; shake hands and part friends. . . .

Friday, October 27th.

The Commons sat again till twelve at night on the Report of the Address, the debate turning on the garrisoning Gibraltar and Port Mahon with Hanoverian troops, which the Opposition cried out against as a glaring breach of the Act of Settlement. Lord North said he did not believe that measure not having the consent of Parliament was illegal, but if it was, there might be an Act of Indemnity. . . .

Saturday, October 28th.

The ministers [have] only provoked and united — not intimidated, wounded, or divided America. Errors in or neglect of execution have rendered everything much worse ; and at this instant they are not sure that the King has a foot of dominion left on that continent. Boston must be, if it is not, abandoned. . . . Canada is in equal danger, and the first letters are likely to say it is gone. The ministers say it will take sixty thousand men to reconquer America. They will as soon have sixty thousand armies. Whether they can get any Russians is not even yet certain ; and, as it is said they must buy them by ceding some post, it is not credible that the other European Powers will wink at that growing puissance becoming a maritime one. . . .

Whether they were frightened themselves, or meant to frighten others, two days before the meeting, the ministers cried out " A plot ! " and took and committed to the Tower a Mr. Sayre, a banker of no great credit, and lately one of Wilkes's sheriffs. A young American officer of still worse character swore Sayre had tried to bribe him to betray the Tower ; and, if that was not trusting him enough, communicated his intention of seizing the King as he should go to the House. The ministers, as grave as they looked, could not keep anybody from laughing — no, though they trebled the Guards. . . . They have blundered in the warrant, just as they did in Wilkes's, must release Sayre, and he will be at liberty, instead of being, as he ought to be, in Bedlam. Earl Rochford will be prosecuted in his room, instead of being shut up for a fool, as he ought to be.

In both Houses the war was brisk and warm ; the Lords sat till eleven, and the Commons till four, and the court was galled, though it kept the field. . . .

Sunday, October 29*th.*

As a lesson to mankind and as a blow to despotism, I could wish to see a private History of the Bastille. M. de Malesherbes, the new Governor of the Police at Paris, is well qualified to furnish materials for such public services. The late Governor, the Duc de la Vrilliere, held his employment nearly fifty years, during which time no inspection was ever made of this prison.

His dismissal produced scenes painful to human nature. In the cells many were found who had lost their senses, from a mere want of means of employing them : others, against whom no one single trace of crime could be found, who had not only outlived in confinement their families and connections, but were even almost strangers to the sounds of their own names. One man, who had lost his liberty by a purchased *lettre de cachet* without any accusation, refused to accept of his permission to be at large but on condition that a proper allowance was made him for his future subsistence. The King humanely ordered him a pension of £150 per annum.

Monday, October 30*th.*

[To Mrs. Kenyon's new house in Lincoln's Inn Fields.]

The entrance is a broad lobby, well lighted by a window over the door and a staircase window. It is wainscot, painted white as far as the arch turned at the bottom of the staircase. On the left hand is a sweet pretty parlour, stuccoed and painted white, marble chimney-piece and hearth ; two windows, and, at the lower end of the room, two pillars on which stand a mahogany sideboard. On the one side stands a *garde du vin*, on the other side a chair. . . . On the side, where the door opens, which is a long way from the window, stands [the] dining table, with one chair on one side near the pillar. Between the windows is a very pretty round glass, ornamented with gilt papier mâché in great taste, two chairs on each side the fire, a handsome cistern of mahogany with brass hoops, etc., under the sideboard and a Turkey carpet. The back room has only one window, which looks into a little flagged court . . . a marble chimney-piece and hearth, a stove grate, the same to the other parlour ; [it] is wainscot, painted white, has a larger dining table for great days, a wardrobe from Chambers for Mr. Kenyon's clothes, a wash-hand-stand, a little closet, dark, but shelved very conveniently, and four chairs, the same as the dining parlour. The room behind that is white wainscot, has two windows, is as large as the little drawing room, but has nothing at all in it yet. There is a fire-place with a marble chimney-piece ; but that and all the back-rooms [have] common fire-places. Behind that is the back staircase, and beyond that a butler's pantry with a dresser that has two drawers and a cupboard under it, shelves over it for glasses, etc., a lead cistern and pipe with water.

So much for that floor. The front staircase is a very good one with a neat mahogany rail to the top of the house. . . . There is a very handsome glass lamp in the passage, another upon the landing and a third by the dining-room door. The dining room is 21 feet and a half long and 17 feet wide, has [a] marble chimney-piece and hearth, a handsome steel grate, etc. ; [it] is to be new-papered this week. . . . The paper is to be a small patterned flock. . . . The back room has at present a bed in it, which is to be removed . . . and that room is to have the old blue flock paper . . . blue moreen curtains, chairs, a toilet and a book-case. . . . a nice breakfast room. In the little room behind that, which is wainscoted and painted white, is a blue moreen bed, a little chest of dressing drawers and two chairs ; then comes [the] little store-room, which is about as large as half the little drawing-room, has two rows of shelves, a table across the end with drawers and cupboards under, [containing] . . . china, glasses, and all [the] stock of groceries ; the plate chest is to be kept there too when it arrives. Through this closet is the water-closet, very convenient and sweet ; it is over the stable.

Up the next story is [their] lodging-room, over the dining-room. It is hung with a green flock paper, has green moreen bed and window curtains, a large chest upon [another] chest . . . a dressing table and glass in one pier, a small chest of dressing drawers in the other pier, a night-table, a wash-hand stand and eight chairs. The back room is wainscoted and is to have the bed from Chambers in. A maid's room behind that . . . another pretty closet with a linen press, and a large light cupboard or small closet through it. The two back garrets have servants' beds in. The front is a landing. All the garrets have flat roofs and are in every respect as good rooms as those below.

November 1775

Wednesday, November 1st.

The Gabrielle . . . has taken a house in Golden Square and has had a brass plate put on the door, with *Mrs* Gabrielle on it. She and Rauzzini seem admirably suited for each other, for let her live ever so much *en princesse*, he will always keep her in countenance by living *en prince*. He has had his drawing room painted after the manner of the card rooms at the Pantheon, with pink and green and finely ornamented. The first opera is to be next Saturday. . . .

Thursday, November 2nd.

The malignancy of the air was tried on Thursday morning last in the Spa fields by fixing a piece of raw meat to the tail of a paper-kite, which (after being suspended about forty minutes) came down quite putrified, and in one part nearly perforated.

Friday, November 3rd.

The present violent Cold and Cough, with which all ranks of people are more or less afflicted, is equally dangerous as general. Thousands are confined to their beds by it ; many have lost their speech by it, and one Weston, a broker on Saffron hill, has totally lost his hearing by it.

There is thought not to be a single family in London of which one or more are not affected with a violent cold. The physical people attribute this disorder to a noxious quality in the air ; and 'tis observed the same person does not catch it twice.

Saturday, November 4th.

La Gabrielli made her first appearance upon the Opera stage last Saturday. She had frequently disappointed the

221

public by deferring the opera, after it was promised ; but she had only heightened expectation by this coquetry ; and the crowd to see and hear her, was prodigious. . . .

The Opera was the *Didone* of Metastasio ; the very same that La Bastardella sung so many songs from, though new set. The entrance of the Gabrielle was noble. The stage was open to the bottom and she appeared at the most distant part and marched forward quite close to the orchestra, amidst the most violent acclamation of applause. She has a pretty figure, rather short, but charmingly proportioned ; her face is also very pretty. She still looks very young, is rather plump and is perfectly graceful. She walks extremely well, and has great dignity in her air. Her voice is feeble but sweetly toned. She has great powers of execution ; but — she is no Agujari !

Sunday, November 5th.

[Letters from] Warsaw, September 26th [say that] several towns of [Poland] are endeavouring to get rid of the Jews. They are, by a publication, ordered out of Cracow in four weeks time on pain of confiscation of their effects if they were found there afterwards. . . .

Tuesday, November 7th.

The desertion of the theatres in consequence of the disease with which so many are afflicted, has been productive of one agreeable effect, that of bringing Mr. Garrick forward in Benedict much earlier than was expected. It cannot be matter of surprise that Roscius should have escaped the infection, as his spirits and constitution seems proof against the attacks of age itself ; after above thirty campaigns, his ardour and execution appears rather to increase ; Benedict owes all its consequence to his attachment ; there is a peculiar turn of humour in this soldier that none but Mr. Garrick has ever been able to enter into the true spirit of. Last night he supported the character with undiminished excellence, and in the speech where he meditates, and then resolves on marriage, he soared beyond himself. Beatrice is Shakespeare's Benedict in petticoats, and very happily has got into the hands of Mrs. Abingdon.

Thursday, November 9th.

The new and old Lord Mayors, accompanied by aldermen Plomer and Smith, and the sheriffs Hayley and Newnham went from Guildhall to the Three Cranes Stairs, near London Bridge, preceded by the Armourers and Brasiers Company, the man in armour, and the Company of Framework Knitters. They took water about half past twelve and proceeded up the river to Westminster Bridge, where they landed and went in procession to Westminster Hall, and his Lordship was sworn into his office for the year ensuing, before the barons of the Court of Exchequer. After which they took water, landed at Blackfriars Bridge and proceeded through the city to Guildhall. The Lord Mayor's coach was drawn by six fine grey horses, decorated with blue and pink ribbons, preceded by six footmen in blue liveries, embroidered with silver lace.

The Lord Mayor has given to all the poor men belonging to the Company of Frame Knitters, blue loose coats, trimmed with white, and blue caps, and they walked yesterday two and two before the livery of that Company, each with a spear in his hand.

The company last night was very numerous at Guildhall, where everything was conducted with propriety and elegance.

Friday, November 10th.

At the play. Garrick acted and the house was so full you could not have thrust your little finger in, notwithstanding [the] " plague " sweeps us away by dozens. . . . Everybody has had cold, and many violent ones too. . . . The sons of Galen have made a harvest of it, and much human blood has been spilt every hour . . . but with the assistance of black currant jelly, warm broth for dinner, egg wine at night, joined to abstinence from malt liquor, I have as nearly got the better of as violent a cold and sore throat as most have had, — a cold . . . that would have produced an apothecary five pounds with good management. . . .

Saturday, November 11th.

Lord North received . . . the commands of the Cabinet to submit to His Majesty the necessity of a large and speedy augmentation of force and the expediency of trying to obtain a corps of foreign troops. They seem to think it not improbable that by offering large terms to the Duke of Brunswick and the Landgrave of Hesse, they might persuade them to permit their troops to serve in America and in that case they prefer employing the Brunswickers in Canada to sending them to Ireland, which may be accompanied with much ill-humour there. Unless we can as soon as the river St. Lawrence is open, pour in a considerable body of troops to Canada, while a strong reinforcement is sent to General Howe, we must have another defensive campaign in America, which will not be easily borne by the nation, and much discontent here, disgrace there, with a possibility of a foreign war will be the consequence. . . .

Sunday, November 12th.

A small but agreeable concert at . . . Dr. Burney's. Lord Bruce, Lady Edgcumb, Mr. and Mrs. Brudenell, and many fine people were there, amongst others General Baur and Count Orloff, this last the most decorated with diamonds I ever beheld. He had the Empress's picture in diamonds. . . .

Monday, November 13th.

General Gage and some other gentlemen arrived in town from Boston. . . .

Tuesday, November 14th.

It seems to be the opinion now that [the Ministers] will think of pacific measures [for America]. They have even talked in Parliament of treating . . . but I doubt peace is not so near. The Parliament grants whatever is asked ; and yet a great alteration has happened in the administration. The Duke of Grafton has changed sides, and was turned out last Friday. Lord Rochford, too, has retired, though not out of humour ; and Lord Dartmouth has quitted the American province and taken the Privy Seal. Lord George Germain is made Secretary of State for America, and Lord Weymouth has taken the southern province. Lord Ashburnham is to be Groom of the Stole, Lord Pelham Master of the Great Wardrobe, and Lord Lyttelton Justice in Eyre. The town is impatient to see whether this change of men implies any change of measure . . . [but] none of the new ministers have ever inclined to the Americans. . . .

Madame Kingston has petitioned the House of Lords for her trial ; but they seem neither eager to acquit or condemn her. . . .

Orloff the Great, or rather the Big, is . . . as proud of his infamous diamonds as the Duchess of Kingston herself. He dances gigantic dances and makes gigantic love ; but no conquests : yet he has quitted his post with honour, for the Empress has appointed two to supply his functions — I suppose they are Gog and Magog.

Wednesday, November 15th.

On Saturday last Henry Thrale, Esq., his lady and daughter, accompanied by Dr. Samuel Johnson, and Mr. Baretti, returned from a tour through France, and the Low Countries.

Thursday, November 16th.

Mr. Burke moved that —" leave be given to bring in a bill for composing the present troubles, and quieting the minds of His Majesty's subjects in America." He prefaced his motion with a speech, which lasted more than three hours and kept up the attention of the House during the whole time. Among other things, he reminded the House how often administration had been told the consequences of those oppressive measures of shutting up the American Ports, revoking their charters, depriving them of trial by the vicinage, taxing them and endeavouring to starve them ; and he warned them for the last time to put an end to the troubles in America by con-ciliatory measures, or, said he, whichever side prevails the Empire of Britain will be undone ; many of his arguments were irresistible ; and those who did not approve could not oppose. . . .

A little before four o'clock in the morning . . . the House divided. Ayes 105, Noes 210.

Saturday, November 18th.

[From] Warsaw, October 28th. The deplorable situation

of the city of Danzig seems to interest the republic very seriously ; in consequence of which complaints have been made to the ministers residing here from Vienna, Petersburgh, London and Copenhagen, of the behaviour of the Court of Berlin to the city of Danzig, and praying them to engage their respective Courts to employ their good offices with His Prussian Majesty, in favour of that unhappy city.

Sunday, November 19*th.*

One Smart, charged with coining and likely to suffer for it, the evidence against him being remarkably strong, contrived to make his escape out of Clerkenwell Bridewell by [an] odd stratagem. His wife went into the prison clothed in two gowns, two pair of stockings, four petticoats, and in short an assortment of clothes for two women ; soon after which the husband passed out, dressed in what the wife had worn as the under suit of clothes, and with his face painted. Soon after he was gone the woman came downstairs, and meeting two men at the door who asked how her husband did, she said very ill in his room, and then went off with them. The woman, however, was soon after apprehended and lodged in New Prison.

Monday, November 20*th.*

Lord North moved the House that leave be given to bring in a bill to prohibit all trade and intercourse with the united colonies (naming them) during the continuance of the present rebellion ; for repealing the Boston Port Bill, the fishery and restraining bills ; and to enable His Majesty to appoint commissioners, and to issue proclamations in the cases and for the purpose therein to be mentioned ; which after a long debate was agreed to without a division. In consequence of this bill every ship in the navy under 40 guns is ordered to be got ready to carry the bill into execution.

Tuesday, November 21*st.*

The new comic opera [by Richard Sheridan, Esq.] called *The Duenna* was . . . received with every mark of approbation that could be given. It will be repeated to-morrow evening with the farce of *The Apprentice.* . . .

Wednesday, November 22nd.

[Dr. Franklin writes to Dr. Joseph Priestley, from Philadelphia, October 3rd :]   Britain, at the expense of three millions, has killed 150 yankees this campaign, which is £20,000 a head ; and at Bunker's Hill she gained a mile of ground, half of which she lost again by our taking post on Ploughed Hill.   During the same time 60,000 children have been born in America.   From these data [Dr. Price's] mathematical head will easily calculate the time and expense necessary to kill us all and conquer the whole of our territory.

Thursday, November 23rd.

In the space of a very few years I have observed a total revolution in the conduct of the common people respecting their diseased friends ; they have learned that most diseases are mitigated by a free admission of air, by cleanliness, and by promoting, instead of restraining, the indulgence and ease of the sick.   Such instruction was new to the poor, though important to their preservation ; and when we consider how late they have acquired this information, we must lament that so many centuries have elapsed before an institution like the General Dispensary became the object of public attention. . . .

Baths for the use of the poor have never yet been constructed, except in a few hospitals, where they are open only to their own patients.   The Dispensary, therefore, which relieves thousands, who either cannot get admitted into an hospital or who do not choose to leave their habitations and families, must remain imperfect, till it is furnished both with a warm and a cold bath ; the expense of which cannot be considered as burthensome to a Charity whose finances are daily augmenting and whose primary design is the good of the poor.

Friday, November 24th.

The Government plan of negotiation with America is to be conducted in the following manner : thirty-six commissioners are to be sent to America, vested with ample powers to treat for peace or push on a war to the utmost extremity.

The leading commissioner nominated for the American negotiation is Lord Howe.

Monday, November 27th.

On Saturday evening Signora Gabrielli, having in a great measure got the better of the reigning influenza, exerted her powers to the admiration of a very splendid and crowded audience. She introduced a Rondeau new set by Giardini, which did infinite credit to the abilities of the composer, as well as to the taste and execution of this foreign siren.

Wednesday, November 29th.

[Mr. John Wesley has] published the following in *Lloyd's Evening Post* :—

SIR,

I have been seriously asked, From what motive did you publish your *Calm Address to the American Colonies* ?

I seriously answer, Not to get money. Had that been my motive, I should have swelled it into a shilling pamphlet, and have entered it at Stationers'-Hall :

Not to get preferment for myself, or my brother's children. I am a little too old to gape after it for myself ; and if my brother or I sought it for them, we have only to show them to the world. Not to please any man living, high or low. I know mankind too well ; I know they that love you for political service, love you less than their dinner ; and they that hate you, hate you worse than the Devil.

Least of all did I write with a view to inflame any ; just the contrary. I contributed my mite toward putting out the flame which rages all over the land. This I have more opportunity of observing than any other man in England. I see with pain to what a height this already rises, in every part of the nation ; and I see many pouring oil into the flame, by crying out, " How unjustly, how cruelly the King is using the poor Americans, who are only contending for their liberty, and for their legal privileges."

Now there is no possible way to put out this flame, or hinder its rising higher and higher, but to show that the Americans are not used either cruelly or unjustly ; that they are not injured at all, seeing they are not contending for liberty ; (this they had even in its full extent, both civil and religious ;) neither for any legal privileges ; for they enjoy all that their charters grant : but what they contend for is, the illegal privilege of being exempt from parliamentary taxation. A privilege this, which no charter ever gave to any American colony yet ; which no charter can give, unless it be confirmed both by King, Lords, and Commons ; which, in fact, our Colonies never had ; which they never claimed till the present reign : and probably they would not have claimed it now, had they not been incited thereto by letters from England. . . .

This being the real state of the question, without any colouring or aggravation, what impartial man can either blame the King, or commend the Americans ?

With this view, to quench the fire, by laying the blame where it was due, the *Calm Address* was written.

I am, Sir,

Your humble Servant,

JOHN WESLEY

[He adds] As to Reviewers, Newswriters, London Magazines, and all that kind of gentlemen, they behave just as I expected they would ; and let them lick up Mr. Toplady's spittle still ; a champion worthy of their cause !

Thursday, November 30th.

Many people are out of town. Amid these bustles stocks keep up. It is said the Americans have paid off large debts by sending the produce of their country, rice, tobacco, &c., hither. We have a very large and profitable trade with Russia and the North of Germany. Our harvest this year has been very plentiful. This plenty and the flourishing state of the manufactures is a reason, and I think a good one, why the recruiting service is not so successful. . . .

DECEMBER 1775

Friday, December 1st.

A gentleman at Greenwich has for some time kept a beautiful young bull, with black and white spots, in training, and has brought him to such a pitch of tameness as to be rode full gallop without a bridle, which he frequently does at Blackheath, and other places.

Sunday, December 3rd.

The Duchess of Kingston was suddenly seized with a fainting during divine service in the Chapel Royal at St. James's, and carried home speechless. Her Grace is since greatly recovered and reported by her physicians to be out of danger. It is not yet certain, whether Her Grace will take her trial before the House of Peers or obtain her release by a *Noli Prosequi.*

Wednesday, December 6th.

Yesterday one of the Bluecoat boys who drew the [State Lottery] numbers at Guildhall, was examined before Sir Charles Asgill, relative to a number that was drawn out before ten o'clock last Friday, which was insured by a person at almost every office in London ; when the boy confessed that he was prevailed on to take out a number the night before, and after the man had wrote it down, the boy the next morning pretended to put it in the wheel and drew it out ; by which the man has been paid upwards of £400 and would have received £3000, had all the offices paid him, but some of them suspected a fraud. Search is making after the man. It is said, that the same person attempted the like scheme at the drawing of the Museum Lottery, but the boy then discovered the affair to the commissioners, which frustrated his intentional fraud upon the office keepers at that time.

Thursday, December 7th.

At Lisbon an Italian, a native of Genoa named John Baptist Pele, was drawn in quarters by four horses after having his hands chopped off, and afterwards burnt to ashes for having plotted the death of the Marquis of Pombal. It is said he denied the fact to the last and though he suffered both the ordinary and extraordinary tortures yet from the beginning to his dying moments he uttered not a groan.

Friday, December 8th.

Came on at the Old Bailey the trial of Margaret Caroline Rudd for feloniously forging on the 24th of December last, a certain paper-writing, purporting to be a bond signed by William Adair, etc. with intent to defraud the said William Adair ; and for feloniously uttering and publishing the same. . . .

The chief witnesses against the prisoner were Mrs. Perreau, wife of Robert Perreau, and John Moody, who lived as servant to Daniel Perreau : the first endeavoured to prove the publishing of the bond ; the latter the forging it. Sir Thomas Frankland proved only the lending the money upon it. The counsel for the prisoner objected to the competency of Mrs. Perreau as a witness, she being interested in the conviction on her husband's account, but that was over-ruled. The material part of her evidence was, that on the 24th of December last, she saw Mrs. Rudd deliver a bond to her husband Mr. Perreau ; that she knew it was a bond because Mr. Perreau laid it down upon the table while he was brushing his coat and she looked at it ; that it was for £5,300 made payable to Robert Perreau and signed William Adair ; and the witnesses were Arthur Jones and Thomas Start or Hart. Being asked when she saw the bond again, she said, the day after her husband's conviction (the 8th of March) it was brought to her with other bonds, to see if she knew it to be the same bond delivered to her husband the 24th of December. She selected it from the rest, she said, and made her mark upon it : that on Mrs. Rudd's delivering it to Mr. Perreau, Mrs. Rudd said, Mr. Adair would be very much obliged to Mr. Perreau to try to raise upon that bond the sum of £4,000 of Sir Thomas Frankland.

Being cross-examined, she said, she did not know that she had ever seen a bond before (the 24th of December) in her life ; that she had no suspicion when she first looked at the bond that anything was wrong. She was then asked, How she came to recollect so particularly every circumstance about the bond in question, so as to know the name of the obligors, to whom payable, the sum for which the bond was given, the name of the witnesses, and that so very exactly as at the distance of three months to be able to select the bond from other bonds by a similitude of circumstances ? Her answer was, I have the happiness to have a good memory. She was asked, if in selecting the bond in question, she had not looked over the other bonds that were presented to her at the same time ? She acknowledged she had. Then said the counsel, Does your excellent memory enable you to remember the date or sum in any one paper produced to you ? Her answer was, *I do not remember.*

John Moody's evidence amounted to this : That he had lived with the prisoner as a servant ; that he had particularly remarked that his mistress wrote two hands, a common and a feigned hand ; that she wrote her feigned hand when she wrote letters to his master as coming from Mr. William Adair, and her common hand in noting the ordinary business of the house ; that he really believed he should know her hand-writing ; and being shown the name William Adair signed to the bond, he said, the name William Adair appears to be the same hand the letters were wrote in which I gave to Daniel Perreau as coming from Mr. William Adair, which I saw Mrs. Rudd write the directions of. Do you believe the name William Adair to the bond is the prisoner's handwriting ? " I believe it is her handwriting." Being asked on his cross examination, if he had ever seen his mistress write the name William Adair ? he said, he never had. On the credibility of these two witnesses the truth of the fact seemed to depend. Sir Thomas Frankland's evidence tended only to prove that Robert Perreau borrowed £4,000 of him upon the bond in question, and that he had given Robert Perreau a draft for £3,890 deducting the discount of £5,000 formerly lent, with the discount of the money then borrowed ; and £15, 10s. for a lottery ticket ; that he had since received, among other things, jewels to the value of £2,800 with women's wearing apparel, etc. which might, for what he knew, be the prisoner's, but were sold to him by the two Perreaus by a bill of sale. The other witnesses produced were equally immaterial with that of Sir Thomas with respect to the bringing home the forgery to the prisoner : a Christian Hart, indeed, proves a paper to have been given her by the prisoner, the purport of which was to show a combination against her life to have been concerted at the witness's house by Sir Thomas Frankland, and the friends of the Perreaus which, though infamous, if Hart's evidence is credited, yet could not at all affect the present prosecution. When put upon her defence her address to the jury was short and pertinent ; and concluded in these words : " Gentlemen, you are honest men, and I am safe in your hands." The jury brought in their verdict very properly. " According to the evidence before us, NOT GUILTY." . . .

Monday, December 11th.

Being the anniversary of the institution of the Royal Academy of Painting, etc. a general assembly of the academicians was held at Somerset House for the purpose of electing officers for the year ensuing, when Sir Joshua Reynolds was re-elected president. . . .

Tuesday, December 12th.

The Bill for destroying the American shipping was passed in the House of Commons by 112 to 16. The Opposition had so deserted (gone to the country) that this was all the force they could muster. . . .

Wednesday, December 13th.

By a letter from an officer in the garrison at Mahon, advice is received, that a frigate belonging to Admiral Mann's squadron has taken a Tunisian piratical Corsair, with a number of English seamen on board chained to the oar, and carried her into Gibraltar.

Thursday, December 14th.

Mr. Sayre has given directions to his solicitor, to commence actions against Lord Rochford, the Under Secretaries of State, and the King's Messengers, that the personal liberty of every Englishman may again be asserted in his person, and the seizure of papers condemned by an English jury.

Friday, December 15th.

It appears to me that American politics are very much altered. Taxation and the exercise of it are totally renounced. You never hear the right mentioned but in order to give it up. The rigid politician of last year, such a man for instance as Welbore Ellis, stands almost single in the House of Commons.

[At the sessions which ended yesterday at the Old Bailey] William Wheeler was indicted for feloniously being found at large in this Kingdom before the expiration of the term for which he had received sentence to be transported. . . .

[The prisoner deposed :] " I was in America last February ; they insisted at Virginia upon my taking up arms against the Regulars at Boston. I told them I would not fight against my King and country. . . . They insisted upon it I should fight, and provided me arms, and put on me a coat with *Death or Liberty* upon one side of it. . . . I made my escape to a seaport town and took shipping and came to London. I had leave to come on shore, and as I was going to return from Darkhouse Lane I was taken."

[He was found guilty and sentenced to death.]

Saturday, December 16th.

Omiah . . . now walks everywhere quite alone, and has lodgings in Warwick Street, where he lives by himself. The King allows him a pension. He has learnt a great deal of English . . . and can with the assistance of signs and action make himself tolerably well understood. He pronounces English quite different from other foreigners and sometimes unintelligibly. However, he has really made a great proficiency, considering the disadvantages he labours under which render his studying the language so much more difficult to him than to other strangers, for he knows nothing of letters and there are so very few persons who are acquainted with his language. . . .

He is lively and intelligent and seems so open and frank-hearted, that he looks everyone in the face as his friend and well-wisher. . . .

Monday, December 18th.

Some very disagreeable news was received yesterday from Canada. Our people have been forced to yield up Fort St. John's to the rebels, for want of fuel and provisions ; and the garrison of near 500 men are made prisoners. General Carleton, who marched to relieve them, has been repulsed and obliged to retreat to Montreal, the fate of which place is greatly to be apprehended. . . .

Thursday, December 21st.

[Mr. Richard Cumberland] has written an Ode, as he modestly calls it, in praise of Gray's Odes ; charitably no doubt to make the latter taken notice of. Garrick read it the other night at Mr. Beauclerk's, who comprehended so little what it was about, that he desired Garrick to read it backwards, and try if it would not be equally good ; he did, and it was. . . .

Saturday, December 23rd.

His Majesty went to the House of Peers and gave the royal assent to the following bills, viz.

The bill to prohibit all trade and intercourse with the North American colonies now in actual rebellion, viz. New Hampshire, Massachusetts Bay, Connecticut, Rhode Island, New York, Pennsylvania, the three lower counties on Delaware, Maryland, Virginia, North Carolina, South Carolina and Georgia, during the continuance thereof.

The bill for the better regulation of His Majesty's marine forces while on shore.

The bill to encourage adventurers to make a discovery of the northern passage from Europe, by British subjects only, to the western or southern ocean of America, and for penetrating to the North Pole. . . .

This morning Brook Watson, Esq., arrived at Lord George Germain's office from Quebec with dispatches from Major General Carleton, dated Montreal, the 5th of November, containing intelligence that General Carleton, not being able to collect a force that might be depended upon for the relief of St. John's, the rebels had taken advantage of the defection of the lower class of Canadians to press forward their enterprize ; and the forts of Chamblée and St. John, upon Richelieu river, the latter of which had stopped the progress of the rebels for above two months, had surrendered and the garrisons were made prisoners upon capitulation.

By a letter from Lieutenant-Governor Cramabé, dated Quebec, Nov. 9, it appears that a party of rebels under the command of one Arnold had invaded the province by way of the river Chaudière ; and that part of them were actually arrived and had taken post at Point Levi opposite to Quebec.

Sunday, December 24th.

[Lately published :]
The Probability of reaching the North Pole discussed. 4to. 2s. 6d.

Journal of the Resolution's Voyage, in 1772, 1773, 1774 and 1775, on Discovery to the Southern Hemisphere. Also, a Journal of the Adventure's Voyage in the years 1772, 1773 and 1774. With an Account of the Separation of the two Ships and the most remarkable Incidents that befell each. 8vo. 5s. boards.

The amazing curiosity which the voyages published, under the name of the late Dr. Hawkesworth, excited will doubtless stamp a value upon this journal. . . . The great point whether the continent towards the southern pole did or did not exist is determined in the negative.

Experiments and Observations on Different Kinds of Air. Vol. II. by Joseph Priestley, LL.D., F.R.S.

[Dr. Priestley writes of his discovery of Dephlogisticated Air:] On the 1st of August, 1774, I endeavoured to extract air from *mercurius calcinatus per se.* . . . Having got three or four times as much as the bulk of my materials I admitted water to it and found that it was not imbibed by it.   But what surprised me more than I can well express was that a candle burned in this air with a remarkably vigorous flame. . . . I was utterly at a loss how to account for it. . . . Being at Paris in the October following . . . I frequently mentioned my surprise . . . to Mr. Lavoisier, Mr. Le Roy and several other philosophers. . . .

Tuesday, December 26th.

General Burgoyne arrived in town [yesterday] from Boston, which he left the 5th instant ; the troops at that time were well supplied.

This day arrived also Lieut. Pringle from Quebec.   He brings advice that Montreal is in the hands of the provincials and that General Carleton, with his garrison, was retired to Quebec. . . .

Thursday, December 28th.

A new museum, under the title of *Spectacle Mechanique*, [has been] opened in King Street, Covent Garden. . . . It consists of three capital mechanical figures and a pastoral scene with figures of an inferior size.—The figure on the left hand side (a beautiful boy as large as life) writes anything that is dictated to him in a very fine hand.— The second on the right hand (of the same size) draws various landscapes, etc., etc. which he finishes in a most accurate and masterly style.— The third figure is a beautiful young lady who plays several elegant airs on the harpsichord, with all the bass accompaniments ; her head gracefully moving to the tune and her bosom discovering a delicate respiration ; during her performance the pastoral scene in the centre discovers a variety of mechanical figures, admirably grouped, all of which seem endued with life.— The last curiosity is a canary-bird in a cage that hops to and fro upon its perch and then whistles two or three airs in the most natural manner imaginable.— Upon the whole, no exertion of art ever perhaps trod so close on the heels of nature.   The ingenious artist is a young man, a native of Switzerland.

Friday, December 29th.

It may be gathered from authentic papers. — That our stage-coaches generally drive with eight inside and often ten outside passengers each. — That there are now of these vehicles, flies, machines, and diligences, upwards of 400 ; and of other four-wheeled carriages 17,000. — That 12,300,000 newspapers are now annually printed. — That the number of packs of cards stamped last year amounted to 428,000 ; and of dice to 3,000. . . .

Saturday, December 30th.

Last night a young lady [Mrs. Sarah Siddons] made her first appearance on a London theatre, in Drury Lane, in the character of Portia, in *The Merchant of Venice*. The most accomplished actress can display little other abilities in this part than a correct elocution, and a knowledge of the author. The lady of last night being thus circumstanced, it is impossible to pronounce what the nature or extent of her powers may enable her to execute when placed in a situation that calls them forth. But from the specimen she gave, there is not room to expect anything beyond mediocrity. Her figure and face, though agreeable, have nothing striking, her voice (that great requisite of all public speakers) is far from being favourable to her progress as an actress. It is feared she possesses a monotony not to be got rid of ; there is also vulgarity in her tones, ill calculated to sustain that line in a theatre she has at first been held forth in ; but as these observations are formed when the lady laboured under the disadvantages of a first attempt in the metropolis, her future efforts perhaps may entirely remove them.

SEVENTEEN SEVENTY SIX

January 1776

Monday, January 1st.

To Mr. Urban, on completing the XLV Volume of the "Gentleman's Magazine"

Close, Urban, close th' historic page
Disgrac'd with more than civil rage ;
And may our annals never tell
To that dire rage what victims fell !
Let dark oblivion hide the plain
O'erspread with heaps of *Britons* slain,
Friends, brothers, parents, in the blood
Of brothers, friends and sons imbrued !
While *Canada* disclaims our sway,
Those laurels withering in a day,
Which scarce whole years of toil could yield,
The growth of many a well-fought field.
For this, with transient glory fired,
Have *Britain's* bravest sons expired ?
For this was *Howe*, was *Wolfe*, decreed
To fight, to conquer and to bleed ? . . .

Griev'd at the past, yet more we fear
The horrors of the coming year,
Ships sunk or plundered, slaughtered hosts,
Towns burnt and desolated coasts.
Yet sever'd by the *Atlantic* main,
Though great, our efforts must be vain :
Resources so remote must fail,
Nor skill, nor valour can prevail :
When winds, waves, elements are foes,
In vain all human means oppose.

At length, when all these contests cease,
And *Britain* weary'd rests in peace,
Our sons, beneath yon Western skies
Shall see one vast republic rise :
Another *Athens*, *Sparta*, *Rome*
Shall there unbounded sway assume ;
Thither her ball shall Empire roll,
And *Europe's* pamper'd states control. . . .

Wednesday, January 3rd.

The father of the runaway siren of Covent Garden Theatre apprehended the little wanton truant at her aunt's in the city, and forcing her into a coach, drove off with her into the country : however she had not been carried above five miles before her cries raised the inhabitants of a village ; whom she soon worked to her purpose by declaring that the man, (her father) was carrying her away by force, in order to ship her for America. . . . The peasants released her, when she run to town across the country, and has not since been retaken by her father.

Saturday, January 6th.

On Sunday morning last was run the famous match between Mr. Hetherington's and Mr. Higgs's ponies (twenty miles on the Uxbridge road) for fifty guineas, each riding his own pony, and his own weight ; which, as it was a crossing and jostling match, afforded great sport to the spectators. It was won by half a head by Mr. Higgs, who jockeyed Mr. Hetherington twice into the ditch. Also the same day Mr. Shedrach's famous horse Shuffler, and Mr. Mishach's famous horse Monkey, trotted two miles on the Romford road, for fifty guineas, which was won with great ease by the former, (by the superior skill of his rider) who trotted the two miles in six minutes and four seconds.

Sunday, January 7th.

The wife of Robert Perreau accompanied by her three children, dressed in deep mourning, presented a petition to the Queen in favour of her husband. It was a picture of distress which surpassed imagination.   Her Majesty seemed much affected.

Friday, January 12*th.*

Yesterday one of the Bath coaches came to town, to the Bear, in Piccadilly, being one out of six that should have been in town the evening before ;   the above coach got to town with fourteen horses, and near Hungerford was dug out of the snow.   It is more than eight feet deep at Marlborough, and several other places in the western road.

Saturday, January 13*th.*

[Mr. Garrick writes to Sir W. Young :]
I have ventured to produce *Hamlet* with alterations.   It was the most imprudent thing I ever did in all my life ;   but I had sworn I would not leave the stage till I had rescued that noble play from all the rubbish of the fifth act.   I have brought it forth without the grave-digger's trick and the fencing match.   The alteration was received with general approbation, beyond my most warm expectations.

I shall play Lear next week and Macbeth (perhaps) in the old dresses, with new scenes, the week after that, and then exit Roscius. . . .

Sunday, January 14*th.*

There are positive orders sent to Lord Howe and General Carleton to send over no more prisoners of war, as the Ministry are in the greatest dilemma imaginable what to do with those they already have.   To try and condemn them would be a mockery, as they afterwards would be afraid to execute them, the Americans having more regular prisoners in number and quality, and would, no doubt, immediately put in force the law of retaliation.

Wednesday, January 17*th.*

This morning the convicts ordered for execution were carried from Newgate to Tyburn. . . . George Lee (for robbing Thomas Cuddin, Esq. on the highway) Saunders, Alexander and Lyon Abrahams, alias Lipe, (for breaking into the house of Mr. Sandford, baker, in Winchester Street, etc.) in a cart : Richard Baker and John Radcliffe, (for counterfeiting the silver coin of this kingdom, viz. half crowns, shillings, and sixpences,) on a hurdle : and Robert and Daniel Perreau, (the former for uttering as true, a forged bond for £7,500 with intent to defraud Messrs Drummonds, and the latter for uttering a bond for £3,500 with intent to defraud Dr. Brooks,) in a mourning coach drawn by four horses, and attended by a gentleman and a clergyman : the Sheriffs preceded them in their carriages. At the place of execution they all behaved becoming their unhappy fate ; and little was said that could be heard owing to the great concourse of people present both in carriages, on horseback and on foot, thousands of whom came away without being able to get near. Hearses attended to receive the bodies of the two unfortunate brothers. Lee, the highwayman was a handsome young fellow, dressed in a crimson suit of clothes, with a gold laced hat, which he pulled off to a young woman in a hackney coach, genteely dressed in white, in Holborn, who immediately burst into tears.

Thursday, January 18th.

The King and Queen entered the ball room at nine . . . at St. James's, when the ball opened with a minuet by the Prince of Hesse and Lady Betty Stanley ; the Prince danced the next with Lady Essex. Lords Stanley, Maynard and Cholmondley danced minuets but very few other gentlemen, so that many ladies were disappointed. The best dressed woman in the room was Lady Stanley, in a mouse-coloured satin embroidered with variegated coloured flowers, with an antique border on the adametic plan. Lady Gideon sported an extraordinary head upon the occasion, which forced a smile from her Majesty ; the lower part of her hair was like a man's wig, the upper part terminated in a lofty peak, like a grenadier's cap, with a bouquet on the top of all. The most elegant dressed gentleman was Lord Monson ; a pink satin suit embroidered with a mosaical white silk and in the centre of each square, a delicate flower of embroidery. Two ladies, Quakers, (one Mr. Barclay's daughter, of Cheapside) were noticed for the elegance and simplicity of their dress. His Majesty was in

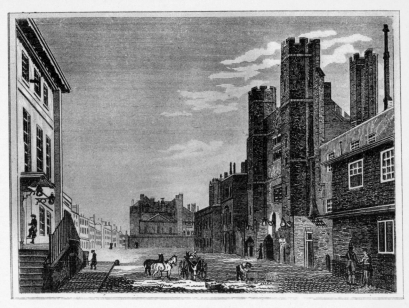

THE GATE OF ST. JAMES'S PALACE IN 1776
From E. W. Brayley's 'Londiniana'

THE MANSION HOUSE
From 'London and its Environs'

light blue and gold ; the Queen (who is always in an undress
on her birthday) in a suit of dark brown satin.

Friday, January 19th.

David Garrick, Esq., has signed and sealed for the sale of
his share in the patent and property of Drury Lane Theatre.
The purchasers are Dr. Ford, Mr. Ewart, Mr. Linley and
Mr. Richard Sheridan.   The purchase money is £35,000.
The public may now, therefore, depend upon it that this will
be the last season of Mr. Garrick's performing.   The new
proprietors, as an act of their own, have stipulated that Mr.
Garrick shall continue to keep that box which has of late years
been set apart for the accommodation of his family.

Mr. Garrick last night intimated to the audience his having
sold his share in Drury Lane Theatre, by answering in the part
of Abel Drugger, on being asked if he had any interest at the
theatre, " I *had* some, I don't know what I may have."

Saturday, January 20th.

So dreadful and impassable are the northern roads that
Lord George Germain's carriage was preceded all the way
from Northampton by a large party of pioneers, who cut
occasional passages for it through the snow, or otherwise his
Lordship could not have arrived in town to have assisted at the
Privy Council, which was held on Monday last.

It is expected every tide that the river will be froze entirely
up between London and Westminster Bridge, the floating
mountains of ice-snow that incessantly come down, afford a
striking though an awful scene. . . .

Monday last the penny-post going from Windsor to Sunning-
wells was lost in the snow, with the bag of letters about him.

Sunday, January 21st.

This evening the remains of the two Perreaus were carried
from the house of Robert Perreau in Golden Square, and after
the usual solemnities deposited in the vault belonging to St.
Martin's Church.   The coffins were covered with black cloth
and black nails, with a black plate on each on which were
inscribed their names. . . . They were carried in separate

hearses, attended by their friends in mourning coaches and by an innumerable crowd of spectators, who behaved with decency till they came to the entrance of the church ; but there they became so rude that it was with difficulty the bodies and mourners could get entrance. . . .

Monday, January 22nd.

Letters of the late Rev. Mr. Laurence Sterne to his most intimate Friends. With a fragment in the manner of Rabelais. To which are prefixed Memoirs of his Life and Family. Written by himself and published by his daughter, Mrs. Medalle. In 3 vols. small 8vo. 7s. 6d. sewed. Becket.

Mrs. Medalle sent to all the correspondents of her deceased father, begging the letters which he had written to them ; among other wits she sent to Wilkes with the same request. He sent for answer, that as there happened to be nothing extraordinary in those he had received, he had burnt or lost them. On which the faithful editor of her father's works sent back to say, that if Mr. Wilkes would be so good as to write a few letters in imitation of her father's style, it would do just as well, and she would insert them. . . .

Wednesday, January 24th.

The dispute so long depending between the Duke of Bridgewater and Sir Richard Brooke is now amicably settled, and his Grace's navigation near Norton will soon be completed and goods conveyed between Manchester and Liverpool without transhipping. The public, by this agreement, will save at least £3,000 per annum, which sum was expended in conveying the merchants' goods between the two ends of the canal ; besides being supplied plentifully and reasonably with excellent coal.

Thursday, January 25th.

Captain Cook in the new voyage which he is going to make, (Captain Clarke, the commander of the second ship) is to take Omiah to Otaheite, and from thence to proceed upon the discovery of the North-west Passage to the Northwards of California. Parliament have just offered £25,000 reward, £20,000 to those who discover the passage, £5,000 to those who

approach within one degree of the Pole ; but there are to be
no men of science, such as botanists, designers, etc. to accompany
them.

Friday, January 26th.

Great reliance is put in the plan of declaring the negroes
in the Southern Provinces free as an encouragement to join
the King's troops destined to act in that quarter. . . .

Saturday, January 27th.

The House of Commons met yesterday with a design to
have chosen a committee to try the merits of the Worcester
petition ; at the usual hour for balloting, the Deputy Sergeant
was dispatched with his Mace to the coffee houses and other
places adjoining to the House of Commons ; he rummaged
every house, avenue and corner without success, and upon his
return the Speaker adjourned, not having above four score
members. It is imagined, that had the Deputy Sergeant gone
to the Serpentine river he might have completed his complement with the Honourable Gentlemen belonging to St.
Stephen's Chapel, who were skating thereon.

Since the execution of the Perreaus the people appear to
be as much divided in their opinions about the guilt or innocence
of Robert Perreau as about the American cause. . . .

Sunday, January 28th.

The Rev. Mr. John Wesley preached in the parish church
of St. Allhallows, in Lombard Street. By particular desire,
Mr. Wesley selected his text from Revelations, Chap. XX,
ver. 12. . . . Mr. Wesley bore his testimony against the horrible
Calvinan opinions of absolute necessity and unconditional
Predestination, which make the Holy God and Judge of all, the
author of Sin, and render the death of Christ a needless thing.
Mr. Wesley earnestly warned his hearers against such diabolical
Creeds and called upon all the ministers of the Gospel of Christ,
and of the Church of England to preach against necessity,
Calvinism, and Antinomianism, the horrible tenets of our day.

Monday, January 29th.

The government is straining every nerve to muster a great army in America, though it must combat for its very landing. Fifteen thousand Hessians and Brunswickers are retained. This force, if half of it can get thither and land, must be maintained from hence. We are not apt to be frugal about our armies abroad. The millions this will cost. . . . Boston is famishing ; what is the fate of Quebec, we do not yet know. The Parliament is met, but two-thirds of the members are frozen in the country.

Omiah . . . breakfasted with Mr. Conway today, and learns to skate. He had no notion of ice, and calls it *stone-water* ; a very good expression. . . .

Wednesday, January 31st.

The finest naval bull that ever hibernized the history of any country, was lately made by Admiral Graves, who commands the fleet on the American station : when General Carleton sent to the Commander-in-Chief at Boston for a reinforcement of a few hundred men, the Admiral was immediately applied to by General Howe, for vessels to carry the said forces to Quebec. However, the prudence of this brave tar superseded all their orders, for he sent a man-of-war to Quebec to assure General Carleton " that His Majesty's ships-of-war could not at that season of the year, make any port in Canada." — *Risum teneatis !* Besides, the single ship that carried this curious bull, would have conveyed nearly the complement of men required, though not a single soldier was sent in her !

FEBRUARY 1776

Friday, February 2nd.

An officer who is just arrived from America, gives an account that so great a respect and veneration do the people of that country pay Lord Chatham, that upon Lord Pitt's first landing there, they got an exact description of his person, which was given in orders to the Riflemen, with an intent to spare him upon all engagements. It was likewise given in constant orders, should he be taken prisoner, to treat him with all imaginable respect, the etiquette of which was even settled in every particular.

The guards are everyday practising the use of the rifle gun in Hyde Park ; the barrels of these new fangled instruments of death are on so particular a construction, that a pistol carries 300 yards ; and some of the men are already so dexterous, that they can hit the centre of a small target at that distance. Whether they will be such good marksmen when there is a rifle gun opposed against them, is another question.

Saturday, February 3rd.

"THE DUENNA, OR DOUBLE ELOPEMENT," A NEW SONG TO AN OLD TUNE

> In the days of Gay, they sing and say,
>   The Town was full of folly :
> For all day long, its sole sing-song,
>   Was pretty, pretty Polly.
>
> So now-a-days, as it was in Gay's,
>   The world's run mad agen-a :
> From morn to night its whole delight
>   To cry up *The Duenna*.

249

One half the Town still talks of Brown,
    The other of Leoni,
While those sly curs, the managers,
    Keeping pocketing the money.

Nor flatters less this strange success
    The modest Master Sherry ;
For strange enough, that such sad stuff
    Should make dull folks so merry.

God save my head !   What have I said ?
    Our gracious King and Queen-a
Already twice, (or may be thrice),
    Have been at *The Duenna*.

Friday, February 9th.

A ship which left Virginia the 12th of January brings an
account that Lord Dunmore had landed, and in attacking
some entrenchments of the Provincials had been repulsed with
the loss of seventy or eighty men and with difficulty regained
his ship.   By their last accounts from Canada General Montgomery was preparing to attack Quebec in a few days.   The
ministry say he had made an attempt and had been repulsed
with loss.   Nothing new at Boston — provisions very scarce,
but it is thought the troops in it may hold out. . . .

Monday, February 12th.

They write from Bath, that no season was ever known to be
near so full as the late one : — lodgings at last were not to be
had for love or money : — the Prince of Hesse, after every
enquiry, was obliged to put up with a single bedchamber on
the second floor at one of the taverns.

Wednesday, February 14th.

The occasion of the Duke of Grafton's disgust with the
Court was owing to a refusal he met with in an application
for a considerable church preferment to Mr. S ——, a relation
of the Duchess of Grafton.   Lord North immediately promised
the thing upon the first mention of it, but upon the Duke's

applying a second time, he found the King had mentioned it for another person ; that person happening to be nearly related to Sir Gilbert Elliot made the Duke endeavour to trace the whole affair to its source, when he found that Sir Gilbert Elliot, after knowing of his Grace's application to Lord North, had gone to the King and desired the same preferment, which he obtained at once. The Duke, as well he might, was infinitely disgusted, and upon finding himself treated in a manner not very well calculated to soothe him, pursued that public line of conduct which has occasioned some surprises in the political world.

Sunday, February 18th.

There is just appeared a truly classic work ; a history, not majestic like Livy, nor compressed like Tacitus ; not stamped with character like Clarendon ; perhaps not so deep as Robertson's *Scotland,* but a thousand degrees above his *Charles* ; not pointed like Voltaire, but as accurate as he is inexact ; modest as he is *tranchant* and sly as Montesquieu without being so *recherché.* The style is as smooth as a Flemish picture, and the muscles are concealed and only for natural uses, not exaggerated like Michael Angelo's to show the painter's skill in anatomy ; nor composed of the limbs of clowns of different nations, like Dr. Johnson's heterogeneous monsters. This book is Mr. Gibbon's *History of the Decline and Fall of the Roman Empire.* He is son of a foolish alderman, is a member of Parliament, and called a whimsical one because he votes variously as his opinion leads him ; and his first production was in French, in which language he shines too. . . .

Monday, February 19th.

The American Congress are adjourned and have appointed an executive committee of five, who are : Doctor Franklin, John Dickenson, Esq., John Jay, Esq., Tho. Johnson, Esq. and Benj. Harrison, Esq.

A deputation of three other members are gone to Canada to consult the Canadians upon a form of government to be established for that province, and to solicit their accession to the General Congress. The rest of the delegates are returned to their respective provinces, to consult their constituents upon a matter which, they say, will not only be surprising to Great Britain, but to all Europe.

Thursday, February 22nd.

News arrived . . . to the Government, by an officer of marines who came in eighteen days from Boston, that on New Year's Day the rebels made a double attack on Quebec, one of which was a feint in order to draw off our troops to facilitate the real attack. From some mistake (as it is supposed) the real attack was made too soon, the rebels were entirely defeated by General Carleton and the garrison, a hundred of them slain, among them their leader Montgomery. In the meantime the feigned attack was made, and the town being on that part without defence and the ditches frozen, the rebels entered it with ease, but were soon surrounded by our victorious troops and made prisoners to the number of 300, together with Arnold their leader, who is said to be wounded. This event 'tis imagined will clear the rebels out of Canada. Arnold has of late been much talked of for leading the New England men through woods and deserts into Canada. . . . Good effects are hoped from this event and those immediate with regard to the Canadians. . . .

Saturday, February 24th.

Miss Linley last night, in *Acis and Galatea*, gave every delight that the ear, the heart, or understanding could receive from music. . . . Miss Linley's manner of delivering Recitative is peculiarly distinct and sensible ; a circumstance of infinite importance in a performance of this nature. Her voice is clear and melodious, and capable of the truest expression as was peculiarly evident in the song of " Must I my Acis still bemoan ? " . . .

Their Majesties' presence and apparent satisfaction lead us to hope that the Royal countenance and encouragement will never again be withdrawn to grace the innovations of foreigners on the only musical ground which is left for English genius to take root and flourish.

Sunday, February 25th.

On the 30th of December, Rear-Admiral Shuldham arrived at Boston, in His Majesty's ship the *Chatham* of fifty guns ; and on the 27th of January following, Vice-Admiral Graves delivered over the command of the squadron to him and sailed for England in the *Preston.*

Monday, February 26th.

Many families within the neighbourhood of St. James's on Saturday last ordered the persons who deliver the daily papers to bring in the evening a Gazette, expecting a glorious account of the victory obtained over the rebels at Quebec, but when they came to inspect the Royal sheet of intelligence, and found no letter authenticating the report of last week, the disappointment spoiled not only the appetite but the night's repose of many loyal politicians.

Tuesday, February 27th.

A fellow who sat on the sixth row of the Upper Gallery of Covent Garden Theatre, threw a keg (which he had brought full of liquor into the house) over the gallery front. It fell upon a lady's head, who sat in that part of the pit which was railed into the boxes, but the lady's hair being dressed in high *ton*, the artificial mountain luckily prevented the mischief that otherwise might have been occasioned. . . . The fellow who threw the cask was carried to the Public-office, in Bow-street, and from thence committed to Tothill-fields Bridewell. As the custom of throwing mugs, bottles, apples, etc., from the galleries of the theatres is equally wanton and wicked and is frequently the cause of great mischief, it is thought the present culprit will be made an example of.

Wednesday, February 28th.

Lord Viscount Pitt, (son of the Earl of Chatham) lately resigned his commission as ensign in the 47th regiment, now at Boston, his lordship being determined not to serve in the present war between the mother country and her colonies.

Thursday, February 29th.

My ingenious friend Mr. George Adams, lately philosophical instrument maker to His Majesty, put into my hands a little apparatus which he called a machine for exhibiting perpetual electricity and informed me that it was the invention of some foreign gentleman. This machine consisted of a circular plate of glass about eight inches in diameter ; covered on one side with a coating of bees-wax and rosin, about the sixteenth part of an inch thick. This coat of wax etc being strongly excited with a dry warm flannel, he placed upon it a circular board of the same dimensions, coated with tinfoil and furnished with a glass handle, screwed to and standing upright upon it. These bodies having remained in contact some seconds the board was raised up by the glass handle, when, applying the knuckle to the tinfoil coating, a snap was heard, a spark seen and a small sensation felt. On replacing the board and permitting it to remain some seconds, as before, having touched the tinfoil with a finger on removing it again and applying the knuckle as at first, the same phenomena were produced, and might, Mr. Adams observed, be repeated for a long time without any renewal of the excitation of the wax, any farther than the replacing of the board might be said to excite it. . . .

I have since learned from Mr. Nairne that Mr. Volta, of Coma, near Milan, was the inventor of it. . . .

MARCH 1776

Friday, March 1st.

Yesterday Lord Hillsborough moved in the Lords whether they had a right to try the Duchess of Kingston and it was agreed they had. Whether her Grace will stay the trial is doubted by many, but true it is that the scaffolding is begun in Westminster Hall, and that she has attended and looked to it more than once ; some say she goes daily.

The *ton* [now] is the game of " Commerce " which the fine people play most immoderately high, sometimes £1,000 the pool, the lowest hand giving ten guineas each deal ; if the highest has a priol of aces all the company give five guineas each.

Saturday, March 2nd.

Yesterday being the day appointed by the Sheriffs for making the declaration of the poll, on the late election for Chamberlain of [the City of London] about twelve o'clock Aldermen Hopkins, Kennet, Esdaile, and Thomas, with about 60 of Mr. Hopkins's Committee, came into Guildhall ; preceded by a band of music from Coopers-hall, with blue cockades in their hats ; and about one o'clock the Sheriffs, the Aldermen Alsop, Bull, Wilkes, Hopkins, Esdaile, Thomas, Kennet, Plomer and Peckham ascended the hustings and after the proper officer had opened the business of the adjourned Hall, declared the numbers on the poll for Chamberlain as follows : for Mr. Alderman Hopkins 2,887, for Mr. Alderman Wilkes, 2,710 : therefore the Sheriffs declared the election to have fallen on Mr. Alderman Hopkins.

A man who was so imprudent as to cry the last dying speech of Mr. Wilkes, after the final close of the poll on Tuesday, in King Street, met with such a severe discipline from the populace, who rolled him in the kennel, and beat him so unmercifully that he died as he was carrying to an hospital.

Tuesday, March 5th.

When the *Eagle*, East Indiaman, arrived last week at Londonderry, she had only three men who could stand on deck, the rest of the ship's company being so very ill of the scurvy. She was fifteen weeks on her passage from St. Helena.

Wednesday, March 6th.

Letters by the *Samuel*, Capt. Shepperd, who arrived in the Downs the 28th ult. from Virginia, mention that the town of Norfolk has been bombarded by the King's ships and great part of it burnt down, upon which the natives set fire to the other part, so that the town is laid in ruins except three houses which are standing.

Thursday, March 7th.

About nine o'clock, the head dress of a lady in high life, who lives in the neighbourhood of Portman Square, accidentally caught fire, but by the timely assistance of three engines and plenty of water, it was got under a little before twelve.

Friday, March 8th.

A letter from Captain James Cook of His Majesty's Ship the *Resolution* to Sir John Pringle, Bart., P.R.S. . . .

SIR,

As many gentlemen have expressed some surprise at the uncommon good state of health which the crew of the *Resolution*, under my command, experienced during her late long voyage, I take the liberty to communicate to you the methods that were taken to obtain that end.

A good deal was owing to the extraordinary attention paid by the Admiralty in causing such articles to be put on board as either by experience or suggestion were judged to tend most to preserve the health of seamen. . . .

We had on board a quantity of malt, of which was made sweet wort and given to such of the men as showed the least symptoms of the scurvy and also to such as were thought to be threatened with that disorder, from one to two or three pints a day, each man ; or in such proportion as the surgeon found necessary, which sometimes amounted to three quarts in the 24 hours. This is without doubt one of the best antiscorbutic sea-medicines yet found out, and if given in time will, with proper attention to other things, I am persuaded, prevent the scurvy from making any great progress for a considerable time. But I am not altogether of opinion that it will cure it at sea.

Sour krout, of which we had a large quantity, is not only a wholesome vegetable food, but in my opinion highly antiscorbutic and spoils not by keeping. A pound of it was served to each man when at sea, twice a week, or oftener when it was thought necessary.

Portable soup or broth was another great article of which we had a large supply. An ounce of this to each man, or such other proportion as I thought necessary, was boiled in their pease, three days in the week. And when we were in places where vegetables were to be got it was boiled with them, and wheat or oatmeal every morning for breakfast, and also with pease or vegetables for dinner. . . .

Rob of lemons and oranges is an antiscorbutic we were not without and the surgeon made use of it in many cases with great success.

Amongst the articles of victualling we were supplied with sugar in the room of oil, and wheat instead of much oatmeal, and were certainly gainers by the exchange. Sugar, I imagine, is a very good antiscorbutic, whereas oil, such at least as is usually given to the Navy, I apprehend has the contrary effect.

But the introduction of the most salutary articles either as provision or medicines will generally prove unsuccessful unless supported by certain regulations.

On this principle, many years' experience, together with some hints I had from Sir Hugh Palliser, the Captains Campbell, Wallis and other intelligent officers, enabled me to lay a plan whereby all was to be governed.

The crew were at three watches, except upon some extraordinary occasions. By this means they were not so much exposed to the weather as if they had been at watch and watch, and had generally dry clothes to shift themselves when they happened to get wet. Care was also taken to expose them as little to wet weather as possibly could be done.

Proper methods were employed to keep their persons, hammocks, bedding, clothes etc., constantly clean and dry. Equal care was taken to keep the ship clean and dry betwixt decks. Once or twice a week she was aired with fires, and when this could not be done she was smoked with gunpowder mixed with vinegar or water. I had also frequently a fire made in an iron pot at the bottom of the well. . . .

Proper attention was paid to the ship's coppers so that they were kept constantly clean. The fat which boiled out of the salt beef and pork I never suffered to be given to the people, as is customary, being of the opinion that it promotes the scurvy.

I was careful to take in water where ever it was to be got, even though we did not want it. Because I look upon fresh water from the shore to be more wholesome than that which has been kept some time on board a ship. Of this essential article we were never at an allowance, but had always plenty for every necessary purpose. I am convinced that, with plenty of fresh water and proper attention to cleanliness, a ship's company will seldom be much afflicted with the scurvy, even though they are not provided with any of the antiscorbutics before mentioned. . . .

These, Sir, were the methods, under the care of Providence, by which the *Resolution* performed a voyage of three years and eighteen days, through all the climates from 52° North to 71° South, with only the loss of four men out of one hundred and eighteen. Two were drowned, one was killed by a fall, and the other died after a long illness, occasioned by a complication of disorders without the least mixture of the scurvy.

I have the honour to be,
 Sir,
  Your most obliged and most humble servant,

            JAMES COOK

MILE END,
5th March, 1776.

Wednesday, March 13th.

[In the House of Commons] Sir Charles Whitworth reported from the Committee to whom the Petition of the Commissioners for carrying into execution the several Acts for paving, cleansing, lighting and regulating the . . . City and Liberty of Westminster. . . . That it is necessary some further regulations should be made with regard to the companies which furnish the inhabitants with water, and that provision should be made for preventing sweeping or raking any dirt or mud into the sewers . . . that the placing of goods, wares and merchandises, carriages, casks, packages, timber, wheels, materials for building and other things in the streets to the annoyance thereof, ought to be prevented . . . that the keeping open holes or funnels, for the purpose of letting down coals or other things . . . wants regulating ; that it is necessary the foot-crossings should be ascertained, and provisions made to prevent their being stopped by carriages or otherwise ; that the digging holes to make vaults and leaving them, as well as areas, open without fencing or placing any lights thereto, is very dangerous and ought to be prevented ; that the driving cattle, carriages, casks and other things on the foot pavements is a very great annoyance, as is also the standing of horses at farriers' shops, and the throwing of bricks, tiles and other things from the tops of houses ; that the . . . sinking dungholes and sawpits . . . are great nuisances, as is the custom of throwing at oranges or other things, and at cocks, pigeons and other fowls, and the making of bonfires and letting off gunpowder in the streets . . . that it would be convenient to have the houses and lamps numbered . . . and that an appeal should be allowed against the rates. . . .

Ordered, that leave be taken to bring in a Bill for remedying some [of these] defects. . . .

Thursday, March 14th.

On Friday last a steam engine constructed upon Mr. Watt's new principles was set to work at Bloomfield Colliery, near Dudley, in the presence of its proprietors, Messrs. Bentley, Banner, Wallin and Westley, and a number of scientific gentlemen whose curiosity was excited to see the first movements of so singular and so powerful a machine, and whose expectations were fully gratified by the excellence of its performance. . . . From the first moment of its setting to work it made about 14 to 15 strokes per minute and emptied the engine pit (which is about 90 feet deep and stood 57 feet high in water) in less than an hour. . . . According to custom a name was given to the machine, viz, Parliament Engine, amidst the acclamations of a number of joyous and ingenious workmen. This engine is applied to the working of a pump 14 inches and a half diameter, which is capable of doing to the depth of 300 feet, or even 360 if wanted, with one fourth of the fuel that a common engine would require to produce the same quantity of power. The cylinder is 50 inches diameter and the length of the stroke is 7 feet. . . . These engines are not worked by the pressure of atmosphere. Their principles are very different from all others. They were invented by Mr. Watt (late of Glasgow) after many years' study and a great variety of expensive and laborious experiments ; and are now carried into execution under his and Mr. Boulton's directions at Boulton and Fothergill's manufactory near [Birmingham] ; where they have nearly finished four of them and have established a fabric for them upon so extensive a plan as to render them applicable to almost all purposes where mechanical power is required, whether great or small, or where the motion wanted is either rotatory or reciprocating.

Friday, March 15th.

It is not easily conceived what attention a certain great personage gives to his old plan of keeping men in power dependent on himself.— Notwithstanding Lord North having so long proved what is thought a successful minister, yet has he not a shadow of authority in court or parliament independent of the royal smile. The members of the junto, all-powerful as they are, feel the effects of the same spirit. They have rivals perpetually rising, who keep them to their obedience. Lord Clare, Mr. Rigby, and the Solicitor General, are the three at present, who speak in a tone which was exclusively assumed by Jenkinson, Ellis, and Elliot. At the opening of the Sessions,

Lord Barrington trod on their heels — but giving himself too many airs of authority, the above three have since arisen. This system is finely calculated to render the court truly independent.

Saturday, March 16th.

A grant of an invention to the ingenious Christopher Pinchbeck, of Cockspur-street, for his new invented, simple addition to those very useful domestic machines called snuffers, by which the disagreeable circumstances of their dropping the wick after snuffing the candle, so generally complained of, is totally prevented, passed the Great Seal on Saturday last.

Friday, March 22nd.

Everybody is on the quest for tickets for the Duchess of Kingston's trial. I am persuaded her impudence will operate in some singular manner. Probably she will appear in weeds with a train to reach across Westminster Hall, with mourning Maids of Honour to support her when she swoons at her dear Duke's name, and in a black veil to conceal her not blushing. . . .

Tuesday, March 26th.

Jolliffe tried to bring a Bill into the House for a tax upon dogs, but it was thrown out. . . . Rigby intended to make an amendment by a tax upon cats. Jolliffe was most violently attacked last night by nine young ladies at once, for his inhuman intention ; these ladies so *worried* him that he had not a word to say and they fairly barked him off.

I hear there are parties among the great world for and against Monsieur Tessier. The Duchess of Manchester says he is not a person fit to be admitted into genteel society. The Duchess of Devonshire has danced with him at Almack's.

Thursday, March 28th.

On Tuesday Lord Townshend and several other general officers made an experiment of a piece of ordnance called the Hand Grenade, in Portman Square. It is round like a common ball, of about the weight of twelve pounds, and filled with shell powder and all sorts of combustibles, and when thrown at any distance, supposed to kill a great number of persons. Many thousands of them are made to send to America and in particular to Quebec.

Saturday, March 30th.

The remains of more than 20 dead bodies were discovered in a shed in Tottenham Court Road, supposed to have been deposited there by traders to the surgeons ; of whom there is one, it is said, in the Borough who makes open profession of dealing in dead bodies and is well known by the name of the Resurrectionist.

Sunday, March 31st.

In the Park . . . we saw the young and handsome Duchess of Devonshire, walking in such an undressed and slatternly manner, as in former times, Mrs. Rishton might have done in Chesington Garden. Two of her curls came quite unpinned and fell lank on one of her shoulders ; one shoe was down at heel, the trimming of her jacket and coat was in some places unsewn, her cap was awry ; and her cloak which was rusty and powdered was flung half on and half off. Had she not had a servant in a superb livery behind her, she would certainly have been affronted. Every creature turned back to stare at her. Indeed I think her very handsome, and she has a look of innocence and artlessness that made me quite sorry she should be so foolishly negligent of her person. She had hold of the Duke's arm, who is the very reverse of herself, for he is ugly, tidy and grave. He looks like a very mean shopkeeper's journeyman.

APRIL 1776

Monday, April 1st.

On Wednesday last a patent passed the Great Seal for an invention by Mr. William Horton, of a new piece of machinery to be fixed to a stocking frame, for making various sorts of knotted and double looped work, in gold, silver, thread, cotton, worsted, etc. This machine, though simple, is capable of making the greatest variety of work ever known. . . .

Tuesday, April 2nd.

The King's speech to both Houses at the opening of this session of Parliament, and the account of the fate of the petition of the Continental Congress, excited in America great rage and indignation which the leading people were careful to inflame. The speech was publicly burnt in the rebel camp before Boston ; and the Congress to show their displeasure, ordered their national colours to be changed from a plain red ground which they had hitherto used, to a flag with thirteen stripes, as a symbol of the number and union of the colonies that had thrown off their allegiance to the British Crown. . . . The passing of the Prohibitory Act, and the intelligence that a large army of foreigners were to be taken into British pay on purpose to serve in America, roused the Congress to adopt vindictive measures. They immediately dispatched instructions to General Washington, whose army was now pretty well formed, to change his mode of conduct and with all possible diligence to commence offensive operations against the town of Boston and the British fleet in its harbour. . . .

Wednesday, April 3rd.

Patrick Hastings and John Clark stood in the pillory at the end of Margaret Street, Cavendish Square, for extorting several sums of money from James Lintott, by charging him with a detestable crime. They were pelted with apples, potatoes, eggs, etc. very severely; and conveyed back to Newgate, to undergo the remainder of their sentence, which is two years' imprisonment.

Thursday, April 4th.

A great number of outwardbound ships, cleared at the Custom House, are detained in the river for want of hands, the sailors having left their ships on a report . . . that press-gangs were gone down to Gravesend in order to stop all ships and take out such sailors as they thought fit. . . .

Advice has lately been received at the East India House that His Majesty's ship *Sea Horse* has taken a French pirate on the coast of India, after a close engagement of five glasses, in which the pirate was so disabled that she could not make her escape. She is said to have been a French frigate; that she sailed about four years ago for the Mauritius; that in her passage the crew mutinied, murdered the Captain, and appointed the second lieutenant their commander; that she then sailed to the South Seas, where she made many captures; that she had been equally successful on the coast of India; and that she is immensely rich.

Easter Sunday, April 7th.

Dr. Kaye, Sub-Almoner, preached at the Chapel Royal, St. James's, in the room of the Archbishop of York.

His Majesty came to St. James's before 12 o'clock, and went to Chapel in the usual state, attended by the Lord Chamberlain, Lord Steward of the Household, the Lord-in-Waiting, Lord Falmouth, and the Heralds at Arms in their vestments and collars. . . . His Majesty appeared in the proper collar of the day. Her Majesty was not at Chapel.

The Sacrament was administered to his Majesty by the Bishop of London, assisted by the Bishop of Winchester, and his Majesty made the Easter offering of the wedge of gold as usual to the Bishop of London, Dean of the Chapel Royal.

Monday, April 8th.

By the report of the state of the city hospitals for the last year, laid before the Lord Mayor this day, as usual, at St. Bride's Church, it appeared,

That all the patients cured, relieved, buried, and remaining under cure in St. Bartholomew's Hospital, amounted to 10,155. Those in St. Thomas's to 7,957.

That, in Christ's Hospital, 142 boys had been put out and provided for, seven had died, and that 1,132 remained.

That in Bridewell, 1,084 vagrants had been provided for, and that 33 apprentices had been maintained at trades, etc.

That in Bethlem 187 lunatics had been admitted, 190 cured, 17 buried ; and 244 remained under cure.

Tuesday, April 9th.

By the act just passed for the better supplying His Majesty's fleet with mariners, it is enacted, that all trading ships shall be allowed to be navigated with 3-4ths of their crew foreigners till the 25th of March, 1777 and no longer.

Wednesday, April 10th.

An express arrived last Monday from Ireland . . . it is said . . . to acquaint the Government with the alarming account of having discovered a great quantity of gunpowder, arms, etc. in some private recesses of the deluded people called White Boys, which it is imagined were transmitted by the French or Spaniards, for reasons too obvious to comment upon. . . .

The last letters brought by the *Northumberland*, Indiaman, are dated so far back as the 19th of May. So that this ship has been above ten months on her passage home. She brings advice of great disagreements among the counsellors who compose the Government ; but adds that the people were generally inclined to Messrs. Hastings and Barwell against General Clavering, Colonel Monson and Mr. Francis, who carried everything by their majority of one.

Friday, April 12th.

On Tuesday at Battersea a number of women ran a race for a Holland smock ; there was a race of asses for a silver-laced hat ; and seven men grinned for three pounds of tobacco, each of the grinners having a horse collar round his neck. This part of the sport afforded abundant diversion. . . . The successful wry-face-monger has a countenance not to be matched, at least in the county of Surrey. . . .

Monday, April 15*th.*

Garrick would make me take his ticket to go to the trial of the Duchess of Kingston ; a sight which for beauty and magnificence exceeded anything which those who were never present at a coronation or a trial by peers, can have the least notion of. . . . At eight we went to the Duke of Newcastle's, whose house adjoins Westminster Hall, in which he has a large gallery communicating with the apartments in his house. . . . Five thousand people getting into one hall ! Yet in all this hurry, we walked in tranquilly. When they were all seated, and the king-at-arms had commanded silence on pain of imprisonment, (which, however, was very ill-observed,) the gentleman of the Black Rod was commanded to bring in his prisoner. Elizabeth, calling herself Duchess Dowager of Kingston, walked in led by Black Rod and Mr. la Roche, courtseying profoundly to her judges. When she bent, the lord steward called out, " Madam, you may rise " ; which was taking her up before she was down. The peers made her a slight bow. The prisoner was dressed in deep mourning ; a black hood on her head ; her hair modestly dressed and powdered ; a black silk sacque with crêpe trimmings ; black gauze, deep ruffles and black gloves. The counsel spoke about an hour and a quarter each. Dunning's manner is insufferably bad, coughing and spitting at every three words ; but his sense and expression pointed to the last degree ; he made her Grace shed bitter tears. . . . The fair victim had four virgins in white behind the bar. She imitated her great predecessor, Mrs. Rudd, and affected to write very often, though I plainly perceived she only wrote as they do their love epistles on the stage, without forming a letter. . . . We had only to open a door to get at a very fine cold collation of all sorts of meats and wines, with tea, etc. a privilege confined to those who belonged to the Duke of Newcastle. I fancy the peeresses would have been glad of our places at the trial, for I saw Lady Derby and

WESTMINSTER HALL IN TERM TIME, ABOUT 1770

From E. W. Brayley's 'Londiniana'

the Duchess of Devonshire with their work-bags full of good things. Their rank and dignity did not exempt them from the " villanous appetites " of eating and drinking.

Foote says that the Empress of Russia, the Duchess of Kingston and Mrs. Rudd are the three most extraordinary women in Europe ; but the Duchess disdainfully, and I think unjustly, excludes Mrs. Rudd from the honour of deserving to make one in the triple alliance. The Duchess has but small remains of that beauty of which kings and princes were once so enamoured. She looked very much like Mrs. Pritchard ; she is large and ill-shaped ; there was nothing white but her face, and had it not been for that, she would have looked like a bale of bombazeen. There was a great deal of ceremony, a great deal of splendour, and a great deal of nonsense : they adjourned upon the most foolish pretences imaginable, and did nothing with such an air of business as was truly ridiculous. . . .

Wednesday, April 17th.

Yesterday was less propitious [for the Duchess]. The Attorney and Solicitor-Generals, and Dunning, refuted the Duchess's counsel, made a very contrary impression, and seemed to have unhinged some of her firmness. She was blooded as soon as she retired, fell into a great passion of tears, and is, or affects to be, very ill. However, the Lords have given her and themselves a respite of two days. On Friday the opinion of the judges is to be asked on her plea against a second trial, which, it is not doubted, will be overruled. All the future is uncertainty ; whether she will be sent back to the Ecclesiastic Court, or whether the Lords will proceed to trial — either of which would produce deep probing into her history ; or whether, to avoid either, she will not plead guilty as soon as the Ecclesiastic Court's decisive jurisdiction is set aside. In fact, this is as much the trial of the Ecclesiastic Court as of the prisoner ; and may, at least ought to, produce a reform of that Popish tribunal. The Earl of Bristol does not stand in a fairer predicament ; and is not the whole burlesque, when, except the foreigners, there could not be one person in the Hall who was not as much convinced of the bigamy as of their own existence ? But the world can make *laws* against crimes, till nobody knows whether there is any crime which may not be committed *legally*.

Monday, April 22nd.

Elizabeth, calling herself Duchess Dowager of Kingston, was this very afternoon *undignified and unduchessed*, and very narrowly escaped being burned in the hand. . . . All the peers, but two or three (who chose to withdraw), exclaimed with great emphasis, " Guilty, upon my honour ! " Except the Duke of [Newcastle], who said, " Guilty erroneously, but not intentionally." . . .

Lord Camden . . . is very angry that the Duchess of Kingston was not burned in the hand. He says, as he was once a professed lover of hers, he thought it would have looked ill-natured and ungallant for him to propose it ; but that he should have acceded to it most heartily, though he believes he should have recommended a cold iron. . . .

Tuesday, April 23rd.

The prodigious inconveniences of the present backstairs mode of governing the affairs of this country are felt more and more every day ; the plan of conducting the war in North America has been changed once a week for eight or nine weeks past. Lord George Germain has been for sending the great force to Canada : Sir Jeffery Amherst's opinion and General Gage's were for making the principal effort from Boston : another party was for having the great force at New York in order to cut the colonies in two. These opinions, with others, have been determined on and rejected several times, which is owing to private advice given by nobody knows who ; and after all these schemes being thoroughly canvassed, none of them are abided by, but orders are given by the Secretary at War, according to the advices of the moment. . . .

Wednesday, April 24th.

Proceedings in the House of Commons. As soon as prayers were over, an amazing crowd of people got into the gallery to hear the opening of the budget, and met with no obstruction till it was so full that an order was given to admit no more. At a little after three Lord North rose, and in a most elaborate speech entered upon the particulars of what is called the Budget, or ways and means of raising such part of the supplies granted for the service of the current year, as are not provided for by the ordinary national revenues. The House was in a Committee of Supply, Sir Charles Whitworth in the Chair, and very full. His Lordship with great ability showed the expediency and economy of raising the sum of two millions by a new fund, bearing interest at three per cent in preference to all other means . . . £1,400,000 by annuities at 3 per cent, £600,000 by Lottery. . . . To raise the annual interest of these funds . . . his Lordship proposed the following taxes, which he said he was happy to think he had contrived to fall upon articles of luxury, that would be hardly felt. . . .

An additional duty of 20s. on Four Wheel carriages. . . . As to Two Wheel carriages, so few were now kept, that it was not an object worth his notice. . . . He then mentioned the number of Four Wheel carriages, entered to pay duty last year to be 18,900, and the number of Stage coaches (which some think he under-rated) to be 400, and made his new tax, together with the new and old to be paid by the Stages, amount to £19,000.

The second tax proposed was an additional Stamp Duty on all Deeds. . . . His third was a tax of an additional half-penny on newspapers ; with this article he made very merry as a great luxury, and expressed his astonishment that under a despotic minister twelve million three hundred and twenty-four thousand newspapers should be stamped yearly at the Office and did not doubt but that rather than not have the pleasure of seeing such a minister daily abused, the curious and the politicians would with pleasure give the other half-penny. . . . The fourth was an additional Stamp Duty of 6d. per pack on cards. . . . The fifth an additional Stamp Duty of 2s. 6d. on every pair of dice. . . . The whole computed produce . . . his Lordship calculated at £73,000. . . .

His Lordship added, that contingencies might arise and unforeseen incidents which might require a larger supply, and therefore he gave notice to the House that he should receive a message from His Majesty to desire a Vote of Credit for one million.

The resolutions were almost unanimously agreed to and ordered to be reported next day.

Thursday, April 25th.

About six in the morning, her Majesty was taken with labour pains, notice of which was immediately sent to the Archbishop of Canterbury, the Secretaries of State, and several of the nobility ; and, at seven o'clock, Her Majesty was safely delivered of a princess, being her eleventh child, and all of them living.

Friday, April 26th.

[Two accounts of naval engagements in American waters :]

Lieutenant Dawson, commanding the *Hope* brig, discovered on the 29th of January, about ten in the morning, a schooner privateer belonging to the enemy at anchor off Plymouth. Upon his standing towards her she immediately got under way and endeavoured, but in vain, to enter several of the harbours on that part of the coast. The *Hope* having frustrated all these attempts, at last forced her ashore about two o'clock. Lieutenant Dawson then brought the brig under his command to anchor as near her as the depth of water would allow, and kept up a smart fire on her until seven in the evening, when she floated, made a push to get into the North River, and sunk in the attempt. At daylight next morning, Lieutenant Dawson endeavoured to burn the part of her which remained above water : but the country people, having by this time assembled in great multitudes, kept up a constant fire on the *Hope* and her boats from small arms and a battery of cannon which they had erected in the night. It was, therefore, judged proper to desist, especially as the privateer had received so much damage as would effectually prevent her from cruising.

The Congress having received information of the defenceless situation of the Island of [New] Providence, the seat of Government of the Bahama Islands, despatched their squadron under the command of Mr. Hopkins in hopes of seizing upon his Majesty's magazine there : but Governor Brown having got intimation of their design, in a great measure disappointed it by having almost all the gunpowder conveyed away in two sloops the day before they appeared off the town of Nassau, (March 3rd). The place, being in no condition to withstand either an attack or a siege, surrendered on the first summons. Here the enemy found plenty of cannon and mortars ; but to their great mortification only fifteen barrels of gunpowder, which they carried off. They also made Governor Brown their prisoner and were on their voyage to New London when their fleet, about two in the morning on the 6th of April, (off Block island) fell in with His Majesty's ship *Glasgow* of twenty guns, Captain Tyringham Howe. About half an hour past two, a large brig of Mr. Hopkins's squadron came so near as to be hailed by the *Glasgow*, but seemed to hesitate what answer to give ; upon which Captain Howe repeated the question, " What are ye ? And what are the other ships in company ? " They then answered " The *Columbus*, and *Alfred* frigate of twenty-two guns " ; and immediately a hand-grenade was thrown out of the brig's top at the *Glasgow* which was returned by a broadside ; and an action commenced. The brig then shot ahead to make room for a large ship with a top-light to come alongside the *Glasgow*. At the same time another of their ships ran under her stern, raked her as she passed and then luffed up under her lee-beam, while a brig took her station on her larboard-quarter, and a sloop kept altering her position continually. At four o'clock the situation of all the enemy's vessels was changed ; their two ships had dropped on each quarter, and a brig lay astern keeping up a continual fire. The *Glasgow* then bore away and made for Rhode Island, when all the rebel fleet were in musket-shot on her quarters or stern. Captain Howe ordered two stern-chase guns to be run out at the cabin windows, from which he kept up a warm fire on the enemy, who at day-break on the 17th, were found to consist of two ships, two brigs and a sloop, all fitted for war, and a large ship and a snow, which had kept to windward from the commencement of the action. At half past six the enemy hauled their wind and steered to the S.S.W. In this action the *Glasgow* had one man killed and three wounded by the enemy's small arms.

Saturday, April 27th.

[Extract of a letter from Cowes, April 24 :]

This morning forty-four sail of transports, with ten thousand Hessian troops on board, bound to America, passed by the back of the Isle of Wight, under convoy of two men of war and three frigates. They have been out from the Weser nine days, which is reckoned a long passage. They are to remain at Plymouth till the guards all sail from Portsmouth, and then are ordered to join them, and to proceed in one fleet to America.

Sunday, April 28th.

[Lately published :]

An Enquiry into the Nature and Causes of the Wealth of Nations. By Adam Smith, LL.D. F.R.S.   2 vols. quarto.

The growth and decay of nations have frequently afforded topics of admiration and complaint to the moralist and declaimer ; they have sometimes exercised the speculations of the politician ; but they have seldom been considered in all their causes and combinations by the philosopher. The French economical writers undoubtedly have their merit. Within this century they have opened the way to a rational theory, on the subjects of agriculture, manufactures, and commerce. But no one work has appeared amongst them, nor perhaps could there be collected from the whole together, any thing to be compared to the present performance, for sagacity and penetration of mind, extent of views, accurate distinction, just and natural connection, and dependence of parts. It is a complete analysis of society, beginning with the first rudiments of the simplest manual labour, and rising by an easy and natural gradation to the highest attainments of mental powers. In which course not only arts and commerce, but finance, justice, public police, the economy of armies, and the system of education, are considered and argued upon, often profoundly, always plausibly and clearly ; many of the speculations are new, and time will be required before a certain judgment can be passed on their truth and solidity.

The style of the author may be sometimes thought diffuse, but it must be remembered that the work is didactic, that the author means to teach, and teach things that are by no means obvious. . . .

The State of the National Debt, the National Income and the National Expenditure. With some short inferences and reflections applicable to the present dangerous Crisis. By John Earl of Stair. Folio. 1s. Almon.

An Enquiry whether the Guilt of the present Civil War in America ought to be imputed to Great Britain or America. [By John Roebuck, M.D.] 8vo. 1s. Donaldson.

Monday, April 29th.

The Congress have ordered 13 frigates to be built with all expedition, of 36 guns each, at Maryland, Philadelphia and Rhode Island, four of which were on the stocks at Philadelphia when Captain Meston sailed. Likewise one floating battery of 105 feet in keel, which is to mount 18 eighteen pounders, row fifty oars and carry 300 men. Also 30 fire-rafts. They have sunk 50 cheveux de frizes in the river to prevent the English ships from going up.

Tuesday, April 30th.

Mr. Wilkes made his motion in Parliament for expunging from the journals of the House, the resolution for his expulsion ; for a more equal representation of the people ; and for shortening the duration of Parliament : it passed in the negative, 186 to 92.

MAY 1776

Wednesday, May 1st.

[Into the City to take note of the May Day observances.]

The young chimney-sweepers with their sooty and chalked faces are dressed out with ribbons and gilt paper, a grotesque and merry-andrew appearance. With their brushes and scrapers they made a kind of musical sound, raising contributions on their employers and others. The milkmaids appeared in fine and fantastic attire, and carried on their heads pyramids of three or four feet in height, finely decorated. In Ave-Mary Lane [I] saw the milkmen and maids with a *garland* so called, being a pyramid consisting of seven or eight stories, in the four angles of which stood a silver tankard and on the sides, between each, lessening in height as the storeys rose, stood a silver salver, the top crowned with a chased silver tea-kettle, round which were placed sundry small pieces of plate ; the whole adorned with wreaths and festoons of flowers, gilt paper, etc. carried on a bier and hand-barrow . . . to collect of the customers a yearly contribution. The wrought silver appeared worth many hundreds of pounds, and is borrowed for the occasion.

Friday, May 3rd.

A few days since Mr. Rowley made a seizure of 2,000 cwt. and upwards of fine teas in Hurstmonceux Castle, an ancient uninhabited seat belonging to the family of the Nailors, near the sea-coast in the county of Sussex. What is remarkable, a man who takes care of the gardens belonging to the castle, and has lived in the gardens as a servant for upwards of seventy years, and is more than ninety years of age, has by laying up goods for the smugglers in the castle for some years past, amassed together between £3 and £4,000, and was never before detected.

Saturday, May 4th.

The House of Commons are determined to do something effective in relation to the enormous increase of the poor tax throughout England ; the late order to have reports of the number of the chargeable poor, and the sums paid, by all the parishes in the kingdom, is an excellent first step.

Sunday, May 5th.

General Howe is driven from Boston by a cannonade and bombardment of a fortnight's continuance, acting in concert with a scarcity of provisions of much longer standing. The Ministers triumph at his escape ; and all things considered, it is surprising that he should have been able to effect it with so much advantage. They say that he has brought off everything with him ; cannon, military stores, and a vast quantity of useful goods of all kinds, with about eighteen hundred of the inhabitants. I saw a letter today which said that they were obliged to quit partly from want of provision, partly that the place was made too hot for them. . . . The office-folks tell us that General Howe writes that he would have gone to New York ; but, from tenderness to the women and children, of whom he had such numbers on board, he thought it better to proceed to Halifax, where his landing would not be opposed. In that nook of penury and cold the proud conqueror of America is obliged to look for refuge. The provincials entered the town on the 24th of March, drums beating and colours flying. There is reason to believe, from some letters by way of Ireland, that the cannonade began almost immediately on the receipt of the Separation Act ; that before that time they did not choose to proceed to extremities. Since then, the most moderate are become eminently outrageous ; and Dickenson of Pennsylvania (the candid man of America) headed a battalion which marched to reinforce General Lee. . . .

Tuesday, May 7th.

Attempted to get into Drury Lane Theatre, to see Mr. Garrick in the character of Archer [in *The Beaux' Stratagem*] ; but the crowd [was] so great that after suffering thumps, squeezes and almost suffocation for two hours, I was obliged to retire without effecting it. . . .

Wednesday, May 8th.

The fleet of American privateers under the command of Commodore Hopkins, which [captured the Island of New Providence] was sent out some months since and supposed to be gone to intercept the homeward bound Indiamen that touch at St. Helena. . . .

The Governor [of New Providence] and his family are gone to St. Augustine. This island is so situated as to command the Jamaica and other West India trade.

Thursday, May 9th.

[Mr. John Wesley writes :]

In travelling through Berkshire, Oxfordshire, Bristol, Gloucestershire, Worcestershire, Warwickshire, Staffordshire, Cheshire, Lancashire, Yorkshire, Westmoreland, and Cumberland, I diligently made two enquiries : the first was, concerning the increase or decrease of the people ; the second, concerning the increase or decrease of trade. As to the latter, it is, within these last two years, amazingly increased ; in several branches in such a manner as has not been known in the memory of man : such is the fruit of the entire civil and religious liberty, which all England now enjoys ! And as to the former, not only in every city and large town, but in every village and hamlet, there is no decrease, but a very large and swift increase. One sign of this is the swarms of little children which we see in every place. Which, then, shall we most admire, the ignorance or confidence of those that affirm, population decreases in England ? I doubt not but it increases full as fast here, as any province of North America.

Friday, May 10th.

Letters from Georgia . . . on Tuesday at Dover . . . bring a confirmation of the strange revolution in that Colony since they have heard of the hiring foreign troops to assist in bringing the Americans to submit to the arbitrary mandates of the British Ministry ; that that circumstance has more exasperated them than all their proceedings before ; and they have no thoughts now but of throwing off the dependency of the mother country.

The Duke of Manchester moved in the House of Lords, " That an humble address be presented to His Majesty, requesting that he would be graciously pleased to order the proper officers to lay before the House copies of all dispatches received by Government from Gen. Howe and Admiral Shuldham since the 1st of March." He urged as a reason for this motion, the mutilated, partial account given in the Gazette of the retreat of the King's troops from Boston, essentially different from authentic accounts received by private persons from officers of the army and other respectable persons on the spot. . . . Passed in the negative, 64 to 27.

Saturday, May 11th.

Lord Denbigh [writes] . . . that he, Lord Sandwich, Lord Mulgrave, Mr. Banks and two or three Ladies of Pleasure had passed five or six days [at the inn at Spine Hill near Newbury] and intended to pass all this week and the next in the same place ; that their chief object was to enjoy the trouting season ; that they had been very successful ; that Lord Sandwich in particular had caught trouts near twenty inches long, which gave him incredible satisfaction ; but that for his part, being a great admirer of sea fish . . . he commissioned my friend to send him up by the London Fly a good cargo of soles, John Dories, and pipers, which would render their happiness complete. I do not remember in all my little or great knowledge of history . . . such another instance, and I am sure such a one does not exist : that the First Lord of the Admiralty, who is absolute and uncontrolled master in his Department, should at a time when the fate of the British Empire is in dependence, and in dependence on him, find so much leisure, tranquillity, presence of mind and magnanimity as to have amusement in trouting during three weeks near sixty miles from the scene of business and during the most critical season of the year. There needs but this single fact to decide the fate of the nation. What an ornament would it be in a future history to open the glorious events of the ensuing year with the narrative of so singular an incident.

Sunday, May 12*th.*

The more admirable [Garrick] is, the more painful it is to reflect that I am now catching his departing glories. He is one of those summer suns which shine brightest at their setting. Within these three weeks, he has appeared in Brute, Leon, Drugger, Benedict, Archer, etc. for the last time ; and it appears like assisting at the funeral obsequies of these individual characters. . . .

On Monday night he played King Lear and it is literally true that my spirits have not yet recovered from the shock they sustained. . . . It was the universal opinion that it was one of the greatest scenes ever exhibited. I called today in Leicester Fields, and Sir Joshua declared it was full three days before he had got the better of it. The eagerness of people to see him is beyond anything you can have an idea of. You will see half-a-dozen duchesses and countesses of a night in the upper boxes : for the fear of not seeing him at all, has humbled those who used to go, not for the purpose of seeing, but of being seen ; and they now courtesy to the ground for the worst places in the house.

Monday, May 13*th.*

Our prisons at present are very full of convicts, for since this American war they know not where to send them. Mr. Eden moved they might be put on board transports on the Thames, to work in irons for the purpose of clearing the river of all rubbish, and all that impedes the navigation, and to be fed with common food, none for less than three years or more than ten. . . .

Lord Stormont was married on Sunday to Miss Cathcart. . . .

Tuesday, May 14*th.*

In the gay circle at Ranelagh on Thursday night, several of those who have the priviledge of giving the *ton*, exhibited their sweet persons in coats à la Polonaise. A smart youth with a cockade was a striking figure indeed, his head was a pyramid of curls ; the cape of his coat, which was lined with yellow, edged with silver and without buttons, was fastened at the breast with two large silver tassels ; the garment which supplied the place of the waistcoat, having neither pockets, flaps or buttons, gave his body the appearance of a bale of yellow silk ; his breeches were black ; his feet covered with plates of silver of enormous size, and from his whole person, but from the white silken gloves in particular, exhaled perfumes that scented the ambient air.

Wednesday, May 15th.

Visited Pinchbeck's to view stained glass ; most elegant figures, finest tints, in the new revived art, by a Mr. Jervais, among which were two full lengths of Christ and Moses, bought at seventy guineas by a clergyman and presented to Westminster Abbey. . . .

The Baron De Wenzel, oculist to His Britannic Majesty is expected at his house in Pall Mall, the latter end of this month, when he will continue to perform his operation of extracting the cataract on the poor gratis.

Thursday, May 16th.

The voyage to the South Sea, to be now prosecuted by Capt. Clarke and Cook, is to attempt a landing on California, whose inhabitants were originally of Japan, and are supposed to have travelled into the remote and western parts of America. . . .

Friday, May 17th.

At a Court of Proprietors of East India Stock [held on Wednesday] the resolution of the Court of Directors to remove Warren Hastings, Esq., the Company's governor of Bengal, and [Richard] Barwell, Esq., one of the Council, was taken into consideration, when Mr. Beecher distinguished himself in defence of the injured gentlemen, particularly in that of Governor Hastings, who, he said, at a time when that country was overrun with venality and corruption, by his good management, attention, and moderation had restored the credit of the Company and increased its revenues ; that his faithful services were upon record ; and that no crime had been directly laid to his charge. . . .

Saturday, May 18th.

Mr. Garrick's foible, the desire of praise, has often been remarked ; and one day, when sitting to Nollekens [in Rome] he was very inquisitive to know what was said of him by his country-men at the English coffee-house in that city : when Nollekens gravely answered, " Indeed, I heard somebody speaking very highly in your praise, as high as possible." " Ah ! ah ! " said Garrick, with great quickness, " pray, who was it — who was it spoke so highly in my praise ? " " Why, it was yourself," answered Nollekens. " Ah, d——d vulgar ! that's St. Giles's wit." replied Garrick.

Sunday, May 19th.

Being the birthday of Her Majesty [the Queen] who but then entered her thirty-third year, the ceremony of the christening of the young princess was performed in the great council chamber, by his Grace the Archbishop of Canterbury. Her Royal Highness was named Mary. The sponsors were Prince Frederick of Hesse-Cassel, represented by the Earl of Hertford, Lord-Chamberlain of his Majesty's Household ; the Duchess of Saxe-Gotha, represented by the Duchess of Argyle ; and the Princess Frederica of Mecklenburgh Strelitz, repre-sented by the Dowager Countess of Effingham.

Tuesday, May 21st.

Mr. Garrick . . . repeated his capital representation of *Lear*, and in consequence thereof drew together a most crowded audience, principally composed of the first people of dis-tinction, who seem resolved to let no opportunity escape them of enjoying the remainder of his inimitable performances. . . . He never appeared so great in the character before.

The curse at the close of the first act,— his phrenetic appeal to heaven at the end of the second on Regan's ingrati-tude, were two such enthusiastic scenes of human exertion, that they caused a kind of momentary petrefaction through the house, which he soon resolved as universally into tears. Even the unfeeling Regan and Goneril, forgetful of their characteristic cruelty, played through the whole of their parts with aching bosoms and streaming eyes. In a word, we never saw before so exquisite a theatrical performance, or one so loudly and universally applauded.

The play received considerable improvement last night from the characters being judiciously habited in old English dresses ; Lear's was more majestic than usual, and in our opinion, was more in character.

Wednesday, May 22nd.

Yesterday some officers of the customs made a seizure of foreign lace, to the amount of £2,000 in a single horse-chaise, in Old Burlington Street, Piccadilly, which they carried as far as Warwick Street, Golden Square, where they were obliged to take refuge in a house, in order to secure the goods, they being closely pursued by the smugglers, who frequently fired at them with pistols, and one of the officers was wounded in the face. They then broke all the windows in the front of the house, and were proceeding to further outrages, but were prevented by the arrival of a party of guards, who obliged the smugglers to retreat ; the goods were put in a hackney-coach and conveyed to the custom-house, guarded by soldiers.

Saturday, May 25th.

The sessions at the Old Bailey ended, when 17 convicts received sentence of death, (besides two for murder, whose sentence was pronounced immediately on conviction) among whom were Joseph Bissel and Thomas Hankey for coining. With these men were tried one Hannah Horner, as an accessory, who having a fine child about four months old at her breast, greatly affected the whole court. . . .

The two men convicted of murder, Benjamin Harley and Thomas Henman, were smugglers, and the man murdered, Joseph Pearson, was a custom house officer. It appeared that the officers, of whom there were four, having previous intelligence that a quantity of tea was to be run in the night, way-laid the smugglers near Deptford Turnpike, but possibly the same person who gave the information to the officers might alarm the smugglers, who having made themselves drunk for mischief, instead of running the tea, armed themselves with clubs and bludgeons to hunt the officers ; the unfortunate deceased in the pursuit was overtaken and beat unmercifully, so that he died after being conveyed to the hospital in great agonies. . . . One Gipsy George, a noted smuggler, was their employer and hired the whole gang, 20 in number, to pursue the officers.

Sunday, May 26th.

[Lately published :]
Epitome of Philosophical Transactions [of the Royal Society], Vol. LXV for the Year 1775. Part II. 7s. 6d. Davies. [This includes] Art. XXIII. *Of the House-swallow, Swift and Sandmartin.* By the Rev. Gilbert White.

This humane and intelligent writer, who seems like M. Buffon, to be very conversant with the manners and even the language of the animal race, has here given a circumstantial and curious detail of the life . . . of the swallow. . . .

And Art. XXXVIII. *An Account of further Discoveries in Air.* By Joseph Priestley, LL.D. F.R.S.

To the marine acid air, before discovered by this writer, he has now added three more, viz. the vitriolic, the nitrous and the vegetable ; and here relates the manner of procuring them. The purest air, he observes, contains the least *phlogiston.* . . .

The Plain Question upon the present Dispute with the American Colonies. Wilkie. 2d.

Hypocrisy Unmasked ; or a short enquiry into the religious complaints of our American Colonies. To which is added a word on the Laws against Popery in Great Britain and Ireland. Nicholl. 2d.

An Examination of the Rev. Mr. John Wesley's Primitive Physic : showing that a great number of the prescriptions therein contained are founded on Ignorance of the Medical Art and of the Power and Operation of Medicines ; and that it is a publication calculated to do essential Injury to the Health of those Persons who may place confidence in it. Interspersed with medical remarks and practical observations. By Mr. Hawes, Apothecary. Dodsley. 8vo. 1s. 6d.

Essays Physical and Chymical ; &c. By M. Lavoisier, Member of the Royal Academy of Sciences at Paris. Translated from the French with notes and an Appendix, by Thomas Henry, F.R.S. 6s. sewed. Johnson.

The Third and Last Volume of *A Tour in Scotland*, being the Second Part of the Year 1772. By Thomas Pennant, Esq. 4to. £1, 11s. 6d. in Boards. White.

Monday, May 27th.

The large smuggler which has lately been on the North coast and bid defiance to the custom house smacks, appeared a few days ago to the southward of Newcastle and is said to have a large cargo on board. She mounts 20 guns, six-pounders and 30 swivels and has 80 men on board ; her keel measures 66 feet, and is reckoned a fine sailor. Yesterday se'nnight, sailed from Harwich His Majesty's armed cutter *Hinchinbroke* in quest of her.

Tuesday, May 28th.

The ensuing campaign in America is likely to be exceedingly bloody ; the humane reply of General Washington to General Howe's request, and the mercy in consequence shown to his half-starved and retreating army, received the universal applause of the whole Provincial soldiery. But such is the spirit of resentment conceived by those troops against the German mercenaries, hired (as they construe the measure) for the express purpose of establishing German slavery in the place of their birth right, American liberty, that the officers will find it impossible to restrain their indignant fury against those devoted legions. . . .

Wednesday, May 29th.

Lady Gr——by . . . is now become the pink of the *ton* and is even looked up to by Devons——re's Duchess with envy and despair ; her ladyship's white and black plumes, which she exhibited the other night at Drury Lane, when Garrick played Richard, resembled those mournful ones which adorn the top of a hearse and struck terror in the mind of every beholder. . . .

The concourse of servants assembled yesterday morning at seven o'clock, at Drury Lane stage door, to take places for the approaching benefit, in which it is said Mr. Garrick will again play Richard the III, was astonishing, amounting to many hundreds, three-fourths of which were not able to succeed in their embassies.

Thursday, May 30th.

To see Hamlet [played by Garrick for the last time]. It was such an entertainment as will probably never again be exhibited to an admiring world. . . . In every part he filled the whole soul of the spectator, and transcended the most finished idea of the poet. The requisites for Hamlet are not only various but opposed. In him they are all united and as it were concentrated. One thing I must particularly remark, that whether in the simulation of madness, in the sinkings of despair, in the familiarity of friendship, in the whirlwind of passion, or in the meltings of tenderness, he never once forgot he was a prince ; and in every variety of situation and transition of feeling, you discovered the highest polish of fine breeding and courtly manners. . . .

To the most eloquent expression of the eye, to the hand-writing of the passions on his features, to a sensibility which tears to pieces the hearts of his auditors, to powers so unparalleled, he adds a judgment of the most exquisite accuracy, the fruit of long experience and close observation, by which he preserves every gradation and transition of the passions, keeping all under the control of a just dependence and natural consistency. So naturally, indeed, do the ideas of the poet seem to mix with his own that he seemed himself to be engaged in a succession of affecting situations, not giving utterance to a speech, but to the instantaneous expression of his feelings, delivered in the most affecting tones of voice, and with gestures that belong only to nature. It was a fiction as delightful as fancy and as touching as truth. A few nights before I saw him in *Abel Drugger* ; and had I not seen him in both, I should have thought it as possible for Milton to have written *Hudibras*, and Butler *Paradise Lost*, as for one man to have played " Hamlet " and " Drugger " with such excellence. . . .

I sat next the orchestra, in which were . . . Edmund and Richard Burke, Dr. Warton and Sheridan.

Friday, May 31st.

On Tuesday Sir William Chambers, Comptroller of His
Majesty's Board of Works, attended by the master tradesmen,
laid the first stone of the intended new buildings at Somerset
House, on which occasion he gave the workmen a handsome
sum to drink His Majesty's health, and success to the undertaking.

JUNE 1776

Monday, June 3rd.

Being His Majesty's birthday, who then entered into the 39th year of his age, their Majesties came from Buckingham House to St. James's, and received the compliments of a numerous and brilliant court on that occasion. The Ode was much admired.

Wednesday, June 5th.

To Drury Lane, to see for the last time Garrick in *Richard III*, by command of their Majesties, but [I was] too late — house filled.

Friday, June 7th.

It [is] something extraordinary that the birthday news, which sounded the triumph of the British arms in America, and the downfall of Lee, Washington, and the Congress, should gain as little credit in the alley as the Birthday Ode. . . .

Three arguments for the authenticity of the birthday news : First, it is not in the *Gazette* ; secondly, the Ministry are modest about it, and thirdly, the Jews disbelieve it. Such good news as this should have raised the stock ten per cent. . . .

Sunday, June 9th.

The night before the last day of [the Duchess of Kingston's] trial, after Sir Francis Molyneux had been some hours in bed (for he slept at Kingston House), he got up in a most violent fright, ran out of his room with nothing on but his shirt, caught a housemaid in his arms, crying out " The Duchess is gone off ! " The maid said he might see the Duchess, for that she was not undressed, as the Councillors had just left her, but recommended his putting on some other garment. So, in his hurry, he threw his powdering dress over his shoulders and

went into the Duchess's room, after which he went down and
" saw that all his *tall beastly fellows* were on duty," and then
went to bed again.

Monday, June 10th.

[This night] Mr. Garrick made his last theatrical appearance in Don Felix, [in *The Wonder*, the comedy by Susannah
Centlivre] generously giving the profits of the night, as a
second benefit this year to the Fund. His performance, as might
be expected, was inimitable ; never were the passions of love,
jealousy, rage, etc. so highly coloured, or admirably set off :
in short, he finished his comic course with as high a theatrical
climax as he did on Saturday evening his tragic one. . . .

The play being ended, came the awful crisis, when the
Roscius of this country was to take leave of this town in his
public capacity — and of all those numberless admirers, who
had followed him for so many years, with a devotion that could
only be equalled by his merits.— The scene was too distressing
to be described. . . . This universal favourite, impressed with
all those nicer feelings which his peculiar situation must call
forth, [advanced] forwards, to bid farewell to that public, who
seemed universally to lament that they should be the melancholy witnesses of their own great loss. Behind him, and
between every scene, stood groups of his mournful subjects,
whose tears spoke their sorrow, and who for once, joined in
one unfeigned tragedy.— After a short pause, as soon as he
recovered a little from the first shock, he thus addressed the
audience : [1]

" Ladies and Gentlemen,
    " It has been customary with persons under my circum-
stances, to address you in a farewell epilogue.— I had the same
intention, and turned my thoughts that way ; but indeed I
found myself then, as incapable of writing such an epilogue,
as I should be now, of speaking it.
    " The jingle of rhyme, and the language of fiction, would
but ill suit my present feelings.
    " This is to me a very awful moment ; it is no less than

---

[1] This address was taken down in shorthand.

The Laſt Time of the **Company's** performing this Seaſon.

At the Theatre Royal in Drury-Lane,

This preſent MONDAY, June 10, 1776,

The WONDER.

Don Felix by Mr. GARRICK,
Col. Briton by Mr. SMITH,

Don Lopez by Mr BADDELEY,
Don Pedro by Mr. PARSONS,

Liſſardo by Mr. KING,

Frederick by Mr. PACKER,
Gibby by Mr. MOODY,
Iſabella by Miſs HOPKINS,

Flora by Mrs. WRIGHTEN,

Inis by Mrs. BRADSHAW,

Violante by Mrs. YATES.

End of Act I. The Grand GARLAND DANCE,
By Signor GIORGI, Mrs. SUTTON,
And Mr. SLINGSBY.

To which will be added a Muſical Entertainment, call'd

The WATERMAN.

The PRINCIPAL CHARACTERS by
Mr. BANNISTER,
Mr. DAVIES,
And Mr. DODD.
Mrs. WRIGHTEN,
And Mrs. JEWELL.

To conclude with the Grand Scene of The REGATTA.

Ladies are deſired to ſend their Servants a little after 5 to keep Places, to prevent Conjuſion.

The Doors will be opened at HALF after FIVE o'Clock.

To begin at HALF after SIX o'Clock.   Vivant Rex & Regina.

The Profits of this Night being appropriated to the Benefit of
The Theatrical Fund, the Uſual Addreſs upon that Occaſion
Will be ſpoken by Mr. GARRICK, before the Play.

parting for ever with those from whom I have received the greatest kindness and favours, and upon the spot where that kindness and those favours were enjoyed."

(Here for a moment he was unable to proceed until relieved by a flood of tears.)

" Whatever may be the changes of my future life, the deep impression I have of your kindness, will always remain here, (putting his hand to his breast) fixed, and unalterable.

" I will very readily agree to my successors having more skill and ability for their station than I have ; but I defy them all to take more sincere, and more uninterrupted pains for your favour, or to be more truly sensible of it, than is, your most obedient and grateful servant."

Here he retired, crowned with never-fading laurels, amidst the blended tears, and acclamations of the most brilliant theatre that ever was assembled ; — all ranks uniting in their invocations for the future happiness of a man, who has so repeatedly, and essentially contributed to theirs.

Tuesday, June 11th.

Major Caldwell, Lieutenant-Colonel Commandant of the British militia in Canada, arrived [yesterday morning] from Quebec in His Majesty's sloop *Hunter* ; by whom was received the following letter from General Carleton to Lord George Germain. . . . [dated] Quebec, May 14, 1776 :

" After this town had been closely invested by the rebels for five months and had defeated all their attempts, the *Surprize* frigate, *Isis* and sloop *Martin* came into the basin the 6th instant.

" As soon as that part of the 29th they had on board, with their marines, in all about two hundred, were landed they, with the greatest part of the garrison, by this time much improved and in high spirits, marched out of the ports of St. Louis and St. John's to see what those mighty boasters were about ; they were found very busy in their preparations for a retreat ; a few shots being exchanged, the line marched forward and the plains were soon cleared of those plunderers ; all their artillery, military stores, scaling-ladders, petards, etc.,

etc. were abandoned : the *Surprize*, *Martin* and a Province armed vessel went up the river, when they also quitted the *Gaspe* and the armed schooner *Mary*. The rear of the rebels have haulted at Dechambault ; and the *Surprize* with the two other vessels are a little upon this side of the falls of Richelieu.

"This ended our siege and blockade ; during which the mixed garrison of soldiers, sailors, British and Canadian militia, with the artificers from Halifax and Newfoundland showed great zeal and patience. . . ."

Wednesday, June 12th.

It is surprising what little seeming effect the loss of American orders has on the manufactories ; they have been in full employ ever since the dispute arose. Stocks are not one jot lessened, the people in general little moved by it ; business and amusements so totally engross all ranks and orders . . . that administration find no difficulty on that score to pursue their plans. . . .

Sunday, June 16th.

Sir Joshua [Reynolds says] that he could instruct any boy that chance should throw his way, to be able in half a year to paint a likeness in a portrait ; but to give a just expression and true character to the portrait was infinitely difficult and rare to be seen, and when done was that which proved the great master ; and of Velasquez, the celebrated Spanish painter, of whose great powers he thought so favourably, he said, "What we are all attempting to do with great labour, he does at once."

Wednesday, June 19th.

The man convicted of perjury at the Hindon election, and sentenced to stand twice in the pillory, was brought from the King's Bench to Fisherton gaol, Wiltshire, and on Thursday was carried to Hindon, where he was placed in the pillory for the first time. He was met on the road by a number of his friends, with two flags and blue ribbons in their hats. The populace treated him very favourably, their attention being taken off in a great measure by a person mounted on a stool who sung and sold an election ballad, much to their entertainment. . . .

Saturday, June 22nd.

On Saturday evening the journeymen carpenters throughout the cities of London and Westminster entered into a joint association (to use their own phrase) not to strike a stroke till their wages were advanced from 18s. to one pound per week ; in consequence of which their masters must either comply with their exorbitant demands, or be unable to get the least work whatever executed for their employers.

Monday, June 24th.

The remainder of the second division of Brunswick troops arrived at Spithead [on Tuesday, and] all the transports with the second division of Hessian troops. . . . The transports with the Waldeck troops on board [arrived on Thursday] ; and they are preparing for their immediate departure for North America.

Tuesday, June 25th.

Several ladies of quality, offended that so many persons of inferior rank should be admitted into all public places with them (so that Almack's, the Festino, Bach and Abel's Subscription, etc. were all pestered with *Bourgeoise*) have determined upon having an assembly by subscription opened next winter, to which none are to be admitted to subscribe but such as are balloted for ; and none allowed to be candidates but people of the first rank and consequence. At the head of this scheme are the three noted beauties, the Duchess of Devonshire, Lady Derby, and the Marchioness of Granby. Difficulties have been found how to determine who are of proper rank. Lady —— was among the first that applied in case the scheme went on, but it was determined that a new made Irish Lord, without his family having been long established, was nobody ; and therefore her Ladyship was rejected in right of her husband, but it is said, is accepted in right of her own family. Plans of this sort have often been thought of and will probably end in the distinction of an old and new nobility, which has taken place in so many countries.

Thursday, June 27th.

The insurrection of the journeymen carpenters is increased to an alarming height ; they met on Tuesday last at Mother Red Cap's, about 4,000 in number, where they entered into certain articles for the support of their schemes : the most material was that no man, under the severest penalties, should work under the advanced price of 20s. a week, and that those who first entered upon those wages should allow three shillings out of his weekly allowance for the support of his brethren who continued out of employ.

Friday, June 28th.

Yesterday came on in the Court of Common Pleas, before Lord Chief Justice de Grey, an action of Damages brought by Stephen Sayre, Esq. ; against William Henry Earl of Rochford, for an illegal seizure of his papers, and false imprisonment, on the 23rd of October last.

The Lord Chief Justice . . . observed on the points of law, and summed up the evidence ; observing that the present decision was of the highest consequence, as the proceedings seemed to have affected the safety of Government on one hand, and the liberty of the subject on the other. . . . One remark was very striking, viz. " That what would be innocent regarding a subject, might become extreme guilt when it respected the King."

The jury then withdrew ; but a point of law being started by the Defendant's Counsel, about the competency of the Jury's bringing in a verdict independent of the after opinion of the court in point of justification : After much battling between the advocates, they all agreed, that the Jury may ascertain what damages they thought proper, subject to the two following questions of law, to be afterwards decided by the court.

1st Question, whether an offer of bail, and refusal, was admissible evidence on the issue joined on the Special Plea ?

2nd Question, whether the evidence was a sufficient proof

of an offer and refusal of bail to make the subsequent imprisonment illegal ?

The Jury being brought back into court to be informed of this, returned, and about six o'clock gave a verdict for the Plaintiff (subject to an after determination of those two questions) of one thousand pounds damages.

JULY 1776

Thursday, July 4th.

The following are the particulars of an engagement between His Majesty's ship the *Rose*, of 20 guns, commanded by Capt. Wallace and two American privateers of Rhode Island : " Capt. Wallace, whose ship was to the windward, as soon as he perceived they were American vessels, cleared his ship for action, bore down to them, and demanded the commander of the largest vessel to hoist out his boat and come on board his ship ; when, on the latter's refusal, an engagement ensued, which continued very hot for upwards of two hours, the smallest vessel lying all the action on the Rose's quarter, and the largest close alongside of her ; however, at length the small privateer receiving several dangerous shot in her bottom, which made her very leaky, sheered off ; and the *Rose* having great part of her rigging shot away and her masts wounded, maintained a running fight with the other till she sheltered herself in Rhode Island."

Friday, July 5th.

[Last Monday] a poor woman, at Earls-Hilton, Leicestershire, that could scarce crawl, was cruelly plunged in a pond by way of trying if she was a witch ; and might have lost her life, had it not been for the neighbouring gentlemen, merely because her suffering blood to be drawn from her body, and blessing another poor woman, who was thought to be bewitched by her, had not the desired effect.

Saturday, July 6th.

That nothing may be wanting to complete the greatness of his political character, his Prussian Majesty is now about to establish a navy more for the honour, he says, than the safety of his territories ; and in consequence thereof several docks are now framing at Emden, and at various ports in his newly acquired Polish dominions. He has . . . already manned and victualled eight armed ships of considerable burden, which are about to sail to the East Indies under the command of the well-known Mr. Botts, late of the English East India Company, who has full powers and instructions to establish a principal settlement in the richest part of Asia : It is well for the peace and prosperity of the European commercial states, that Frederick of Prussia — has one foot in the grave !

Tuesday, July 9th.

The journeymen carpenters, notwithstanding it is with the greatest difficulty that they can, even at this time of the year, maintain themselves and their families ; yet, as they have in vain petitioned their masters for redress, they are determined to submit to their present fate, and return to work ; but that they will take the first opportunity to offer an humble petition to Parliament to obtain relief under their present circumstances by getting the wages between themselves and their masters to be settled by the Justices of the Peace at their Quarter Sessions ; and in the meantime they are resolved to work for no master who collects his journeymen together on a Saturday night to pay them their wages at a public-house, commonly called a pay-table, where they are obliged to spend a great part of the wages they have earned in the week by the sweat of their brows, to the injury of their families ; for at these pay-tables they are often kept till near twelve o'clock before they receive their wages. This evil prevents their wives from going to market till Sunday morning, which gives common informers, who are a disgrace to human nature, an opportunity of betraying good-natured tradesmen from their compassion into a violation of the law ; but whenever any master tradesmen pays his men at an alehouse, it is always supposed that the publican furnished the money to pay the wages ; in return for which the master, out of compliment to the publican, keeps his men drinking as long as he can. The event ultimately is this : the publican lends his money to the builder, the journeymen make long scores, and move to other parts of the town ; so that at last the whole comes out of the pocket of the brewer, who, if he was wise, would never serve a public-house where there was a pay-table, which is as destructive to him as a gaming-table would be.

Wednesday, July 10th.

Mr. Foote, at the Little Theatre in the Haymarket, appeared (their Majesties being present) in the character of Lady Pentweazle, with a head-dress stuck full of feathers in the utmost extravagance of the present mode, being at least a yard wide. Their Majesties laughed immoderately ; and to heighten the ridicule the whole fabric of feathers, hair and wool dropped off as Foote waddled off the stage, which continued the roar for some time. The elegant, becoming manner in which Her Majesty's head was dressed, was, however, the severest satire on the present filthy fashion.

Thursday, July 11th.

Yesterday a commission passed the Great Seal appointing Henry Strachey, Esq., Secretary to his Majesty's Commission for restoring peace to his Colonies in North America, and for granting pardons to such of his subjects now in rebellion as shall deserve the royal mercy, with a salary of £587 per ann. during his life, out of the 4½ per cents at the Exchequer. . . .

Friday, July 12th.

[There died] lately Mr. James Ashley, aged 78, master of the punch-house on Ludgate-Hill, which he had kept forty-five years. He was the first to introduce the selling of punch in small quantities, by which he not only made a large fortune, but greatly promoted the interest of the British Islands, and the increase of the revenue.

Sunday, July 14th.

A riotous mob of weavers assembled at Shepton Mallet, in Somersetshire, [on Wednesday] to destroy some machines [called the Spinning Jenny] lately erected there for expediting their work. They had scarce accomplished their purpose when a party of soldiers appeared, and some of the ring leaders were apprehended, whom the mob endeavoured to rescue by attacking the soldiers. This brought on a serious action, in which seven persons were either killed or wounded.

Monday, July 15th.

Captain Bromfield of the *Salisbury* East Indiaman now in the River, has brought over one of the largest and most beautiful tigers ever beheld in this country, as a present to Lord North ; he was so ferocious on his passage as to bite off a hand from each of his two feeders, but by being kept on the open deck in a large coop, he is become somewhat more tame.

The notorious smuggler called Gipsy George who stands charged with the murder of Pearson, the Custom House officer, was apprehended at Portsmouth [on Friday].

Wednesday, July 17th.

London could put Florence into its fob-pocket ; but as they build so slightly, if they did not rebuild, it would be just the reverse of Rome, a vast circumference of city surrounding an area of ruins. As its present progress is chiefly north, and Southwark marches south, the metropolis promises to be as broad as long. Rows of houses shoot out every way like a polypus . . . so great is the rage of building everywhere. . . . America and France must tell us how long this exuberance of opulence is to last ! The East Indies, I believe, will not contribute to it much longer. Babylon and Memphis and Rome probably stared at their own downfall. Empires did not use to philosophize, nor thought much but of themselves. Such revolutions are better known now, and we ought to expect them. . . . This little island will be ridiculously proud some ages hence of its former brave days, and swear its capital was once as big again as Paris, or — what is to be the name of the city that will then give laws to Europe — perhaps New York or Philadelphia.

Saturday, July 20th.

[Some account of Captain Cook's departure :]
Having received a commission to command His Majesty's sloop the *Resolution* [Captain Cook] went on board [on February

10th] . . . and began to enter men. At the same time the *Discovery*, of 300 tons burthen, was purchased into the service and the command of her given to Captain Clarke. . . . These two ships were in the dock at Deptford . . . being ordered to be equipped to make further discoveries in the Pacific Ocean. . . .

With the benevolent view of conveying some permanent benefit to the inhabitants of Otaheite, and of the other islands in the Pacific Ocean, whom [they] might happen to visit, His Majesty having commanded some useful animals to be carried out [they] took on board . . . a bull, two cows with their calves, and some sheep, with hay and corn . . . with a sufficient quantity of such of our European garden seeds as could not fail to be a valuable present to our newly-discovered islands. . . .

Nothing was denied to [the ships] that could be supposed in the least conducive to health, or even to convenience. . . .

Omai left London with a mixture of regret and satisfaction. When we talked about England, and those who, during his stay, had honoured him with their protection or friendship, I could observe that . . . it was with difficulty he could refrain from tears. But the instant the conversation turned to his own islands his eyes began to sparkle with joy. He was deeply impressed with a sense of the good treatment he had met with in England. . . .

He was furnished by His Majesty with an ample provision of every article [likely to be held in estimation in Otaheite]. He had, besides, received many presents of the same nature from Lord Sandwich, Mr. Banks [and others]. . . . In short, every method had been employed . . . to make him the instrument of conveying to the inhabitants of the islands of the Pacific Ocean the most exalted opinion of the greatness and generosity of the British nation. . . .

On the 30th [of June, the *Resolution*] anchored in Plymouth Sound, where the *Discovery* had arrived only three days before. . . . [The *Resolution* sailed on July 12, and was followed a few days later by the *Discovery*.] . . .

Without being liable to any charge of want of zeal for the public service [Captain Cook] might have passed the rest of

his days in the command [of] Greenwich Hospital, there to
enjoy the fame he had dearly earned. . . . But he cheerfully
relinquished this honourable station . . . [for] the toils and
perils of a third circumnavigation, by a track hitherto un-
attempted. . . .

Sunday, July 21st.

The thought of visiting a gaol is shocking to most people,
and few have philanthropy enough to do it ; therefore they
have been suffered to run into the greatest disorder. . . . It is
well known what sort of people many of the gaolers are, and
when such people are left to themselves what else is to be
expected but oppression, debauchery and confusion ? And
how is this to be known ? . . . Besides the danger of infection
attending the visitation of gaols, few accustomed to any degree
of cleanliness could bear the stench of such places, or stand the
shock of such misery. Vagrants and disorderly women of the
very lowest and most wretched clan of human beings, almost
naked, with only a few filthy rags almost alive and in motion
with vermin, their bodies rotting with the bad distemper and
covered with itch, scorbutic and venereal ulcers ; and being
unable to treat the constable even with a pot of beer to let them
escape, are drove in shoals to gaols, particularly to the two
Clerkenwells and Tothill-fields. There thirty and sometimes
near forty of these unhappy wretches are crowded or crammed
together in one ward, where in the dark they bruise and beat
one another in a most shocking manner.

In the morning, before the turnkeys open the doors of the
different wards, which are more like the black hole in Calcutta
than places of confinement in a Christian country, they are
obliged to drink a glass of spirits to keep them from fainting,
for the putrid steam or miasma is enough to knock them
down. . . .

The benevolent Mr. Howard has taken an infinite deal of
pains to come at a perfect knowledge of gaols, and will soon
publish his discoveries, which cannot fail to awaken the
attention of the legislature and prevail upon them to supply
some effectual remedy for so alarming grievances. . . . What
can be of greater consequence to a nation, or greater glory to a

king than to prevent the wretched from being still more so, to reclaim the profligate and abandoned and to render them useful members of society, to defend the lives and liberties of the innocent and to make the criminal's punishment contribute to the general good of society ?

Wednesday, July 24th.

[Yesterday] evening Mary-le-bone Gardens exhibited a scene equally novel and agreeable, namely a representation of the Boulevards of Paris. The boxes fronting the ball-room, which were converted into shops, had a very pleasing effect . . . — Crotchet, a music-shop ; a ginger-bread shop (no name over it), the owner in a large bag-wig and deep ruffles *à la mode de Paris* : Medley (from Darley's) a print shop ; New-fangle, a milliner ; a hardware shop and lottery office in one (the price of tickets £11. 14. 0) ; *La Blonde*, a milliner ; Pine, a fruiterer ; Trinket, a toyshop . . . *Tête*, a hair-dresser . . . Madame Pine, Messrs. Trinket and *le Marchand de Gingerbread*, ran away with the custom . . . Mr. *Tête* indeed would have had a good share of trade, but that the ladies were previously provided . . . If his head-dresses were as big as a peck, many of theirs could not be crammed into a bushel.

The ball-room was illuminated in an elegant manner with coloured lamps ; and at one end of it women attended, selling orgeat, lemonade, and other cooling liquors. This was intended as a representation of the English coffee-house at Paris. . . . The number of persons present is thought to be about 600.

Friday, July 26th.

During this recess of the performances at Covent Garden and Drury Lane theatres . . . the managers are not idle. . . . It will be a very harmonious winter. Indeed, the success of the *Duenna* last season was so extraordinary that we may reasonably suppose there will be many poetical candidates in the same line. In the meanwhile, Mr. Foote entertains the town in the Hay Market, and although he has, as yet, produced nothing new but the *Contract* and a new scene in the *Cozeners* he has had great success, playing generally to crowded houses. This may, in some measure, be ascribed to their Majesties frequently honouring him with their presence.   The company at Richmond has also produced good houses and met with applause, there being among them some of the best performers that have appeared in that agreeable spot for some years. . . .

Saturday, July 27th.

On Wednesday last died, at its apartments near St. James's Park, the Queen's elephant and on Thursday Dr. Hunter, attended by six of his pupils, anatomized that animal.

Sunday, July 28th.

[Lately published :]
An account and description of an improved steam-engine, which will with the same quantity of fuel and an equal space of time raise above double the quantity of water than any lever engine of the same dimensions. By N. D. Falck, M.D.   2s.   Law.

The British Chronologist ; comprehending every material occurrence, ecclesiastical, civil or military, relative to England and Wales, from the invasion of the Romans to the present time, &c.   3 vols.   8vo.   18s. Kearsley.

The Gentleman and Lady's Gardener ; containing the modern method of cultivating the kitchen garden, flower garden, and for raising of forest trees.   2s.   Edmeades, seedsman.

Monday, July 29th.

An express was received at Lord George Germain's office on Saturday, and printed in the *Gazette*, which thereby delayed the publication till 2 o'clock on Sunday morning ; giving an account of Sir Guy Carleton's having taken possession of Montreal and burning all the buildings and vessels at St. John's.

Tuesday, July 30th.

The eclipse . . . which was many years since prognosticated, with a remarkable degree of precision, by that great master of the astrological science, Sir Isaac Newton, began to be observable at ten minutes after ten in the evening.   At that time the face of the moon (which was uncommonly bright and luminous) commenced gradually to be obscured by a shadow of the earth, it was wholly covered with the shade at half after twelve, and from that period recovered its natural lustre in the same proportion of time in which it lost it.

Wednesday, July 31st.

[On June 28th] Sir Peter Parker made an attack upon Sullivan's Island, the key to Charles-Town, the capital of South-Carolina ; but was repulsed with great damage to his ships, and great loss of his men. Among the killed was the brave Captain Morris, commander of the *Bristol* man of war. . . .

AUGUST 1776

Friday, August 2nd.

Died . . . Matthew Maty, M.D. Principal Librarian of the British Museum, and secretary to the Royal Society, a very learned and ingenious gentleman ; and well-known, as such, in the literary world.

[And lately,] Mrs. Mary Yates, of Shiffnal, aged 128 years. She walked to London after the fire in 1666, married a third husband in her ninety-second year, and was hearty and strong at 120.

Saturday, August 3rd.

[On Thursday] both Houses of Parliament met pursuant to their last prorogation, and were further prorogued to the 5th day of September.

List of ships ordered to be got ready immediately viz. *Prince George*, *Queen* and *Sandwich* of 90 guns ; *Bedford*, *Courageous*, *Culloden* and *Hector*, of 74 guns ; *St. Alban's*, *Augusta*, *Biensaisant* and *Ripon*, of 64 ; the three last to be sheathed with copper.

Monday, August 5th.

The curious in this city have now an opportunity of examining the wonderful powers of the Gymnotus Electricus, commonly called the Electric Eel, as Mr. George Baker, mariner, who last year made an unsuccessful attempt to bring some alive from the equinoctial parts of America to London, indefatigable to gratify the public in this particular, has now succeeded in landing here five living Gymnoti, all taken by himself 150 miles up the river of Surinam : he is probably the first who has landed any of the kind alive in Europe, and has thereby afforded a striking instance of the industry of this country in matters of science, particularly as the Gymnotus, though common in the American Colonies of other European States, is not to be met within those of Great Britain. On Thursday the President and many gentlemen of the Royal Society were present at an exhibition of the effects of these extraordinary fish ; and on Friday Mr. Walsh, whose observations on the Electricity of the Torpedo have been published in the Philosophical Transactions [of the Royal Society], made some experiments on them, and obtained from the Gymnotus the electrical spark, which he never could procure from the Torpedo ; by which event an entire agreement in the natural effect of these animals, and the artificial effect of the Leyden phial, is established.

Tuesday, August 6th.

Dr. Robertson's long expected work, the History of Spanish America, was sold we hear, a few days ago, for two thousand seven hundred pounds ; it is to be comprised in two volumes quarto, and is expected to be published next Spring.

Wednesday, August 7th.

Monday last a very large number of journeymen carpenters assembled in Stepney fields, for the purpose of raising their wages ; but Justice Sherwood having had previous notice of such meeting, he, with two other magistrates, Mr. Blackmore and Mr. Curtis, attended by the High Constable and peace officers, met them near Bow Common, where the men drew up in a ring, and received the Justices with great respect, acquainted them with their supposed grievances, etc. and of the occasion of their meeting. To which the justice told them, if they would leave at Mr. Sherwood's office, their case, or any plan they could wish to have put in force, they would give any assistance, but feared nothing but a bill in parliament to regulate their wages would do, as in the case of the weavers ; but . . . insisted on their immediately dispersing, which they instantly complied with cheerfully, without the least indecent or irregular behaviour.

Commission superseded.

John Carr, of Scotland-yard, Coal-merchant, (Partner in Trade with James Farrer and Edward Arrowsmith, of the same Place, Coal-merchants.)

Bankrupts enlarged.

James Farrer, Edward Arrowsmith, and John Carr, of Scotland-yard, Coal-merchants and Partners, to surrender Aug. 29, at Guildhall.

Dividends to be made.

Sept. 3. John Gardner, late of Romsley, in Hants, Clothier, at the Angel in Romsey.

11. Richard Ford, of Coalbrookdale, in the County of Salop, Ironmaster, at Mary Corbett's, in High-street, Bridgnorth, Salop.

20. Benjamin Cooper, late of Walsall, in Staffordshire, and Joseph Hodgkin, late of Aldridge, in the said County, Merchants and Traders, at the King's-head in New-street, Birmingham.

Certificate to be granted.

Aug. 31. William Richardson, of Fenchurch-street, London, Linen-draper.

LONDON.

Advice is received that the Congress resolved upon independency the 4th of July; and, it is said, have declared war against Great Britain in form.

When General Thompson was conducted in the guard-room at Montreal with the rest of the prisoners of that day, he requested an audience of his brother. General. Carleton, and a subaltern waited on him with the message, which Carleton refused complying with, and returned for answer, " that he never held any conversation with rebels."

A letter from Paris received on Saturday, says, " that the French Court have absolutely

On Tuesday last was married at Ash, in Kent, the Rev. Mr. Hutchinson of No-bourn, to Miss Elizabeth Beale Pery, of Ash.

On Saturday last was married at Crayford, in Kent, Mr. Essex, of Southampton-street, Covent-Garden, to Miss Nancy Wright, of Crayford.

Yesterday was married Mr. Samuel Penn, of this City, to Miss Tate of the Old Change.

On Friday last died at Greenwich, Captain Francis Minshull.

On Saturday last died, at his house in St. James's-street, Mr. Matthew Crane, Apothecary to the Houshold.

At Shrewsbury affixes John Herbert for sheep-stealing, was capitally convicted, but afterwards reprieved.

H. M. The Nabob, with Tate.

This Day was published, Price 1s. 6d.

A New Edition, corrected to the present time, on a broad sheet of elephant paper, proper for framing, with an elegant engraved border,

A COMPLETE TITHE-TABLE: Wherein are shewn at one view the nature of tithes, and all things tithable, with an account of compositions; custom, prescription, and privilege, distinguished under their proper heads; with reference to abridged cases, and statutes relating to tithes.

Proper for all Vestries, Halls of Clergymen and Gentlemen, as well as Attornies.

Printed for J. F. and C. Rivington, No. 62, in St. Paul's Church-yard.

Or, whom may be had,

A Sporting Table: Wherein all the laws touching game are shewn at one view. Price 1s. 6d.

SOCIETY for the Discharge and Relief of Persons imprisoned for Small Debts.

Craven-street, Strand, July 31, 1776.

BENEFACTIONS since the last report, l. s. d.
viz.

	l.	s.	d.
Mr W. w. a Lady	100	0	0
Lord Chief Baron Smythe, annual	5	5	0
Lady Smythe, ditto	2	2	0
Mr. Hull, ditto	2	2	0
W. d. 3d benefaction	5	5	0
A. R.	2	2	0
B. B.	0	10	6
D. C. July 18	3	3	0
J. H. by J. R.	1	1	0
	122	12	6

Discharged from the several prisons in the metropolis, and other parts of the kingdom, 26 Debtors, who could not be relieved by the Insolvent Act, for 39 l. 6 s. 2 d.

Approved the recommendations of 24 Petitioners.
Referred for Enquiry 19 Petitions.

The books may be seen by any person inclined to promote this undertaking, between the hours of Eleven and Three, at No. 7, Craven-street, where benefactions are received, and where the Society will meet on Wednesday the 22d of August, at Six o'Clock in the Afternoon.

Benefactions are also received by Mr. Willis, at the Thatch'd-house Tavern; the London Exchange Banking Company; and Mr. Nield, the Treasurer, in St. James's-street; by Messrs. Dorrien and Co. in Finch-lane, Cornhill; Messrs. Hoares, in Fleet-street; Messrs. Biddulph and Cocks, at Charing-Cross; Messrs. Fullers; and Messrs. Lowry and Co. in Lombard-street; and Mr. Leacroft, Bookseller, at Charing-Cross.

Saturday, August 10th.

DECLARATION BY THE REPRESENTATIVES OF THE UNITED
STATES OF AMERICA, IN GENERAL CONGRESS ASSEMBLED,
JULY 4 _____

When in the course of human events, it becomes necessary
for one people to dissolve the political bands which have connected them with another, and to assume among the powers
of the earth the separate and equal station to which the Laws
of Nature and of Nature's God entitle them, a decent respect
to the opinions of mankind requires that they should declare
the causes which impel them to the separation.

We hold these truths to be self-evident, that all men are
created equal, that they are endowed by their Creator with
certain unalienable rights, that among these are life, liberty,
and the pursuit of happiness.   That to secure these rights,
governments are instituted among men, deriving their just
powers from the consent of the governed.   That whenever any
form of government becomes destructive of these ends, it is
the right of the people to alter or to abolish it, and to institute
new government, laying its foundation on such principles and
organizing its powers in such form, as to them shall seem most
likely to effect their safety and happiness.   Prudence, indeed,
will dictate that governments long established should not be
changed for light and transient causes ;   and accordingly all
experience hath shown, that mankind are more disposed to
suffer, while evils are sufferable, than to right themselves by
abolishing the forms to which they are accustomed.   But when
a long train of abuses and usurpations, pursuing invariably the
same object, evinces a design to reduce them under absolute
despotism, it is their right, it is their duty, to throw off such
government, and to provide new guards for their future security.
Such has been the patient sufferance of these Colonies ;   and
such is now the necessity which constrains them to alter their
former systems of government.   The history of the present King
of Great Britain is a history of repeated injuries and usurpations, all having in direct object the establishment of an absolute
tyranny over these States.   To prove this, let facts be submitted
to a candid world.

He has refused his assent to laws, the most wholesome and necessary for the public good.

He has forbidden his Governors to pass laws of immediate and pressing importance, unless suspended in their operation till his assent should be obtained ; and when so suspended, he has utterly neglected to attend to them.

He has refused to pass other laws for the accommodation of large districts of people, unless those people would relinquish the right of representation in the legislature, a right inestimable to them and formidable to tyrants only.

He has called together legislative bodies at places unusual, uncomfortable, and distant from the depository of their public records, for the sole purpose of fatiguing them into compliance with his measures.

He has dissolved representative houses repeatedly, for opposing with manly firmness his invasions on the rights of the people.

He has refused for a long time, after such dissolutions, to cause others to be elected ; whereby the legislative powers, incapable of annihilation, have returned to the people at large for their exercise ; the State remaining in the meantime exposed to all the dangers of invasion from without and convulsions within.

He has endeavoured to prevent the population of these States ; for that purpose obstructing the laws for naturalisation of foreigners ; refusing to pass others to encourage their migration hither, and raising the conditions of new appropriations of lands.

He has obstructed the administration of justice, by refusing his assent to laws for establishing judiciary powers.

He has made judges dependent on his will alone, for the tenure of their offices, and the amount and payment of their salaries.

He has erected a multitude of new offices, and sent hither swarms of officers to harass our people, and eat out their substance.

He has kept among us, in times of peace, standing armies without the consent of our legislatures.

He has affected to render the military independent of and superior to the civil power.

He has combined with others to subject us to a jurisdiction foreign to our constitution, and unacknowledged by our laws ; giving his assent to their acts of pretended legislation :

For quartering large bodies of armed troops among us :

For protecting them, by a mock trial, from punishment for any murders which they should commit on the inhabitants of these States :

For cutting off our trade with all parts of the world :

For imposing taxes on us without our consent :

For depriving us in many cases of the benefits of trial by jury :

For transporting us beyond seas to be tried for pretended offences :

For abolishing the free system of English laws in a neighbouring Province, establishing therein an arbitrary government and enlarging its boundaries so as to render it at once an example and fit instrument for introducing the same absolute rule into these Colonies :

For taking away our Charters, abolishing our most valuable laws, and altering fundamentally the forms of our governments :

For suspending our own Legislatures, and declaring themselves invested with power to legislate for us in all cases whatsoever.

He has abdicated government here, by declaring us out of his protection and waging war against us.

He has plundered our seas, ravaged our coasts, burnt our towns, and destroyed the lives of our people.

He is at this time transporting large armies of foreign mercenaries to complete the works of death, desolation, and tyranny, already begun with circumstances of cruelty and perfidy scarcely paralleled in the most barbarous ages, and totally unworthy the head of a civilized nation.

He has constrained our fellow citizens taken captive on the high seas to bear arms against their country, to become the executioners of their friends and brethren, or to fall themselves by their hands.

He has excited domestic insurrections amongst us, and has endeavoured to bring on the inhabitants of our frontiers the merciless Indian savages, whose known rule of warfare is an undistinguished destruction of all ages, sexes and conditions.

In every stage of these oppressions we have petitioned for redress in the most humble terms : our repeated petitions have been answered only by repeated injury. A prince whose character is thus marked by every act which may define a tyrant, is unfit to be the ruler of a free people.

Nor have we been wanting in attention to our British brethren. We have warned them from time to time of attempts by their Legislature to extend an unwarrantable jurisdiction over us. We have reminded them of the circumstances of our emigration and settlement here. We have appealed to their native justice and magnanimity, and we have conjured them by the ties of our common kindred to disavow these usurpations, which would inevitably interrupt our connections and correspondence. They too have been deaf to the voice of justice and consanguinity. We must, therefore, acquiesce in the necessity, which denounces our separation, and hold them as we hold the rest of mankind, enemies in war, in peace friends.

We, therefore, the Representatives of the United States of America, in General Congress assembled, appealing to the Supreme Judge of the world for the rectitude of our intentions, do, in the name, and by authority of the good people of these Colonies, solemnly publish and declare, That these United Colonies are, and of right ought to be, Free and Independent States ; that they are absolved from all allegiance to the British Crown, and that all political connection between them and the State of Great Britain is and ought to be totally dissolved ; and that as Free and Independent States they have full power to levy war, conclude peace, contract alliances, establish commerce, and to do all other acts and things which independent States may of right do. And for the support of this declaration, with a firm reliance on the protection of Divine Providence, we mutually pledge to each other our lives, our fortunes and our sacred honour.

Signed by order and in behalf of the Congress,

JOHN HANCOCK, President

Attest,   CHARLES THOMPSON, Secretary

Sunday, August 11th.

Ann Cruttenden, for the wilful murder of her husband was
burnt at Horsham, in Sussex, [on Thursday]. She showed
marks of insanity to the last.

Monday, August 12th.

The great cricket match between Surrey and Hampshire,
on Laleham Burway, was on Thursday afternoon, at four
o'clock, determined in favour of Surrey. The players on that
side had eight wickets to go down, and wanted 110 notches to
tie. The first three or four who went in, were exceedingly
unfortunate, getting but very few ; the two last (Lumpy and
Wood) had 43 left for them to get. Bets ran more than twenty
to one against them, six guineas being laid to two shillings and
sixpence, by some persons, and other bets equally extravagant.
To the astonishment, however, of all present, Lumpy got 19,
and Wood 19, and 5 bye-balls gave them the victory. This is
beyond example the most extraordinary game of cricket that
ever was played.

Tuesday, August 13th.

Friday se'nnight last, at the Ball at Tunbridge, the ladies
were thrown into the most ludicrous consternation by the
inclemency of the evening : the thunder and lightning were so
tremendous, that every gentleman in course became anxious
for the safety of her he beloved best ; one beau in particular
entreated his partner for the love of God and him, to pull the
black pins out of her hair, for fear they should attract the
lightning to blast her brilliant eyes ; — the Lady, alarmed at
the exhortation, instantly set about it, and with a violent
scream cried out, Ladies, pull out your black pins ! — The
effect of this word of command was astonishing, and the
manoeuvre consequently beyond any executed by the most
dextrous Prussian Regiment of Infantry ; for in less than a
minute ten thousand black spears were grounded on the
floor, together with Cushions ! Wools of divers colours and
assortments ! — fore curls — and hind curls in abundance ! —
in short, what with the dishevelled locks and piercing shrieks

of young virgins, and the long faces of the bald dowagers, there never was so frantic an exit from an Assembly-room exhibited before in either of the three kingdoms.

Thursday, August 15th.

The fate of New York, and, in all probability, of the lives of thousands of his Majesty's British and American subjects, will depend entirely upon the answer that will be given by the commander of the provincial forces to Lord Howe's terms of accommodation, which were to be carried by a flag into New York previous to the intended bombardment : — it is earnestly to be wished that these propositions may breathe a temper of mercy and forgiveness which may save that general and dreadful carnage that must otherwise succeed.

Thursday, August 22nd.

Tuesday morning last their Majesties made a visit to the Bishop of Winchester, at Farnham Castle, in Surrey ; his Majesty drove the Queen there in his phaeton, and his white horses ; where they stayed some time, drank chocolate, and afterwards returned to Windsor to dinner.

Sunday, August 25th.

[David Hume, Esq., died at Edinburgh, about 4 o'clock in the afternoon. Adam Smith, Esq., writes :]

Upon his return to Edinburgh [from Bath], though he found himself much weaker, yet his cheerfulness never abated and he continued to divert himself as usual, with correcting his own works for a new edition, with reading books of amusement, with the conversation of his friends ; and sometimes in the evening with a party at his favourite game of whist. His cheerfulness was so great, and his conversation and amusements ran so much in their usual strain, that notwithstanding all bad symptoms, many people could not believe he was dying. " I shall tell your friend Colonel Edmonstoune," said Dr. Dundas to him one day, " that I left you much better, and in a fair way of recovery." " Doctor," said he, " as I believe you would not choose to tell any thing but the truth, you had better tell him I am dying as fast as my enemies, if I have any, could wish,

and as easily and cheerfully as my best friends could desire." ...
Mr. Hume's magnanimity and firmness were such that his
most affectionate friends knew that they hazarded nothing in
talking and writing to him as to a dying man ; and that so far
from being hurt by this frankness, he was rather pleased and
flattered by it. . . . He said that . . . when he was reading,
a few days before, Lucian's *Dialogues of the Dead*, among all the
excuses which are alleged to Charon for not entering readily
into his boat, he could not find one that fitted him : he had no
house to finish, he had no daughter to provide for, he had no
enemies upon whom he wished to revenge himself. " I could
not well imagine," said he, " what excuse I could make to
Charon, in order to obtain a little delay. I have done every
thing of consequence which I ever meant to do, and I could
at no time expect to leave my relations and friends in a better
situation than that in which I am now likely to leave them : I
therefore have all reason to die contented." He then diverted
himself with inventing several jocular excuses, which he supposed he might make to Charon, and with imagining the very
surly answers which it might suit the character of Charon to
return to them. " Upon further consideration," said he, " I
thought I might say to him, ' Good Charon, I have been
correcting my works for a new edition. Allow me a little time
that I may see how the public receives the alterations.' But
Charon would answer, ' When you have seen the effect of
these, you will be for making other alterations. There will be
no end of such excuses ; so, honest friend, please step into the
boat.' But I might still urge, ' Have a little patience, good
Charon, I have been endeavouring to open the eyes of the
public. If I live a few years longer, I may have the satisfaction
of seeing the downfall of some of the prevailing systems of
superstition.' But Charon would then lose all temper and
decency. ' You loitering rogue, that will not happen these
many hundred years. Do you fancy I will grant you a lease
for so long a term ? Get into the boat this instant, you lazy,
loitering rogue.' " . . .

Concerning [his] philosophical opinions men will no doubt
judge variously . . . but concerning [his] character and
conduct there can scarce be a difference of opinion. . . . I

311

have always considered him, both in his lifetime, and since his death, as approaching as nearly to the idea of a perfectly wise and virtuous man as perhaps the nature of human frailty will admit.

Monday, August 26th.

[Extract of a letter from Brighthelmstone, August 23rd :]

This town is still as full as it possibly can be ; the company seems to increase instead of decrease. Last night we had, what is called here, a dress ball ; and indeed I never saw at any of the watering-places, a more polite and better dressed assembly. Our macaronies here are in the utmost pink of the *ton*, and vie with each other in dress, phaetons, and gambling. They have lately introduced a new species of the latter, which is by raffling for diamonds, bracelets, toys and jewels of every sort. If three or four of them chance to meet at Nodes's, or Jones's, one of them immediately swears he wants such a bijou for his mistress : another says, he was just going to declare the same thing ; so does a third and fourth. Well, what's to be done ! Why, raffle for it.— Agreed. What's the price, Sir ? — Forty guineas. They immediately subscribe, and raffle for it, then he who wins puts up something else ; thus the jeweller sells most of the articles in his shop, and if by accident a Duke, a Lord, or woman of style, happens to be in the shop, then every one of the Bucks strive to excel the others in absurdity and extravagance.

Our ball last night was very elegant, and we had a great number of very pretty women, some who are come here for husbands, and others to perform quarantine, and undergo their annual wash and exercise.

The prettiest women we have here are Lady Margaret Fordyce, Lady Bridget Douglas, Miss Mordaunt, Miss Philips, and Miss Ellikers ; there are some others, whose names I do not recollect ; and the fortune-hunters are very busy after the Miss Fredericks, who are rated at £150,000 each ; Miss Lanson at £70,000, the Miss Ellikers at £50,000 each, and Miss Philips at £20,000.— The men who were at the ball were, the Duke of Fitzjames, Lord Peterborough, Lord Mordaunt, Lord Kelly, Sir J. Warren, Sir A. Leith, Sir T. Mills, Sir J.

Rous, Mr. Onslow, Mr. Beauclerc, Mr. Hare, Mr. Dashwood, Mr. Stewart, Captain Brown, Capt. Watson, Mr. Wilkes, etc. etc. . . .

Tuesday, August 27th.

On Sunday upwards of 200 journeymen carpenters left London in order to work in the different country towns ; 40 also shipped themselves for Ireland, being determined not to comply with the masters' terms.

Wednesday, August 28th.

[Extract of a letter from Judge Morris to Governor Legge, dated Halifax, Nova Scotia, July 8th :]

The army has sailed from hence about four weeks, but we have not heard where destined ; part of the Hessians and the Guards arrived last week and sailed on Saturday for the general rendezvous ; they parted with the remainder on the banks of Newfoundland. Canada is in a manner evacuated by the rebels, Montreal is in possession of the English troops, and the army in pursuit of their main body, consisting of 6,000 men, and who were retreating to Fort St. John's on the river Sorell as we were informed by the last advices from Canada. The Americans seem determined in their opposition, but a report has prevailed here that upon the Congress attempting to declare the Provinces independent, great numbers in Philadelphia opposed them, and that many rose in arms. I hope this report has some foundation in truth ; it's possible this may be the turning crisis, for it cannot be supposed that independency can be the aim of the Americans in general.

Friday, August 30th.

The last arch of the fine stone bridge at Richmond, is now turning, and will be passable in a few months, tho' not two years since it was begun ; a circumstance that is uncommon in a public work.

SEPTEMBER 1776

Tuesday, September 3rd.

About seven in the evening, Governor Eden, of Maryland, arrived express from Portsmouth with fresh dispatches to Lord George Germain's office. He came from Virginia in the *Levant* transport, Capt. Thomas, and was only 28 days in his passage.

The Lord Mayor, sheriffs and city officers proclaimed Bartholomew Fair in the usual manner ; but all interludes were strictly forbidden, and none have since been exhibited.

Wednesday, September 4th.

Gaming among the females at Chatsworth has been carried to such a pitch, that the phlegmatic Duke has been provoked to excess at it ; and has spoken to the Duchess in the severest terms, against a conduct which has driven many from the house, who could not afford to partake of amusements, carried on at an expense of £500 or £1000 a night.

Friday, September 6th.

The Lord Mayor of London was robbed near Turnham Green in his chaise and four, in sight of all his retinue, by a single highwayman who swore he would shoot the first man that made resistance or offered violence.

Monday, September 9th.

I went to see [the convicts] at work upon the Thames. They are confined on board the hulk of an old West India ship about 300 tons burthen, which lies at anchor close in shore, a little below Woolwich. There are 89 convicts, chained two and two, on board. . . . Each of the overseers or ship's company is armed with a broadsword, horse pistol and gun. The convicts behave with great submission and discover no unwillingness to work. . . .

314

The hulk . . . has a cabin with two beds, a steerage for the ship's company, two small rooms, one of which is appropriated for an hospital-room, and a hold for the rest, where they lie chained in pairs night and day, except when at work in the lighters. About a dozen, in consequence of their good behaviour, have their chains taken off. They eat in messes. Each mess, which consists of six convicts, has an allowance of half a bullock's head, four pound of biscuit, and broth thickened with bread and oatmeal every twenty-four hours. . . . Their drink is water. . . . They at present lie on the bare boards, and the chain which fastens each to his companion admits of their being two or three feet asunder. . . . No person is admitted on board ; no letters, etc. given or received. The hulk is smoked with sulphur and washed with vinegar twice a week. No clergyman visits them, nor have they any medical assistance : twelve are now sick and unable to move their heads from the boards on which they lie. Most of them complain of a diarrhoea ; few are free from scorbutic patches, some with bad sores and venereal complaints, and all look thin and pale. . . .

Saturday, September 14th.

Lord Shelburne being in town, to present a distant relation at the King's Levee, his Majesty conversed some time with him upon his improvements at Bowood, and at last asked him somewhat suddenly what he thought of the Americans ? This was so much out of the common turn of the King's conversation with Minority Lords, that Lord Shelburne hesitated for a moment, but quickly recovering from his surprise, replied, " I think your Majesty's troops will not be able to effect what a little condescension would do at once." — " Why, what is that, my lord ? " " Conquer them, sir. A little mildness would do the business, force never will." " Do you use mildness with your tenants, my lord, when they refuse to pay your rents, but threaten to burn their houses down ? " And then turned the conversation with a laugh, to Dr. Priestley's experiments.

The King is informed minutely of everything that is done or said by the principal Nobility, even in their country residences. If they alter a lake, or improve a lawn, or pull down a part of their house, it comes out to him in the course of his questions to some of their neighbours; and then he talks familiarly with them upon circumstances which they are surprised how he came to know anything of; and these minutiae serve for drawing-room chat the whole winter, which is the King's forte. He can chat and smile with any monarch in Europe.

The Queen, very contrary to her own inclination, it is said, is under the necessity of making an extraordinary distinction in the drawing-room, in her conduct to the Ladies of the Opposition Lords.— She will speak a quarter of an hour to somebody, that nobody knows, standing by the Duchess of Richmond, for instance, slightly speak to the Duchess, and again pause with some other nobody, in order to mark the inattention to the person in question.

Monday, September 16th.

This morning a highwayman was shot on Finchley Common, in attempting to rob the Derby machine. His accomplice has since been apprehended, but there not being proof sufficient of the identity of his person, he has been discharged.

Tuesday, September 17th.

The sessions ended at the Old Bailey, when eleven convicts received sentence of death, viz. one for coining; four for house-breaking, one of them while the family of the house was in the country; two women for shop-lifting; one for horse-stealing, of which he made a practice, in order to kill them, and boil their flesh, etc.; one for street robbery; one for forgery; and one for returning from transportation; thirty-four were ordered to hard labour for three years on the river Thames, among whom were nineteen capital convicts, who had received his Majesty's pardon on that condition; five were ordered to be sent to the house of correction; twelve to be imprisoned in Newgate for different terms; three to be branded in the hand; fourteen to be whipped; and forty-eight were discharged by proclamation.

At this sessions a gentleman was tried for perjury, in

polling twice for Mr. Wilkes at the late election for Chamberlain [of the City] ; but it appearing that what he did was the effect of an habitual intoxication or rather permanent stupidity thereby produced, he was acquitted. . . .

Thursday, September 19th.

Lord George Germain discovered, by means of some private agents he employed, that the engineers whom the Americans have certainly in their pay, were Germans, and sent to America by the King of Prussia.   Orders were given upon this to our Minister at Berlin to remonstrate ; but obtaining no answer to his memorial, he spoke to the King of it, who answered him dryly, " You are fond of colonies in England — these people emigrated — they are German emigrants."   Nor could any other answer be obtained than this, which ought to be deemed an insult.

Monday, September 23rd.

Lord North in taking an airing in Bushy Park, had the misfortune to be flung from his horse, and his arm broke.   It was soon after set, and his Lordship is in a fair way of recovery.

Friday, September 27th.

Yesterday morning about ten o'clock, were married at St. Margaret's Church, Westminster, by the Lord Bishop of Chester, William Eden, Esq., of Downing Street, Principal Secretary to the Earl of Suffolk, to Miss Eleanor Elliot, of Great George Street, youngest daughter of Sir Gilbert Elliot ; the two eldest daughters of Lord North, and Miss Elliot, attended as Bridesmaids ; Sir Gilbert Elliot, his son, and several young people of fashion, were likewise present.   As soon as the ceremony was over, and the new married couple had got into their coach, Mr. Eden threw a handful of silver among the crowd who surrounded the door in Margaret Street. This created much confusion for a little time, several old women being pushed down and trampled under foot.

Mr. and Mrs. Garrick, after staying for a few days with his Grace the Duke of Devonshire at Chatsworth, left that delightful place last week ; and after visiting Matlock, Buxton, and other parts of Derbyshire, proceeded to Litchfield, where that great actor was educated.

Saturday, September 28th.

[Lately published :]

The Physical Friend ; pointing out the symptoms of every distemper incident to man, with those in every stage of the disease. By J. A., M. D. & F.R.S. 2s. 6d. Baldwin.

Free Thoughts on Quacks, and their Medicines ; occasioned by the deaths of Dr. Goldsmith and Mr. Scawen. 2s. 6d. Wilkie.

Omiah's Farewell. Inscribed to the Ladies of London. 1s. Kearsley.

The Annual Register ; or, A View of the History, Politics and Literature, of the year 1775. Dodsley.

An Essay on the Rights of the East India Company to the perpetuity of their trade, possessions and revenues in India, &c. 1s. Payne.

Sunday, September 29th.

Major Creed, of Lord Cornwallis's regiment, and Lieutenant Roberts of the navy, arrived [today] at the Secretary of State's, and the Admiralty offices, with dispatches from their Excellencies Lord Howe and General Howe at New York, and had the honour of being immediately admitted to an audience of his Majesty at the Royal palace at Kew. . . .

Major Creed and Lieutenant Roberts were near six weeks on their passage, and brought word that the Americans will not hear of a reconciliation with the Mother-country on any terms. . . . The Howes wrote word by the above mentioned gentlemen, that their force amounted to 30,000 men, not above twenty of whom were sick, and the rest in good spirits. . . .

Tobacco is now selling at Glasgow at sixpence a pound, such as sold three years ago for threepence, and lately fourpence. It is supposed that the Glasgow merchants will make great fortunes by the high prices of tobacco, as there is a large quantity on hand.

Monday, September 30th.

At the performance of *The Beggar's Opera*, at Covent Garden

Theatre. . . . The orchestra [was disappointing.]   Mr. Fisher
. . . in avoiding one extreme, has run into another equally
unjustifiable, in accompanying the airs only with a first and
second fiddle, and Merlin's new forte piano.— By this super
delicate pianissimo, the melody and harmony of the matchless
airs in this celebrated opera were filtered down to nothing, but
the obligato flourishings of the first fiddle, and the chord of the
new invented harpsichord . . . [were] more absurd, if possible, than the old style of overpowering the voice with the full
force of a large band. . . .

OCTOBER 1776

Tuesday, October 1st.

Administration are at present as busy as possible in securing that sort of majority in Parliament, that shall stand staunch to them, whatever changes of fortune or ill success may attend them ; with this view they have doubly rewarded their old friends, and have made such formidable attacks upon the integrity of several members of the opposition, that it is thought they are brought into such a situation of temptation as Lord Clive described,— that flesh and blood cannot stand it. The conduct, in particular, of Mr. Townshend, Mr. Fox, Governor Johnstone, Lord Shelburne, Colonel Barré, and Mr. Dunning, is at present much suspected.

Wednesday, October 2nd.

A gentleman at a public feast . . . gave as a toast, Hancock and Adams. One of the company, in the Commission of the Peace, threatened to commit him — " You be d——d (said the other) they were both my schoolfellows at Cricklade, and I dare say they are now in congress over a bottle of Wiltshire ale."

Friday, October 4th.

Mr. Brown, the coal merchant, whose daughter eloped from him some months since, attempted to seize her as she stopped in a coach at the end of the Playhouse Passage in Bow Street. The little siren was accompanied by her aunt who made a great outcry, and told the populace Mr. Brown was mad ; the alarm presently reached the Playhouse, and the theatrical garrison sallied out in great numbers, headed by Messrs. M——, B——, W——, and S——, to relieve the distressed damsel. The thieves in *The Beggar's Opera*, armed with pistols, &c. made a most formidable appearance, and the crowd was so numerous, that for a considerable time the

320

street was impassable. At length, however, the lady was handed into the Playhouse in triumph, and, notwithstanding her great agitation of spirits performed the part of Polly greatly to the satisfaction of a very numerous and brilliant audience, who received her with repeated shouts of applause.

Monday, October 7th.

Thirty-two convicts made their escape from on board a transport lying at Limehouse Hole. They had lain six months in the river without knowing where they were to go.

Tuesday, October 8th.

By the last dispatches from Quebec Government has received very agreeable accounts of General Burgoyne's expedition across the Lakes. The vessel building for Lake George was so near completed that Captain Douglas had set off to take the command of her. All the seamen and marines belonging to the ships at Quebec offered to go as volunteers in the expedition ; and all the boats belonging to the ships, amounting to above 300, are to go up the rivers as far as they can, and then are to be carried over land, which will expedite Gen. Burgoyne's expedition greatly, as he may then get his men across the Lakes without waiting for the making of batteaus, so that there is now a certainty of that expedition being accomplished this season in time to answer the most sanguine wishes of Government.

Wednesday, October 9th.

The cruel inhuman practice of bull-baiting was [today] put in execution in Tottenham Court Road, where the beast was no sooner chained, and the dogs let loose at him, but he pulled up the stake, which was but lightly put in the ground, and set off amongst the numerous spectators, several of whom were run over, and some much hurt. It is a pity the civil magistrates don't put a stop to such iniquitous practices, especially when exercised so near town, where people innocently going about their business are in great danger of their lives.

Thursday, October 10th.

The army under General Howe, after he had made, on the 18th, some further proposals to the provincials, but without effect, being previously joined by a large body of Hessians, made good their landing on Long Island ; and, on the 27th, part of the Provincial army, commanded by General Sullivan, was totally routed ; upon which the whole body, the next day, quitted their entrenchments on Long Island, and retreated to New York. . . .

Friday, October 11th.

Liverpool Diligence, in two days, will for the future set out from the [Swan with Two Necks Inn, Lad Lane] every afternoon at four ; fare as usual. . . . By setting out at so early an hour . . . it will be entirely out of danger of being stopped by robbers, who of late have infested the several roads about town, as it will be upwards of 20 miles from London before the dusk of the evening ; and on its return will be in London every day to dinner.

Saturday, October 12th.

One Mary Barnes has, for some time past, robbed on the highway. She rides a bay mare of the race breed, and dresses in a green coat and waistcoat and leather breeches.

Tuesday, October 15th.

The House being met, pursuant to the last prorogation, and Mr. Speaker being in the country, a message was brought from the Lords, by Mr. Quarme, Yeoman Usher of the Black Rod :

Gentlemen of the House of Commons,

The Lords, authorized by virtue of His Majesty's Commission, desire the immediate attendance of this Honourable House, in the House of Peers, to hear the Commissions read.

Accordingly the House, with the Clerk Assistant, went up to the House of Peers, where the Commission was read, for the further proroguing of the Parliament until Thursday the

31st day of this instant October : and the Parliament was accordingly prorogued until Thursday the 31st day of this instant October.

Monday, October 21st.

During the Mayorality of the present Lord-mayor, John Sawbridge, Esq., eighty-eight persons received sentence of death, and thirty-nine were executed, six of them for murder.

Friday, October 25th.

It was imagined, by the numerous appearance of the clergy . . . at St. James's, that a bishop had died suddenly.

Saturday, October 26th.

On Monday the 28th of October at 7 in the evening in the Anatomical Theatre, Great Windmill Street, will be begun a Course of Lectures on the Principles and Practice of Surgery by J. Hunter, F.R.S., Surgeon Extraordinary to the King, Surgeon to the Army and to St. George's Hospital. Proposals will be seen and tickets for the Course delivered at his house in Jermyn Street, St. James's. The Course will take up the whole winter : the lectures will be given on Mondays, Wednesdays and Fridays. . . . No public introductory lecture.

Sunday, October 27th.

[Lately published :]

An Oration delivered at the State House at Philadelphia, on Thursday, August the 1st, 1776. By Samuel Adams, one of the members of the General Congress. 1s. Johnson.

Letters on the American Troubles. Translated from the French of Mr. De Pinto. 1s. 6d. Boosey.

The Total Refutation and Political overthrow of Dr. Price ; or Great Britain successfully vindicated against all American rebels, and their advocates, &c., &c. By James Stewart. 1s. 6d. Bew.

A Treatise on Artificial Electricity. In which are given solutions of a number of interesting electric phenomena, hitherto unexplained. To which is added, an essay on the mild and slow Electricity, which prevails in the atmosphere during serene weather. Translated from the original Italian of Father Giambatista Beccaria, Professor

of Natural Philosophy in the University of Turin. 4to.
Nourse.

Monday, October 28th.

In consequence of press warrants sent to the several sea
ports through the Kingdom, a very hot press took place, and
in the Port of London alone, it is said, 800 men were impressed.
They swept from the ships all but the master, mate and boys.
Some men as usual lost their lives in the conflict, and among
them a lieutenant of the navy, who was shot dead.

Ten sail of the line are put in commission and ordered to
be manned with the utmost expedition.

Tuesday, October 29th.

[On] Saturday morning Mr. Akerman, the Keeper of Newgate, with the proper officers, conveyed a person from that
gaol to Enfield, where he is sentenced to stand on the pillory,
for deer-stealing. He has been punished for the same offence
before, and was so much pitied by the populace, that they
collected for him a sum of money ; on which he entertained
them with several songs, which produced repeated plaudits
from the merry multitude.

Wednesday, October 30th.

By the King.

A PROCLAMATION FOR A GENERAL FAST
George, R.

We, taking into our most serious consideration the just and
necessary measures of force which we are obliged to use against
our rebellious subjects in our colonies and provinces in North
America, and putting our trust in Almighty God, that He will
vouchsafe a special blessing on our arms, both by sea and
land, have resolved and do, by and with the advice of our
Privy Council hereby command, that a Public Fast and
Humiliation be observed throughout that part of our Kingdom
of Great Britain called England, our Dominion of Wales, and
Town of Berwick-upon-Tweed, upon Friday the 13th of
December next, that so both we and our people may humble

ourselves before Almighty God, in order to obtain pardon of
our sins and may, in the most devout and solemn manner, send
up our prayers and supplications to the Divine Majesty for
averting those heavy judgments which our manifold sins and
provocations have most justly preserved, and for imploring
His intervention and blessing speedily to deliver our loyal
subjects within our colonies and provinces in North America
from the violence, injustice and tyranny of those daring rebels,
who have assumed to themselves the exercise of arbitrary
power ; to open the eyes of those who have been deluded, by
specious falsehoods into acts of treason and rebellion ; to turn
the hearts of the authors of these calamities ; and finally to
restore our people in those distracted provinces and colonies
to the happy condition of being free subjects of a free state,
under which heretofor they flourished so long and prospered
so much. . . .

Given at our Court at St. James's the 30th of October,
1776, in the 17th year of our reign.

God save the King.

Thursday, October 31st.

On Monday evening the Captain of a press-gang, attempting to gain admission upstairs at a public-house not far from
Dark House Lane, Billingsgate, on pretence of searching for
seamen, was resolutely withstood by the mistress of the house,
who insisted he had no authority, unless his warrant was backed
by the Lord Mayor, on which the hero very imprudently
drew his sword, but the woman, unterrified, kept her ground,
till at length the officer and his crew were obliged to sheer off,
convinced, though reluctantly, by a woman, that the military
power ought on all occasions to be subservient to the civil.

The press continued upon the river till nine o'clock [on
Tuesday] morning ; and 'tis said that upwards of 1000 able
seamen were obtained. However violent this mode of procuring seamen for the defence of the nation may be, yet until the
legislature provides a more equitable substitution, it is wise to
adopt it when necessity requires.

The gangs took several persons from Billingsgate within the

Lord Mayor's jurisdiction, which occasioned his Lordship to issue out his order for apprehending the officers of all press gangs, unless they have legal warrants.

A Lieutenant having boarded an outward-bound Grenada ship, lying off Wapping, the sailors immediately ran to the arm chest, broke it open, and fired several times at the gang. The Lieutenant persisting that he would go down the hatchway, one of the ship's crew swore if he attempted it, he would shoot him, and on his proceeding the sailor fired, and lodged the whole of the charge in his body ; he lingered a short time, and then expired. Seven or eight seamen were drowned in endeavouring to swim to shore to avoid being pressed.

NOVEMBER 1776

Sunday, November 3rd.

The strange admiration that empirics, or pretenders to physic, are held in by the common people is really astonishing. An ignorant quack shall roll in his chariot from Ludgate Hill, while a doctor of physic shall walk on foot. If you will believe the advertisements with which the daily papers are filled, their nostrums are a cure for all diseases. Thus the populace are cheated of their money and their health : and the College of Physicians take no notice of it. Yet it is expressly provided by law that if any person, not regularly bred to the practice of physic or surgery, nor licensed to practice, shall undertake any cure, and the patient lose his life by it, such person shall be deemed guilty of felony and suffer accordingly. . . .

Monday, November 4th.

[From] *The London Gazette Extraordinary*, Whitehall, November 4th, 1776 :

The following letters from the Honourable General Sir William Howe to Lord George Germain, were received in the evening of the 2nd instant, by Captain Balfour, second Aid de camp to General Sir William Howe, who arrived in the *Lord Halifax* packet from New York.

My Lord,   Head Quarters, York Island, Sept. 21, 1776.

I have the satisfaction to inform your lordship of His Majesty's troops being in possession of the city of New York.

Upon the rebels abandoning their lines at Brooklyn, the King's army moved from Bedford, leaving Lieutenant-General Heister encamped upon the heights of Brooklyn with two brigades of Hessians, and one brigade of British at Bedford, and took five positions in the neighbourhood of Newton, Bushwick, Hell Gate and Flushing.

The two islands of Montresor and Buchanan were occupied and batteries raised against the enemy's work at Horen's Hook, commanding the passage at Hell Gate.

On the 15th instant in the morning, three ships of war passed up the North River as far as Bloomingdale to draw the enemy's attention to that side, and the first division of troops, consisting of the light infantry, the British reserve, the Hessians, grenadiers and chasseurs under the command of Lieut. Gen. Clinton, having with him Lieut. Gen. Earl Cornwallis, Major Gen. Vaughan, Brigadier Gen. Leslie and Colonel Donop, embarked at the head of New Town Creek and landed about noon upon New York Island, three miles from the town at a place called Kepp's Bay, under the fire of two forty-gun ships and three frigates . . . Commodore Hotham having the direction of the ships and boats.

The rebels had troops in their works round Kepp's Bay; but their attention being engaged in expectation of the King's troops landing at Stuyvesant's Cove, Horen's Hook and at Harlem, which they had reason to conclude, Kepp's Bay became only a secondary object of their care. The fire of the shipping being so well directed and so incessant, the enemy could not remain in their works, and the descent was made without the least opposition.

The conduct of the officers of the navy does them much honour; and the behaviour of the seamen belonging to the ships of war and transports employed to row the boats was highly meritorious. Much praise in particular is due to the masters and men of six transports that passed the town on the evening of the 14th under a heavy fire, being volunteers to take troops on board for the more speedy disembarkation of the second division.

The British immediately took post upon the commanding height of Inclenberg, and the Hessians moving towards New York fell in with a body of rebels that were retiring from Stuyvesant's Cove; some firing ensued, by which a Brigadier General, other officers and several men of the rebels were killed and wounded, with the loss of four men killed and eight wounded on the part of the Hessians.

As soon as the second embarkation was landed, the troops

advanced towards a corps of the enemy upon a rising ground three miles from Inclenberg, towards King's Bridge, having McGowan's pass in their rear, upon which they immediately retired to the main body of their army upon Morris's height.

The enemy having evacuated New York soon after the army landed, a brigade took possession of the works in the evening.

The prisoners made in the course of this day were about 20 officers and 300 men.

The position the King's army took on the 15th in the evening was with the right to Horen's Hook and the left at the North River, near to Bloomingdale ; the rebel army occupying the ground with extensive works on both sides of King's Bridge, and a redoubt with cannon upon a height on the west side of the North River, opposite to the Blue Bell, where the enemy have their principal work, in which positions both armies still continue.

On the 16th, in the morning, a large party of the enemy having passed under cover of the wood, near to the advanced posts of the army by way of Vanderwater's height, the 2nd and 3rd battalions of light infantry, supported by the 42nd regiment pushed forward and drove them back to their entrenchments, from whence the enemy observing they were not in force, attacked them with near 3,000 men, which occasioned the march of the reserve with two field pieces, a battalion of Hessian grenadiers and a company of chasseurs to prevent the corps engaged from being surrounded ; but the light infantry and 42nd regiment with the assistance of the chasseurs and field pieces repulsed the enemy with considerable loss and obliged them to retire within their works.   The enemy's loss is not ascertained, but from the accounts of deserters it is agreed that they had not less than 300 killed and wounded and among them a colonel and major killed.   We had eight officers wounded, most of them very slightly, fourteen men killed and about seventy wounded.

Major General Vaughan was slightly wounded in the thigh, on the 15th by a random shot, as he was ascending the heights of Inclenberg with the grenadiers ; and I have the pleasure of informing your lordship that Lieut. Colonel

Monckton is so well recovered, he has been walking about for some days.

Captain Balfour, my second aid de camp, will have the honour of delivering your lordship this dispatch ; and with the most profound respect,

I have the honour to be, etc.,

W. HOWE

Tuesday, November 5th.

Yesterday a most elegant picture, painted by Gainsborough, of the Right Hon. Lord Folkestone, in his Coronation robes, was put up in the Great Room of the Society for encouraging Arts, Manufactures, and Commerce. His Lordship was the first President of that Society.

Wednesday, November 6th.

[In the] Debate in the Commons on a Motion for the Revisal of all the Laws by which the Americans think themselves aggrieved . . . Mr. Burke [said] :

The honourable and learned gentleman [the Solicitor-General, Mr. Wedderburn] has called to his assistance the bayonets of 12,000 Hessians ; and as he thinks it absurd to reason at present with the Americans, he tells us, that by the healing, soothing, merciful measure of foreign swords, at the breasts of those unhappy people, their understandings would be enlightened, and they would be enabled to comprehend the subtleties of his logic. It was well said, on another occasion, that your speech demands an army ! — and I may say, that the learned gentleman's demands blood. Reasoning he says is vain ; — the sword must convince the Americans, and clear up their clouded apprehensions. The learned gentleman's abilities surely desert him, if he is obliged to call such a coarse argument as an army to his assistance ; — not that I mean anything reflecting on his parts. I always esteem, and sometimes dread his talents. But has he told you why commissioners were not sent sooner to America ? Has he explained that essential point ? Not a jot. Why, after the act passed for them, were they delayed full seven months, and not permitted to sail till May ; and why was the commission appointing them delayed till the sixth of that month ? Answer this. The blood and devastation that followed was owing to this delay ; upon your conscience it ought to lay a heavy load. If the measure was right and necessary in order for conciliation, as the king declared in his speech at the opening of that session, why was it not executed at a time in which it could be effectual ; instead of being purposely deferred to one when it could not possibly answer any end but that of adding hypocrisy to treachery, and insult and mockery to cruelty and oppression ? By this delay you drove the Americans into the declaration of independency ; not as a matter of choice, but necessity ; and now they have declared it, you bring it as an argument to prove, that there can be no other reasoning used with them but the sword. What is this but declaring, that you were originally determined not to prevent, but to punish rebellion ; not to use conciliation, but an army ; not to convince, but to destroy ? Such were the effects of those seven months cruelly lost, to which every mischief that has happened since must be attributed.

Thursday, November 7th.

Tuesday evening the remains of Mr. Edward Shuter were interred in the burying ground of St. Paul's, Covent Garden, close by the grave of the late Mr. Dyer, comedian of Covent Garden ; his pall was supported by Messrs. Hull, Clarke, Mattocks, Reinhold, Dunstall and Baker, of the same theatre, who joined their tributary sigh with those of the numerous, and melancholy spectators, that flocked from all parts of the town to pay their last respect to the ashes of their comic favourite, and retired pensively exclaiming — Alas ! poor Ned !

Friday, November 8th.

It appears by Lloyd's books, that since the commencement of the unnatural war with the Americans, they have taken 90 sail of our merchant ships.

Saturday, November 9th.

The seamen here are a generation differing from all the world. When one goes into Rotherhithe and Wapping, which places are chiefly inhabited by sailors, but that somewhat of the same language is spoken, a man would be apt to suspect himself in another country. Their manner of living, speaking, acting, dressing and behaving are so very peculiar to themselves. Yet with all their oddities they are perhaps the bravest and the boldest fellows in the universe.

Sunday, November 10th.

Since the theatrical resignation of Roscius, the rage for dramatic entertainments in private families has increased astonishingly ; scarce a man of rank but either has, or pretends to have, his *petit théâtre*, in the decoration of which the utmost taste and expense are lavished. . . .

Monday, November 11th.

The Proprietors of the *Morning Post*, considering the late attack made on this paper, not only as an invasion of their property, as individuals, but as an insult, and injury to that public, which has so long, and so liberally protected it, determined to apply to the laws of their country, to suppress this daring and infamous attempt ; they did accordingly, on Saturday last, by their Counsel, the Attorney General, apply to the Lord Chancellor to restrain by his authority these lawless invaders, who so basely imitated this extensive paper,— from printing, or publishing a *Morning Post* : this application was supported by such arguments, as fully convinced, not only the Chancellor, but a very numerous audience, that it was founded on the strictest principles of justice and equity. . . .

The wanton and impudent address, of E. Cox, and G. Corrall, to the public, respecting the proprietors of this paper, delivered through the metropolis, in a hand-bill, on Saturday last, will be fully refuted this day, in another hand-bill, attested by Mr. Biggs, late partner to the above Mr. Cox. . . .

All letters and articles of Intelligence are requested at present to be sent down Blake Court, to prevent their falling into the hands of the Piratical Confederacy.

Tuesday, November 12th.

I heard drums and trumpets in Piccadilly ; I looked out of the window and saw a procession with streamers flying. At first I thought it a pressgang, but seeing the corps so well dressed, like Hussars, in yellow with blue waistcoats and breeches, and high caps, I concluded it was some new body of our allies, or a regiment newly raised, and with new regimentals for distinction. I was not totally mistaken, for the colonel is *a new ally*. In short, this was a procession set forth by Mr. Bate, Lord Lyttleton's chaplain, and author of the old *Morning Post*, and meant as an appeal to the town against his antagonist, the new one. I did not perceive it, but the musicians had masks ; on their caps was written the *Morning Post*, and they distributed handbills. I am sure there were at least between thirty and forty, and this mummery must have cost a great deal of money. . . . The new *Morning Post* . . . exceeds all the outrageous Billingsgate that ever was heard of. What a country ! . . . A solemn and expensive masquerade exhibited by a clergyman, in defence of daily scandal against women of the first rank, in the midst of a civil war ! and while the labouring poor are torn from their families by pressgangs ! and a foreign war is hanging over our heads ! And everybody was diverted with this ! . . .

Wednesday, November 13th.

This day the State-lottery began drawing, when No. 57,470 was drawn a prize of £20 and being the first drawn ticket, was entitled £1,000.

Thursday, November 14th.

Saturday se'nnight Henry Liddle, Esq., of Newton, with his fox-hounds, unkennelled a fox at Cassop-hills, near Durham, and run him to Thornly, from thence down to the sea ; reynard, smelling the press-warrants, returned back again to Sherburn-hills, from thence to Shincliff-wood, passed Bishop Auckland, and quite through the county to Raby Castle, and through the Sir Ralph's Park ; after a chase upwards of fifty miles, thought to be the longest that has been run this century, he was obliged to yield. Out of a very numerous company, only three were in at the death.

Friday, November 15th.

I read Mr. Bolt's Account of the Affairs in the East Indies.

333

I suppose much the best that is extant. But what a scene is here opened ! What consummate villains ! What devils incarnate were the managers there ! What utter strangers to justice, mercy, and truth ! to every sentiment of humanity ! I believe no heathen history contains a parallel. I remember none in all the annals of antiquity : not even the divine Cato, or the virtuous Brutus, plundered the provinces committed to their charge, with such merciless cruelty, as the English have plundered the desolated provinces of Indostan.

Saturday, November 16*th.*

Covent Garden is the great square of Venus, and its purlieus are crowded with the votaries of this goddess. One would imagine that all the prostitutes in the Kingdom had pitched upon this blessed neighbourhood for a place of general rendezvous. For here are lewd women in sufficient numbers to people a mighty colony. And that fuel for the natural flame may not be wanting, here is a great variety of open houses whose principal employment it is to minister incitements to lust. The jelly-houses are now become the resort of abandoned rakes and shameless prostitutes. These and the taverns afford an ample supply of provision for the flesh ; while others abound for the consummation of the desires which are thus excited. For this vile end the bagnios and lodging-houses are near at hand. . . . The neighbouring Strand is so frequented at night by wretched objects of this caste, reduced to the most abject misery, as must awaken a sense of horror and of pity at the same time in every thinking person. . . .

There are miscreants of both sexes on the watch to seduce the fresh country maiden, with infinite protestations of friendship, service, love and pity, to prostitution, shame and misery. For this purpose the very carriages which convey them are hunted and examined ; the inns, where they are to alight, are beset by these infernal hirelings. . . . If she applies to an office of intelligence 'tis odds but she falls into the hands of some procuress or bawd. . . . So that in fact it is not safe for any blooming young creature to set out for the great city, without letters of recommendation from known friends in the country.

MORNING IN COVENT GARDEN
William Hogarth

Monday, November 18th.

On Friday last Mr. Dunning moved the Court of King's Bench for an information against two Justices of the Peace for Middlesex, for refusing to compel two persons to take the oaths, who had been charged to be Roman Catholics, when Lord Mansfield refused Mr. Dunning's motion ; at the same time [he] expressed his disapprobation at this attempt to revive the severities of those very penal laws.

Friday, November 22nd.

Wednesday an extraordinary General Court of East India Proprietors, called by the Duke of Richmond, Governor Johnston, and some other gentlemen, was held in Leadenhall Street. The chief business upon which the court assembled was to enquire into the regularity of the late resignation made by Mr. [Warren] Hastings of his important employments in the service of the Company. . . .

Saturday, November 23rd.

Yesterday at noon a Messenger arrived at the Right Hon. Lord George Germain's Office express from Sir Guy Carleton, Governor of Quebec, with an account that his Majesty's forces under his and General Burgoyne's command had gained a complete victory over the Americans in crossing the Lakes at Lake Champlain, and had destroyed a number of their vessels ; after which they marched to Crown Point, which the rebels had reduced to ashes : His Majesty's forces then marched to Ticonderoga, where the rebels, under the command of Col. Arnold, were defeated and he himself taken prisoner. . . .

Sunday, November 24th.

I am not at all surprised that Lord Chatham, however retired, both sees and feels the critical and perilous state of the Kingdom. The American affairs speak for themselves notwithstanding all the disguise of Ministers and their unprecedented suppression of all private letters.

I have reason to believe, that no engagement was entered into between France and America, as far as the month of

October ; but fresh messengers were certainly then arrived with fresh powers, and what they may have done, it has not come in my way to know. If France chooses to avail herself of her advantages, she has most undoubtedly gained in her present armament three months ; which, in the opinion of the best professional authorities, no diligence can recover on our part for the approaching spring. On the other hand, the imbecility of the person at the head of that country, the triflingness of M. de Maurepas, with whom the power rests, though he is incapable of taking a lead in any line, their natural levity, besides that they have the air throughout of a *sunk* people, makes me believe it within the reach of possibility, by an instant change of councils, to avert our fate ; particularly if it took place before the Spanish fleet sails against the Portuguese ; which otherwise, I am afraid, will be found to involve all the rest, and England will be to look for safety in the clouds.

Wednesday, November 27th.

The Crown Lawyers, having been consulted on the legality of Pressing within the City of London, have unanimously given their opinion, that there is no necessity for the warrants being backed by the Lord Mayor to render them legal ; and in consequence of this opinion, warrants for the City are forthwith to be issued by the Lords of the Admiralty.

Friday, November 29th.

About a quarter past eight o'clock [on Wednesday morning] the shock of an earthquake was felt at Canterbury, Sandwich, Ashford and all over east Kent particularly on the coast. Its direction was from south to north, it lasted about eight seconds and was attended by a distant rumbling noise. The morning was gloomy and perfectly calm, wind south, Fahrenheit's barometer (at Sandwich) 29.8, thermometer within doors, at the side of an east window on a staircase, 37.3. Some china on a chest of drawers at Folkestone was moved an inch or two each piece and two bits of wood were shaken from under the feet of a table. At Dover the shock caused a bell in the church to sound, as did a handbell on St. Martin's Hill, near Canterbury. The same shock was very sensibly felt at Calais.

Saturday, November 30th.

Since Lord North has been at the head of the Ministry, the King has had the satisfaction of seeing his whole pack of political hounds keep to their respective scents. The three Secretaries of State are each confined strictly to their department. The Navy is in Lord Sandwich's hands; and the Army in the King's, for Lord Barrington is a cypher. The disposition of small places is left to the head of each department, but great ones are given away not as formerly by the Prime Minister *ex officio*, but reserved for the King's pleasure, who consults with Mr. Jenkinson chiefly. Great transactions of a secret and delicate nature, in which the Premier and the Sovereign formerly alone participated, are now settled in the King's cabinet by himself and Mr. Jenkinson. By means of this disposition of the Royal power, the whole is in his Majesty's hands, as the degree of importance which each Chief holds in his own department, depends entirely on the orders he receives from the King alone.

December 1776

Sunday, December 1st.

[Lately published :]

Psalms and Hymns for Public and Private Worship. Collected (for the most part) and published by Augustus Toplady, A.B. Vicar of Broad Hembury. 12mo. 2s. 6d. in boards. Dilly.

A General History of the Science and Practice of Music, from the Establishment of a System thereof to the Present Time, &c., &c. By Sir John Hawkins. 5 vols. 4to. £6, 6s. in boards. Payne.

State of the Gaols in London, Westminster and the Borough of Southwark. By Wm. Smith, M.D. 1s. 6d. Bew.

Monday, December 2nd.

On Saturday last, being St. Andrew's Day, the Royal Society held their Anniversary meeting at their house in Crane-court, Fleet Street ; when the President, Sir John Pringle, Bart., in the name of the Society, presented the gold medal, called Sir Godfrey Copley's, to James Cook, Esq., Captain in his Majesty's Navy, for his useful discoveries in the South Seas. The President on this occasion delivered an elegant discourse on the means of preserving the health of mariners, in consequence of Capt. Cook's paper on that subject.

Friday, December 6th.

Mr. Hume's History of England turned out so very well for his booksellers, that after his retirement to Scotland (where he carried down with him in annuities and interest of money near £1000 per annum) he was applied to to write a continuation of it up to the present times, for which they offered him very handsomely. Mr. Hume, for some time, in general terms, declined it ; but being pressed on the subject, and told he might make his own terms, he gave them the following definitive answer : " I must decline not only this offer, but all others of a literary nature for four reasons : Because I'm too old, too fat, too lazy, and too rich."

Tuesday, December 10th.

In Sir Joshua [Reynolds's] seventh Discourse, delivered [to-day] . . . his object was to prove the existence of a real standard of taste ; this he considered as absolute as one for corporeal beauty, and as an immutable truth in itself, although at the same time, it did not preclude the existence of certain variable and secondary truths, differing according to circumstances, in their influence as well as in their stability, and therefore particularly requiring the artist's close attention.

At the commencement of this oration, he again recommended *industry* most strenuously to the students, but with this happy distinction, that it was not " the industry of the *hands* but of the *mind*." He then marked the precise definition of the art itself, which, though " not a divine gift, so neither is it a mechanical trade." . . .

As great learning is not absolutely necessary for a painter, he recommended his youthful hearers not to be terrified at the want of it, but still to keep in mind that a certain degree of cultivation, such as was in their power, was nevertheless essential ; and he therefore pointed out the propriety of being tolerably conversant with the poets, even in English, so as to imbibe a poetical spirit. . . .

" The true spirit of philosophy," said he, " by giving knowledge, gives a manly confidence, and substitutes rational firmness in the place of vain presumption. A man of real taste is always a man of judgment in other respects ; and those inventions which either disdain or shrink from reason, are generally, I fear, more like the dreams of a distempered brain than the exalted enthusiasm of a sound and true genius. In the midst of the highest flights of fancy or imagination, reason ought to preside from first to last, though I admit her more powerful operation is upon reflection."

Wednesday, December 11th.

General Burgoyne arrived in town Monday night from Quebec in good health. The cause of his leaving Canada is variously reported ; some say a dispute with General Carleton, others, that as the latter does not mean to quit the Province, the command of course remains with him, and the presence of General Burgoyne is therefore not necessary. 'Tis said, however, that he will return in Spring.

Thursday, December 12th.

Our Ministry do not seem to entertain a doubt, but that the fire at Portsmouth, was another stroke of French policy ; intended to recover, by so base a scheme, that naval advantage, which they certainly had over us, about nine months ago ; but now have lost ; — thanks to a gracious and superintending Providence, their diabolical projects have a second time miscarried.

The men who were apprehended at Portsmouth, on suspicion of setting fire to the rope-house, etc. of that dock-yard, on Saturday evening last, have been examined, and from what has been already drawn from them, it seems pretty clear, that they were certainly the instruments set on to do this desperate deed, by some more interested foreign agents.

Friday, December 13th.

Today, on account of the fast ordered by royal proclamation, there will be no Levée at St. James's, nor play at either of the theatres ; and, on the same account, the lottery will discontinue drawing till tomorrow morning.

Saturday, December 14th.

The solemnity of yesterday was strictly observed by all ranks of people through the cities of London and Westminster, all the churches of which were crowded with attentive congregations, who seemed to join with great fervency in the occasional prayers which were offered up to the Deity ; pathetical interceding for a speedy termination of the unhappy contest between the mother country, and her rebellious colonies. . . . The House of Peers and Commons attended divine service at the Abbey, and St. Margaret's ; the Lord Mayor, Sheriff, and Court of Aldermen at St. Paul's ; at each of which places very excellent sermons were preached on the occasion. The

Lord Mayor and his suite appeared in mourning, and the Sword of State was likewise carried in a sable scabbard. . . .

Tuesday, December 17*th.*

About a quarter past eleven o'clock, Sir John Fielding, with the high-bailiff, etc. assembled on the hustings in Covent Garden. When they had sat there till twelve, silence was proclaimed, and the high-bailiff declared a seat in parliament for Westminster to be vacant, by Earl Percy's becoming a peer in his own right, in consequence of the death of his mother, the late Duchess of Northumberland ; on which Lord Petersham, now in America, was nominated a candidate, and, no other candidate appearing, declared duly elected.

About ten minutes after the election was over, Sir Watkin Lewes appeared on the hustings, and was received with great applause. He declared himself a candidate, and demanded a poll, which being refused on account of his not appearing at the declaration, a warm dispute arose in respect to the time allowed by act of parliament, before they proceeded to elect.

Sir Watkin afterwards invited such of the electors as were desirous of bringing this business before the House of Commons, to the Swan in New-street, for the purpose of drawing up and signing a protest against the proceedings of the day.

Wednesday, December 18*th.*

The crowd of people was so great in Westminster Abbey, to see the funeral of her Grace the late Duchess of Northumberland, that the Lord Bishop of Rochester and the gentlemen and boys of the choir could not perform the service. Although the corpse entered the Abbey a little before eleven o'clock, it was not interred till between one and two o'clock. The old Gothic screen or fence belonging to St. Edmund's Chapel, supposed to have been built between four and five hundred years, by the number of people climbing upon it, fell down. The Lord Bishop of Rochester, narrowly escaped being dangerously hurt ; one man had his leg broke, as had a woman her arm, and three other persons were carried out of the Cathedral very much bruised, to be taken care of by their friends, and considerable damage was done to the monuments. . . .

Thursday, December 19th.

It looks very much as if we should know soon whether America is to be subdued or saved by a French war. We heard on Tuesday last that Dr. Franklin himself was landed in France — no equivocal step ; and on Wednesday came a full explanation. General Howe had made two movements, that threatened enclosing Washington, and cutting him off from his magazines : a small engagement ensued, in which the Americans were driven from a post without much loss on either side. Washington has since retired with his whole army to other heights, about five miles off, seeming to intend to protract the war, as was always thought would be their wisest way ; but, as the Americans do not behave very heroically, and as the King's fleet will now be masters of the coast, it is supposed that Washington must retire northward, and that the Howes will make great progress in the south, if not prevented by the rigour of the season. . . . Dr. Franklin must have sailed a day or two after Washington's retreat ; and therefore it is natural to conclude that he is come to tell France that she must directly interpose and protect the Americans, or that the Americans must submit to such terms as they can obtain. . . .

Friday, December 20th.

Mr. Selwyn being at the King's Levee, soon after the execution at Tyburn, and his Majesty having been told of his extraordinary passion for public executions, said to him, " Well, Mr. Selwyn, did they die hard, as usual ? — *You* doubtless were at Tyburn, — you study human nature there, Mr. Selwyn." " No," said Lord Sandwich, who was present, " he goes to practice an entrée which he intends to make himself." Upon any other subject Mr. Selwyn's wit would not have been wanting in repartee, but he does not like to be touched upon this peculiarity of his, and therefore turned aside the conversation, by joining in the laugh himself.

Saturday, December 21st.

The accounts which have been received of the late operations of His Majesty's forces are to the following effect :

That on the 12th of October, the guards, light infantry and reserve together with Colonel Donop's corps of Hessian grenadiers and chasseurs marched from the advanced posts of New York island and embarking in boats at Turtle Bay passed up the East River through Hell Gates and landed on Frog's Neck. That having crossed the Neck they found the bridge which joined it to the main had been broken down by the rebels, who had thrown up some works on the opposite side. That being joined by the 1st, 2nd, and 6th brigades from Long Island, the troops embarked again in boats, and landed in Pelham's Manor the 18th without opposition ; and marching on through a random fire of the rebels from behind stone walls, gained the road which leads from Connecticut to King's Bridge. The rebels, apprehending their communication to the eastward would be cut off, moved from the camp at King's Bridge, and extended their left to the White Plains, a chain of stoney hills so called. On the 21st His Majesty's light troops took possession of the heights of New Rocheli. Colonel Rogers, with his New York companies, having taken post at Maramack was attacked by a party of the rebels which he drove back with considerable loss.

On the 25th the advanced corps moved forward to the road which leads to the White Plains, where the rebels appeared determined to make a stand ; but on the 27th, the party that was posted there struck their tents in the night and moved off to the entrances to the White Plains, where the main body of the rebels was entrenched having the Bronx's River in their front, the banks of which are swampy and the river deep, except at the ford where the banks are steep and rocky. On the 28th in the morning, our army marched in columns to attack the rebels, who, seeing the troops in motion, a body of about eight thousand came out of the lines and posted themselves on the top of a very steep hill above the ford. The second brigade consisting of the 5th, 28th, 35th and 49th regiments, with a battalion of Hessians and a party of the light dragoons marched down and crossing the ford, though much annoyed by the rebels' grapeshot, ascended the hill with the greatest intrepidity, attacked and routed the body of rebels that were posted there, driving them to their entrenchments in the entrances to the

343

White Plains where General Howe was preparing to attack them on the morning of the 1st of November ; but being prevented by a very heavy rain, the rebels quitted their entrenchments in the night following and retired towards Connecticut and the Highlands, abandoning their camp at King's Bridge, after setting fire to their huts and barracks they had built for their winter quarters, which was immediately taken possession of by a detachment of the King's troops, where they found between sixty and seventy pieces of cannon, a large quantity of provisions, which the rebels had spoiled and a great number of hogsheads of rum, which the General ordered to be destroyed. There is no exact return of our loss in the different attacks, but it is supposed to have been between one hundred and ninety and two hundred killed and wounded.

Sunday, December 22nd.

On Wednesday last Lord Dunmore arrived in town from America, and yesterday waited on his Majesty at the levee ; and had afterwards a long conference with him.

The Hessians solicited the honour of attacking and reducing Fort Washington, which General Howe complied with : — the event of this attack is expected to be brought over by every ship that arrives. This, it is supposed, would be the last stroke, struck by the King's troops in the campaign of 1776.

Tuesday, December 24th.

Lord Rockingham is so much interested in the success of Mr. Burke's eloquence, that though no orator himself, he has undertaken to advise him as a friend, from the joint opinions of all their acquaintance, to bring his flighty speeches to bear more immediately to the points in question. He reminded him, that all Charles Fox's success is owing to this circumstance. Edmund took the advice in very good part, which, by the way, was not of the best, not at all adapted to the poetic abilities of his Irish friend, who might have answered with Lord Chesterfield, that out of the 540 members, the odd forty might have the understandings to follow, and judge of Mr. Fox's reasoning, but the 500 have ears to be tickled with the music of Burke's periods.

Wednesday, December 25th.

This being Christmas Day there was a numerous and splendid appearance at court to compliment their Majesties, when the Knights Companions of the several Orders appeared in their respective collars. At noon their Majesties went to the Chapel Royal and heard a sermon, after which they received the Holy Sacrament, and made the usual offering. . . .

The day has been kept with more strictness, by all ranks of people in this metropolis, than for some years past.

Saturday, December 28th.

Dr. Franklin . . . will doubtless try to persuade France to acknowledge the independence of America. My opinion has always been that France will not declare *openly* till 1778, at which time our treaties with Brunswick and Hesse will expire and our finances be pretty well exhausted. But she will assist the Americans *privately*, by permitting her merchants and all her subjects to do it in whatever way they find most advantageous to themselves ; and by making all her ports in Europe and America so many asylums for the American privateers. . . . Some regulations of this kind, either temporary or permanent, I think Dr. Franklin is come to frame and establish. . . . And he is come early, in order that the articles wanted for the war may be in America by the opening of the next campaign. Will the two prizes he has carried into Nantes be sold there ? That will mark a good deal. It is certain that both France and Spain have ordered more ships of the line to be fitted out. . . . France certainly means to have a part of the American commerce and is therefore preparing to protect it. . . .

Sunday, December 29th.

The conduct of the American cause at this time . . . attracts particular attention. They were seemingly reduced to a very low ebb, being left almost without an army and encompassed with dangers and difficulties ; notwithstanding which, they preserved a firm and undaunted countenance, never making any advances for peace. . . . They had experienced the inconvenience of levying troops for a short period only ; and determining in future to avoid it, near the end of autumn they set about raising eighty-three battalions to serve during the continuance of the war. To encourage these levies, a bounty of twenty dollars per man was offered and an allotment of land was destined to every soldier who should serve until the ratification of a peace, and to the representatives of those who should be slain in action. Five hundred acres were the highest and one hundred the lowest allotment. To prevent improper advantages from being taken of the thoughtless or necessitous soldiers, by artful or designing men, the lands so allotted were declared to be unalienable during the continuance of the war. Previous to this enactment they had instituted a law, which entitled all soldiers and sailors disabled in action, to half-pay during the remainder of their lives. Notwithstanding all these encouragements, their new levies went on heavily ; so that Congress in November was obliged to change the proposed term of service to a period of three years only : allowing the same bounty but withholding the allotment of lands. Still, their progress in recruiting was far from answering their expectations and intentions ; until the success of the indefatigable Commander-in-Chief of their armies at last gave a spur to their efforts. . . .

Congress also finding the sums raised by the colonies owning their authority, to be inadequate to the purposes of carrying on the war, resolved to borrow four millions of dollars, at four per cent interest, on the faith of the United States ; which was pledged to the lenders for the payment of both principal and interest. . . .

Many complaints were made to Congress of the irregularities committed in the provinces of New York and New Jersey, by the King's troops, particularly by the Hessians. These they were careful to publish, no doubt with circumstances of aggravation, the more to discredit their enemies among their associates in arms : and this expedient was successful in heightening the detestation of the revolted Americans against the military, especially against the Hessians, whom they were taught to regard with horror.

Tuesday, December 31st.

Yesterday, at twelve o'clock, Capt. Gardiner, First Aid-de-camp to General Howe, arrived at Lord George Germain's with the important news of the taking Fort Washington by storm on the 25th of Nov. and two thousand seven hundred . . . made prisoners. The place has been closely invested (ever since Washington's retreat to Courtland's Manor) by Lord Percy's brigade, and all the Hessians. It is said we have lost near five hundred men, killed and wounded, the greater part of whom are Hessians. . . . It is likewise said, that the fort on the other side Hudson's river has surrendered ; and that a body of ten thousand men are marching to Bruns-wick, on the road to Philadelphia, in order to beat up the quarters of the Continental Congress.

APPENDICES

LIST OF SOURCES

For explanations of the abbreviations see the Index of Sources. Events occurred on the dates under which they appear unless otherwise stated. Some extracts are antedated ; e.g. Shelburne's letter of 3.2.1774, describing the events of 29.1.1774, is quoted under the latter date. Biographical details of many persons mentioned are given in the General Index.

Prologue.—Ambulator. From the Introduction iv-x, xxii.

January 1774

1. L.C. 2.1.1774.
5. M.C. 5.1.1774 and A.W.C. 11.1.1774.
6. P.A. 6.1.1774.
8. P.L. 15.1.1774.
10. D.A. 10.1.1774.
11. Malmesbury, I, 278-279. Mrs. Harris to her son at Berlin, from Piccadilly, 14.1.1774. This son, James Harris, was English minister at Berlin, 1772-76 : first Earl of Malmesbury, 1800. Mme. Cornelys organised the concerts, etc., at Carlisle House, Soho.
13. L.M. 1774, 46 and L.G. 11-15.1.1774.
15. P.A. 15.1.1774. Advertisement. By the candle = an auction held while a short piece of candle was burning, the bid accepted being the last received before the candle went out.
17. P.A. 17.1.1774.
18. First para. G.M. 1774, 43. Second, Malmesbury I, 280-281. Mrs. Harris to her son at Berlin, 18.1.1774. The Queen's actual birthday was May 19.
22. G.M. 1774, 27-28. Extracted from a five-column article.
23. M.R. vol. 50, 30.
24. B.L.J. 24.1.1774.
25. G.M. 1774, 44.
27. P.A. 27.1.1774.
28. First two paras. P.A. 28.1.1774. Third, G.M. 1774, 45.
29. Chatham Corres. IV, 322-324. Shelburne to Chatham from London, 3.2.1774. Last para. G.M. 1774, 89. " The proceedings of January 29th, 1774, turned the ablest colonial representative, who hitherto had believed in the possibility of a compromise and the maintenance of the imperial connection, into an irreconcilable foe. Franklin kept the resolve made while he listened unmoved to Wedderburn and the laughter of the councillors. The plain brown suit that he wore that day was folded up and next worn when he put his signature to the treaty that ratified the independence of the thirteen colonies."—Sir Charles Grant Robertson, *England under the Hanoverians.*

30. Gibbon Letters, I. 201-202. Gibbon to J. B. Holroyd, 29.1.74. The British Coffee House, in Cockspur Street, was a favourite resort of Scotsmen. *Got a verdict* : The attitude of the first-night audience decided whether a play would be repeated. The decision was announced from the stage. Second para. M.C. 18.1.1774.
31. Walpole, VIII, 413-414. Walpole to the Countess of Upper Ossory, 29.1.1774. " Magdalen " because Dodd (a popular " Society " preacher, nicknamed the " macaroni parson ") was Chaplain of the Magdalen House, a home for reformed prostitutes.

February 1774

1. First para. Walpole Journal, I, 300. Second, L.C. 1.2.1774.
4. T.C.M. 1774, 76.
5. First para. G.N.D.A. 5.2.1774. Second, M.C. 5.2.1744. Donaldson, an Edinburgh bookseller (=publisher and bookseller), had opened a shop in London and sold cheap editions of popular books which London booksellers claimed as their copyright. Becket had obtained a decree in Chancery from Lord Mansfield (see under Feb. 23) that copyright was perpetual to the author and his assigns (hence " monopoly "), not limited to the 14 or 28 years prescribed by the statute of Queen Anne. Donaldson appealed to the Lords. See P.H. XVII, 953 ff.
6. L.M. 1774, 55.
7. George III Papers. King to Lord North, from Queen's House, 4.2.1744.
8. P.A. 5.2.1774.
10. G.M. 1774, 91.
11. G.M. 1774, 91.
12. L.M. 1774, 102-103.
13. L.M. 1774, 88.
14. G.M. 1774, 91.
17. G.M. 1774, 92.
19. P.A. 19.2.1774.
23. First para. Chatham Corres. IV, 327-328. Shelburne to Chatham, from London, 27.2.1774. Second, G.N.D.A. 23.2.1774. See under Feb. 5.
24. Walpole, VIII, 428-429. Walpole to Sir Horace Mann from Arlington Street, 23 and 24.2.1774. The partitioners were Russia, Prussia and Austria. The Prince was Adolphus Frederick (1774–1850), created Duke of Cambridge in 1801.
25. G.N.D.A. 24.2.1774.
26. M.C. 26.2.1774. Handel died in 1759.
28. G.M. 1774, 137.

March 1774

1. First para. P.A. 1.3.1774. Second, Walpole Journal, I, 326.
2. G.M. 1774, 60-62, much abridged.
3. L.C. 3.3.1774. *Gin* is a contraction of *Geneva*.
4. G.M. 1774, 138, checked by Malcolm, I, 79-80.
5. G.N.D.A. 5.3.1774. Caudle = a hot drink of spice, sugar and wine.

6. G.M. 1774, 142.
7. First three paras. P.H. XVII, 1159. Remainder, Walpole Journal, I, 328-330. "This day was the era of the American War" (Walpole).
8. Walpole Journal, I, 331. This bill was to make perpetual the Act for deciding disputed elections by referring them to committees of M.Ps.
10. T.C.M. 1774, 166. Second para. P.L. 10.3.1774.
11. A.R. 1774, Chronicle, 102.
12. G.N.D.A. 12.3.1774. Chatham was now an invalid with manic depression and gout.
13. L.M. 1774, 153.
14. Walpole Journal, I, 332-333. Last para. P.H. XVII, 1170.
15. P.A. 14.3.1774.
17. M.C. 17.3.1774.
20. T.C.M. 1774, 130-132.
23. Franklin Writings, VI, 223. Letter from London, 22.3.1774.
24. Walpole Journal, I, 333-334.
25. Walpole Journal, I, 337-339.
26. Chatham Corres. IV, 336-338. Chatham to Shelburne, from Burton Pynsent, 20.2.1774.
27. G.M. 1774, 173, 181, 182, 178. Last entry, T.C.M. 1774, 156. Published=edited.
28. Walpole Journal, I, 340-343.
29. Walpole, VIII, 436-437. Walpole to Sir Horace Mann from Arlington Street, 28.3.1774. Last para. P.A. 28.3.1774. The Sir John Moore who was killed at Coruña in 1809, now 13 years old. Cornet=standard-bearer in a cavalry troop. Tanjore, in Madras.
30. Chatham Corres. IV, 339. Shelburne to Chatham, from Bowood Park, 4.4.1774.
31. G.M. 1774, 185. Last para. M.C. 1.4.1774.

April 1774

1. G.M. 1774, 185. Fielding (half-brother of the novelist) was a magistrate of Westminster.
2. G.M. 1774, 186.
5. P.A. 5.4.1774.
7. L.C. 7.4.1774.
10. Walpole, VIII, 439-441. Walpole to Rev. William Mason, rom Strawberry Hill, 7.4.1774.
13. Reynolds (Northcote), I, 325-327, and (last para.) L.M. 1774, 204. See also May 8. The lady was Goldsmith's "Jessamy Bride," Mary Horneck.
15. Walpole Journal, I, 349-350.
17. Walpole, VIII, 442-443, 446. First para. Walpole to Rev. William Mason, from Strawberry Hill, 7.4.1774. Second, the same to the same, 17.4.1774.
18. P.A. 20.4.1774.
19. First para. G.M. 1774, 188. Second, T.C.M. 1774, 219.
20. A.R. 1774, Chronicle, 111.

April 21st–June 2nd, 1774

21. P.A. 21.4.1774.
22. Walpole Journal, I, 352-356. Last para. G.M. 1774, 188.
23. First para. P.A. 23.4.1774. Second, A.R. 1774, Chronicle, 112.
25. L.M. 1774, 207.
26. L.M. 1774, 194-195. From a full-page review.
27. L.M. 1774, 187. The murder was the lynching of Captain Porteous.
28. A.R., Chronicles, 113-114.
29. P.A. 29.4.1774.
30. M.C. 30.4.1774.

May 1774

1. Walpole, VIII, 450-451. Walpole to Sir Horace Mann, from Strawberry Hill, 1.5.1774.
2. A.R. 1774, Chronicles, 117-118.
3. First two paras. Walpole Journal, I, 357. Third, P.L. 3.5.1774.
4. Gibbon Letters, I, 215-216. Gibbon to J. B. Holroyd, 4.5.1774.
5. M.C. 5.5.1774.
6. T.C.M. 1774, 245-246.
7. M.C. 7.5.1774.
8. Goldsmith (Hawes), 25-26, 17-18. Dated here arbitrarily.
9. M.C. 9.5.1774. George III was nominally King of France.
11. L.M. 1774, 211, 212.
12. P.A. 12.5.1774.
14. A.R. 1774, Natural History, 74, 72, 73. Much abridged. Some paragraphs transposed.
15. Walpole, VIII, 452-456. Walpole to Sir Horace Mann from Strawberry Hill, 15.5.1774. Lord Stormont was British Ambassador at Paris.
16. G.M. 1774, 235.
17. M.C. 17.5.1774.
18. A.R. 1774, Chronicles, 121-122.
19. P.A. 19.5.1774. The Bill extended " the province southward to the banks of the Ohio, westward to the banks of the Mississippi, and northward to the boundary of the Hudson's Bay Company " (G.M. 1774, 284).
21. P.A. 19.5.1774.
22. T.C.M. 1774, 255. Opening paragraph of a long article on the value and methods of " inoculation."
23. P.A. 23.5.1774.
26. First para. M.C. 26.5.1774. Second, A.R. 1774, Chronicle, 124. George Colman the elder, dramatist.
27. M.C. 27.5.1774.
28. P.A. 31.5.1774.
29. G.M. 1774, 225, 229, 230 ; L.M. 1774, 245 ; Goldsmith, *Retaliation.*
30. G.M. 1774, 281.

June 1774

1. P.A. 1.6.1774.
2. First para. Walpole Journal, I, 372. Second, G.M. 1774, 281.

3. Walpole Journal, I, 372.
4. P.A. 3.6.1774. Recorded more briefly by Boswell.
5. A.R. 1774, Miscellaneous Essays, 185.
7. Walpole Journal, I, 373.
8. L.E.P. 7.6.1774. The party got no farther than Paris, in the autumn of 1775.
10. G.M. 1774, 263-265. Last para. P.L. 10.6.1774. The *Fête* celebrated the marriage of the Earl of Derby and Lady Betty Hamilton.
13. L.M. 1774, 299.
15. L.M. 1774, 300. " Marylebone " is written " Marie-la-bonne."
16. P.A. 16.6.1774.
17. G.M. 1774, 282.
20. P.A. 20.6.1774.
22. First three paras. A.R. 1774, Chronicle, 130. Fourth, Walpole Journal, I, 379. Fifth, P.A. 23.6.1774. " No Popery " because the Quebec Bill gave tolerance to Roman Catholics in Quebec, and was interpreted in some quarters as the first move towards re-establishing Roman Catholicism in England.
24. P.A. 22.6.1774.
25. P.A. 25.6.1774.
26. G.M. 1774, 269-270, 277, 278 ; L.M. 1774, 292, 293, 294.
29. G.M. 1774, 285-286.

July 1774

1. P.A. 4.7.1774.
2. P.A. 2.7.1774.
3. L.M. 1774, 351.
4. P.A. 4.7.1774.
5. L.E.P. 5.7.1774. See *A Philosophical Dissertation on the Diving Vessel projected by Mr. Day and sunk in Plymouth Sound . . .* by N. D. Falck, M.D., 1775 ; and see 18.8.1774.
7. L.C. 7.7.1774.
8. A.R. 1774, Chronicles, 134-135.
9. P.A. 9.7.1774. The " Noble Lord "= North.
10. Walpole, IX, 15, 16. Walpole to Sir Horace Mann from Strawberry Hill, 10.7.1774. Elizabeth Chudleigh, Countess of Bristol, who called herself Duchess of Kingston, a " beautiful but weak-minded and illiterate " woman, was secretly married in 1744 to Augustus John Hervey, a naval lieutenant, brother of the second Earl of Bristol. She concealed the birth and death of a son in November 1747. Later she obtained a separation from her husband, and in 1760 she appeared publicly as the mistress of Evelyn Pierrepoint, second Duke of Kingston. Her husband threatening divorce, she denied her marriage on oath in 1769, was legally declared a spinster and married the Duke of Kingston, who left her his property on his death in September 1773. She went to live in Rome. The charge of bigamy was brought against her by the Duke's nephew in 1774. Her husband succeeded to the Earldom of Bristol in 1775. For the account of her trial etc., see General Index.

11. P.L. 11.7.1774.
14. A.R. 1774, Chronicle, 136. Otaheite=Tahiti. Two spellings, Omiah (Fanny Burney, etc.) and Omai (Boswell, etc.), are used by contemporaries. The editor has retained the inconsistency.
15. First para. L.M. 1774, 309. Remainder, T.C.M. 1774, 349, much abridged.
20. P.A. 20.7.1774.
20. L.E.P. 21.7.1774.
25. L.M. 1774, 346, 347, 348.
26. L.E.P. 26.7.1774.
27. L.M. 1774, 356.
29. L.C. 29.7.1774.
30. P.A. 30.7.1774.
31. Beatson, IV, 44-45.

August 1774

4. Walpole, IX, 23, 24, 25. Walpole to Sir Horace Mann from Arlington Street, 3.8.1774. Branding on the hand was part of the punishment for bigamy.
10. M.C. 10.8.1774. Malta was in possession of the Knights of St. John.
11. P.L. 11.8.1774.
13. M.C. 13.8.1774.
14. G.M. 1774, 381.
15. M.C. 15.8.1774.
16. P.A. 16.8.1774.
18. M.C. 18.8.1774. See 5.7.1774.
19. G.M. 1774, 387.
20. P.L. 20.8.1774. Baker was provincial Commander-in-Chief in *Bengal*. East Indies includes India.
21. L.M. 1774, 407.
22. Beatson, IV, 46-47.
23. M.C. 23.8.1774.
24. P.A. 24.8.1774.
25. T.C.M. 1774, 500.
26. M.C. 26.8.1774.
29. A.R. 1774, Chronicle, 195.
30. M.C. 30.8.1774.
31. G.M. 1774, 389.

September 1774

2. P.A. 2.9.1774.
6. L.E.P. 6.9.1774.
7. P.L. 7.9.1774.
9. M.C. 9.9.1774.
10. L.E.P. 10.9.1774.
14. George III Papers. King to Lord North, from Kew, 11.9.1774.
16. A.R. 1774, Chronicles, 146-147.

18. G.M. 1774, 434 ; L.M. 1774, 448, 451.
25. T.C.M. 1774, 492-493. Much abridged.
27. Burke Corres. I, 473-474. Burke to Rockingham, from Beaconsfield, 16.9.1774.
29. G.M. 1774, 489.
30. G.M. 1774, 490.

October 1774

6. Walpole, IX, 61, 62, 63. Walpole to Sir Horace Mann from Strawberry Hill, 6.10.1774.
7. G.M. 1774, 491.
8. G.M. 1774, 491.
9. Franklin Writings, VI, 249-250. Letter from London, 6.10.1774.
12. Franklin Writings, VI, 253-254. Franklin to Joseph Galloway, from London, 12.10.1774.
13. First para. M.C. 13.10.1774. Second, Walpole, IX, 65-66. Walpole to Rev. Wm. Mason, undated. Walpole's nephew, Lord Orford, had borrowed money from Macreth.
14. L.C. 14.10.1774.
18. G.M. 1774, 492.
21. M.C. 21.10.1774.
22. First para. P.A. 22.10.1774. Second, Walpole, IX, 74. Walpole to Sir Horace Mann, from Strawberry Hill, 22.10.1774. Wilkes had been four times previously elected for Middlesex and his elections annulled.
23. T.C.M. 1774, 548. Misnumbered 448 in the editor's copy.
27. D.A. 27.10.1774.
28. G.M. 1774, 493.
30. G.M. 1774, 531-532, 532-533 ; L.M. 1774, 503 and 502. *The Patriot* was written by Dr. Johnson.
31. G.M. 1774, 537.

November 1774

2. P.L. 2.11.1774.
3. P.A. 2.11.1774.
5. L.C. 5.11.1774.
7. Walpole Journal, I, 430.
8. First para. Burke Corres. I, 498. Burke to his sister, Mrs. French, from Bristol, 2.11.1774. Second, Johnson (Piozzi), 242.
9. L.M. 1774, 560.
10. L.C. 10.11.1774.
11. G.M. 1774, 538-539.
13. Malmesbury, I, 284. Joseph Warton (1722–1800), brother of the historian of English Poetry, was a " conspicuously unsuccessful " headmaster of Winchester, 1766–93.
14. T.C.M. 612 and 670.
15. G.M. 1774, 540.
21. George III Papers. King to Lord North, from Queen's House, 18.11.1774.

22. M.C. 21.11.1774.
23. L.M. 1774, 551, 555. The play, almost certainly by Burgoyne, was apparently based on the *Fête Champêtre* of June 9.
24. Walpole, IX, 99. Walpole to Sir Horace Mann, from Strawberry Hill, 24.11.1774. See also November 28.
25. Walpole, IX, 99, 100. Walpole to Sir Horace Mann, 24.11.1774.
26. M.C. 26.11.1774.
27. A.R. 1774, Chronicle, 164.
28. First para. Walpole, IX, 102-103. Walpole to Hon. Henry Seymour Conway, from Arlington Street, 27.11.1774. Second, Gibbon Letters, I, 238. Gibbon to J. B. Holroyd, 29.11.1774. There are conflicting accounts of Clive's death.
29. G.M. 1774, 591.
30. G.M. 1774, 591-592.

December 1774

1. Burney Diary, I, 321-322, 333-334, 335, 336. James Burney, Fanny's brother, had sailed with Captain Cook. *Bag*=bag-wig.
2. G.M. 1774, 593.
3. P.A. 3.12.1774. Presumably Clive and Alexander Wedderburn, Solicitor-General, who defended Clive.
4. A.R. 1774, Chronicle, 175.
5. G.M. 1774, 593, 594.
6. A.R. 1774, Chronicle, 167. Hastings was Governor-General of India, 1773-84.
7. T.C.M. 1774, 611.
9. M.C. 9.12.1774.
11. M.C. 11.12.1774.
12. L.C. 12.12.1774 and G.M. 1774, 595.
13. M.C. 13.12.1774.
14. M.C. 14.12.1774.
15. Walpole, IX, 106-107. Walpole to Hon. Henry Seymour Conway, from Arlington Street, 15.12.1774.
19. L.M. 1774, 639.
22. G.M. 1774, 601. Burke's speech on American Taxation. (P.H. XVII, 1215.) See also Jan. 10, 1775.
25. G.M. 1774, 628.
26. P.A. 26.12.1774. Advertisement ; much abridged.
28. G.M. 1774, 611. For a full discussion of the accuracy and value of the London Bills of Mortality see M. Dorothy George : *London Life in the Eighteenth Century*.
30. G.M. 1774, 628.
31. L.C. 31.12.1774.

January 1775

1. G.M. 1775, 43.
4. M.C. 4.1.1775.
7. D.A. 7.1.1775.

9. Lloyd's E.P. 9.1.1775.
10. Walpole Journal, I, 442-443. See Dec. 22, 1774.
11. M.C. 10.1.1775.
12. L.C. 10-12.1.1775.
16. First para. A.R. 1775, Chronicle, 83. Second, M.C. 16.1.1775.
17. First two paras. Lloyd's E.P. 18.1.1775. Third and fourth, M.C. 18.1.1775. Fifth, L.C. 19.1.1775. Sixth, M.P. 18.1.1775. See 28.1.75.
18. First para. B.C. 20.1.1775. Second, Walpole, IX, 147. Walpole to the Countess of Upper Ossory, from Arlington Street, 21.1.1775. Third, M.P. 19.1.1775.
19. G.M. 1775, 44.
20. Boyd, Vol. I, pp. 255-275. Much abridged. Boyd's are probably the most accurate records of Chatham's speeches which exist.
21. L.C. 21.1.1775. The present book is set in Monotype Baskerville.
22. Johnson (Boswell), II, 298. Footnote and facsimile. Mr. Powell's transcription of the original letter.
23. M.P. 21.1.1775.
24. M.P. 24.1.1775. Becket, Macpherson's former publisher, had publicly stated that the original MSS. of the Ossian poems were in his possession for some months in 1762.
25. First para. G.M. 1775, 97. Second, M.C. 25.1.1775, advertisement.
26. M.C. 21.1.1775.
27. M.P. 27.1.1775. Refers to a pamphlet giving a false version.
28. First three paras. L.C. 31.1.1775. Fourth, B.C. 30.1.1775.
29. Walpole, IX, 146. Walpole to the Countess of Upper Ossory, from Arlington Street, 21.1.1775.
30. First para. G.M. 1775, 45. Second, Walpole, IX, 155. Walpole to Sir Horace Mann, from Arlington Street, 21.1.1775.
31. G.M. 1775, 45. The editor has been unable to find the authors of *Harlequin's Jacket* and *The Druids*. *Alexander* is probably *The Rival Queens*, by Nathaniel Lee. Older plays, including Shakespeare's, were usually performed in adaptations.

February 1775

1. Malmesbury, I, 287-288. Mrs. Harris to her son at Berlin, from Piccadilly, 3.2.1775. John Christian Bach again.
2. Walpole, IX, 162-163. Walpole to the Countess of Upper Ossory, 2.2.1775.
3. Walpole Journal, I, 453-454, 455.
4. Malmesbury, I, 290. Mrs. Harris to her son at Berlin, from Piccadilly, 6.2.1775.
5. Franklin Writings, VI, 305. Franklin to Charles Thomson, from London, 5.2.1775.
6. Burke Corres. I, 509-514. Abridged. Letter from Lee to Burke, from Annapolis, 16.12.1774, sent c/o Sir Joshua Reynolds.
7. Malmesbury, I, 291. Mrs. Harris to her son at Berlin, from Piccadilly, 6.2.1775.
9. M.C. 10.2.1775.

10. Walpole Journal, I, 460.
11. L.C. 11.2.1775.
14. First para. George III Papers. King to Lord North, from Queen's House, 11.2.1775. Second, W.E.P., 14.2.1775.
15. Walpole, IX, 164-165. Walpole to Sir Horace Mann, from Arlington Street, 15.2.1775.
16. A.R. 1775, Chronicle, 83.
17. First para. M.P. 17.2.1775. Second, Malmesbury, I, 292. Mrs. Harris to her son at Berlin, from Piccadilly, 17.2.1775.
18. Walpole, IX, 166-167. Walpole to Rev. Wm. Mason, from Arlington Street, 18.2.1775. Given out=announced for further performances.
20. Garrick Corres. II.
21. Malmesbury, I, 292. Mrs. Harris to her son at Berlin, from Piccadilly, 21.2.1775.
24. A.R. 1775, Chronicle, 93.
25. G.M. 1775, 86, 93.
27. Burney Diary, II, 10. Mrs. R. B. Sheridan (née Elizabeth Linley), famous as a singer before her marriage.
28. M.C. 27.2.1775.

March 1775

5. Burney Diary, II, 20, 21, 7-8. The " History " is Dr. Burney's *History of Music*. Merlin made various harpsichords and early pianos.
8. P.A. 8.3.1775. The papers burnt were *The Crisis*, No. III, a periodical, and *The Present Crisis with respect to America*, a pamphlet. See G.M. 1775, 147.
12. G.M. 1775, 131 (a letter dated February 25th).
13. Bath C. 9.3.1775.
14. Campbell, 29-30.
15. Lady's M. 1775, 166.
16. G.M. 1775, 150.
17. Malmesbury, I, 296. Mrs. Harris to her son at Berlin, from Piccadilly, 16.3.1775.
19. Campbell, 39. Two burlesque plays, Henry Fielding's *Tom Thumb* and Henry Carey's *Chrononhotonthologos*.
20. Walpole, IX, 171, 172. Walpole to Sir Horace Mann, from Arlington Street, 20.3.1775.
21. First two paras. Campbell, 40-41. Third, Malmesbury, I, 297. Mrs. Harris to her son at Berlin, Piccadilly, 21.3.1775.
22. First para. Walpole Journal, I, 478. Remainder, Burke Speeches, 286-287.
23. Lloyd's E.P. 24-27.3.1775.
24. G.M. 1775, 133, 134-135.
25. M.C. 25.3.1775.
26. M.P. 24.3.1775.
27. Johnson (Boswell), II, 324-325. *Bon Ton*, or *High Life above Stairs*, a farce in two acts by David Garrick.
28. L.C. 28.3.1775.

30. Lady's M. 1775, 162.
31. G.N.D.A. 31.3.1775.

April 1775

1. Johnson (Boswell), II, 331.
2. Johnson (Boswell), II, 337.
3. Malmesbury, I, 299. Mrs. Harris to her son at Berlin, from Piccadilly, 31.3.1775. The embalmer was probably William Cruikshank.
4. S.J.C. 4.4.1775.
5. M.P. 5.4.1775.
6. G.M. 1775, 202-203.
10. D.A. 10.4.1775. Advertisements.
11. Lloyd's E.P. 12.4.1775, and (last para.) Malmesbury, I, 302. Mrs. Harris to her son at Berlin, from Piccadilly, 14.4.1775.
13. G.M. 1775, 203.
16. First and third paras. G.M. 1775, 141. Second, Walpole, IX, 177. Walpole to Rev. W. Cole, from Arlington Street, 11.4.1775. Fourth, Walpole, IX, 181. Walpole to Rev. Wm. Mason, from Arlington Street, 14.4.1775.
17. First para. M.P. 17.4.1775. Second, Walpole, IX, 184. Walpole to Sir Horace Mann, from Strawberry Hill, 17.4.1775.
18. Malmesbury, I, 302-303. Mrs. Harris to her son at Berlin, from Twickenham, 20.4.1775.
19. M.P. 19.4.1775.
22. Walpole, IX, 186-187. Walpole to Sir Horace Mann, from Arlington Street, 22.4.1775.
23. George III Papers. Lord North to King, from Downing St. ? 21.4.1755, and King to Lord North, from Kew, 21.4.1775.
25. M.C. 26.4.1775. Anker=a liquid measure. A Dutch anker=about 8½ gallons.
26. G.N.D.A. 26.4.1775. James Watt.
27. A.R. 1775, Chronicles, 110-111.
28. Lloyd's E.P. 28.4.1775.
29. G.M. 1775, 206. Last para. G.E.P. 27-29.4.1775. Advertisement.
30. G.M. 1775, 189, 192.

May 1775

1. M.C. 2.5.1775.
2. M.C. 3.5.1775. Much abridged. Sheridan's play.
3. G.M. 1775, 251.
4. L.C. 1.5.1775.
8. M.C. 8.5.1775.
9. Watt (Muirhead), II, 89, 8.5.1775, Watt to his father, from London. (Fire-engine=steam engine.)
10. L.C. 10.5.1775.
12. M.P. 12.5.1775.
13. M.C. 13.5.1775.
14. L.C. 11.5.1775.

15. G.M. 1775, 252.
17. Boswell Letters, 194. To Temple, from Thrale's villa at Streatham, 17.5.1775. Topham Beauclerk.
18. Lady's M. 1775, 277-278.
19. Walpole Journal, I, 489-490.
20. G.N.D.A. 19.5.1775.
22. M.C. 23.5.1775. Second para. M.P. 25.5.1775.
23. A.R. 1775, Chronicle, 122.
24. First para. Walpole Journal, I, 490. Second, A.R. 1775, Chronicle, 126. Eclipse, the most famous of English racehorses, belonged to Dennis O'Kelly, an Irish adventurer who became a Count of the Holy Roman Empire and made a fortune by gambling and horse-breeding. The saying " Eclipse first and the rest nowhere " arose from his first race, the Queen's Plate at Winchester. Eclipse died in 1789, aged twenty-five. He was never beaten.
26. G.M. 1775, 253.
30. Walpole, IX, 203-204. Walpole to Sir Horace Mann, from Strawberry Hill, 5.6.1775. This skirmish at Lexington on April 19th, 1775, was the first engagement between the regular troops and the Americans. See June 10.
31. A.R. 1775, Chronicles, 127-128.

June 1775

1. First para. G.M. 1775, 300. Remainder, 148-150.
2. G.M. 1775, 254.
5. First para. M.P. 5.6.1775. Second, Walpole, IX, 205. Walpole to Sir Horace Mann, from Strawberry Hill, 5.6.1775. According to G.M. 1775, p. 301, " his most Christian Majesty " was crowned in the cathedral at Rheims on June 12th " with the greatest magnificence and regularity."
7. G.M. 1775, 300.
9. Burney Diary, II, 79-80. This at Dr. Burney's. " She came before 7, and stayed till 12, and was singing almost all the time ! "
10. Lady's M. 1775, 332.
11. Beatson, IV, 69-70.
15. G.N.D.A. 15.6.1775.
19. H.M.C. Dartmouth, 378-379. Wesley to Dartmouth, " in the way to Dublin," 14.6.1775. But compare 29.11.1775.
20. A.R. 1775, Chronicle, 131.
21. G.M. 1775, 301.
22. First para. A.R. 1775, Chronicle, 132. Second, M.C. 23.6.1775.
23. G.M. 1775, 302.
24. G.M. 1775, 302.
25. First para. Walpole Journal, I, 493. The rest, M.P. 24.6.1775.
28. G.M. 1775, 302-303.

July 1775

3. George III Papers. Lord North to the King, from Bushy Park, 1.7.1775.

4. G.M. 1775, 347.
5. G.M. 1775, 347-348.
8. George III Papers. King to Lord North, from Kew, 5.7.1775.
10. G.N.D.A. 10.7.1775.
11. Burke Corres. II, 36-37. Rockingham to Burke, from Grosvenor Square, 11.7.1775.
15. M.P. 15.7.1775.
25. T.C.M. 1775, 390. The Battle of Bunker's Hill. The American losses were half the British.
26. Garrick Corres. II, 68. J. and D. Hoadly to Garrick, from St. Maries, 25.7.1775. Puffy Pensioner is of course Dr. Johnson.
27. First para. M.C. 27.7.1775. Second, G.M. 1775, 350.
29. M.C. 29.7.1775.
31. First para. Lloyd's E.P. 31.7.1775. Second, G.M. 1775, 350. Third, Gage, I, 407.

August 1775

1. P.A. 2.8.1775. Edward Alleyn (1566–1626) founded Dulwich College. Doggett (*d.* 1721) founded this competition in 1716. It is still held.
3. First para. M.P. 3.8.1775. Second, Walpole, IX, 227. Walpole to Sir Horace Mann, from Strawberry Hill, 3.8.1775. Foote, who made a practice of putting caricatures of well-known people of the day on the stage, wrote a play about the Duchess which was banned from performance but was printed. For an account of the passage of arms between Foote and the Duchess see G.M. 1775, 390-392.
4. G.M. 1775, 403.
6. A.R. 1775, Chronicle, 143.
7. G.N.D.A. 7.8.1775.
9. Walpole, IX, 227-228. Walpole to Rev. Wm. Mason, from Strawberry Hill, 7.8.1775.
11. Lloyd's E.P. 11.8.1775.
12. Lloyd's E.P. 12.8.1775.
14. Lloyd's E.P. 14.8.1775. But see 9.5.1776.
15. A.R. 1775, Chronicle, 139. Nephew of Sir William Johnson.
16. G.M. 1775, 404. George III's second son, Frederick Augustus (1763–1827), Duke of York and Albany, was elected Bishop of Osnaburg, or Osnabrück, in Hanover, in 1764. By the Treaty of Westphalia this Bishopric was occupied alternately by a Catholic prelate and a Protestant secular prince of the House of Brunswick-Lüneburg.
17. T.C.M. 1775, 444.
18. M.P. 18.8.1775.
19. P.A. 19.8.1775.
20. G.M. 1775, 372, 374, 376.
21. Lennox, I, 244. Lady Sarah Bunbury to Lady Susan O'Brien, from Castletown, 21.8.1775.
22. First para. Burke Corres. II, 43. Burke to Arthur Lee, from Beaconsfield, 22.8.1775. Remainder, G.M. 1775, 397.
23. Walpole Journal, I, 500.

24. Burke Corres. II, 47-50. Burke to Rockingham, 23.8.1775. The " foreigners " were German mercenaries.
25. Lloyd's E.P. 25.8.1775.
26. Franklin Writings, VI, 408-409.
27. Sheridan (Moore), I, 140. Letter from Mary Linley to her sister, Sheridan's wife, from Bath, 22.8.1775.
28. M.P. 29.8.1775. Presumably Thomas Arne, the composer. A not uncommon method of extorting money.
29. Harrison, 692.

September 1775

2. G.M. 1775, 451.
4. G.M. 1775, 450.
13. George III Papers. King to Lord North, from Kew, 10.9.1775.
15. A.R. 1775, Chronicle, 156.
16. L.C. 16.9.1775.
17. G.M. 1775, 451.
19. M.P. 19.9.1775.
20. M.P. 21.9.1775. So far as the editor can discover this is the earliest known reference to " *Hamlet* without the Prince of Denmark."
21. G.N.D.A. 21.9.1775.
22. First para. T.C.M. 1775, 491. Second, L.C. 23.9.1775. Advertisement.
23. A.R. 1775, Chronicle, 160.
24. Burke Corres. II, 69. Rockingham to Burke, from Wentworth, 24.9.1775.
25. L.C. 27.9.1775.
27. George III Corres. III, 242, 244. The last paragraph goes to the heart of the problem. Burgoyne apologises to his unspecified correspondent for writing " loosely."
28. Lady's M. 1775, 498.
29. G.M. 1775, 496-497.

October 1775

2. M.P. 2.10.1775.
6. First para. Lloyd's E.P. 6.10.1775. Second, M.P. 6.10.1775.
7. Lady's M. 1775, 556.
9. M.J. 7-9.10.1775.
13. Lady's M. 1775, 557.
16. M.C. 16.10.1775.
21. L.C. 21.10.1775.
23. Lady's M. 1775, 554.
25. Lady's M. 1775, 553. Caravel and xebec.
26. Walpole Journal, I, 510, 512, 513, 514. Last para. Hume, II, 300-301. David Hume to his publisher, William Strahan, from Edinburgh, 26.10.1775.

27. Walpole Journal, I, 514.
28. Walpole, IX, 277-278. Walpole to Sir Horace Mann, from Arlington Street, 28.10.1775.
29. Malmesbury, I, 325-326. Dr. Jeans to James Harris, M.P., from Paris, 19.10.1775.
30. H.M.C. Kenyon, 505-506. Letter from Mary Kenyon to her mother, 30.10.1775.

November 1775

1. Burney Diary, II, 86.
2. P.A. 4.11.1775.
3. P.A. 3.11.1775.
4. Burney Diary, II, 100.
5. Lady's M. 1775, 553.
7. G.N.D.A. 7.11.1775.
9. T.C.M. 1775, 612.
10. Cumberland Letters, 98-99. George Cumberland to his brother, Richard Dennison Cumberland ; cousins of the playwright.
11. George III Papers. Lord North to King, from Downing Street, 12.11.1775.
12. Malmesbury, I, 330. Mr. Harris, senior, M.P., to Mr. James Harris, from Gerrard St. 14.11.1775.
13. T.C.M. 1775, 612.
14. Walpole, IX, 282-283. Walpole to Sir Horace Mann, from Arlington Street, 14.11.1775. Orloff was one of Catherine II's lovers.
15. Lloyd's E.P. 15.11.1775.
16. G.M. 1775, 8, 56.
18. T.C.M. 1775, 610.
19. A.R. 1775, Chronicles, 174-175.
20. G.M. 1775, 550.
21. P.A. 22.11.1775.
22. Priestley, I, 277-278.
23. Lettsom, 51, 53-54. Dated here arbitrarily.
24. T.C.M. 1775, 613.
27. M.P. 27.11.1775.
29. Wesley Journal, IV, 60-61.
30. Malmesbury, I, 335. Mr. Harris, Senior, M.P., to Mr. James Harris, from Gerrard St. 28.11.1775–2.12.1775.

December 1775

1. M.C. 30.11.1775.
3. G.M. 1775, 602.
6. Lloyd's E.P. 6.12.1775.
7. G.M. 1775, 550.
8. G.M. 1775, 603, 604-605. See London Sessions Papers.
11. A.R. 1775, Chronicle, 184.

12. Walpole Journal, I, 528.
13. L.C. 11.12.1775.
14. L.C. 14.12.1775.
15. First para. Selwyn Letters, 107. Anthony Storer to Lord Carlisle, from Portugal Street, 14.12.1775. Second para. London Sessions Papers. First Session in the Mayoralty of Sawbridge, No. 1, Part III, 86-87, Dec. 1775.
16. Burney Diary, II, 130.
18. Malmesbury, I, 337. Mr. Batt, to James Harris, Senior, M.P., from Lincoln's Inn, 18.12.1775.
21. Walpole, IX, 306. Walpole to Rev. Wm. Mason from Arlington Street, 21.12.1775. Cumberland the playwright, original of Sir Fretful Plagiary in Sheridan's *The Critic*.
23. First para. A.R. 1775, Chronicle, 187. Second, T.C.M. 1775, 669.
24. T.C.M. 1775, 708. Priestley : Experiments, II, 34-36. Acting on Priestley's remarks, Lavoisier made many experiments with this new gas, which he named oxygen.
26. G.M. 1775, 636.
28. A.R. 1775, Chronicle, 191.
29. Ibid. 191.
30. M.J. 30.12.1775.

January 1776

1. G.M. 1775, ii. " Sylvanus Urban, Gent." was the pseudonym of Edward Cave (1691–1754), who founded G.M. in 1731, and it was retained by subsequent editors. Vol. XLV was that for 1775.
3. M.P. 5.1.1776. See also 3.2.1776 and 4.10.1776.
6. M.P. 6.1.1776.
7. G.M. 1776, 44.
12. Lloyd's E.P. 12.1.1776.
13. Garrick Corres. II, 126. Letter dated 10.1.1776.
14. G.N.D.A. 12.1.1776.
17. T.C.M. 1776, 53.
18. M.P. 20.1.1776.
19. M.C. 19.1.1776.
20. M.P. 17.1.1776.
21. G.M. 1776, 45.
22. First para. G.M. 1776, 27. Second, More, I, 67. Letter from one of Hannah More's sisters to an unnamed person, " London, 1776."
24. M.C. 24.1.1776. Para. dated " Liverpool, Jan. 19."
25. M.P. 25.1.1776.
26. G.N.D.A. 25.1.1776.
27. First para. M.C. 27.1.1776. Second, G.M. 1776, 45.
28. L.P. 31.1.1776.
29. Walpole, IX, 321-322. Walpole to Sir Horace Mann, 28.1.1776.
31. M.P. 31.1.1776.

February 2nd–March 30th, 1776

February 1776

2. First para. Lloyd's E.P. 2.2.1776.   Second, G.N.D.A. 2.2.1776.
3. Ballad sheet quoted by R. Crompton Rhodes in *The Plays and Poems of R. B. Sheridan*, I, 177-178.   The phenomenal success of Gay's *Beggar's Opera* was exceeded only by that of *The Duenna*.   Polly was Gay's heroine.   Miss Brown and the Jewish singer Leoni appeared in *The Duenna*.   See also 3.1.1776 and 4.10.1776.
9. Priestley, I, 289.   Priestley to Rev. C. Rotheram, from London, 9.2.1776.
12. M.P. 12.2.1776.
14. M.P. 14.2.1776.
18. Walpole, IX, 329.   Walpole to the Rev. Wm. Mason, 18.2.1776. Gibbon had sent his *History* to Walpole : Vol. I only.   Vols. II and III appeared in 1781, IV–VI in 1788.
19. T.C.M. 1776, 109.
22. Malmesbury, I, 339-340.   Mrs. Harris to her son at Berlin, from Piccadilly, 23.2.1776.
24. M.C. 24.2.1776.
25. Beatson, IV, 114.
26. M.C. 26.2.1776.
27. Lloyd's E.P. 29.2.1776.
28. A.R. 1776, Chronicle, 123.
29. R.S.L.P. (in MS.), Decade VI, 180.   Part of a copy of a long letter from William Henly to Rev. Dr. Horsley, F.R.S., dated 4.3.1776, beginning " On Thursday last my ingenious friend . . ."   Endorsed " Redde May 16th 1776."

March 1776

1. Malmesbury, I, 340-341.   Mrs. Harris to her son at Berlin, from Piccadilly, 1.3.1776.
2. G.N.D.A. 2.3. and 1.3.1776.
5. M.C. 5.3.1776.
6. T.C.M. 1776, 164.
7. M.P. 9.3.1776.
8. R.S.L.P. (in MS.), Decade VI, 163.   From the original letter, the corrections in which show the writer's care for style and for exactness of expression.
13. J.H.C. XXXV, 649-650.
14. A.B.G. 11.3.1776, as quoted in *James Watt and the Steam Engine*, by H. W. Dickenson and Rhys Jenkins.
15. M.P. 14.3.1776.
16. M.C. 18.3.1776.
22. Walpole, IX, 339.   Walpole to Sir Horace Mann, 22.3.1776.
26. Malmesbury, I, 342.   Mrs. Harris to her son at Berlin, from Piccadilly, 26.3.1776.   Tessier was a professor of agricultural science.
28. M.C. 28.3.1776.
30. G.M. 1776, 188.

31. Burney Diary, II, 138-139. Georgiana, Duchess of Devonshire, the famous beauty painted by Gainsborough and Reynolds.

April 1776

1. M.P. 1.4.1776.
2. Beatson, IV, 129.
3. A.R. 1776, Chronicle, 130.
4. First para. M.C. 4.4.1776. Second, G.M. 1776, 235.
7. M.P. 7.4.1776.
8. A.R. 1776, Chronicle, 132.
9. G.M. 1776, 189.
10. G.N.D.A. 10.4.1776.
12. Lloyd's E.P. 12.4.1776.
15. More, I, 81-83. Hannah More to her family, "Adelphi, 1776." For a full account of the trial see G.M. 1776, 179-187.
17. Walpole, IX, 348-349. Walpole to Sir Horace Mann, from Arlington Street, 17.4.1776.
22. More, I, 84-85. Hannah More to her family, "Adelphi, 1776." Camden's remarks to her were actually made a few days later than the 22nd. Branding on the hand was part of the punishment for bigamy.
23. M.P. 23.4.1776.
24. Lloyd's E.P. 24.4.1776.
25. A.R. 1776, Chronicle, 134.
26. Beatson, IV, 133-135.
27. G.N.D.A. 27.4.1776.
28. First item, A.R. 1776, Account of Books, 241. Remainder, M.R. LIV, 326.
29. T.C.M. 1776, 222.
30. G.M. 1776, 235.

May 1776

1. Curwen, 54.
3. G.N.D.A. 3.5.1776.
4. M.P. 4.5.1776.
5. Burke Corres. II, 102-104. Burke to Rockingham, 4.5.1776.
7. Curwen, 55.
8. T.C.M. 1776, 275.
9. Wesley Journal, IV, 73-74.
10. First para. M.P. 10.5.1776. Second, G.M. 1776, 237.
11. Hume, II, 319. David Hume to William Strahan, from Bath, 10.5.1776. See note under 3.8.1776.
12. More, I, 89-90. Hannah More to Mrs. Gwatkin, " Adelphi, 12.5.1776."
13. Malmesbury, I, 345-346. Mrs. Harris to her son at Berlin, from Piccadilly, 10.5.1776.
14. M.P. 11.5.1776.
15. Curwen, 56. Second para. M.P. 15.5.1776.

16. M.C. 16.5.1776.
17. G.M. 1776, 238.
18. Reynolds (Northcote), II, 36 ; footnote to year 1776. Dated here arbitrarily.
19. A.R. 1776, Chronicle, 134. For the official anniversary see 18.1.74 and 75.
21. M.P. 22.5.1776.
22. M.P. 22.5.1776.
25. G.M. 1776, 282-283.
26. G.M. 1776, 222, 223, 270, 224, 225, 226, 228.
27. Lloyd's E.P. 27.5.1776.
28. M.P. 28.5.1776.
29. M.P. 29.5.1776.
30. More, I, 85-87. Hannah More to her family, " Adelphi, 1776."
31. G.N.D.A. 30.5.1776.

June 1776

3. G.M. 1776, 283.
5. Curwen, 56.
7. G.N.D.A. 7.6.1776.
9. Malmesbury, I, 347. Mrs. Harris to her son at Berlin, from Salisbury, 9.6.1776. Molyneux, Usher of the Black Rod, had charge of the Duchess.
10. M.P. 11.6.1776 and Garrick (Davies), II, 321-322. The Fund was for distressed players. Garrick was a generous contributor.
11. T.C.M. 1776, 332. Letter much abridged.
12. Curwen, 58. Letter from Curwen to Dr. Charles Russell, Antigua, dated London, June 10, 1776.
16. Reynolds (Northcote), II, 49. Dated here arbitrarily.
19. G.M. 1776, 285.
22. M.P. 24.6.1776.
24. G.M. 1776, 284-285.
25. M.P. 24.6.1776.
27. M.C. 27.6.1776.
28. Lloyd's E.P. 28.6.1776.

July 1776

4. T.C.M. 1776, 387.
5. A.R. 1776, Chronicle, 158.
6. M.P. 6.7.1776.
9. G.N.D.A. 9.7.1776.
10. G.M. 1776, 334.
11. M.P. 11.7.1776.
12. A.R. 1776, Chronicle, 169.
14. G.M. 1776, 334. " Called the Spinning Jenny " is taken from M.P. 15.7.1776, a fuller account.
15. First para. M.P. 15.7.1776. Second, G.M. 1776, 334.
17. Walpole, IX, 392. Walpole to Sir Horace Mann, from Strawberry Hill, 17.7.1776.

20. Cook, I, 1-13 (Cook's own journal, very much abridged) and, last para. Introduction, xxx.
21. Smith, 8-10, 17. Page 68 : " A penny loaf a day, the present gaol allowance, is an uncertain quantity and insufficient to support a man in health ! " Dated here arbitrarily.
24. Malcolm, II, 291-292, quoting from a newspaper of July 1776.
26. T.C.M. 1776, 377.
27. Lloyd's E.P. 27.7.1776.
28. G.M. 1776, 325.
29. T.C.M. 1776, 390.
30. L.C. 1.8.1776.
31. A.R. 1776, Chronicle, 156.

August 1776

2. A.R. 1776, Chronicle, 176.
3. G.M. 1776, 382. The navy was in a sad condition, and Sandwich's administration at the Admiralty was lax and corrupt.
5. G.N.D.A. 5.8.1776.
6. M.P. 5.8.1776.
7. M.C. 7.8.1776.
10. G.M. 1776, 361-362. Checked with S. E. Morison's *Sources and Documents illustrating the American Revolution* (1923).
11. G.M. 1776, 383.
12. M.P. 12.8.1776.
13. S.J.C. 13.8.1776.
15. M.P. 15.8.1776.
22. M.P. 22.8.1776.
25. Hume, II, 450-452. Adam Smith to William Strahan, from Kirkcaldy, 9.11.1776.
26. M.C. 26.8.1776. "Brighthelmstone" became "Brighton" about 1800.
27. G.N.D.A. 27.8.1776.
28. H.M.C. Dartmouth, 409.
30. M.P. 30.8.1776.

September 1776

3. G.M. 1776, 432. Interludes=short plays.
4. M.P. 4.9.1776. The Duke of Devonshire.
7. G.M. 1776, 433.
9. Smith, 83-85. Dated here arbitrarily.
14. M.P. 14.9.1776.
16. G.M. 1776, 434.
17. A.R. 1776, Chronicles, 179-180.
19. M.P. 19.9.1776.
23. G.M. 1776, 434.
27. M.C. 27.9.1776.
28. G.M. 1776, 426. For nearly thirty years Edmund Burke wrote the survey of events in the *Annual Register*.

29. L.C. 1.10.1776 and 7.9.1776.
30. M.P. 2.10.1776. For Merlin see Index and note to 5.3.1775.

October 1776

1. M.P. 1.10.1776.
2. L.C. 4.10.1776.
4. M.C. 7.10.1776. See under 3.1.1776 and 3.2.1776.
7. G.M. 1776, 480.
8. T.C.M. 1776, 556.
9. M.C. 11.10.1776. Bull-baiting was very popular and bull-wards, or bullards, led their bulls from place to place to secure the patronage of the local " sportsmen." Cock-fighting was more popular still.
10. A.R. 1776, Chronicle, 173.
11. D.A. 11.10.1776.
12. L.C. 11.10.1776.
15. J.H.C. XXXV, 812.
21. A.R. 1776, Chronicle, 187.
25. L.P. 26.10.1776.
26. G.N.D.A. 26.10.1776. John Hunter, the great surgeon and anatomist.
27. G.M. 1776, 473.
28. G.M. 1776, 481-482.
29. G.N.D.A. 28.10.1776.
30. G.M. 1776, 505.
31. First para. M.C. 31.10.1776. Second, M.P. 30.10.1776. Third, L.P. 30.10.1776. Fourth, Lloyd's E.P. 30.10.1776.

November 1776

3. Brief Description, xxxii. Dated here arbitrarily.
4. T.C.M. 1776, 611-612.
5. Lloyd's E.P. 5.11.1776.
6. P.H. XVIII, 1441-1442, and Burke Speeches, 364-365.
7. M.P. 7.11.1776.
8. M.C. 8.11.1776.
9. Brief Description, xv. Dated here arbitrarily.
10. L.P. 5.11.1776. Garrick was often referred to as Roscius.
11. M.P. 11.11.1776.
12. Walpole, IX, 439-440. Walpole to the Countess of Upper Ossory, 13.11.1776, from Arlington Street.
13. G.M. 1776, 529.
14. L.C. 12.11.1776.
15. Wesley Journal, IV, 90.
16. Brief Description, xxix, xxvii-xxviii. Dated here arbitrarily.
18. L.C. 18.11.1776.
22. M.P. 22.11.1776.
23. P.A. 23.11.1776.
24. Chatham Corres. IV, 428-429. Shelburne to Lady Chatham, 23.11. 1776.

27. P.A. 27.11.1776.
29. G.M. 1776, 574.
30. M.P. 30.11.1776.

December 1776

  1. G.M. 1776, 522.   Toplady's volume contained " Rock of Ages."
  2. Lloyd's E.P. 2.12.1776.
  6. N.M.P. 6.12.1776.
10. Reynolds (Northcote), II, 65-66, 69-70.
11. M.C. 11.12.1776.
12. M.P. 10.12.1776.
13. M.P. 13.12.1776.
14. M.P. 14.12.1776.
17. A.R. 1776, Chronicle, 201.
18. P.A. 20.12.1776.
19. Walpole, IX, 450.   Walpole to Sir Horace Mann, from Arlington Street, 20.12.1776.
20. M.P. 20.12.1776.
21. T.C.M. 1776, 671, quoting the *London Gazette*.
22. M.P. 21.12.1776.
24. M.P. 24.12.1776.
25. Lloyd's E.P. 25.12.1776.
28. Almon, 97-98.   Letter from Almon, apparently to John Lloyd, from Piccadilly, 28.12.1776.   He proved a true prophet.
29. Beatson, IV, 190-191.
31. G.N.D.A. 31.12.1776.

INDEX OF SOURCES

The editions named are those which the editor has used, not necessarily the first editions.

Biographies and memoirs are indexed under their subjects.

Curwen. Journal and Letters of the late Samuel Curwen, Judge of Admiralty, etc., an American refugee in England from 1775 to 1784, [edited by] G. A. Ward. 1842.

D.A. The Daily Advertiser.

Franklin Writings. The Writings of Benjamin Franklin, edited by A. H. Smyth. New York. 10 vols. 1905–1907.

Gage. The Correspondence of General Thomas Gage with the Secretaries of State, 1763–1775. Edited by C. E. Carter. New Haven, 2 vols. 1931.
Garrick Corres. Private Correspondence of David Garrick, edited by James Boaden. 2 vols. 1831–32.
Garrick (Davies). Memoirs of David Garrick, by Thomas Davies. 2 vols. 1780.
George III Corres. The Correspondence of George III with Lord North, from 1760 to 1783, edited by the Hon. Sir John Fortescue. 6 vols. 1927–28.
George III Papers. In the Royal Archives at Windsor Castle.
G.E.P. The General Evening Post.
Gibbon Letters. Private Letters of Edward Gibbon, edited by R. E. Prothero. 2 vols. 1896.
G.M. The Gentleman's Magazine.
G.N.D.A. The Gazetteer and New Daily Advertiser.
Goldsmith (Hawes). An Account of the late Dr. Goldsmith's illness, by William Hawes. 4th ed. 1780.
Goldsmith : Retaliation. Retaliation, a poem by Dr. Goldsmith, including epitaphs on the distinguished wits of the Metropolis. 1774.

Harrison. A New and Universal History Description and Survey of the Cities of London and Westminster, the Borough of Southwark and their adjacent parts . . . by Walter Harrison, 1775.
H.M.C. Dartmouth. Historical Manuscripts Commission : 11th Report, Appendix, Part V, MSS. of the Earl of Dartmouth. 1887.
H.M.C. Kenyon. Ditto. 14th Report. Appendix, Part IV, MSS. of Lord Kenyon. 1894.
Hume. The Letters of David Hume, edited by J. Y. T. Greig. Oxford, 1932.

Johnson (Boswell). The Life of Samuel Johnson, by James Boswell, edited by G. Birkbeck Hill, revised by L. F. Powell. 6 vols. 1934–   .
Johnson (Piozzi). Anecdotes of the late Samuel Johnson, by H. L. Piozzi. 1786.
J.H.C. Journals of the House of Commons, reprinted by order of the House of Commons. 1803–1804, etc.

Lady's M. The Lady's Magazine.
L.C. The London Chronicle.

Lennox. The Life and Letters of Lady Sarah Lennox. 2 vols. 1901.

L.E.P. The London Evening Post.

Lettsom. On the Improvement of Medicine in London on the Basis of Public Good, by J. C. Lettsom, M.D., F.R.S. 2nd ed. 1775.

L.G. The London Gazette.

Lloyd's E.P. Lloyd's Evening Post.

L.M. The London Magazine.

London Session Papers. The whole Proceedings on the King's Commission of the Peace, Oyer and Terminer and Gaol Delivery for the City of London and also the Gaol Delivery for the County of Middlesex. . . .

L.P. The London Packet.

Malcolm. J. P. Malcolm : Anecdotes of the Manners and Customs of London during the Eighteenth Century. 2 vols. 1810.

Malmesbury. A Series of Letters of the First Earl of Malmesbury, his family and friends, 1745–1820, edited by his grandson, the Earl of Malmesbury. 2 vols. 1870.

M.C. The Morning Chronicle.

M.J. The Middlesex Journal.

More. Memoirs of the Life and Correspondence of Mrs. Hannah More, by William Roberts. 4 vols. 3rd ed. 1835.

M.P. The Morning Post. (See also *New Morning Post.*)

M.R. The Monthly Review, or Literary Journal.

N.M.P. The New Morning Post, *i.e.* the second one, published by G. Corral. See Nov. 11th and 12th, 1776.

P.A. The Public Advertiser.

P.H. The Parliamentary History, printed by T. C. Hansard for Longman, etc. Vols. 17-19. 1813.

P.L. The Public Ledger.

Priestley. The Life and Correspondence of Joseph Priestley, by J. T. Rutt. 2 vols. 1831–32.

Priestley : Experiments, II. Experiments and Observations on Different Kinds of Air, Vol. II., by Joseph Priestley, LL.D., F.R.S. 1775.

Reynolds (Northcote). The Life of Sir Joshua Reynolds, by J. Northcote. Revised ed. 2 vols. 1819.

R.S.L.P. Royal Society : Letters and Papers in MS.

Selwyn Letters. George Selwyn, His Letters and his Life, edited by E. S. Roscoe and Helen Clergue. 1899.

Sheridan (Moore). Memoirs of the Life of the Rt. Hon. Richard Brinsley Sheridan, by Thomas Moore. 3rd ed. 2 vols. 1825.

S.J.C. St. James's Chronicle.

Smith. The State of the Gaols in London, Westminster and the Borough of Southwark, by William Smith, M.D. 1776.

T.C.M. The Town and Country Magazine.

Walpole. The Letters of Horace Walpole, Fourth Earl of Orford, edited by Mrs. Paget Toynbee. 16 vols. Oxford, 1904–5.

Walpole : Journal. A Journal of the Reign of King George III, 1771–1783, edited by Dr. Doran. 2 vols. 1859.

Watt (Muirhead). The Origin and Progress of the Mechanical Inventions of James Watt, illustrated by his Correspondence, by J. P. Muirhead. 3 vols. 1854.

W.E.P. The Whitehall Evening Post.

Wesley Journal. The Journal of the Rev. John Wesley, edited by F. W. Macdonald. 4 vols. 1909.

DRAMATIS PERSONAE

The leading persons who are mentioned in the Journal. The ages given are those on January 1st, 1774.

	AGE
King George III	35
Queen Charlotte	29

	AGE
Lord North, *First Lord of the Treasury and Chancellor of the Exchequer : Prime Minister*	41
Earl of Rochford, *Secretary of State for the Northern Department* * : *to November 1775*	56
Viscount Weymouth, *Secretary of State for the Northern Department : from November 1775*	39
Earl of Dartmouth, *Secretary of State for the Colonies : to November 1775. Lord Privy Seal : from November 1775*	42
Lord George Germain, *Secretary of State for the Colonies : from November 1775*	57
Duke of Grafton, *Lord Privy Seal : to November 1775*	38
Earl of Sandwich, *First Lord of the Admiralty*	55
Viscount Townshend, *Master General of the Ordnance*	49
Viscount Barrington, *Secretary at War*	56
Earl of Mansfield, *Lord Chief Justice*	68
Edward Thurlow, *Attorney-General*	42
Alexander Wedderburn, *Solicitor-General*	40
Sir Fletcher Norton, *Speaker of the House of Commons*	57

IN OPPOSITION

	AGE
William Pitt, Earl of Chatham	65
Lord Camden	59
John Wilkes, *M.P., Middlesex ; Lord Mayor of London, 1774*	46
Edmund Burke	44
Marquis of Rockingham	43
Earl of Shelburne	36
Lord Temple	34
Charles James Fox	24

* The Northern Department was reorganised as the Foreign Office in 1782, the Southern Department as the Home Office.

377

Dramatis Personae

INDIA

	AGE
Lord Clive, *retired*	48
Warren Hastings, *Governor-General*	41
Philip Francis	33

ARMY AND NAVY

	AGE
Lt.-General Thomas Gage, *Governor of Massachusetts, 1774–75, Commander-in-Chief in America, 1775*	52
Major-General John Burgoyne	51
Major-General Guy Carleton, *Governor of Quebec, 1775–77. K.B. 1776* .	49
Lt.-General William Howe, *Commander-in-Chief in America, 1775–78. K.B. 1775*	44
Lt.-General Earl Cornwallis	35
Vice-Admiral Samuel Graves, *Commander-in-Chief on American Station, 1774–75*	60
Rear-Admiral Molyneux Shuldham, *Commander-in-Chief on American Station, 1775–76*	?56
Vice-Admiral Earl Howe, *Commander-in-Chief on American Station, 1776–78*	47

AMERICANS

	AGE
Benjamin Franklin	67
Major-General Israel Putnam	55
Samuel Adams	51
Major-General Charles Lee, *Second in command* . . .	42
General George Washington, *Commander-in-Chief* . .	41
Brigadier-General Richard Montgomery . . .	37
John Hancock	36
Colonel Benedict Arnold	32

LITERATURE AND DRAMA

	AGE		AGE
Samuel Johnson	64	Thomas Warton	45
David Hume	62	George Colman the elder	41
William Whitehead, *Poet Laureate*	58	Richard Cumberland	41
		James Beattie	38
David Garrick	56	James Macpherson	37
Horace Walpole	56	Edward Gibbon	36
Gilbert White	53	Hugh Kelly	34
Samuel Foote	53	James Boswell	33
William Robertson	52	Hannah More	28
Adam Smith	50	R. B. Sheridan	22
Hester Chapone	46	Sarah Siddons	18
Oliver Goldsmith	45		

PRINTING AND PUBLISHING

John Baskerville	67	Thomas Cadell the elder	31
William Strahan	58	John Bell	28

Dramatis Personae

MUSIC

	AGE		AGE
Thomas Arne	. . 63	Thomas Linley .	. 41
K. F. Abel .	. . 48	John Christian Bach .	. 38
Charles Burney	. . 47		

PAINTING, SCULPTURE, ARCHITECTURE, ETC.

Sir Joshua Reynolds, P.R.A.	50	Josiah Wedgwood .	. 43
Thomas Gainsborough	. 46	Joseph Nollekens .	. 36
Francesco Bartolozzi .	. 46	Benjamin West .	. 35
Robert Adam .	. . 45	Philip Loutherbourg .	. 33

EXPLORATION

James Cook .	. . 45	James Bruce .	. . 43

RELIGION AND SOCIAL REFORM

John Wesley .	. . 70	John Howard	. ? 47
Sir John Fielding	. 52		

MEDICINE, SCIENCE, ENGINEERING

Sir John Pringle, P.R.S.	. 60	Nevil Maskelyne, *Astronomer-*	
William Hunter	. 57	*Royal* . .	. 41
Joseph Priestley	. 50	James Watt . .	. 37
John Hunter .	. . 45	J. C. Lettsom . .	. 29

Louis XV of France (*died*		Charles Edward Stuart, the	
1774) . .	. 63	Young Pretender	. 53
Frederick the Great of		Catherine II of Russia	. 44
Prussia . .	. 61	Louis XVI of France	. 19

GENERAL INDEX

GENERAL INDEX

The ranks and appointments given in the biographical notes are those held during the period 1774–76 unless otherwise stated.

General Index

Pele, John Baptist, tortured, 231
Pelham, Lord, 42
penal laws, reform needed, 82
penance, public performance of, 62
Pennant, Thomas (1726–98), traveller, 70, 142, 283
Pennsylvania. See American Colonies
" Pennsylvania Farmer," 115
penny post, 5-6, 245
Pentweazle, Lady, 296
Percy, Lord (Sir Hugh Percy, later 2nd Duke of Northumberland), (1742–1817), M.P. Westminster (1763–1776), 104-107, 183-184, 347
perpetual electricity, 254
perpetual motion, 22
Perreau, Robert and Daniel, trial of, 179-181 ; conviction, 182 ; Mrs. Robert's petition for, 242 ; execution, 244 ; disorder at their funeral, 245 ; their guilt disputed, 247
Peru, 116
pest-houses, 5
Peterborough, Lord, 182
Petersham, Lord, 341
phaetons, 152, 310, 312
Philadelphia. See American Colonies
Philips, Ambrose (1675 ?–1749), poet, 143
Philosophical Transactions (of the Royal Society), 15, 282
Phipps, Capt. Constantine John (1744–1792, R.N., 106
phlogiston, 282. See also dephlogisticated air
Physical Friend, The, 318
Physicians. See Royal College of Physicians
piano, Merlin's new forte, 319
Piccadilly, 243
pickpocket maltreated, 87-88
pictures, rage for, 55-56
Pigot, Brigadier-General Robert (1720-96), 193-195
pillory, 263, 290-291, 324
Pinchbeck, Christopher (1710 ?–83), inventor, 67, 261, 279
Pirates, Moroccan, 26 ; English, 175 ; French, 264 ; Tunisian, 233
Pitt, Lord (son of William Pitt, Earl of Chatham), 249, 253
Pius VI, Pope, 163
Plomer, Sheriff and Alderman, 189, 190-191, 223, 255

plough for mending roads, 67
Poland, Partition of, 25, 352 ; election riots, 90 ; reduced to slavery by Prussia, 91 ; Prussian naval dockyards in, 294
Pole, North, 236 ; Government reward offered for reaching, 246 ; and see Arctic
Pole, South. See Antarctic
police, need of, 12 ; defects of, 208
Polly (in *The Beggar's Opera*), 249, 321
Pomfret, Earl of, 12
poor relief, 275
Pope, Alexander (1688–1744), poet, Warburton's edition, 208-209
Pope, the, burned in effigy, 131
Pope, election of, 163
population, British, increasing, 276
Porte. See Turkey
Port Mahon (Minorca : in British possession), 200, 202, 215, 217
Porteous, Captain, 354
porters, character of, 84
Portia, 238
Portsmouth Dockyards, sabotage at, 340
post, penny, 5-6, 245
pottery, 174
Poussin, Nicholas, 150
Pownall, Governor Thomas (1722–1805), Governor of Massachusetts Bay (1757–59), of South Carolina (1759–60), 41, 50, 100
Present Crisis with respect to America, 360
press, freedom of the, 213
press-gangs, 264, 324-326, 332-333, 336
Preston, H.M.S., 93
Pretender, the Young, the Chevalier Charles Edward Stuart (1720–88), in Tuscany, 96 ; rumoured to be in America, 116 ; burned in effigy, 131 ; his poverty and drunkenness, 174
Price, Dr. Richard (1723–91), nonconformist writer on morals, politics, etc., and friend of Franklin, 227, 323
Priestley, Joseph (1723–1804), theologian and man of science, *Experiments and Observations on Different Kinds of Air*, 66, 236 ; *An Examination of Dr. Reid's Enquiry into the Human Mind*, etc., 115 ; letters

General Index

from Franklin, 203, 227 ; discovery of oxygen, 236, 366 ; *An account of further discoveries in air*, 282 ; George III talks of, 315
Prince of Wales, 244
Pringle, Sir John (1707–82), physician, P.R.S., 256, 338
prison hulks in the Thames, 278
Pritchard, Mrs., actress, 267
Privy Council, Franklin before the, 17
prize fights, 168-69
prostitutes, 18, 127, 204, 277, 334
Prussia and Danzig, 48, 88, 91, 206-207, 226
Prussia, to fight France, etc., 96 ; and Holland, 91 ; and Malta, 90 ; and Poland, 93, 96 ; and Russia, 93 ; all males in, born military slaves, 91 ; building a navy, 294 ; seeking colonies in Asia, 295 ; sends volunteers to America, 317
Prussia, Frederick the Great, King of (reigned 1740–86), " a thorough-paced villain," 25 ; gracious to General Conway, 90 ; invades Poland, 96
Public Advertiser. See Woodfall publishers. See booksellers
punch, 296
Punch of Shaftesbury, 163
Putnam, Major-General Israel (1718–1790), American army, 184

Quacks and their Medicines, 318
quacks, prosperity of, 327
Quakers, 132, 156, 176, 244
Quebec. See under American Colonies, and Canada
Queen Charlotte Sophia (of Mecklenburgh - Strelitz) (1744 – 1818), married George III in 1761, her birthday, 14, 135, 244, 280 ; her children born, 26, 270 ; portrait of, in fireworks, 135 ; receives Mrs. R. Perreau's petition, 242-243 ; her elephant, 301 ; driven in King's phaeton, 310 ; discriminates against Ladies of the opposition, 316 ; her Palace, 6
Queensberry, Duke of, 166

races, horse, 55 ; asses, women, 265
raffle, 312
Ranelagh, 59, 162, 188, 278

Rauzzini, composer, 156, 221
reading society, a, 157
recruiting, 106
Reddish, Samuel (1735–88), actor, 124, 150, 214
regatta, a new thing, 188
Regatta, The, 288
Reinhold (probably Charles Frederick, 1737–1815, singer), 331
Report of the Lords Committees on Massachusetts, 66
Resistance no Rebellion, 195
Resolution, H.M.S. (Cook's sloop), 86, 196, 236, 256, 297-299 ; and see Cook, James
resurrectionist, 262
Retaliation, 66
Reynolds, Sir Joshua (1723–92), portrait painter, P.R.A., grieves for Goldsmith, 45 ; designs Goldsmith's monument, 46 ; his " canvas," 51 ; his Discourses, 122, 339 ; re-elected P.R.A., 122, 233 ; at dinner with Johnson and Boswell, 168 ; his pictures of Mrs. Sheridan, etc., 152, 368 ; at the play, 162 ; a great painter, 169 ; his colours fade, 169 ; on Garrick as Lear, 278 ; on Velasquez, 290 ; Lee's letter, 359
Rice, George (1724–79), M.P. for Carmarthenshire (1754–79), 32
Richard III, 143, 150
Richelieu River. See Canada
Richmond, 3rd Duke of (1736–1806), in opposition, 118, 176, 335
Richmond, Duchess of, 316
Richmond, new bridge, 313
Richmond Theatre, 301
riding dresses, 57
Ridley. See under booksellers
rifle, the new-fangled, 249
Rigby, Richard (1722–88), Paymaster of the Forces (1768–84), 260, 261
riots. See sailors, weavers
Rivals, The. See Sheridan, R. B.
Rivington. See under booksellers
Robertson, William (1721–93), historian, 251, 304
" Robin Hood " Tavern, discussions at, 174
Robinson. See under booksellers
Rochford, Lord (4th Earl) (1717–81),

401

THE END

Printed in Great Britain by R. & R. CLARK, LIMITED, *Edinburgh.*